# APPROACHING THE PAST

# Approaching the Past

HISTORICAL ANTHROPOLOGY
THROUGH IRISH CASE STUDIES

Edited by

Marilyn Silverman
P. H. Gulliver

COLUMBIA UNIVERSITY PRESS

New York

The editors of the present volume gratefully acknowledge the financial support of the Social Sciences and Humanities Research Council of Canada (SSHRC), the Wenner-Gren Foundation for Anthropological Research, New York, and the universities of the contributors.

Columbia University Press
New York      Oxford
Copyright © 1992 Columbia University Press
All rights reserved

Library of Congress Cataloging-in-Publication Data

Approaching the past : historical anthropology through
Irish case studies / edited by Marilyn Silverman, P.H. Gulliver.
p. cm.
Includes bibliographical references and index.
ISBN 0-231-07920-6 (cl).
—ISBN 0-231-07921-4 (pa).
1. Ireland—Historiography—Case studies.
2. Anthropology—Ireland—Case studies.
I. Silverman, M. (Marilyn), 1945–   .
II. Gulliver, P.H.
DA908.A67   1992   941.5'0072—dc20
92-21772
CIP

Casebound editions of Columbia University Press books
are Smyth-sewn and printed on permanent and
durable acid-free paper.

Printed in the United States of America

c 10 9 8 7 6 5 4 3 2 1
p 10 9 8 7 6 5 4 3 2 1

# Contents

   *P. H. Gulliver*

6. The Early Twentieth-Century Irish Stem Family: A Case Study
   from County Kerry                                          205
   *Donna Birdwell-Pheasant*

7. Making the Documents of Conquest Speak: The Transformation
   of Property, Society, and Settlement in Seventeenth-Century
   Counties Tipperary and Kilkenny                            236
   *William J. Smyth*

   PART III:  APPROACHES TO THE PAST IN ANTHROPOLOGY,
   SOCIAL HISTORY, AND HISTORICAL SOCIOLOGY

8. Colonialism and the Interpretation of Irish Historical
   Development                                                293
   *Joseph Ruane*

9. Historical Anthropology, Historical Sociology, and the Making
   of Modern Europe                                           324
   *Samuel Clark*

10. The Anthropological Turn in Social History                325
    *Nicholas Rogers*

    References                                                371

    Index                                                     405

# Contributors

DONNA BIRDWELL-PHEASANT: Associate Professor of Anthropology, Lamar University, Beaumont, Texas

SAMUEL CLARK: Associate Professor of Sociology, University of Western Ontario, London, Ontario

P. H. GULLIVER: Distinguished Research Professor of Anthropology, York University, Toronto, Ontario

NICHOLAS ROGERS: Associate Professor of History, York University, Toronto, Ontario

JOSEPH RUANE: Lecturer in Anthropology, University College Cork, Cork, Republic of Ireland

MARILYN SILVERMAN: Associate Professor of Anthropology, York University, Toronto, Ontario

WILLIAM J. SMYTH: Professor of Geography, University College Cork, Cork, Republic of Ireland

LAWRENCE J. TAYLOR: Professor of Anthropology, Lafayette College, Easton, Pennsylvania

JOAN VINCENT: Professor of Anthropology, Barnard College, Columbia University, New York

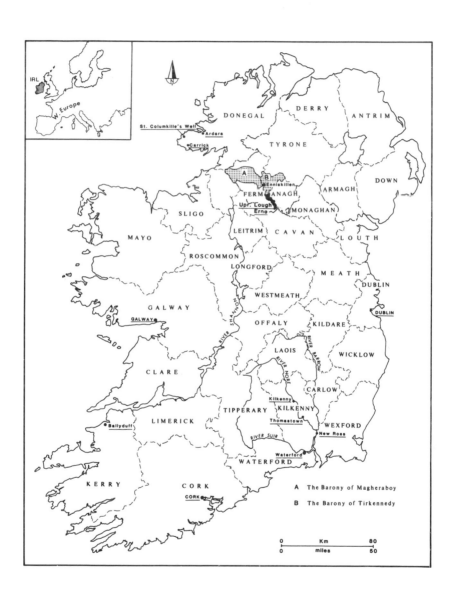

IRL

W Europe

N

DONEGAL          DERRY        ANTRIM

St. Columkille's Well
•Ardara                 TYRONE                      DOWN
•Carrick
                              A  B
                          •Enniskillen          ARMAGH
                      FERMANAGH
              SLIGO       Upr. Lough    •MONAGHAN
                          Erne

        MAYO          LEITRIM   CAVAN          LOUTH

                      ROSCOMMON
                              LONGFORD
                                              MEATH
                          WESTMEATH              DUBLIN
                RIVER SHANNON
        GALWAY                                      DUBLIN
GALWAY•                    OFFALY        KILDARE
                                    RIVER BARROW
                              LAOIS                WICKLOW
                            RIVER NORE
        CLARE
                                              CARLOW

                              Kilkenny
                    TIPPERARY  KILKENNY
                          Thomastown            WEXFORD
        LIMERICK                                New Ross
•Ballyduff            RIVER SUIR
                          Waterford
                      WATERFORD

    KERRY        CORK              A   The Barony of Magheraboy
              CORK•                B   The Barony of Tirkennedy

                      0        Km        80
                      0       miles      50

# I

# INTRODUCTION

# I

# Historical Anthropology and the Ethnographic Tradition: A Personal, Historical, and Intellectual Account

■

MARILYN SILVERMAN AND
P. H. GULLIVER

Although the simple chronology behind the present volume is that it developed out of a conference held in April 1989, its origins lie in a convergence of more complex experiential and intellectual routes. These were traveled by anthropologists who were working with Irish ethnography and who, while so doing, felt obliged to deal with the past and somehow, therefore, "to do history"—because a strong historiographic tradition in Ireland could not be ignored, because the present on its own failed to make sense, and because anthropology itself was changing. In preparing this essay, we have tried to capture the interplay of experience and ideas, of anthropology and history, of the personal and the intellectual. Although our aim is to construct a context within which the papers in the present volume can be located, we are equally concerned to present a historical viewpoint that might stimulate anthropologists like us who, wherever they work, are trying to approach the past.

## "Doing History": A Personal and Anthropological Odyssey, 1979–89

We first came to the Republic of Ireland for a few weeks in the summer of 1979 to find a rural locale for a lengthier stint of field research the following year.[1] Having done some background reading in Irish history, we had concluded that the general historical context of rural Ireland was fairly straightforward—for the delineation of this context was located in a well-established historiographic tradition that had its roots in the nineteenth century, was linked to an impressive array of organizations dedicated to the study of Irish history, and even generated historical overviews of its own historical writings.[2] From this literature, we had learned that rural Ireland was a land of farmers and that its past was one of unremitting nationalism led by agrarian agitation and fallible leaders. The more recent literature added an important subtlety: this came from the ideas of economic and cultural "dualism" and regional variation. The Republic, it seemed, contained at least two regions: the east-southeast and the west. In the former could be found commercially viable agriculture, "modern" values, and vibrant community life. In the latter were subsistence or marginal agriculture, "traditional" values, and decaying community life.[3]

We believed at that time, in 1979, that the explanation for such regional variation did not lie in functionalist explanations, in notions of cultural persistence or breakdown, or in the structure of the agricultural sector alone. Instead, so we believed, it was necessary to explore social, cultural, and economic factors together and to link them all to a broader world context. Most important, we believed that it was essential to look at the past to understand the structural and cultural differences of the present. In the late 1970s, this meant "doing local-level political economy": both the present and the past were explicable through an analysis of political economy as applied to local-level and regional arenas. The central foci, and the analytical thrusts, were the concepts of "articulation" and "class formation" in the context of dependency and world systems theory.[4] This concern with local-level political economy also meant that we were determined to avoid the usual anthropological predilection in Ireland of turning a locality, a parish, a village, or an island into a "community"—a bounded, closed, and culturally homogeneous place.[5]

At the beginning of our sabbatical in June 1980, we established ourselves in a rural locale called Thomastown in County Kilkenny. We had purposefully located in the southeast, away from the main anthropological traffic in the supposedly traditional and presumably esoteric west.[6] Because we needed to set boundaries within which to collect data, we deliberately defined Thomastown using two administrative-electoral units that contained the small town of Thomastown and a rural hinterland around it.[7] We did this so that we could use offical materials: population censuses, agricultural reports, electoral returns, and poor law union records were all compiled using such units.[8] Our intention was to study this local area exhaustively, from 1901—the date of the earliest census for which individual household returns had survived—until 1980. We intended to do the usual participant observation and informal interviewing, and to collect all available documents for the period from 1901 to 1980.[9]

We began by obtaining permission from the parish priest to copy the parochial records of baptisms and marriages. Every morning for several months we sat in his dining room generating hundreds of index cards.[10] We also began to seek people out, to become involved as participant observers. But because, like most anthropologists in the early stages of fieldwork, we knew few people who would talk seriously with us, we spent many an afternoon immersed in Irish history books. We were looking for documentary source materials; equally important, we were trying to pin down the outline of "Irish history." In both endeavors, we had little difficulty, for the history books provided not only numerous archival references but also a coherent chronology of events that appeared to form a connected thread through Irish history. Seemingly, a great deal began with the famine of 1845–49, which was followed by a period of economic recovery, and then, in sequence, by economic depression, Land Wars and Parnellian politics, renewed prosperity and political conciliation, the War of Independence and the Civil War, the polarization of the 1920s, the so-called Economic War of the 1930s, World War II, economic depression, and finally, membership in the EEC and economic expansion.

From this reading of Irish history, 1901 did not appear to stand out in any way. It marked no major event or process, and we soon came to think that it was not a good base point. So we decided to step back a bit and established a new base point in 1879, the year the Land Wars began—the political agitation that led to agrarian land reform and the creation of a landowning "peasantry" in Ireland. We decided to read the newspapers for the Land War period and to look for news about Thomastown and possibly County Kilkenny. We started with the nationalist papers published in Dublin. What we found were reports from various parts of Ireland but almost nothing from County Kilkenny. So we searched out the two county newspapers from the period. Even they contained reports only of events, meetings, and violence from other parts of Ireland—mainly the west—with only an occasional story about a Land League meeting near Thomastown or in south Kilkenny.

We concluded that the Land Wars had not been a major event in Thomastown and again decided to push back our temporal boundaries. This time we picked the years just preceding what some of our history books declared to be the "great watershed of modern Irish history"—the 1845–49 famine.[11] Once again we approached the County Kilkenny newspapers:[12] they were filled mainly with reports of famine from other parts of Ireland. Then, over the following months, as we read the newspapers for all the years between 1840 and 1980, looked at other archival materials, and elicited stories from people about the past, it began to seem that—regardless of what we looked at—either very little or "nothing ever happened in Thomastown."[13]

We raised this issue at a multidisciplinary seminar at University College, Cork, in 1980. We expressed great perplexity: seemingly, Thomastown lay outside Irish history. The historians were somewhat amused. They knew, and readily admitted, that so-called Irish history was an amalgam of local and regional events combined to create a unified and coherent whole held together by nationalist (and later, revisionist) ideology. They did not find it surprising that a particular local area or region never experienced all or even any of the events that later became part of so-called Irish history. They also conceded that such lacunae were more likely in the southeast.

What the historians told us was what we had already concluded from our experiences over the previous months. However, what we found most disconcerting, and intriguing, was that the historians seemed utterly untroubled by our objections and concern. This experience crystallized for us the fragility of the past, the capriciousness of historiography. For surely Thomastown, although it had been placed outside historiography, was located in history and had a past.

To recover this past, to do this history, we faced two immediate problems. First, we realized how serious it was that the primary sources (such as newspapers, parliamentary commissions) were not only patchy but also contaminated in indeterminate ways. They had focused not only on the newsworthy at the time but also on the issues and events of concern to the producers of such documents.[14] Consequently, during the famine and Land Wars, Kilkenny county newspapers carried little of local interest, compared with extensive coverage about these events from other parts of Ireland. Thus, even as the past was happening, the skeleton of "national history" was being

constructed while the experiences of localities such as Thomastown
were being ignored.

Second, for Thomastown, the particular locality on which we
focused, many of the kinds of documents that historians use had
never existed or had not survived. For example, we unearthed no
estate papers, personal diaries, letters, or memoirs from the nineteenth century, and important British parliamentary commissions
often had not solicited evidence from property owners or inhabitants
of the Thomastown area.

With such constraints, we had four questions:

1. What events, if any, were experienced at the local level in
   Thomastown and in what ways were local experiences affected by events in other localities—by so-called national and
   international events—and by Thomastown people's knowledge of them?
2. How can so-called national history be used by anthropologists if its construction is arbitrary and its content uneven?
3. Since Thomastown's history was not a localized reflection of
   the events that had been constructed into a national history,
   what was it?
4. If the Irish past was partly made up from Thomastown's
   history and the histories of many other similar local levels,
   how could all these histories be made congruent?

To continue our work, we realized that we had to confront what
history was; we could not simply study the past or do history. In
1980, in anthropology, this was still a relatively unexplored idea, and
it raised two central problems. First, in doing history, Irish historians
have expanded the quantity and range of their documentation by
unconcernedly using materials from numerous and dispersed local
areas. A historian studying, for example, landlordism might have
used estate papers from one part of a county, valuation records from
another part, and conveyances from another county altogether. However, as anthropologists with our local focus, the vagaries of documentation on the past meant that we were severely limited in our
ability to explore the key issues that formed the topical and chronological agenda of Irish history—such as, in the nineteenth century,
the nature of landlordism, the trajectory of rents and evictions, tenant
land purchases, and so on.

Second, through documents and participant observation, we began
to find categories of people in Thomastown who had seldom made it
into the Irish history books. The clearest case was that of the rural,
industrial proletariat, some members of which, as far as we could tell,

had been landless for at least two centuries. We also encountered the millers, maltsters, brewers, and tanners who had hired these laborers and the numerous, often self-employed, artisans who had lived and worked in the locality. At the same time, we discovered many economic and political activities, organizations, and cultural ideas never mentioned by Irish historians. Clearly, Irish historians, in their concern with events related to their own topical and chronological agenda, had constructed their own very partial version of society.

The problems with Irish historiography and its relation to our own concerns at the time were not solved by referring to the sociological or anthropological literature on Ireland. There we found three biases unacceptable. First, we found a heavy concentration of social studies in the west. It was partly this western bias that had led to a general view of rural Ireland as poor, "peasant," and demoralized. From our Thomastown vantage point in the southeast, rural Ireland looked very different: good tillage land, large farms, a retail sector, and an articulation with an international market that extended centuries into the past, local industries founded during an industrial revolution at the end of the eighteenth century, and the presence in 1980 of foreign-owned enterprises. Instead of drawing from the social science literature, therefore, we found that we had to confront its assumptions about rural Ireland as these had been generalized from studies done west of the river Shannon.[15]

However, the image of a poor and demoralized rural Ireland that came out of anthropology and sociology at the time was not simply a reflection of regional differences. It was also the result of the particular approach that underlay these studies and that provided a second reason for our sense of isolation from Irish ethnography. This was the approach of anthropologists who viewed rural Ireland as comprised of distinct "communities" and who therefore took a so-called community as a basic and natural unit and studied its contemporary culture to ascertain whether "tradition" was persisting, wearing away, or being reinforced. To us, as political economists, the idea was absurd that there could be bounded and isolated local places that had culture but no economy, tradition but no history.[16] As we tried to approach the past in the context of a particular locality, we found little help in these stereotypical "community studies."

A third bias underlay anthropology and these community studies in the west. This was the theory of modernization that also informed, both implicitly and explicitly, the vast majority of economic, social, and historical analyses of Irish society. In this view, Ireland was in the process of "catching up" with the rest of Europe, and it was only a matter of time before it "developed." In direct contrast, we had notions from political economy and dependency theory that, at best, regarded modernization assumptions as wrong and, at worst, postulated that Irish conditions had more in common with the structural underdevelopment of Third World societies than with the developed countries of Western Europe.[17] At the time of our research, however, only a few macrostudies used this model, and certainly no local-level studies in Ireland analyzed dependency on the micro level.

Thus, with our southeastern study of a rural locality in both past and present, with concepts from political economy and dependency theory, we found ourselves confronting history, sociology, and anthropology. In this effort, we decided, as an early task, to write a local history for Thomastown people. This is what we had promised our informants, friends, and curious onlookers. We also thought to use the opportunity to try an initial and comprehensive survey of our data before approaching more purely academic and theoretical issues. For this task, doing history was a sorting through and a review of our ethnographic materials. However, as we were to realize only later on, this overview of our data from 1840 to 1983 became a way not only of doing history but also a way of creating it.

We wrote *In the Valley of the Nore: A Social History of Thomastown, 1840–1983*. To do so we combined three elements that, at the time, seemed straightforwardly and simply derived from our own interests and predilections. First, we took the events and chronology of so-called Irish history as our major section headings. These were the categories Thomastown people used when they talked about the past and were those they had learned in school. So they spoke about bad landlords and evictions, about good landlords who helped people; they also spoke about the War of Independence and the Civil War, the economic war and hard times of the 1930s, and so on. Local people very clearly conceptualized the *chronology* of their past in the same way as did their history books.

Yet it also was clear that sometimes what people remembered or took care to remember had not necessarily happened, whereas they had forgotten (or failed to remember) things that had happened.[18] A striking case was a large farmer who spoke vehemently, as did many farmers, about the numerous tenant farmers who had been evicted by landlords in the nineteenth century; again, like most farmers, he was unable to name a single case in the Thomastown locality. When pressed, he asserted somewhat impatiently that the evictions had all happened "up Kilkenny way." Interestingly, this farmer did not know (although we had learned it from a document) that his great-grandfather had indeed been evicted in 1850. Thus, the chronological periods of Irish history with which people compartmentalized the past only partly corresponded to what they knew, or did not know, to be actual events and particular people. These two ways of structuring and conceptualizing the past coexisted in Thomastown. In writing *In the Valley of the Nore,* we provided actual events and the names of real people, as best we could, in the context of the accepted and dominant historical chronology.

There was a third element. Throughout our time spent living in Thomastown, we were struck, virtually every day and in numerous ways, by the centrality of class differences in the locality. In fact, Thomastown people had their own explicit categories that they used to organize a *class-based, social map* for their everyday interaction.[19] The map contained laborers, artisans, shopkeepers, and farmers; once there were landlords and gentry as well. An important feature of these categories was that they involved fixed structural ideas, not temporal ones. They were never used to organize chronology or to order sequences of events in time. Instead, the categories were timeless—they had always existed, they continued to exist; therefore, they were descriptive as well as explanatory. This meant that the categories could be, and were, extrapolated backward in time both to describe and to explain, simultaneously, the past and the present. To take an example: several laboring men, independently, while trying to tell us about the intensity of class difference in Thomastown, illustrated it by telling us that their fathers had never received IRA pensions after the War of Independence because of discrimination against workers. They also always added that "no laboring man ever got his pension." In other words, an unchanging, timeless class structure—seen through a personal event and a general principle—both described the past and the present while it explained that past and this present. A timeless past and present intersected in the here and now through the use of class categories.[20]

In writing *In the Valley of the Nore,* we linked these categories to actual local events and people and to national chronologies. As a result, Thomastown's history was for the first time constructed in the partial ways that it probably was experienced: that children during the economic war had no shoes was the experience of laborers and small farmers; that some Thomastown men became British soldiers during World War I was true only for the working class and the gentry; that emigration was central after World War II was true for everyone, but laborers tended to emigrate to England, whereas farmers and shopkeepers had sufficient capital to go to North America.

In making these kinds of linkages—among chronology, event/ people, and class—we essentially constructed a new and different way of seeing Thomastown's past. In doing history, we had created history. Children from Thomastown's schools have borrowed our book from the local library and have painstakingly copied our story in which the key actors were class based and in which real events only partially confirmed the dominant chronology. Similarly, Thomastown's parish newspaper has reproduced sections of the book for a more general readership.

Our aim in writing the local history had been to reciprocate the help we had received in Thomastown over the years and to have a first go at our materials. It was only after the book was completed in 1985 that we slowly realized that we had "made history."[21] When we began to question why this had occurred (in other words, when trying, still and once again, to understand how to do history) we decided to hold a conference[22] on anthropology and history. Through it, we hoped to discover the different ways in which other anthropologists approached the past using Irish ethnography.

### An Overview of Historical Anthropology: From the Past to the Present

Our struggles with the past in both Ireland and Thomastown were but a single instance of a general trend in anthropology and of a growing concern among anthropologists with history. This did not, of course, happen overnight; it was a result of attempts by anthropologists to get away from earlier, increasingly unsatisfactory frameworks.

It is scarcely necessary once again to describe and criticize an erstwhile anthropology (and sociology) that was monopolized by synchronic, structural studies and analyses in which both dynamic process and history were either simply ignored or positively eschewed. The case against that earlier kind of work in anthropology, as in the social sciences generally, has been sufficiently, and repetitively, made, although too often without sufficient recognition of the importance of the detailed, perceptive, and often empathetic studies that were produced within that framework during the 1930s, 1940s, and 1950s. Indeed, it would not be difficult to argue that the foundation of present-day anthropology was well laid as a result. However, for present purposes it is sufficient to recognize that the neglect or rejection of history was not the consequence of any single theoretical approach in earlier anthropology, although too often, misguidedly, the cause of this neglect has been attributed solely to functionalist theory.[23] Rather, it was the result of a general, ill-considered approach to the description of sociocultural milieux that, inter alia, offered the apparent ease and simplicity of the snapshot of the "here and now" or the "there and then" in other societies.[24]

At the same time, it would be a historical mistake to assume that anthropologists have only recently turned to a consideration of dynamic process and of history and their implications for research, analysis, and understanding. The explorations into Boasian culture history and neoevolutionism and the emergence of the so-called ethnohistory of the 1930s, 1940s, and 1950s stimulated concern for one kind of history, although these can scarcely be seen as forerunners of a later historical anthropology, which is our present concern. In that matter, a crucial moment came in 1949 with the publication of Evans-Pritchard's historical monograph on the Bedouin of Cyrenaica.[25] This was followed in the next year by the same author's declaration that anthropology and history shared common methods and aims despite some differences in technique and perspective.[26] In 1961, Evans-Pritchard reaffirmed Maitland's century-old assertion that anthropology had to choose between becoming history or being nothing.[27] The message was only gradually heeded, but a trickle of anthropological studies began, in the 1950s and 1960s, in which sociocultural change through some period of time was a major preoccupation, even though it was sometimes uncomfortably linked with synchronic analysis.[28] Then, during the 1970s and 1980s, historical anthropological studies became a flood, to the extent that they have undoubtedly established a mode in ethnographic presentations.

This gradually increasing interest in historical studies was, of course, a product of and a part of a number of trends and innovations in anthropology. This is not the place for a history of anthropological thinking and experimenting, and it must suffice briefly to note the trends (with a few illustrative references)[29] that seem to have been particularly influential in the growth of historical anthropology. Setting them out starkly creates a danger of seeming to present them as discrete intellectual developments; but of course they have overlapped and influenced each other in manifold ways. These trends began at different times from the 1950s onward, and most are still active genres in social and cultural anthropology.

One trend was a growing concern, after World War II, for the study of social and cultural change. This was not a purely intellectual and theoretical development, for it was also related to practical and ethical issues and to ideas about the political relevance of anthropology in the poorer parts of the world, particularly the non-Western parts. Initially at least, the concern was for the consequences of regimes of colonial domination.[30] Anthropologists shared with other interested parties[31] a desire to know what was happening to particular social and cultural institutions in empirical contexts: to households and kin groups, chiefship, patterns of cooperation, religious practices and beliefs, for example, and to economic production and standards of living. By the 1950s, it had become increasingly difficult for anthropologists to ignore what was actively occurring among the peoples they were studying, and it began to be unacceptable to concentrate on a so-called traditional stable order, relegating remarks on contemporary changes to a section or chapter tacked on to the main analysis. This concern for recent social change, and the need to make it integral to research and analysis, encouraged anthropologists to investigate further back in time and to acknowledge the importance and the possibilities of the extended collection of historical materials and of diachronic studies.

Unfortunately, this kind of interest led some anthropologists to conceive of social change (other than minor adjustments) as tantamount to a breakdown of the social system.[32] This conception has been particularly prominent in Irish studies, which purported to show how "tradition" was crumbling and becoming lost. A later example of this persisting viewpoint was Brody's 1976 description of Inishkillane. In his composite and allegedly typical "community" in the west of Ireland, he presented a picture of demoralization, anomie, and disintegration, quite failing "to recognise the diversely creative and innovative processes through which people currently constitute their economic and political lives."[33] With such processes in mind, anthropologists have more realistically investigated and described what innovations have been imposed or offered, how and why, and with what consequences.[34] From such specific and empirical interests, the acknowledged need for analytical and theoretical sophistication has arisen.[35]

More or less separately, a concern for social processes and the dynamics of social life began to develop. The early stage of this concern can conveniently be linked to Firth, who proposed, in 1951, the concept of social organization—people's choices and actions and the processes involved—in contrast to an underlying social structure. At first this concern was manifested in studies of repetitive processes within an essentially static structure, for example, in the domains of kinship, politics, and dispute management.[36] However, the artificial limitations of this soon became apparent and unacceptable; and a positive concern grew for such processes through time and in real life, together with a recognition that social reproduction did not necessarily lead to mere repetition. That is, as social anthropologists sought to understand various social processes, it became necessary for them to look at ways in which social systems, institutions, roles, values, and patterns of interaction actually operated through time; and that required anthropologists to take account of real time, the passage of time, and history.[37]

Another development occurred as some anthropologists came to study peasant societies. Initially, following the lead of Redfield in Mexico, attention focused on synchronic studies or analyses of recent social change.[38] However, as peasant studies were extended, particularly to Europe, anthropologists entered a novel situation in which their units of study—peasant villages—had long been part of political states whose hegemonic rule had produced archival materials. These allowed anthropologists to extend their inquiries further back in time than had hitherto been possible, taking them beyond short-term studies of current social change and inducing a greater awareness and concern for the past.

The introduction of the Marxist paradigm into anthropology in the late 1960s brought new concepts that were amenable to local analysis (e.g., petty commodity production) while it provided others that required considerable modification before they could be applied to local studies (e.g., mode of production, class, superstructure).[39] The efforts to apply or revamp such concepts required a practical recognition of the significance of historical and regional analysis in the context of a wider social formation. New conceptual and empirical vistas opened up in anthropology. The commitment to historical anthropology through the approach of political economy (in varying degrees influenced by Marxist theory) has been apparent in the large proportion of historical ethnographies written under its influence from all geographical areas.[40]

The Marxist paradigm converged with the growing anthropological concern with dependency and world systems theory.[41] This too demanded a historical orientation. But it also brought a positive reaction from anthropologists against studying history from the top down and against the implication that local and regional populations merely reacted and adapted to national and world movements, almost in automatic and identical fashion. Such assumption was unacceptable to the specialists in local-level studies who saw that it was unjustified. As Cole and Wolf put it:

> We know that a study of small populations will not reveal all there is
> to know about the total societies in which they are embedded, and we

are similarly aware that the study of total societies will not in and of itself provide grounds for predicting how small populations react to more wide-ranging systematic processes . . . a small settlement [is not] a replica of a larger whole in miniature.[42]

Moreover, because of different local and regional conditions, local populations have been affected and have reacted in different ways.[43] Thus, in the context of dependency and world systems theory, anthropologists reasserted the importance of microanalysis and of local and regional variations. They have called attention to the value of the study of history from below and have sought to demonstrate it in their studies.

Meanwhile in Europe, historians and sociologists had begun investigating family structures, household composition, and social life in "past time." The early work by Laslett[44] led historians[45] into kinship and domestic domains that had generally been the peculiar specialism of anthropologists in their studies of contemporary societies. This incursion, in turn, induced anthropologists to bring to the past their expertise on kinship,[46] and conferences brought anthropologists and historians together to examine household and domestic processes.[47] Further cross-disciplinary fertilization occurred as anthropologists began to look explicitly to social history[48] and "people's history"[49] for ideas and stimulation. All this has influenced anthropological thinking, sometimes specifically and overtly, as, for instance, in Kertzer's study of kinship in late-nineteenth-century Italy[50] and in the case studies in this volume.

At the same time, anthropologists were becoming more self-critical and self-reflexive, more aware of the historical and contextual conditions in which their discipline had developed. Whether anthropology has simply been a "child of imperialism" and the degree to which a scholarly discipline has been controlled by the sociocultural context of its practitioners have been, and are, matters of considerable debate.[51] The point here, however, is that anthropologists have been induced to consider the historical context within which they worked and, therefore and by extension, the historical dimensions of the peoples they studied.

With the flood of monographic studies in historical anthropology during the 1980s, and from both sides of the Atlantic, it is reasonable now to assume that for many anthropologists it has come to be taken for granted that it is both necessary and invaluable to look for and at the past—to "do history." However, although this is the case, it does not mean that anthropologists are clear or agreed about the range of implications of those now accepted necessities. How should anthropologists deal with time, in research and in description and analysis? What are the results likely to be for theory and understanding?

Historical anthropology has become sufficiently well established that a range of interests and foci is fairly clear. In presenting here what looks suspiciously like a firm typology, we have in mind only to facilitate an overview of current interests by suggesting categories that are not intended to be watertight and discrete. Thus, we identify two broad categories within historical anthropology—historical ethnography and the anthropology of history.[52] Although some particular studies fall more or less clearly into one or another of our categories, most studies have the characteristics of more than one as data and interests have required.

| I. *Historical ethnography* | II. *Anthropology of history* |
|---|---|
| (a) How the past led to and created the present | (c) How constructions of the past are used to explain the present (history as ideology) |
| (b) Synchronic and diachronic studies of a past time | (d) How the past is created in the present (the invention of tradition) |
| | (e) How the past created and recreated the past |

A *historical ethnography* provides a description and analysis of a past era of the people of some particular, identifiable locality, using archival sources and, if relevant, local oral history sources. The ethnography may be general, covering many aspects of social life during that era, or it may concentrate on specific features, such as social ecology, politics, or religion. It was this kind of ethnography that at last brought anthropologists away from long-established, clumsy devices and assumptions such as the ethnographic present, autarchic "communities," and stable "tradition."

Most commonly, and for good working reasons, social anthropologists have been concerned to link past and present, chronologically and processually, in order to explain and understand the present by reference to the past. That past may have been a generation, several decades, a century, or a longer period, as anthropological interests and the availability of data dictated. As some anthropologists have said during field research, in an explanation to the people involved, there was a desire not merely to record the past for its own sake but to discover and show "how things have come to be the way they are now." Thus, the anthropologist in her or his work among a contemporary, living people, not only garnered information about the "way they are now" but also, for fuller understanding, worked back in time, constantly relating contemporary conditions and institutions to past events, conditions, and processes. In the final historical ethnography, as it appeared in published form, the anthropologist, like any historian, may well have presented data and analysis more or less chronologically. This has not disguised the historiographical intent to explain the present through understanding the past. Therefore, this kind of historical ethnography has given a bias in the articulation of the historical process. This is an orientation and a concern rarely shared with historians.

In addition, there have been historical ethnographies of periods entirely in the past for which only archival materials were available. Such materials usually included the views and ideas of some of the individuals of that past time. Whether the ethnography was in synchronic or diachronic form depended a great deal on the availability of data. Such historical ethnographic work has been, of course, a more straightforward invasion of the historian's field and not directly related to conventional anthropological research in a present-day situation. As a result, these kinds of ethnographies have been less common. However, a few anthropologists have ventured away from a present-day attachment to make a diachronic study of a wholly past period (e.g., Hastrup's Icelandic ethnography, 1400–1800).[53] In some cases, the period was chosen largely as a matter of convenience (e.g., Vincent's analysis of marriage, religion, and class in nineteenth-century Fermanagh, Northern Ireland). In other cases, the period was dictated by the historical conditions, as in Silverblatt's study of Inca and colonial Peru or Dening's study of the Marquesas from 1774 to 1880 (the end date being the year that French colonial domination was finally established).[54]

Synchronic ethnographies of a particular past time for which archival materials happened to be available have attracted much less anthropological interest. Historians seem to have been readier to undertake that kind of study (typified by Le Roy Ladurie's well-known works).[55] Perhaps the reason may have been the growth of anthropological concern for social dynamics, process, and change, which has made an account of a petrified society scarcely attractive. If, because of limitations of historical materials, it was impossible to take account of major changes through a period of time, it has come to be expected that the ethnography should nevertheless depict a society in which people were active and interacting, making decisions, following or avoiding "rules," and creating adjustments. Thus, Donham advocated first the identification of the underlying structure—an "epochal analysis"—before proceeding to a "historical analysis" that was dynamic in character but concerned with changes within the system rather than with fundamental changes or changes of the system: "What I mean by historical explanation is not simply an account of the connections between events over a period of time. A leads to B leads to C. . . . Historical analyses must be located *in* time. They must capture what might be called historicity, but they do not necessarily have to deal with large-scale changes *through* time."[56]

As monographs and journal articles in historical anthropology have proliferated since about 1970, it is obvious that the production of historical ethnographies has been the principal interest in historical anthropology. The aim has been to compile analytical histories that, ultimately, have been outsiders' constructions. Thus, although properly cautious, historical ethnographers have not been afraid to exercise responsible authorial authority. Nevertheless, they have neither advocated nor practiced neglect of the so-called native point of view concerning the history of the people involved. Oral history, human memory, and native explanations have invariably augmented archival sources in valuable ways. Moreover, these historical ethnographers have been prominent in demonstrating the gross error of assuming a single "native point of view" in an assumed homogeneous society or culture. Any society, large or small, is heterogeneous with regard to status, class, age, gender, group affiliation, and distribution of power and resources. Therefore, the anthropologist always needs to consider many "native points of view," which provide an entry into the complexities of real social life and real people.

This does not mean that historical ethnographers have produced artificial syntheses of all the "native points of view" into a single version of history. Rather, it suggests that they have explored the variety of points of view, of native versions of history, together with empirical archival material that may well have been unfamiliar to or rejected by the people under study and possibly contradictory to some or even all native points of view. Indeed, the nature and causes of such contradictions have become important in the construction of a dynamic history. It is clear, then, that historical ethnography has gone beyond "native points of view" as a result of both access to archival materials and use of analytical expertise. Thus, it is clear that any particular historical ethnography has been a construction by the anthropologist—a suggested version of a possible reality—which, however, did not willfully ignore or contradict native points of view and did not claim to present any final, complete truth or reality.

However, some historical anthropologists have gone beyond taking serious account of native points of view to focus primarily on the ways and the cultural rationale by which a particular people have envisioned, created, and re-created their own past and related it to their perceived present. This we call the *anthropology of history*. Its concern has been to record and describe the insiders' views, assumptions, and perceptions and to show them in the insiders' own sociocultural terms. There has been, then, little or no attempt to produce an "objective" history. Rather, the interest has been in what people know and remember about their past, and how and why, and how people make sense of the past and relate it to the present.

It is important to recognize that the anthropological concern here has been more than just history for history's sake. People's own versions and evaluations of their past are a retrospective product of their present. Moreover, those versions tend to change from generation to generation. Thus, they are important for the anthropological understanding of a people and of changes in their sociocultural contexts.

The most straightforward endeavor has been for the anthropologist to set down the native versions of their own past, linking these to their contemporary cultural conceptions and social arrangements. In an extreme case, the anthropologist may consider available archival materials irrelevant and therefore ignore them. For instance, Sharp and Hanks related that, for the Thai village they studied, there were few documentary materials

> and most of them were never consulted. A visit to the district office
> . . . revealed a thousand neatly tied bundles of yellowing land deeds.
> In the deeds were listed changes of ownership that had long been
> forgotten in Bang Chan [the village studied], but more serious for our
> study were the transfers of ownership that were acknowledged in Bang
> Chan but unrecorded at the district office.[57]

It appears that, for these anthropologists, only the information retained in the village was considered relevant and usable in the discovery of the villagers' current visions of their own history. Logically, Sharp and Hanks may have been correct insofar as the introduction of documentary evidence from earlier years was not pertinent to their avowed purpose. On the other hand, consideration of such evidence could have led to a recognition that villagers' own history could itself change and that, for whatever reasons, villagers were selective in what they remembered and put together and what they ignored and forgot.

People explain the past to themselves, just as they explain, rationalize, and justify their present. From this perspective, history is ideology, and like any ideology, it is open to manipulation and reformulation while it is believed by many to be "true" and correct. In this matter, Parmentier called for and sought to practice an "ethnographic study of the modalities of history," taking account of the connections between notions of time; historical memory; the distribution of power to control, create, and destroy historical ideology; and the range of cultural codes involved in historical consciousness.[58] Moreover, he emphasized that the "inclusion of the intentionality of people who create and interpret their own past is essential, rather than supplementary, to adequate ethnographic study."[59] Parmentier used and demonstrated his ideas through his exploration of the local story about the establishment of the political order in Micronesian Belau.

It is not easy to generalize cross-culturally about the degree of deliberate action by those with power to reinforce and/or re-create historical knowledge and perception to their own expected advantage. In at least some documented cases (but surely in many others too), the initial invention of tradition and history was begun by individuals with little or no power who must have seen some advantage to be gained from their invention and some prospect of its being accepted. In successful cases, their inventions proved most congenial to those with power or seeking to gain it who therefore promoted them. A well-known example was that of the creation of the Highland tradition in Scotland described by Trevor-Roper.[60] There, for a variety of reasons, those with influence and the general population colluded, so that the new tradition was universally accepted. Another instance, among many that could be cited from the current literature,[61] has been the creation by Indonesian historians (under the protection and encouragement of political leaders) of new culture heroes (as, of course, was often done in Europe in the thirty or forty years before World War I).[62] Hoskins described the elevation of a headhunter and famous warrior to the status of Indonesian hero. In 1909, this man led opposition to the Dutch "pacification" of one part of a smaller island in what later became Indonesia. "The rebel who opposed Dutch control has, with some irony, been used as a tool of a new kind of ideological control: the integration of distant regions into the [new] nation state through [invented] assertions of a shared past."[63]

A weakness in the many studies of the invention of tradition and of new visions of the past has been the impression often given that, once tradition was invented, that was more or less the end of the story. However, if the past can be invented once in response to changes in the present, then it can be (and has been) reinvented later on in further response. There is no need to posit inevitably continuous reinvention or to deny its possibility. It depends, in any case, on what is meant by invention: something wholly new or modifications in various degrees of preceding visions of the past. It has been a long time since it was said that each generation rewrites its history. True as this may be, the rewriting can occur in less than a generation, or it may take longer. Contemporary anthropologists have been strongly reminded by Sahlins of the potentiality of the continuous re-creation by a people of their own history.[64] He introduced his *Islands of History* by noting that history "is culturally ordered, differently so in different societies, according to meaningful schemes of things. The converse is also true: cultural schemes are historically ordered, since to a greater or lesser extent the meanings are revalued as they are practically enacted."[65] What Sahlins called "practical revaluations" of sociocultural things may be a continuous process as people live their lives, make decisions, and act with ineluctable reference to their culture and therefore to their past, whether or not they are conscious of this. There is a "symbolic dialogue of history—dialogue between received categories and perceived contexts, between cultural sense and practical reference." Thus, "there is always a past in the present, an a priori system of interpretations" and, therefore, always a present in the past as that in turn is interpreted.[66]

## Engaging Other Disciplines: "Little Localities" and "Big Problems"

Locality has been a key concern in contemporary anthropological analysis.[67] Whereas an earlier anthropology focused mainly on "a people," "a culture," or "a society," most anthropologists today are concerned with "a place." This emphasis probably developed alongside the growing anthropological interest in so-called peasants during the 1950s and 1960s. The early anthropological (and evolutionary) classification of non-Western peoples was based on a juxtaposition of mode of livelihood, settlement pattern, and political regime. Hunter-gatherers, pastoral nomads, and swidden agriculturalists—in so-called acephalous societies—were physically mobile; they may have moved within a large and known territory, but they did not have small, permanently settled hamlets, villages, or towns. Anthropologists took sociopolitical groups, not locality, as the framework of society. Where tribal peoples were in permanently settled locales, usually in the context of more centralized political regimes (chiefships), anthropologists continued to emphasize the groups that comprised the society or culture: territory and space were regarded as secondary—as reflections of the kinship and political system. In contrast, so-called peasants were defined as permanently settled agriculturalists linked in various ways to a wider state and/or urban-based society. By anthropological definition, then, the peasant mode of livelihood was inextricably linked to a fixed, settled locale and to a wider political regime or "great tradition."[68] When anthropologists moved in—both with their definition of peasant and with peasants—they reinforced the importance of locality both for themselves and for peasantries. During the conference, historian Nicholas Rogers commented several times that he was truly struck by the fact that "anthropologists have a compelling sense of place."

At best, we have found that this anthropological commitment to locality has raised questioning eyebrows among historians and sociologists. More often, though, we have found that the anthropological concern with a "little locality" has been severely criticized, and most seriously, it has been used as a reason for dismissing anthropological findings and understandings. Samuel Clark, a historical sociologist, insisted at the conference that "anthropologists ignore the major transformations, the big problems. They also don't look at what's happening outside the community which they're studying."

We believe that much of the criticism and dismissal has come from the fact that nonanthropologists have often failed to understand the ways in which anthropologists nowadays are trying to use locality. The former often have the outmoded idea that an anthropological study based on a locality was associated with closed boundaries and with a reification of the notion of community.[69] In fact, we argue later that the anthropological use of space contains a theoretical logic and only seldom, today, implies closed systems and esoteric findings. We also argue that the contemporary anthropological use of space and spatial boundaries is no more and no less arbitrary than the conceptual management of space in other disciplines.

Anthropologists in the field have tended to surprise other academics, local people, and archivists with the doggedness with which they have pursued every lead that might provide information on a particular locality. When offered a newly discovered, 150-year-old census tract or a 90-year-old informant from two parishes over, an anthropologist may only with reluctance pursue the lead, bemoaning all the way there the ill luck that made such a document or such a person not survive from his or her more immediate place.[70] Local historians, or social historians, seem to have been less rigid. When there have been no data for a particular locality, then materials from an adjacent or other nearby localities have been used. In producing one of the very few local studies at the parish level by a historian in Ireland, O'Neill routinely used material from parishes all over County Cavan to study the parish of Killashandra.[71] In historical sociology, another tack has been followed: a sufficiently large political unit or region has been delineated that, deliberately or not, obviated problems of data shortages.[72]

The unique (and seemingly neurotic) anthropological fixation on relatively small-scale localities has a rationale that can be summarized succinctly as *contextualization* and *comprehensiveness*. It has three key aspects. First, the intensive focus on the small scale allows a deep understanding of the phenomena being analyzed, and which constitute the true purpose of the study. This permits the inclusion of "real people" along with an exploration of the interdependencies of sociopolitical patterning, economic conditions, and cultural belief. As the essays by Birdwell-Pheasant and Gulliver in this volume illustrate, this can raise serious questions about the validity of conclusions based on data that have been drawn from larger and less contextualized areas. Documentary or oral evidence from and about an adjacent locality is always only of limited utility because its sociological and cultural context is not known or only incompletely known and, therefore, its meaning cannot be adequately assessed and its implications entirely understood.[73]

Second, the focus on a particular place allows anthropologists to expand into a wider area as they follow the relevant processes, networks, or constraints outward from the particular locality. For example, in this volume, Silverman moves from Thomastown (inward and outward, up and down) to the appropriate arenas and levels, following the processes of privatization in the inland salmon fisheries. Thus, contrary to the popular image derived from an earlier anthropology, an anthropologist today often varies the way in which locality is delineated according to the specific analytical interest being pursued at any particular point. This has the effect of giving the anthropologist's locality an organic, living quality; it also means that the anthropologist is *not* analyzing it as a closed, insular system. Indeed, by choosing a small-scale locality, the anthropologist maintains the option of keeping the boundaries permeable because an expansion outward is manageable. Ironically, that other disciplines choose larger regions to study does not resolve the issue of boundaries, permeability, or closed systems; it just hides the issue under the guise that a bigger area is a better area. For just as there are no closed localities, there are no closed regions; and just as there are no closed regions, there are no closed nation-states.

Third, the anthropological use of little localities should allow for the explanation of phenomena. Indeed, anthropologists have often been criticized for not explaining why. Part of the problem is, of course, how causality is conceptualized;[74] another part of the problem is that anthropologists have not been listened to. For insofar as it is the anthropologist who is closest to real people, events, and cultural meanings; who has an intimate knowledge of so many interdependent variables; and who sees the intersection of structure and agency in action; then clearly those in the social sciences who seek historical explanation for the "big problems" should find some of what they want in historical anthropology.

What this means, of course, is that anthropologists today seldom study a locality purely for its own sake—to do yet another stereotypical, so-called community study or to provide even more descriptions of the esoteric minutiae of everyday life. It is equally important to recognize that any so-called local level is differently defined, depending on the particular anthropologist, the purpose of the study, and the availability of data sources. To take examples from historical anthropology, Cole and Wolf, the Schneiders, and Stoler each began their analyses at what geographers would call a regional level and then moved to smaller units as they traced out the logic of their particular research problems.[75] In contrast, other anthropologists began more locally and expanded outward as the need arose, or as they moved between localities, or as they used comparative data from other localities.[76] Therefore, it is crucial to recognize that no longer do the majority of anthropologists work with analytically closed, local systems. Indeed, we argue that the contemporary concern with historical anthropology is a definitive statement about the final demise of the primordial anthropological notion that closed local systems can exist anywhere. By moving back in time, historical anthropologists discover that they are unable to find true beginnings for the phenomena that they are studying,[77] and therefore true boundaries in space.[78]

"Little localities" thus form a context within which "big" sociological and cultural problems can be investigated. For such big problems or so-called major transformations as the rise of capitalism, the founding of the modern world system, and the decline of the landed aristocracy had local manifestations and unintended as well as intended consequences that are visible only from a micro perspective. In addition, the sociospatial networks that encompassed the globe had terminal nodes within local places.

This idea that localities are where networks intersect was suggested in the 1950s by Wolf: "Communities which form parts of a complex society can . . . be viewed no longer as self-contained and integrated systems in their own right. It is more appropriate to view them as the local termini of a web of group relations which extend through intermediate levels from the level of the community to that of the nation."[79] Since then, however, it has proved exceedingly difficult to conceptualize and to elaborate on this multidimensional idea.[80] Thus, thirty years later, in 1985, when Carol Smith criticized the anthropological use of the world systems approach in which all local change was treated as exogenous, she asked, once again, "How does one examine and analyze a dialectical process that involves the articulation of different layers in a multi-layered system?" Smith's solution was to analyze "structures that mediate between the local community and the world system."[81] Indeed, the concept of "mediation" has perhaps been the most fruitfully used over the years to cope with this dilemma of levels, layers, and local termini; and often it has been used in historical analyses.[82] However, the dilemma remains, as does the fact that "local nodes," and what happens there, are crucial and somehow must be treated as such. The Catholic Church in Ireland, for example, was (and is) both international and local, as was the operation of the network of economic relations. Conversely, that Thomastown's farmers traveled to Brussels as part of an Irish agricultural lobby was an example of local networks engaging the world system. Particular localities, then, were—and continue to be—where such myriad networks intersected and where the effects can be clearly traced. The local level thus is a context for testing ideas, for generating new interpretations, and for developing new hypotheses. Local case studies, therefore, can provide the framework for comparative analyses in the future.

Most important, though, is the fact that the response and actions from a myriad of local places propel the so-called big processes and major transformations.[83] To say this does not of course resolve the problems of conceptualization that have plagued all disciplines. However, this does mean that the experiences of localities must be made congruent with the findings of the macro-oriented people from other disciplines.

Thus, with roots in a local unit, anthropologists find it possible, desirable, and necessary to analyze large-scale processes. By locating in a local place, an anthropologist not only achieves expertise in the problem at a manageable and contextualized local level but also can use this as a base for casting both the spatial and conceptual net more broadly. Thus do anthropologists adjust the boundaries of their unit spatially and/or conceptually as they explore the local manifestations of big processes and networks. An excellent example of the kind of contribution that can be made with this strategy has been in the study of local-level political economy of the past two decades, which has done much to explain the nature of agrarian transformation—both in the present and in the past, in Europe and elsewhere. There is now a vast amount of literature telling us, for example, how—and why— peasants become (or do not become) proletarians. We have learned that this process has not been a simple one; it has had numerous permutations, depending on particular contexts and on how the groups were demarcated and the processes conceptualized in the first instance. This literature provides an excellent example of what can be the anthropological contribution to the big problems, dealing as it does with big political-economic processes in the context of open, little localities.[84]

How does this fit with the "big problems" that have formed the basis of Irish historiography? How do we, as historical anthropologists, fit in? As historical anthropologists working in Ireland—or indeed in any state with an extensive and entrenched historiographic tradition—we believe that we must address Irish history and historiography. However, we do not believe that this requires us as anthropologists either to write local histories to provide data for historians or to rewrite national history. The former would have little analytical utility and would be of limited interest, whereas the latter is buried under too much interpretive argument, ideological debate, and hegemonic construction. Equally important, and perhaps as a result, is our recognition that, in the Irish context, so-called national history has consistently failed to engage the fact of local experiences and local histories. One historian put it as follows:

> Almost universally, Irish historians have been guilty of what is best termed the "fallacy of cross-grouping." That is, almost all groups within Irish society, even deviant and dissident groups, have been studied in terms of the nation-state or the national culture. . . . Unfortunately, this perspective . . . has woven yet another deep-running fallacy into Irish historiography, namely an ethnomorphism wherein the entire nation has been conceptualised in terms of the Dublin administrators. Historians of Irish life in the nineteenth century, even the most nationalistic, have taken the same viewpoint as the former British

administration in Dublin in emphasising patterns discernible only from that imperial centre. By focussing upon national patterns of governmental and religious administration, we have wrongly projected upon local communities the belief that national concerns, not local issues, should be at the forefront of local consciousness.[85]

At the same time, national historians have constructed a past that has entered the local level and has formed the lenses through which people in local places see and in turn interpret their own local experiences.[86] The result is that complex inside views of the past coexist with, and affect, our complex outside perspectives.[87]

To state the obvious, events in a locality such as Thomastown occurred not in a vacuum but in response to events elsewhere and to impositions, opportunities, and ideas coming not only from more macro levels but also from other localities. For example, the series of Land Acts after 1880 that progressively gave Thomastown farmers ownership of the land on which they had been tenants owed very little to anything that Thomastown people did. The sources were in London, Dublin, and other parts of Ireland. At the same time, Thomastown's tenant farmers obtained their farms not at the national level but at the local level,[88] in interaction with particular landlords and land agents in the context of local political, agroeconomic, and cultural frameworks. Such local conditions subsequently played a large part in affecting the success of farm reproduction over time. The patterning of these successes and failures from varying, diverse, and numerous localities was later aggregated into a unified and homogenized Irish agricultural history that could say little about what had actually happened in Thomastown and about the conditions that had produced the aggregated patterns.[89] Moreover, the culmination of what some historians have seen as the "revolutionary" event that created a so-called peasantry had little meaning in Thomastown.[90] In 1981, most farmers were scarcely aware, first, that they had recently made a last payment to the Land Commission and, second, that this gave farmers unencumbered tenure for the first time in over seven hundred years. As another example, marriage and residence patterns have been the grist of many a historical mill. Yet marriage choices occurred at the local level, not at the national or regional level at which generalized patterns have often been discerned;[91] and such choices have been very much subject to prior household histories as well as to particularly local socioeconomic and local demographic conditions.[92]

What this means is that any national history has to be perceived as constructed partly from, and therefore made congruent with, Thomastown history and the histories of many other local levels. Thus, we are arguing that locality-based history must be taken as a building block of national history and that historians must account for the "dependency" of national history upon local histories.[93] Moreover, they must simultaneously confront their own past and the historical constructions of their own making.[94]

At the same time, it is essential to recognize that the historical anthropological endeavor is not to provide grist for Irish historians. As a participant aptly said during the conference, "I don't see my work as an effort to fill in the gaps in Irish history." Thus, as historical anthropologists working in Ireland we believe that Irish history and historiography require work to which historical anthropologists can make a contribution. However, historical anthropology in Ireland has its own past, its own present, and its own agenda, which makes it distinct from that of Irish historiography. More important, it links historical anthropology in Ireland, via the cross-cultural tradition of anthropology in general, to the historical anthropology currently being done, and that has been done, in other cultures, societies, and periods.

## Historical Anthropology as a Strategy for the Past: From the Cases, the Commentaries, and the Anthropological Present

In approaching the past, anthropologists have brought with them a distinctive cross-cultural tradition rooted in the academic and political history of the discipline, in the personal and professional histories of its practitioners, and in the internal differences—both theoretical and empirical—that always have characterized, and continue to affect, the "doing of anthropology." The intellectual heterogeneity of anthropology in both the past and the present has centered on several key domains that, like hydra's head, cannot be laid to rest. Issues of space, time, voice, and power have been carried forward from our intellectual past into our present. These issues continually emerged during discussions at our conference, they underlie the papers in the volume, and they thread through the growing body of literature in historical anthropology.

> SILVERMAN: What . . . is the anthropological approach to the past? Why are we different?

GULLIVER: We do field work. We engage the present with the past.

TAYLOR: We use case material to build theory.

BIRDWELL-PHEASANT: We look at the past to explain the present.

SMYTH: You do ethnographies of the past.

VINCENT: Through ethnohistory, we have a long tradition of historical anthropology. Yet today, it's different; what is it in 1989? Perhaps it's a strategy for the past.

RUANE: But what is the strategy?

## A Compelling Sense of Place

That "anthropologists have a compelling sense of place" is very much reflected in the historical case studies in this volume. For anthropologists now working in Ireland, this "sense of place" probably derived from the imperatives that resulted when they confronted a settled agriculture and fixed property matrix in both the past and present; from an earlier anthropology in Ireland with its notions of tradition and community; and, most important, from a more general and contemporary tendency within anthropology, and historical anthropology, to use locality as a central fulcrum: the "local is interesting precisely because it offers a *locus* for observing relations."[95] At the same time, the essays in this volume illustrate that the ways in which local space may be conceptualized and organized can differ dramatically.

Currently in anthropology there are ethnographers who have been concerned with the cultural construction of particular places, of particular localities. Works from the margins of Western Europe (e.g., Cohen [in Whalsay, Shetland Islands],[96] Parman [in a "Gaelic-speaking crofting community . . . on the island of Lewis in the Scottish Outer Hebrides"],[97] and Ennew [also in Lewis][98]) are examples of recent efforts in the British Isles to construct the historical bases for a "culture of community." What is interesting about these studies, and what makes them similar, is that the localities were designated as peripheral—defined as such by the people living there, by emigrants and outsiders, and by the tenets of certain dependency theories. In such studies, the local place was seen as a "community of the periphery" and the anthropologists were concerned to explore the cultural responses to marginality and to learn, therefore, how meanings about the present were constructed using notions about the past. These studies fall into the genre we have called the anthropology of history. According to Parman, the "position taken in this book is that history and myth should be compared not for their factuality but for their meaning. That is, history should be intepreted not as a recording of what 'really' happened but as a cultural construction that is meaningful in the present to the people interpreting the past."[99]

This kind of approach contrasts sharply with that taken by the authors of the case studies in the present volume and therefore with their conceptualizations and uses of locality. Peripherality, in the ethnographic cases here, is never taken as a fixed condition but as an aspect that alters in time. As a result, cultural constructions of locality are treated as temporally specific, partial, and variable. Ethnographers in the present volume therefore refute the idea that there is a structurally based inevitability about the seeming peripherality of little localities. Instead, they treat peripherality as dependent on the historical trajectory of the so-called geography of domination.[100] Clearly, then, the case studies presented here lean more toward the historical genre that we have called "historical ethnography."

Interestingly, several contributors to this volume explicitly chose fieldwork sites in order to confront conventional assumptions about place. At the conference, Birdwell-Pheasant explained how she purposefully went to the west of Ireland—to a prosperous farming area— to provide an alternate view to the dominant stereotype of the west as poor and marginal. Silverman and Gulliver chose the southeast for similar reasons: to show "another Ireland"—without its stereotypical accoutrements of poor people and so-called traditional culture.

None of the papers in this volume, then, is concerned with the marginality of local places or with the historical construction of a culture of fixed marginality. Instead, the meanings associated with place are seen as changing over time; perhaps more important, a central feature of the cases is that they all look to a wider spatial or analytical context within which local meanings were generated.

Vincent's essay is concerned with the morality of famine behavior and the culture of dearth as these were rooted in a "culture of neighborhood" in County Fermanagh. However, Vincent makes clear that this culture was hierarchically organized and that "the neighborhood" did not conform to a fixed space. Instead, the culture of neighborhood was linked to the structure of landholding and to the changing microeconomies of two different regions on either side of Lough Erne.

Vincent's inductive construction of localness, which she builds

from archival materials, contrasts with those contributors who selected their place and then defined an analytical problem. Gulliver and
Birdwell-Pheasant both are concerned with testing "received wisdoms" and the findings of other researchers. Gulliver confronts sociological and historical conclusions about the relationships between
shopkeepers and farmers and about the political roles that shopkeepers played in agrarian and nationalist protest. Birdwell-Pheasant confronts interpretations about the "stem family" concept in the Irish
farming context. Gulliver uses data from the parish of Thomastown,
County Kilkenny; Birdwell-Pheasant uses data from twenty-six contiguous townlands in County Kerry. In both cases, particular localities form the context within which models and hypotheses are tested
and sociopolitical and economic processes are investigated.

The two other anthropological essays in the volume provide additional ways of integrating locality in the context of historical ethnography. Taylor analyzes the relationship between meaning and power
using three kinds of competing religious discourse found in southwest
County Donegal in the middle to late nineteenth century. His concern
is to shed light on "popular Catholicism" and on the "devotional
revolution" that was occurring at the time throughout Ireland. For
Taylor, locality is a broad and general "region" within which his
theoretical interests can be pursued. Yet he remains very much rooted
in locality. For the nineteenth-century organizational context (of new
market towns and associated class structure) and the devotional bases
of local society (focused on holy wells) were very much part of a
northwest Irish context. Taylor's description would not fit most of
southeastern Ireland at the time.

In contrast with Taylor, Silverman begins with a smaller place—
the town and hinterland of Thomastown on the river Nore. She
focuses on the various classes that were represented in order to describe the political process—of encroachment and protest—by which
the burgeoning rights of private property gradually criminalized the
customary, common right to fish during the nineteenth century. She
follows the action, spatially, as it waxed and waned over the century,
to incorporate larger and smaller spaces at different times and for
different reasons.[101]

Overall, then, each historical ethnographic case is rooted in a
locality; but what is done with place—and how it is defined—varies.
No one, however, reifies a particular locality by making it synony-
mous with community. Indeed, in a conference session, participants
agreed that a community is not a place but an ideological construct.
It therefore is not surprising that no one takes a place or locality as

the object of analysis. Instead, locality is a flexible context for the analysis of historical problems, while peripherality, when addressed, is treated as a historical question requiring investigation and not as an inevitable state of being a small place.

## Locality, Holism, and Narrative Sequences in Past Time

A corollary of locality in anthropology has been the notion of holism: if the place was small enough, then it seemed self-evident to many anthropologists that everything that was relevant should be included and that nothing should be omitted, even if its significance was not immediately obvious. When this anthropological view is associated with a time sequence, an inherent problem emerges: historical ethnography may get lost in its own density.

In studying the past, the importance of presenting a sequence of events over time—a narrative in consecutive order, a chronology—can be of central importance. This is different from the frequently used anthropological method of delineating a series of consecutive time periods and presenting an ethnographic snapshot of each. Such a strategy stopped the chronology at different times, so that a description, however complex or analytical, could be inserted.[102] Another contemporary textual method has been to subordinate chronology to the multifaceted aspects of a particular cultural or social form (e.g., a ritual, political movement, resistance, system of oppression). With such a strategy, historical and chronological transformations in the form have been traced by focusing, separately, on the various aspects that comprised it (e.g., symbol, meaning, structure, agency, social relations). Then the conjunctures—the various transformations in the various aspects—have been brought together and described.[103] A third textual strategy has been to specify a period in the past and to show the various sociopolitical and cultural strands that comprised or contributed to the chronology.[104] What happens, though, when the ethnography itself is a series of chronological events and not a description of relations within one or several time periods or a description of events/time within a sociocultural form? In other words, how can the historian's use of narrative be combined with the anthropological notion of holism?

In the essays by Vincent and Silverman in the present volume, the combination of chronology and holistic ethnography threatens to become overwhelming. Silverman originally set out to describe the nature of protest among salmon fishers against the privatization of the inland fisheries along the river Nore at Thomastown in the nine-teenth century. Her concern was to link Thomastown to social history, to the literature on peasant and working-class protest. However, in organizing her data, what slowly began to emerge was a narrative—a long, complicated story of a process that had both local and nonlocal origins. This process generated varying responses from among local class segments that in turn affected the patterning of privatization while simultaneously stimulating new local responses, alliances, and meanings. To tell this story, Silverman has to present overlapping chronologies across several axes simultaneously: sociologically, as individuals acted as parts of particular groups or class segments at varying times; spatially, as the action moved back and forth between different places and localities in the river system; and institutionally, as the process moved through and into different arenas—land law and policy, fisheries policy and administration, and the various layers of the legal system. Telling this complicated story, presenting the chronology, creates a paper that several conference participants described as "dense."

Rogers had earlier mentioned, in relation to Vincent's paper, the problems in trying "to layer the analysis," for Vincent too has to manage multiple strands of data as she links changes in the culture of dearth and locality with several simultaneous and overlapping sequences of events—in a local meeting, in the economy of the region, and in the politics of colonial and capitalist domination. She also has to move among actors located—sometimes simultaneously in terms of their interests and roles—in rural townlands, Enniskillen town, Dublin, and London.

Both Vincent and Silverman are able to grasp the complexity of process because both are rooted in a locality and committed to holism. Yet these same features strain the narrative mode as both grapple with the logistical problems of presenting numerous and simultaneous events, agents, and meanings within a linear tale. Silverman explained at the conference that she still had left out important things, such as the microsociology of the fishers and the wider political economy of the working class of which they were part. Vincent explained that she had barely touched upon the complexity of the political process among the varying groups—gentry, bourgeoisie, peasantry, and laboring poor. Samuel Clark, a historical sociologist, insisted that the omissions were serious: Vincent should have included the politics of the landlords and the British administration, and Silverman was reminded that much of the impetus underlying privatization was "not local" and should have been pursued.

Thus, the commitment to anthropological holism in the context of locality and in association with the need for a sequential ordering strains the narrative mode at the same time that the anthropologist must leave out what others regard as the "important things." There is, therefore, an inherent tension between three key features—locality, holism, and narrative sequence—which together comprise one way of doing historical ethnography.

## "Being There": Engaging the Present with the Past

Taylor's essay in this volume is concerned with the "processes by which a text was responded to by listeners" and the fields of meaning that were generated in the process. He is concerned not with the production and transmission of culture but with its reception. Taylor described at the conference how fieldwork alerted him to this process. While in Donegal, he heard people telling stories over tea. Being there allowed him to juxtapose the teller with the story itself: the story was a lived experience for the narrator, and Taylor was able to learn what the editing was, to hear different interpretations, and to begin to understand that in southwest Donegal, stories and language had become a way by which people supported varying religious views. They did this by sustaining multiple, and often contradictory, religious discourses. In addition, being there allowed Taylor to recognize the importance of many of the elements that comprised the content of the narratives: holy wells, for example, which were an important part of many stories, were peripheral in space and in formal Catholic discourse; however, they were central places and key narrative components in the local life that Taylor encountered.

Contemporary fieldwork thus underlay Taylor's approach to the past: the experience alerted him to the importance of particular historical texts; it made him query how these were connected to the social processes within the church at the time; and it led him to explore the more general and theoretical link between meaning and power in past time. In other words, it was fieldwork that led Taylor to historical texts, a research question, and a theoretical problem.

Although Taylor's field experience enabled him to recognize the importance of discourses in the past, the more common anthropological experience of "being there" has been that the anthropologist was inspired or impelled to move back in time in the effort to make sense of the present. All the anthropologists writing for this volume had done "fieldwork" in their areas, and all were concerned to link the past with the present—if not in the case studies in the volume, then certainly in the long-term development of their projects. Indeed, in some cases, the fact of being there allowed anthropologists to approach the past in the first instance. This was not simply because anthropologists used or were interested in oral accounts of the past; it was also because many documents on and from the past were "purely local"—buried in an old cupboard of a village office in Guyana,[105] in the home of the current president of the village council in Spain,[106] or in the bottom drawer of a sideboard in a farmer's living room in Ireland.[107]

More generally, this linking of the past with the present seems to be distinctly anthropological.[108] It marks an essential difference between anthropology and social history; it also contains certain dangers. Social historians, said Rogers at the conference, do not use the present and, apart from oral historians, they do not interview the subject. He expressed a historian's dismay at the way anthropologists accept oral testimony about the past. He recalled an incident at the conference when an anthropologist, in answer to a question as to how he knew a piece of information, said, more or less, "Mrs. Murphy told me." What astounded him, said Rogers, was not just the statement but that all the anthropologists around the table simply nodded in acceptance! He argued that for a historian dealing with a document, this was unacceptable. "There must be a critical interrogation of the sources," he said; information cannot simply be used. Rogers was assured by the anthropologists that it was known who Mrs. Murphy was, what her interests and concerns were, the nature of her social and cultural milieu, and so on. Therefore, the anthropologists claimed that what she had said had a material context that gave her information as much validity as a document properly interrogated and contextualized. Rogers remained unconvinced, and he remained uncomfortable with oral materials. "I would feel better if I could hear the tapes," he said, "or if your field notes were in a public archive instead of in your personal filing cabinet, so that they could be rechecked." "Maybe," said Gulliver, "but when that archive is at the other end of the world, perhaps requiring months to obtain research permission simply to enter the archive, it surely is only tokenism amongst historians that the document is presumed to be available to others."

Rogers did concede, however, that anthropologists are "ahead of historians" because they are concerned with how things were told them and not simply with the truth or falsity of information.[109] At the same time, he pointed to a potential danger. Because anthropologists often do history in order to project backward, he suggested that they may unduly emphasize continuities and cultural resilience instead of ruptures. We would add that it may lead anthropologists to ignore the historical trajectory caused by the dialectic between the two.

In fact, backward projections in historical ethnography already have yielded studies of continuity. For example, Behar responded to earlier studies of social change in Spain by focusing on history and continuity. She wrote: "For the most part, anthropological accounts of rural life in Spain have been studies of contemporary social change rather than studies of long-term cultural continuity."[110] She attributed the concern with change to conditions within the village itself during the 1960s and 1970s—emigration, new agricultural technology, decline of formal religion. However, when she arrived in the 1980s, "things had changed to a point where one could take a longer perspective on village life." She therefore "set [her]self the task of seeking out those aspects of the old rural culture that had endured, that had not been lost in the midst of change."[111] Behar thus studied "long-term persistence" and how the people "forged an adaptation to the profound social, economic and political changes that are so often assumed to have destroyed the old agrarian regime."[112]

For Behar and others, linking the past with the present while doing history became a study in continuity.[113] For some, such continuity also was linked to the ever-present cultural anthropological idea of adaptation. There is, of course, nothing inherently inappropriate about seeking out persistence. The danger lies in positing dichotomies and in studying one side of them (e.g., persistence as opposed to change; continuity as opposed to discontinuity). It also lies in assuming that the present, because it exists, must be linked to a continuous past. Moreover, the danger lies in seeing "social change" (discontinuity) as the opposite of "history" (continuity) and in challenging old studies of sociocultural change by doing new studies of historical continuity. As Sahlins most usefully noted, it is unecessary and erroneous to set up a dichotomy of change and continuity as if there had to be either one or the other, but not both. Clearly, what results is a complex amalgam: the more things change, the more they stay the same; and the more they stay the same, the more they change. Moreover, the subtle synthesis in any particular period and context calls for careful scrutiny, but we must always remember that this is not the end of the story (it might be thought of as only a chapter), for the story continues and requires persisting attention.[114]

A related danger when anthropologists link the present with the past is that they do a kind of Whig history—with its interest in survivals and with its projection of contemporary structures and ideas backward into time. Said Lamphere:

> It is important . . . not to project present-day analysis into the past in some straightforward manner. In other words, the strategies of resistance that I isolated in a contemporary apparel plant may lead us to look for similar strategies during the 1920s and 1930s, but it would be inappropriate to suggest that these particular strategies were used. . . . Continuity occurs at a more abstract level.[115]

In addition, E. P. Thompson's review of Macfarlane's study *The Family Life of Ralph Josselin* is an example of the kind of critique that anthropological methods may engender among historians for what may be a peculiarly anthropological type of so-called Whig history. For anthropologists not only work with the present of their own particular place and therefore run the danger of extrapolating present meanings onto the past but they also work with cross-cultural understandings—that is, with the present of other places, which has been derived, perhaps from their own experiences, but more likely from the ethnographies of colleagues. Thus, Thompson wrote of Macfarlane's study: "It is by no means self-evident that studies of *Nupe Religion* and of *The Sherpas of Nepal* can serve as 'models' for understanding funeral rites in seventeenth-century Essex."[116] He added:

> The discipline of history is, above all, the discipline of context; each fact can be given meaning only within an ensemble of other meanings; . . . it is most unlikely that any "sociological concept" can be taken, raw, from twentieth century suburbia (or from Melanesia) to seventeenth-century England, since the concept itself must be modified and refined before it will be appropriate to the ensemble of 17th-century meanings.[117]

Clearly, then, as anthropologists approach the past, they would do well to leave behind their well-worn dichotomy of continuity as against discontinuity, and they must tread carefully when carrying concepts from place to place, cross-culturally. Yet most anthropologists would disagree with Thompson's embargo on cross-cultural applications. For he ignored the extent to which anthropologists are self-critical in their application of concepts cross-culturally. He also ignored the fact that there are different levels of abstraction among different concepts and different degrees of precision in their use. The anthropological notion of "lineage" is of a different order from a "political game" and both are very different kinds of concepts from that of, say, "power."[118]

What all this means is that a historical anthropology must be based on a critical awareness of how the past is being conceptualized—that there are problems inherent in endeavors to link the present with the past, from efforts to use experiences of "being there" as a historical tool, and from anthropology's essential cross-cultural outlook, experience, and assumptions.

## The Dearth of Data from the Past Time:
Temporal and Analytical Boundaries

Although the experience of being there was central for the anthropologists in this volume, both Taylor and Gulliver expressed great frustration about the limitations of data when approaching the past. Of the three historical texts that he used, Taylor admitted to having different degrees of success in describing their effect in past time. Similarly, in his analysis of shopkeepers, Gulliver bemoaned the paucity of data prior to the late nineteenth century. He commented wryly at one point: "Do you realise that no one today even knows what the inside of a shop looked like in Thomastown in 1900!"[119]

The dearth of ethnographic data is clearly exacerbated by the anthropological rootedness in locality. Indeed, this can directly affect the definition of locality. For example, in Peletz's historical ethnography of Malay kinship, he necessarily focused—given the availability of data on the past time—on the district for the nineteenth and early twentieth centuries, but he concentrated on "his village" for the period after independence in 1957.[120] This kind of changeover may be inevitable, even though it may distort the analysis. In addition, because there is more contextualized data for a smaller locality in the recent past, social and cultural structures in the more distant past may look more homogeneous and more normative, whereas those of the more recent past and present may appear more heterogeneous, more optative.

At the conference, Rogers expressed concern at the kinds of temporal boundaries drawn by the five anthropological case studies: all are located in the nineteenth century and later. Was this, he asked, because they felt they had to engage the present with the past and this temporal boundary represented the absolute outer limit of human or cultural memory? Was it because the anthropologists wished to give a diachronic dimension to a contemporary analysis and therefore only went as far back (about four generations) as necesary? Was it because in Ireland, the documents that survived were from that period?

To all these questions, the answers were yes.[121] Ruane also picked up this question when commenting on Taylor's paper. If "fields of religious experience" were differentiating in the late nineteenth century, was it not relevant to seek out the temporal roots of this process? How far back did the anthropologist need to go?

Part of the answer to this question is linked to how far the anthropologist can go back, given the dearth of data from the past. For a French Alpine village, Rosenberg was able to construct a detailed family history from the mid-seventeenth century;[122] Netting, with his interest in historical demography and ecology, had systematic population data from 1700 onward for his Swiss Alpine village;[123] and for Belmonte de los Caballeros (Spain, population 1,300), Lison-Tolosana noted that "after 1550 the history of the town can be followed satisfactorily in the manuscripts of the parochial archives."[124]

In contrast, in his study of ideology in the circumcision ritual of the Merina (Madagascar), Bloch was able to look at the "history of the ritual, which, with difficulty, can be traced back almost two hundred years." To do this, Bloch did not focus on a "little locality," and he used colonial sources. Rosaldo, in attempting to do Ilongot history using small residential groups and native "stories," pushed back to the late 1880s, although

> my reconstitution of the . . . past before 1905 is based on what Lakay and his age-mates remembered of what their parents or grandparents had told them long ago. Usually these received memories were lists of place names where people had lived, stories about the sources of kinship . . . and episodes from feuds. Like Lakay and the others, I have no direct access to the early . . . past.[125]

The differences between these studies may be related to two features: the former ethnographies were about "peasantries"; the latter were about "tribal" peoples. The former were located where there were in-depth archives, in Europe; the latter were not. These features also seem to have affected the kind of study that was done. While Rosenberg produced a narrative history grounded in political economy and Netting gave an ecological and kinship analysis over three centuries, Bloch and Rosaldo dealt with ideology and the cultural construction of ritual and warfare, respectively, over a far shorter time.

Thus, a series of interconnected features seems to affect directly the kinds and quantity of data and therefore to condition our boundaries in time. Very schematically, this can be represented by co-occurring continua.

| | | |
|---|---|---|
| data sources | in depth archives ——————— | no archives |
| society type | state peasants ——————— | stateless (tribes) |
| place | Europe[126] —— early colonized —— | late colonized |
| temporal boundaries | early time ——————— | recent time |

Moreover, while the availability of data constrains the temporal boundaries that we can use, it simultaneously conditions our use of space and affects our mode of analysis. For as we decide on the time period, so we concomitantly either constrain the size of the locality or fix on the particular place that can be analyzed. As these constraints on temporal and spatial boundaries are experienced, so constraints are exerted on the kind of analysis that may be undertaken. Generally speaking, whether a study can rest on socioeconomic relations as opposed to cultural forms and whether it can move toward narrative history-demography-kinship, into political economy, or into culture transformation will depend on the constraints created by the availability of data on the past and on the temporal and spatial boundaries we set. Conversely, of course, it is important to realize that preexisting anthropological interests—in the context of the kind of data that are accessible—will affect how we bound both time and space. For example, if the anthropologist's concern is, say, demographic analysis, then this may constrain the temporal and/or spatial boundaries according to the availability of adequate data. If the concern is for a longer range of time, in a locale without census materials or their equivalent, this will preclude demography altogether, although it may allow a more thorough study of cultural meanings.[127] Thus, we have a schema that postulates causal relationships among data sources, spatial-temporal boundaries, and theoretical-empirical interests. In suggesting this, we are aware that we underemphasize the ef-

Data (kind and quantity) { Time → Space → Mode of Analysis

fects of personal histories and theoretical predilections on anthropological choices.[128] The schema therefore shows only what may be possible in particular contexts; it does not define what anthropologists choose to do. However, it does make explicit the fact that some of our theoretical predilections may be less a product of choice and a search for—or ignorance of—"the other" than a product of happenstance and necessity. If so, it may make us less critical of those anthropologists who choose to do history somewhat differently.

The cases in the present volume, which reflect Irish historical ethnography today, incorporate the preceding constraints, possibilities, and boundaries. Irish historical materials are heavily weighted for the nineteenth century and later.[129] Moreover, for the period after 1850, it becomes possible to interconnect different data sources. For example, parish records begin to intersect with land records, and both overlap with the 1901 and 1911 household (census) returns. In addition, much can be linked to newspaper reports that increasingly became more concerned with local news and events after 1850.[130] Finally, in the 1980s, elderly people could remember back to the turn of the century. All this probably has conspired to locate historical anthropology in Ireland, and perhaps elsewhere, in the more recent past—a past that anthropologists have explicitly connected with the present, with "being there."

To explore this more fully, it is useful to look at how the dearth of data and its relation to the themes of continuity and discontinuity have been manifested in adjacent disciplines. In this volume, Smyth, a historical geographer, is concerned with reconstructing society and settlement patterns in seventeenth-century, pre-Cromwellian Ireland and with describing the processes of transformation that occurred as a result of the subsequent conquest. At the conference Smyth bemoaned the dearth of data: he could never obtain the ethnographic detail that an anthropologist would want and, apart from contemporary folklore, he had had to use the "documents of conquest"— produced by the conquerors as they went about displacing and reorganizing local society. From their property surveys and tax records, however, Smyth argued, a geographer could analyze "arcal distributions" as the "key to understanding the process of change." The documents of conquest therefore could be made to speak to historical anthropologists and to deal with the pre- and postconquest periods and with the present.

Smyth chooses two counties (Tipperary and Kilkenny), largely because they were the most completely documented, and he builds a series of typologies—of ecological, cultural, and settlement varia-

tion—that capture regional differences within the two counties during the preconquest period.[131] Most generally, the preconquest property matrix contained three types: 1) landowning areas held by those of old English descent, linked to each other in a wide-ranging kin net and containing a hierarchy of towns, villages, and hamlets as part of a "commercialized world" (south and east Tipperary, County Kilkenny); 2) areas organized by a hierarchy of Gaelic land units shared by kin and partners (north and west Tipperary); and 3) buffer areas held by assimilating and modernizing Gaelic families.

This typological strategy allows Smyth to move into the postconquest period to show the process of social change—how the "material bases for the old order were disrupted and, along with it, the associated settlement infrastructure." Tracing the distribution of Cromwellian surnames in both town and country after the conquest, Smyth pinpoints areas of continuity and discontinuity within the two counties: places where villages disappeared counterpose areas where the "residual power of the older society remained" and where today "villages persist from the seventeenth century."

In analyzing places and patterns of continuity and discontinuity, Smyth is clearly aware of the limitations of the typological approach imposed by the kind of data he has. Using a "time 1" and a "time 2" contrast is not the best way to understand change. He also is aware that the dearth of data limits his ability to address the "local level" as distinct from more regional ones. Yet Smyth maintains a careful balance in assessing continuities and discontinuities, thereby illustrating that a dearth of data does not have to lead to a homogenization of social and cultural structures in the more distant past.

Moreover, if the documents of conquest can be made to speak about the seventeenth century, what can they say to the present and to historical anthropologists working with materials more than a century older? If the rootedness of certain economic formations is accepted, can Smyth's analysis provide a base for anthropological studies in the nineteenth century and later? For example, can the apparently unusual patterns that Gulliver traces among Thomastown's shopkeepers be linked to the town's role as a node in the old English trade network from the thirteenth century onward, a function that survived—and indeed was enhanced by—the increased commercialization wrought by the Cromwellian conquest? Conference participants agreed that a link could be hypothesized if a very general notion of continuity were accepted. Yet they also were uneasy at the conceptual and temporal leaps required—from the seventeenth to the nineteenth centuries, from macropatterns to microdata, from spatial distributions to social relations. The anthropologists felt dislocated

from place and time; interestingly, Smyth and Clark—the historical geographer and the historical sociologist—did not. Vincent argued that it was more important for anthropologists to work from the present backward. Birdwell-Pheasant agreed: "We do history to find out what really happened," she added.[132] It also was Birdwell-Pheasant who most strongly supported the plausibility of the conjectural linkages to the Gaelic past in her own analysis of early twentieth-century household and kinship patterns.

This issue of continuity over extensive time periods will probably become a point of great contention among historical anthropologists. An early example, in 1976, concerned the study by Schneider and Schneider who—to the discomfort of many—traced cultural codes from Roman times to the contemporary mafia. Yet cultural constructs—more particularly, reputed "cultural survivals" and Herskovits's idea of "old forms, new meanings"—are especially amenable to analysis in the long term;[133] social relations, culture practices, and the material conditions of life are less so, given the dearth of data.

### Inside and Outside Voices: Contextualized Understandings and Aggregated Data

Birdwell-Pheasant's essay is a response to what others have written about kinship in rural Ireland. She looks at the stem family "model" for which Irish farmers have served as a classic ethnographic example in Western European studies, and she tests its applicability in Ballyduff using data from the 1901 and 1911 census returns, parochial records, land registry records, and interviews. To do this she divides the model into its "ideal" component parts—how it has been said to work ideally. She then compares this to what Ballyduff people have done in relation to premortem property transmission, male primogeniture and impartible inheritance, marriage patterns, three-generational residence patterns, and sibling dispersal. She finds what she calls a "flexible" condition in Ballyduff—a flexibility linked to a hierarchy of values held by Ballyduff people. With this hierarchy, and in the face of economic and demographic realities, farmers have managed the transmission process as best they could—trying to hold firm to their primary goal of maintaining the family on the farm while aiming, secondarily, for ensuring father-son inheritance, and finally, for giving a start to as many of the children as possible.

The range of patterns that Birdwell-Pheasant finds clearly raises questions about the use of rural Ireland as an archetype of the so-called stem family. Perhaps most important, it suggests the importance for anthropologists, when studying the past, of maintaining two key distinctions with which they generally are careful when using nonhistorical materials—that between (outsiders') models and (insiders') norms and that between insiders' norms (ideal) and insiders' (real) behavior. Indeed, it has been the confusion among models, norms, and behavior that probably has created the archetype in the first instance: "We don't really know what we mean by the so-called stem family," said Birdwell-Pheasant. "Is it a model? A norm? An idea? And whose?"

The issue of "whose" that Birdwell-Pheasant raised parallels Gulliver's questions when he explores two generalizations about rural shopkeeping that, like the archetype of the Irish stem family, have been made by historical sociologists and historians and that have been accepted as "true." The generalizations are the following: shopkeepers were (are) recruited from, and had (have) key links to, farm families; and shopkeepers always were (are) key activists and leaders in nationalist and agrarian politics.

These "truths" about shopkeepers have been put forward in numerous studies. Virtually all of these used data aggregated for large units (county, province, and/or state); they used data from diverse sources (e.g., police reports of arrests, lists of county councillors); and they used data that pertained to very different time periods and events or contexts after the mid-nineteenth century. Most important, the data were derived from documents that did not, and could not, have a common definition or understanding of what a shopkeeper was.

In contrast to these studies, Gulliver works with locally based documents and recollections from Thomastown. He looks at actual decision-making preferences, real social networks, and recorded political participation. He also aims, despite the difficulties, for a coherent use of the concept of shopkeeper. For *shopkeeper* was an insider's category in Thomastown, and its application and usage were complex—depending on situation, personal histories, and historical context.[134] If Thomastown is typical in this respect, it is unclear whom and what the historical sociologists and historians have caught in their net of aggegated data—derived not only from numerous locales and times but also from conflating inside and outside categories and from combining such diverse terms as *merchant, publican, trader, shopkeeper, commercial sector, townsman, employer, manager, contractor, small business class,* and *gombeenman*.[135] Not surprisingly, Gulliver's findings, with only a few exceptions, depart radically from the established truths.

Gulliver does not want to suggest that Thomastown was either typical or atypical. Instead, he argues for more local-level or contextualized studies associated with a greater sophistication in the use of categories and categorizations[136]—all in order to test properly the conflicting conclusions derived from historical anthropology, from so-called national and regional trends, and from a historiography that has been rooted in large regions and in the seemingly major political events and institutions.

Studying, and knowing about, particular contexts in order to use documentation coherently are necessary for making generalizations that can form the basis for cross-cultural comparison; and such a comparison was an important goal for all conference participants. It also is one that has long been associated with anthropology. However, applying the cross-cultural method to the past is more complicated than applying it to the present.

In the discussion on Gulliver's paper, participants were intrigued by his seemingly unusual findings, despite the problems of comparison. They began to explore possible explanations. It was suggested that class structure and relations in the southeast were different from those in western regions and thus constituted a different context for shopkeeping. Farming was too "important" to be left to shopkeepers (and vice versa), said Smyth; Silverman added that the large numbers of laborers may have provided the main clientele of the shops. It was then suggested that discussion ought to move away from interregional comparison—that the key factors were not rooted in the east-west distinction that has permeated the comparative method in Irish studies. Instead, it was suggested that the key factors were located in the particular histories of particular localities—that is, in precisely those relations that were lost from view when aggregated data from regions were compared. Participants then proposed criteria that might have intersected in different ways—in particular localities and at particular times—to create the peculiar histories within which variations in shopkeeping might have occurred. These included the presence or absence of a gentry class and of local industry (milling, tanning, and so on); the nature of the agricultural hinterland (farm sizes, extent of commercial farming, cropping patterns, and so on); the availability of money, capital, and credit; the pattern of exchange within and between classes; demographic patterns, such as population size and structure, the proportion of shopkeeers to other occupational groups and its implications for recruitment, and so on.

If all these variables have changed over time in their relation to each other, then clearly the potential complexity of local histories is immense. Yet the resulting variability clearly constituted, for participants, an argument in favor of more contextualized, local studies. On the other hand, some participants became uncomfortable with the implications, for cross-cultural comparison, of dealing so intensively with particular localities. Some suggested that the absence of a sufficiently large, quantitative data base with which to test hypotheses would constrain comparison. Others added that the possibility of "unique" findings for each locality would preclude comparison altogether.

This issue was not simply a division between quantitative and qualitative approaches, nor was it the issue of typicality. Rather, it was how the comparative method could be used in the past time. Should it be based on the comparison of contextualized histories or on the comparison of variables? The essays by both Gulliver and Birdwell-Pheasant provide a combination of strategies, but there also have been examples in historical anthropology that have aimed at comparison using multiple contextualized places[137] or time periods.[138] In addition, there have been those, largely kinship and household, studies, that have focused more on the controlled comparison of variables.[139] What all this suggests is that the strategy for cross-cultural comparison in the past time can vary. However, to allow for the possibility of future comparisons among studies carried out by different anthropologists, there must be a firm application of the distinction between inside and outside categories and a contextualization—in time and place—of all data, even those that are aggregated.

## Locality and the Wider Analytical Context: Time, Space, and Power in Cross-Cultural Perspective

Ruane's essay in the present volume can be located in the preceding anthropological litany that the local level is rooted in a context that must be integrated into any analysis.[140] For one model of this wider context, colonialism, is explored by Ruane as he reviews the literature on Ireland's past and assesses the divergent opinions on, and varying usages of, the colonial theme. At the conference, Ruane argued that a colonial model could provide a "middle-range conceptualization or level" in historical analyses. Such a level, he argued, was missing from contemporary studies of Irish historical processes even though it may have set key parameters as to how Irish society in general, and particular localities, developed over time. Ruane also argued that such a model might provide a unifying theme for all disciplines that study the Irish past while providing a point at which the varying interests of different disciplines could meet and articulate. At a minimum, said

Ruane, if historical anthropologists were to use their comparative method and materials, they had to decide if the Irish past had parallels with the non-Western, colonized contexts in which they have tended to do most of their work.

However, after exploring in his essay how the colonial model has been used to study the Irish past by practitioners in several disciplines, Ruane concludes that we cannot yet assess the relevance and applicability of the colonial model to Irish historical processes. This is because it has been used too uncritically and inconsistently by both anthropologists and others. At the same time, though, Ruane's review outlines the elements of an approach—which combines theoretical analysis, ideological critique, and a style of empirical research (holistic, contextual, and comparative)—that might allow the question of colonialism in the Irish past to be addressed and resolved. Moreover, such elements apply to any effort to characterize and analyze the wider context, however defined. On a more general level, of course, Ruane's essay addresses the debate between historians and social scientists over the use of theoretical models to interpret historical processes. Given the reluctance of historians to import concepts and models, Ruane's essay—and his concerns—illustrate that anthropologists are not only sensitive to the reasons underlying such reticence by historians but they also are acutely conscious of the problems that ensue when concepts and models are, in turn, imported into historical anthropology.

However, in questioning the relevance of a wider context that may be conceptualized as colonial, Ruane raises an important issue in historical anthropology. For colonialism, in its fundamental guise, is about power. Yet the case studies in this volume, and indeed in historical anthropology generally, fail to address power in any direct, explicit, or systematic way. For example, the vast majority of monographs in historical anthropology that we have cited so far in this essay did not list *power* in their indexes.[141] This does not mean that it was absent from the analyses; rather, it has been hidden under other rubrics, which have changed over time as the vocabulary of the discipline has changed along with its main paradigms. Power, therefore, has often been subsumed as an attribute within particular institutions or of certain individuals—as evidenced by such terms as *political power, symbolic power, spiritual power,* and *discursive power.* It often has been implied by such notions as ideology, oppression, and control. Most recently, it has been included in such concepts as domination and hegemony.

At the conference, Rogers made a similar observation about anthropology and power. He said that anthropologists have tended to use the concept, albeit often skilfully, in a "noninstrumental way"—in contrast with political scientists and historians, who have been more likely to see power as instrumental.[142] In other words, anthropologists have embedded their ideas about power in other concepts and domains (e.g., in networks, notions of authority, and symbols). Yet when they did this, Rogers added, they often lost sight of its centrality and were unable to define its role and its boundaries explicitly. So, for example, some anthropologists have used the concept of class, but its key constituent element, power, has not been made clear.[143] As a result, class has often been used as a static category rather than as, following Thompson, a "coming into being"—as a dynamic formation in process.

In fact, four of the six cases in this volume are about the dramatic workings of power. Smyth describes a conquest; Vincent describes the destruction wrought by the state through the imposition of the Poor Law; Silverman describes the victory of private property in one arena; and Taylor describes the discourse, and its source, which competed with hegemonic religious power. Although these cases focus either on the local effects of power or on the narrative behind its imposition as experienced from below, none focuses on the history of that power itself.

This fact constitutes the central theme in Clark's essay. For him, how Ireland entered the so-called modern world is the key contextual issue, and the problem that must underlie any historical analysis. He argues that anthropologists have failed to study this. Interestingly, the anthropologists at the conference in turn criticized the modernization model that centered Clark's own concerns. Echoing a debate from the anthropological past and present,[144] they argued that a colonial interpretation would be more congenial were the anthropologists to approach the so-called making of contemporary (modern) Ireland.

Clark then reiterated his more general point: the case studies had failed to locate themselves in an explicitly wider context (e.g., colonialism, modernization, and so on). In response, Taylor argued—and the other anthropologists agreed—that so-called models of process and of Irish history were embedded in the anthropological case studies and could be found if anyone wanted to do so. Said Rogers in support: "A local study can be both particular and general. The building of theoretical paradigms can be implicit."

From this perspective, it can be argued that the essays in this volume do address the processes that contributed to, and the issues underlying, the making of contemporary Ireland. Moreover, when linked together, the case studies comprise a cumulative, lineal, and historical picture of much of that making; and they do so using an implicit colonial model. Thus:

| Centuries | Essays and Issues |
|---|---|
| Seventeenth | Conquest (Smyth) |
| Early to mid-nineteenth | Expansion of the state (Vincent) |
| Mid to late nineteeeth | Extension of private property (Silverman) |
| | Catholic hegemony: contested meanings (Taylor) |
| Nineteenth and twentieth | Fracturing of local classes: farmers distinguished from shopkeepers (Gulliver) |
| | Hierarchy of values and property transmission (Birdwell-Pheasant) |

What is missing, of course, and what makes this effort different from historical sociology, is that the cases remain discrete and the linkages between them remain implicit, awaiting a synthesizer. Also missing is an explicit use of the concept of colonialism and its associated notion, the concept of power.

Yet such an avoidance may have advantages. It may preclude seeing the so-called wider context as the cause of local histories, and it may prevent making colonialism or "capitalism too determinative."[145] Indeed, a "new kind of functionalist reasoning"[146] and a "new kind of global functionalism"[147] have often been associated with macro concepts. Thus, in the same way that the anthropologists at the conference were uncomfortable about conjectural leaps required to bring the distant past forward to the present, they also were wary of using power as part of the kind of explanation that may ensue when overarching concepts, such as world system or colonialism, are used to elucidate local places. The concern was with the ways in which both the prior and later histories, and historicities, of localities and real people are homogenized or lost within such overarching constructs. At the same time, no one denied the relevance of such contexts. Rather, the problem was to handle them so that they could be made appropriate to the histories and historicities of localities.

Wolf made a recent attempt to do this. He distinguished four levels of power: power as potency, power in social interaction, tactical or organizational power, and structural power. He argued that history, process, and signification all involve "considerations of power," particularly the latter two types of power.[148] This focus on power—in a

single context where history, process, and meaning are treated together—may provide a middle-range conceptualization that integrates
the "local" and "wider" context. For although the distinction between *local* and *wider* has been pronounced untenable, the absence of
workable, alternative conceptualizations remains a key problem.[149]
We agree with Rosenhaft that the "adequate comprehension of social
developments on a larger scale and a higher level of discourse and its
integration with the explication of everyday life . . . represents the
greatest challenge to anthropology."[150] Rosenhaft saw the concept of
hegemony as possibly performing this function; others have agreed.[151]
But as Rosenhaft noted, although the concept "directs us more clearly
than any other term in current use to examine 'culture' as an arena of
class domination and negotiation, . . . it does not instruct us as to
what we will find or even how to go about it."[152] There is also the
danger that in the context of doing history, the term may become
description, cause, and effect all at the same time and thus of limited
analytical use.

From another perspective, the discussion about power and the
wider context at the conference, illustrated the difference between
social history and historical sociology. Said Rogers, a social historian:

> Thompson and Tilly for example are explicit about theory building.
> Others emphasize texture and empiricism. Social historians usually
> begin with an historiographic problem to be tested, with an hypothe-
> sis. So although some historians are theoretical, most prefer their working
> paradigms to be implicit. But in any case, they do not work with a
> high level of theory; they work instead with "conceptual clarities."

In contrast, Clark said, "sociologists do not begin with a clear notion
of history. In fact, their notion changes as they work with the data.
And their hypotheses are post facto." Moreover, said Clark, they
prefer so-called jumbo history—macrobased in both space and time—
because "it juxtaposes different types or varying levels of data for the
purpose of elucidating general processes and explicit paradigms."
Rogers disagreed with such an approach. He pointed out how historians choose a group, a location, or a period in order to deal with the
complexity of the past and to explore the issues that have been raised
from a broader intepretative level. He called these "middling issues"—less grand than Tilly's, he said, but interesting all the same.
Moreover, Rogers argued that local studies can be used in comparative perspective to control for certain variables that have been designated by these middling issues.

More generally, it was Clark, the historical sociologist, who had the greatest difficulty with what he saw as the anthropological propensity to ignore the wider context. He found problems with the smallness of scale in the anthropological case study approach. He was intrigued by our "up-down" metaphor—how we saw ourselves as moving "up" from our local areas to wider levels of analysis and how we saw ourselves as moving "down" again. He wondered if anthropologists still assumed that their local-level studies were typical, representative, or unique. "How is an area chosen," he asked, "because it's unusual, or because it's typical? How do you generalize? By replicating local studies? What else can be done with them?"

Clark's questions crystallized, for the anthropologists, the way in which the discipline still was perceived by many outsiders, much in terms of discredited viewpoints. Yet as anthropologists approach the past time, they inevitably and often will meet such opinions—from those in other disciplines who are working in the same archives, using the same data. During much of our past, we were off somewhere else, in a locality (exotic) and time period (now) that only occasionally overlapped with the interests of other disciplines. As the disciplines now meet (e.g., in the National Library or Public Record Office in Dublin), anthropologists may often find themselves on the defensive—accused by others of "messing around with detail" in places where nothing much ever happened. Yet, given the problem with conventional wisdoms that both Birdwell-Pheasant and Gulliver found and given the silence of the historical record on the rural, nonagricultural laborers and fishers, on the complexity of life and death during the famine in Enniskillen, and on the competition among religious discourses and beliefs in Donegal local life, the anthropologists were inclined to agree with Rogers's more sympathetic and understanding viewpoint. However, this interchange signaled two features: first, the communication difficulties that necesarily will ensue as anthropologists continue to approach the same past as other social scientists; and second, a growing rapport between historical anthropology and a certain kind of history.

## A Distinctive Anthropological Tradition

The problematic nature of such rapport, however, becomes manifest when an apparent convergence, or a division of labor, among disciplines is mooted. For example, in 1980, Hobsbawm wrote, with reference to LeRoy Ladurie's work: "There is nothing new in choosing to see the world via a microscope rather than a telescope. So long as we accept that we are studying the same cosmos, the choice between microcosm and macrocosm is a matter of selecting the appropriate technique."[153] From the historian's point of view, insofar as anthropology often is located in small contexts and frequently provides "a worm's eye view," historical anthropology may emerge as a handmaid to, or a segment of, history.[154] From an anthropological perspective, it has been suggested that "to juxtapose historians and anthropologists . . . is simply to reify an artificial boundary and to negate the 'blurred genres' of the contemporary academic scene (Geertz 1983)."[155]

Yet, wrote Tilly, the "discipline of anthropology is far broader than ethnography" and the kind of work done by Le Roy Ladurie.[156] Moreover, many historians have been skeptical of rapprochement.[157] In any case, and from the other side, we maintain that sociocultural anthropology contains more than a series of discrete conceptual items that can be consumed at will by historians, that it is more than a type of textual or discursive analysis that converges with other like efforts from other disciplines,[158] and that it is more than a "genre." Therefore, historical anthropology cannot be a small-scale variation of history, a useful repository of useful concepts, or just a technique. Rather, it approaches the past with a coherence that is derived from its own histories, the persistence of (and rebellions against) its own traditions, and the long-term conflicts (some old, some new) among its component parts.

Looked at from the perspective of the historian's past and present, fundamental differences between anthropology and history are clear. For example, there remains today an important division between narrative history and a history that uses social concepts around which to frame a case study.[159] In anthropology, such a distinction has little meaning. Any anthropological ethnography, whether historical or not, has invariably contained conceptual categories (both insider and outsider ones) while a conceptually based study always has had some narrative—to delineate a genealogy, to describe microevents, to construct a life history, to set the stage in the past about the present, to explicate developmental cycles, or to deal with sociocultural change and continuity in the present.

This inevitable overlap between narrative and concept has had many strands in anthropology, most of which have had a lengthy history. The use of situational analysis (or social drama) is an example, and it is compellingly used by Vincent in her case study here.[160] Another example is the continuing anthropological struggle to link the actions of individuals to the formation of groups—an effort found in the case studies by both Silverman and Gulliver. A third example is the century-old concern with kinship systems and how they operate, a theme that Birdwell-Pheasant pursues. A fourth example is the ongoing anthropological concern with change. Early efforts were Fortes's notion of developmental cycles, Firth's distinction between social structure and social organization, and the studies of culture contact and acculturation in the 1950s. The concern continued, leading to Sahlins's question in 1981 ("How does the reproduction of a structure become its transformation?")[161] and to Wolf's question in 1990 ("How do we get from viewing organization as a product or outcome to understanding organization as process?").[162] In this volume, the essays by Smyth, Vincent, and Silverman provide case studies on the theme of change; Ruane explores a general theoretical context within which historical anthropology might locate change. A final example of the overlap between narrative and concept in anthropology is the endless discussion on the relation between culture and social relations. This has found its way into historical anthropology, resulting, inter alia, in the two genres noted here—historical ethnography and the anthropology of history.

More generally, as historical anthropologists work through their case materials—from archives and from participant observation—the various issues that have been peculiar to the anthropological past are combined in various ways, which reflect the distinctiveness of anthropology and give a particular hue, direction, and content to historical anthropology. Thus, in this volume, Vincent integrates the narrative mode, situational analysis, and the production of culture at a critical juncture. Her effort complements, but is different from, Taylor's use of textual and discourse analysis in a particular historical context. Similarly, yet somewhat differently, Silverman moves between social relations and individual actions, on the one hand, and class action, on the other. She uses concepts from political anthropology as well as the idea of culture as a mediating factor in the context of a complex narrative over a long period of time. Gulliver and Birdwell-Pheasant address variations in kinship and political patterns, using concepts of stratification, values, and interests.

As Vincent pointed out at the conference, and as we do here, all these ideas, concepts, approaches, techniques, and so on, derive from anthropological work in other places and times and for other purposes. Moreover, "we do not all do the same anthropology," said Vincent tellingly. Thus, the elements that comprise the history of the discipline, and the personal histories of anthropologists, all provide distinctive perspectives on, and approaches to, the past. Yet, although such variations occur, it is important to recognize that they do so with a coherence derived from a shared, albeit often internally contested, intellectual tradition.

In addition, when anthropologists bring their conceptual baggage to the past, they combine it with a distinctive use of source materials. Oral testimony, and the linking of present with past, are of course the obvious examples.[163]

VINCENT: Anthropologists see sources differently. For example, a debate recorded in Hansard. An anthropologist looks not only at the context, as does the historian, but at the interactional and situational dimensions of the context—who's speaking? who's listening?

GULLIVER: . . . and who's there?

SMYTH: Anthropologists also ask different questions of the sources.

ROGERS: That's true. Anthropologists tend to ask *how*, not simply *why*, unlike a good many historians.

GULLIVER: Then there is the interface between archival materials and ethnographic data about the present. Historians do not make this connection.

CLARK: Which do you do first?

VINCENT: We do the "archive in the field"—they go both together, hand in hand. Taylor and Gulliver did this systematically.

BIRDWELL-PHEASANT: And if the present doesn't link directly with the past . . .

SMYTH: . . . stories, songs survive.

VINCENT: There is a layering of the past, and a transformation of the past, as in Taylor's paper; and you can use this to come up to the present. In other words, there is a present which incorporates the past and yet, also, there remains the possibility of isolating the past.

SILVERMAN: But that creates difficulties with the idea that there are always "different histories."

RUANE: In the north, for example, there are Protestant and Catholic histories.

TAYLOR: Yes. This raises issues about narrative and knowledge . . .

ROGERS: . . . and whose knowledge? I think an ethnographer is more likely to respect "other knowledge" for itself than is a historian.

VINCENT: At the same time, today, no anthropologist can or would ignore the archives. Malinowski's view that "the past is in the minds of the informants" is simply no longer tenable.

## Toward a Historical Anthropology

In approaching the past, then, anthropologists bring with them a distinctive tradition rooted in the academic history of the discipline and in the professional histories of its practitioners. A corollary is that they also bring their theoretical and intellectual problems, ethical dilemmas, and interpretative arguments that have both plagued and intrigued them for decades. As Ortner noted, "Insofar as history is being amalgamated with virtually every kind of anthropological work, it offers a pseudointegration of the field that fails to address some of the deeper problems."[164]

That, we would argue, is only part of the issue. For many anthropologists who "do history," the past has become just another "foreign country," yet another society or culture. Indeed, this place called "Thepast" has been added to the long list of exotic places in which anthropologists may do fieldwork. However, it is important to recognize that we not only arrive there with our "deeper problems" but also inevitably encounter new kinds of analytical issues precisely because "Thepast" is unlike other anthropological fieldwork sites. This means that historical anthropology cannot be used simply as a means of avoiding or, more likely, of intensifying old conflicts.

For example, what we would call the "misuse" of the past and the reification of history is apparent from the following exchange. Ortner cautioned, in her concern for culture "practice," that, "History is not simply something that happens to people, but something they make within, of course, the very powerful constraints of the system within which they are operating."[165] Roseberry countered that political economists place "anthropological subjects at the intersections of local and global histories." In so doing, "they offer a fundamental challenge to those who discuss culture, history, and practice without sufficient consideration of class, capitalism, and power."[166] Clearly, the divisions are intense, but they are not helped by using "history" as an epithet or by opposing gross concepts (e.g., *people, system, class, power*) that may symbolize but not really address, or allow us to address, the complexities, subtleties, and new problems of doing history and approaching the past.

Thus, we see historical anthropology both as a strategy for the past and as an opportunity to expand the way in which we do anthropology—with stimulus from the new problems raised by approaching the past, with ideas from those who bring different anthropological understandings to the task, and with encouragement from those of other disciplines who have been visiting it before us. Said Smyth, the historical geographer at the conference, with the optimism of a sympathetic outsider: "Anthropologists should not be concerned with doing history. They are approaching the past and that's what's important. They should do anthropology." We agree. For we too see anthropology as a "cumulative undertaking, as well as a collective quest."[167]

## NOTES

1. Most of the time, anthropologists have not described how experiences of various kinds combined to produce their finished product. Comaroff wrote: "The connection between text and context is largely one of 'silent development,' and the conventional acknowledgements of authors tells us little about the actual formation of any intellectual product" (1985:xi). Indeed, even in the few cases where nods in the direction of describing their pasts have been made, anthropologists still provided far too little background—as did Comaroff—about the underlying "material and conceptual relations" (Comaroff 1985:xi). This certainly has been true for historical anthropology. We therefore feel that we need not apologize for including our own odyssey here. Instead, we expect that it may be useful for some who are on a similar route. We certainly could have used, many times over, the experiences of others.

2. For example, *The Bulletin of the Irish Committee of Historical Sciences* was first issued in 1939. "Its purpose was to keep members and associates of the Irish Historical Society and Ulster Society for Irish Historical Studies informed of work in progress. It provided notes and news of Irish historical interest and abstracts of papers read before both societies" (McGuire 1981:225). In 1971, a "survey of Irish historiography sponsored by the Irish Committee of Historical Sciences, the body representing Irish Historical interests on the Comité International des Sciences Historiques," reviewed works published between 1936 and 1970 (Lee 1981a:vii). In 1981, historian Joseph Lee edited a similar book of essays that surveyed historical works published between 1970 and 1979.

3. The idea of economic dualism—of a "dual economy"—in Ireland came out of the work of economic historians (e.g., Lynch and Vaizey 1960), but it was soon replaced by a more complex notion of regionally based, economic variation (e.g., Cullen 1972). Geographers were already using the latter idea

(e.g., Hughes 1963; Smyth 1975), although they were mainly concerned with agriculture (e.g., Gillmor 1967; O'Carroll 1978; Ross 1969). However, it was the idea of cultural "dualism"—of the south/southeast versus the west of Ireland—that entered into analyses of social and community relations (e.g., Hannan 1979), and it certainly underlay the community studies done by anthropologists at the time.

4. A review of this approach was provided by Roseberry (1988). For Silverman it was a continuation of her earlier work in agrarian systems and class formation in Guyana (1979) and Ecuador (1987) and in archival research (1980). For Gulliver it provided the opportunity to research the past—as compared with what had been possible in much of his earlier field research in East Africa (1955b, 1963); to deal more concretely with issues of social change (1955a, 1958, 1969); and to follow up an emerging theoretical interest in linking the present to the past (1971).

5. This of course typified anthropological analyses at the time. It began with Arensberg (1937) (republished in 1988) and included such works as Cresswell (1969), Messenger (1969), Harris (1972), Symes (1972), Brody (1973), Bax (1976), Leyton (1975), Kane (1977), Fox (1978), and Scheper-Hughes (1979a, 1979b). An early critique of this community study approach was made by Gibbon (1973) in reviewing Brody. A later critique, from the perspective of dependency theory, was made by Ruane (1978).

6. Apart from the Harris and Leyton studies listed in n. 5, the anthropological community studies at the time had been done almost entirely in the west of Ireland.

7. The variable and complex meanings of the term *Thomastown* were described in Gulliver and Silverman (1990).

8. These administrative units ("district electoral divisions," or DEDs) did not correspond to the parish, although they were contained within it, together with other parts of other DEDs. In any case, Thomastown parish itself did not correspond to any administrative or legal unit, either in the present or past time. In 1981, the population of the two DEDs was 1,932, and the parish contained 2,670 people, or 716 households. This population was about one-third what it had been in 1841 (Silverman and Gulliver 1986: 18–27).

9. At the time, the archival sources that we knew about were the parish records, parliamentary papers, and census materials. As time passed, our archival arsenal additionally came to include local business and farm records, minutes and correspondence from local organizations, local school records, county and national newspapers, poor law union records, land valuation records, memorialized deeds, encumbered estate court papers, wills and probate papers, land registry materials, and so on. For more detail, see Gulliver (1989).

10. Canon Dr. Michael O'Carroll, P.P., was an unstinting supporter of our work. We owe him a great deal—not simply because of the parochial records but because his early and immediate acceptance of our presence in

Thomastown, and of our research, allowed us to approach more easily other Thomastown people for their help.

11. For example, Ó Tuathaigh (1972). Although other historians denied that it had been a watershed (such as Crotty 1966:46–51), the fact that there was academic dispute inclined us to think that, at the very least, it was a "key event." See Daly (1986:117–24) and Ó Gráda (1988) for discussions of its variable, and debatable, impact.

12. It is curious that we had such difficulties with temporal boundaries as compared with spatial ones. In fact, neither one was ever drawn to our complete satisfaction. In relation to our spatial boundaries, we found—midway through our 1980–81 sabbatical year—that our two DEDs were heavily concentrated on "lowland" areas and that this had implications for farming and settlement patterns. So we began to include other parts (townlands) of the parish that contained "upland" areas (and two farming villages; see Smyth, this volume). This meant that we had failed to collect some data for these (such as newspaper reports). However, in most cases (such as parish records, probate papers, etc.), we actually went back to the sources to collect the materials. Similarly, our temporal boundaries were once again pushed back—to 1800—largely because we found the parochial records for 1798 and beyond, Tighe's 1802 publication, newspapers, and 1833 tithe lists. We then found memorials of deeds and county newspapers for the late eighteenth century. Essentially, we have never firmly fixed our temporal boundaries, although, clearly, different kinds of data apply to different periods. Our spatial boundaries have remained far firmer, although as we go back in time, we occasionally have had to take other geographical units—such as baronies—that were used in the records; and we did collect surviving estate papers for areas adjacent to Thomastown parish. This has meant that we have spent the summers subsequent to 1980–81 reviewing old archives for new areas and times. "Doing history"—as Price (1990:xix) and others have noted, is time-consuming and tedious. For more detail see Gulliver (1989).

13. For example, not only did the Land Wars pass by with only two or three meetings of a land committee in Thomastown, but neither battles nor skirmishes occurred in the War of Independence (1919–21) or the Civil War (1922–23). As a reflection of this, few older people had any personal recollections at all of anything happening—things they saw or heard, about people whom they knew or knew of—in connection with those events.

14. Although this seems self-evident, it is a hard fact to accept about the past when there are so few documents that the researcher wants each one to be of some use. The historians' idea of "interrogating the sources" is useful, but it does not solve the problems of unknown bias and, of course, omission.

15. See n. 5. In fact, by the 1980s, the focus of anthropological research had shifted somewhat to Northern Ireland, largely because of anthropology departments there. However, the western bias remained. In a 1989 collection of seventeen essays by anthropologists on Ireland (edited by Curtin and Wilson), six were located in the west (including Donegal), five were in the

north, three were in the east-southeast (including one by Silverman and one by Gulliver), two were located in Dublin, and one was in Kilkenny city. The urban focus was, of course, new.

16. A recent example of this kind of study—of customs and tradition—was that by Shanklin (1985). For an analysis of the confusion between *history* and *tradition,* see Herzfeld's discussion of the "aboriginal European" in Greek ethnography (1987:56–61).

17. Part of our recognition of this position came from our Canadian roots and from dependency theory that pertained particularly to Canada and the work of Harold Innis (e.g., Melody 1981). As citizens of what we believe to be the "richest underdeveloped country in the world," we found a great many structural and historical parallels in the Irish context. Therefore, that Ireland might be similar to a Third World country (and to Canada) did not require any great conceptual leap on our part. It was, however, very dismaying to most Irish people with whom we discussed this. (See Ruane's essay in this volume.)

18. We are very sure that these were not cases in which "Thomastown people" engaged in a community-based, collective process of historico-cultural amnesia/recall. This has been suggested for other places (e.g., Collard 1989). First, Thomastown people—assuming one can ascertain what that means in the first instance (see Gulliver and Silverman 1990)—did nothing collectively and never have done. Second, we found that different people—depending on age, sex, class, locality, personal history, social networks, and personal predilections—remembered or forgot different things and different categories of things (e.g., Silverman 1989) Third, dramatic and traumatic events that actually had been witnessed by living people, and that were linked to events in the national chronology (such as the funeral, during the War of Independence, of a Thomastown lad who joined the IRA and was killed in action in north Kilkenny) were very clearly remembered and spoken about by eyewitnesses. In general, the process of remembering *events that were actually witnessed* very much depended on the person's interests and personal involvement and on us, the anthropologists, being able to elicit memories by asking the right questions. The process of remembering events prior to living recall was very undeveloped in the Thomastown area. We learned very early on that people's knowledge of events scarcely predated their birth. In contrast, informants could go a little further back in time if *facts about people* were being elicited by us. This was because informants had heard about individuals who had been old when the informants were young. We suggest that the limited time depth in the recall of events and in the recall about people might have been related to the fact that national, and hegemonic, chronologies were so deeply entrenched.

19. This was explored in more detail in Gulliver and Silverman (1990).

20. In fact, with only minor variations in meaning and, occasionally, with additional categories appended, this class-based social map was of very long standing and fairly broadly distributed. We have found it in early nineteenth-

century documents for both southeastern Ireland and England. Interestingly, the structure was used in nineteenth-century sources to describe the past as well as the present!

21. We had "made history" in two senses: not only had we created a new version of the past, but we had also become a part of, and an element in, Thomastown's past after 1979.

22. The conference was held April 4–9, 1989, at Seneca College, King City Campus, Ontario. It was funded by the Social Science and Humanities Research Council of Canada (SSHRC); by the Wenner-Gren Foundation for Anthropological Research, New York; and by contributions from the universities of the participants. Two other participants, not included in this volume, were Chris Curtin (University College Galway) and Thomas Wilson (United Nations International School, New York).

23. Recently, the cause has been identified differently. "In hindsight, anthropologists' previous failure to tackle history seriously was due to their colonial *mentalité*" (Ohnuki-Tierney 1990a:2). We argue, however, that any single-cause explanation is inadequate.

24. Use of the "ethnographic present" has been both a symptom and a partial cause of anthropological failures to consider processes through time, change, and history. Indeed, its use in ethnographic writings has been amply criticized. However, the ways in which academic language and discourse perpetrates the ethnographic present has seldom been discussed. Thus, it is virtually an unquestioned convention to state: "Dr. X writes that . . ." — even though Dr. X wrote in, say, 1972. This use of the academic, ethnographic present is misplaced, misleading, and indicative of ahistorical bias. It also has probably been at least as responsible for ill-considered slides into the easy and convenient ignoring of the dynamics of social life, as have been the more frequently cited causes—ethnocentrism and paternalism among anthropologists in relation to those they have studied. In this volume, because our concern is with history, we have made a careful and deliberate effort to respect temporality. Things that happened in the past are described in the past tense—whether that was yesterday, last year, or last century and whether that was in the ethnographic case studies or in reference to scholarly works. Therefore, when we write about the present volume, we use the present tense, but when we refer to past work(s), events, fieldwork, and so on, we use the past tense. We write, for example, that s/he "described," "explained," or "put forward the view." It is interesting that the conceptual difficulties that we had, as editors, in expunging the present volume of all misleading tenses suggested to us how deeply ingrained is the academic, ethnographic present. It is also interesting, as a telling anthropological footnote, that our severest editorial difficulties came in editing tenses with reference to scholarly works (i.e., not to "the other" but to "ourselves") and to folklore in Taylor's essay (i.e., so-called tradition).

25. Evans-Pritchard (1949).

26. Evans-Pritchard (1962:24ff).

27. Evans-Pritchard (1961:20). It is worth noting that so many critics of an earlier anthropology chose to take Evans-Pritchard's 1940 monograph on the Nuer as an archetype (e.g., Rosaldo 1990) and as a prime example of the absence of concern for diachrony and history. Those critics then ignored both the historical ethnography of the Cyrenaican Bedouin (1949) and the study of the dynamics of local-level processes among the Nuer (1951).

28. Some examples were Barnes (1951, 1954) on the Ngoni of northern Rhodesia (Zambia), Fallers (1956) on the Soga of Uganda, Stenning (1959) on the Fulani, Smith (1960) on political developments in the Hausa chiefdoms of northern Nigeria, Bailey (1960, 1963) in Bihar (India), Mintz (1974) on the Caribbean, Redfield (1962) on a village in Yucatan, Cohen (1965) on Arab villages in Palestine and Israel, Béteille (1965) on an Indian village in Tanjore, Lison-Tolosana (1966) on a Spanish town, Friedrich (1970) on a Mexican village, Wallace (1970) on the Seneca. An exhaustive listing would be rather longer than this and much longer than stereotypical assumptions have allowed. In the same genre, although somewhat different, were the studies in culture history. For example, Mintz and Wolf (1950) first described the historical antecedents of *compadrazgo* in Latin America and then proceeded to a functional analysis of the contemporary institution. See also Wolf (1957).

29. Here and elsewhere in this essay, we do not attempt an exhaustive review of all published works that might fall under the rubric of historical anthropology. The particular studies cited are intended only to be illustrative.

30. Early examples were Gulliver (1958) and the studies in Southall (1962). Later examples were Gough (1981) and Kottak (1980)

31. Scholars in other disciplines (political scientists, sociologists, economists, etc.) and nonacademics—such as aid and development planners and administrators, politicians, and educators, and, of course, local residents.

32. This approach was conditioned by an adherence to functional theory; see Wilson (1945).

33. Peace (1989:106).

34. See the references in n. 28.

35. See Lewis (1968), Ruane (1978), and Peace (1989).

36. For example, political processes analyzed by Leach (1954), Turner (1957), and Swartz et al. (1966); processes in domestic and kinship fields described in Goody (1958) and Gray and Gulliver (1964); jural and dispute management processes in Gulliver (1963).

37. For example, Silverman (1980) and Schryer (1980).

38. See, for example, Redfield (1930, 1955), and Arensberg and Kimball (1940).

39. This was begun by a number of French anthropologists—for example, Meillassoux (1964), Godelier (1966, 1967), Terray (1969)—and became widespread in the 1970s.

40. Some examples have been Nash (1979), Vincent (1982), Stoler (1985), Sider (1986), Bloch (1986), Silverblatt (1987), Rosenberg (1988), G. Smith (1989), and Donham (1990).

41. Mintz (1985); Wolf (1982).

42. Cole and Wolf (1974:3).

43. Cole and Wolf (1974) demonstrated this by contrasting two adjacent villages in northern Italy, one German-speaking and one Italian-speaking. A comparable demonstration was given by Carol Smith (1984) using data from Guatemala.

44. Laslett (1965).

45. For example, Plakans (1984) and Casey (1989).

46. For example, Goody (1983).

47. Laslett et al. (1972); Wachter et al. (1978); Netting et al. (1984).

48. Cohn (1987a, 1987b, 1987c).

49. For example, Samuel (1981) and Medick (1987).

50. Kertzer (1984).

51. From Gough (1968) and Asad (1973) to Marcus and Fischer (1986).

52. Rather more limited categories were suggested by Chapman et al. (1989:1) when they asked two questions: "How did the past lead to the present?" and "How does the present create the past?"

53. Hastrup (1990).

54. Vincent (1984); Silverblatt (1987); Dening (1980).

55. Le Roy Ladurie (1978, 1979).

56. Donham (1990:206, his italics).

57. Sharp and Hanks (1978:31).

58. Parmentier (1987:5).

59. Parmentier (1987:7).

60. Trevor-Roper (1983).

61. Some recent examples have been Rappaport (1985), Farriss (1987), Feinup-Riordan (1988), Bowen (1989), Buckley (1989), Davis (1989), and Silverblatt (1989).

62. See, for a useful review, Hobsbawn (1983).

63. Hoskins (1987:619).

64. It may be added that the envisioned past of a particular people as seen by outsiders can also be re-created, as with Westerners' views of the past in Asia and Africa.

65. Sahlins (1985:vii).

66. Sahlins (1985:144, 152).

67. In recent time, historical anthropologists have carried out general thematic analyses over very broadly defined spaces. For example, Wolf (1982) and Mintz (1985) studied commodities and world systems; Goody (1983) and Segalen (1986) explored principles of kinship in Europe; Macfarlane (1987) produced a series of essays on the "culture of capitalism" largely in Europe. There also have been historical anthropological works that were regionally based: for example, Comaroff (1985), Smith (1985), Bloch (1986), and Silverblatt (1989). However, the majority of historical anthropologists have tended to concentrate their data collection on places that corresponded more with what we are calling "little localities."

68. Whether peasantries should be analyzed within the context of a state as against a city, and whether they should be seen as linked primarily to a dominant political regime as against a wider culture, became crucial points of difference in the analysis of peasants (e.g., Wolf [1966] as compared with Foster [1967]). More Marxist-oriented approaches added their own opinions (e.g., Shanin 1971). Regardless of viewpoint, though, no one questioned the centrality of locality for analyzing settled agriculturalists who were incorporated within a complex society.

69. Certainly this criticism could be made of an earlier anthropology. We ourselves make it in relation to Irish ethnography in the first section of this essay. We do not feel, however, that such a critique is warranted in relation to most contemporary anthropological endeavors. However, the possibility of misunderstanding, criticism, and dismissal remains. For example, Simmons wrote that "historically minded anthropologists, like their structural-functional predecessors, run the risk of pursuing theoretical questions in times and places that may seem to be of little or no importance to historians and others. . . . This is to be expected. Historians concern themselves with a different kind of problem," with "larger scale orders of data" and with "different and larger contexts" (Simmons 1985:182).

70. These examples are taken from our own experience in Thomastown. The document was a copy of the household returns from the 1831 census for the Tighe estate, Inistioge (eight miles from Thomastown). There may be only three such documents that have survived for the entire Republic; none survives from County Kilkenny. We made a copy of the returns, thanks to a local network of local historians that works to keep everyone informed of all new "finds" before they "disappear," as local people would say, irretrievably, into the hegemonic bowels of the Public Record Office in Dublin. However, as we note later, such documentation—from outside one's intensively studied locality—is of limited use to the anthropologist.

71. O'Neill purposefully chose Killashandra parish because the household returns for the 1841 census survived, thus providing the main source for a "unique data base" (1984:25). Rogers pointed out (in a personal communication, February 1991) that historians generally tend to accept the validity of using documents from so-called comparable areas. He added, however, that some historians—such as Hoskins and his students (the Leicester school) and the *Annales* historians—"have a better sense of place and are more sensitive to locality than are other historians."

72. See the essay by Clark, this volume. In political science, historical analyses have followed a similar tack. For an Irish example, see Walker (1983).

73. More specifically, this is because the data in such documents, however rich and scarce, lack a socioeconomic and cultural context in both time and space: they are unlinked to other information, such as births and marriages, property conveyances, and so on. Using such documentation on its own can lead to a timeless snapshot of structure, which is precisely what most anthro-

pologists today are trying to avoid. For a more detailed discussion of this, see Gulliver (1989).

74. For example, Rosenhaft stated that "ethnography, like all forms of structural analysis, is better at describing than explaining, and better at accounting for a situation than at predicting its outcome" (1987:102).

75. Cole and Wolf (1974); Schneider and Schneider (1976); Stoler (1985).

76. For example, Blok (1974), Kottak (1980), Kertzer (1984), Lan (1985), and Donham (1990). In addition, some historical anthropologists have used only a state or regional level (e.g., Tambiah 1976; Sider 1986; Hastrup 1990). Others, in the context of a so-called tribal society, have used a "people" (e.g., Vincent 1982; Comaroff 1985; Bloch 1986).

77. See n. 12 for our experience with boundaries in Thomastown.

78. Although there have been exceptions, these usually had an explicit reason or goal. For example, in his study of a Portuguese village, Brian O'Neill stated: "I have worked with the community-study framework despite the methodological problems that choosing a bounded 'community' raises. Macfarlane has pointed to the utility of a revised definition of the community as an object of analysis (1977); I have followed his tack by attempting to expand the community-study framework diachronically" (1987:19). O'Neill was addressing a very precise ethnographic problem as he tried to deconstruct a dominant idea in Iberian ethnography—that villages had been and were egalitarian. The "most essential task at this moment is to provide solid empirical data which will serve to banish once and for all the myth of the egalitarian hamlet community" (p. 2). The fact that O'Neill had a particular ethnographic purpose in bounding a so-called community and the fact that he regarded it as necessary to explain why he was dealing with "community" suggests that the current trend in anthropology is to avoid what we have here called closed systems and esoteric findings.

79. Wolf (1971:51).

80. Wolf, in the previously quoted article, illustrated his point by providing a historical and political description "of the ways in which social groups arranged and rearranged themselves in conflict and accommodation along the major economic and political axes of Mexican society. Each rearrangement produced a changed configuration in the relationship of community-oriented and nation-oriented groups" (1971:62). However, Wolf's more complicated ideas about a "web of group relations," "local termini," and "intermediate levels" remained unsatisfactorily explored.

81. Smith (1985:194).

82. For example, Sydel Silverman (1965), Blok (1969), and Marilyn Silverman (1979).

83. This was Carol Smith's point as well. She argued that "capitalism [is] a social and cultural phenomenon as much as an economic one . . . that can be and is affected by class struggle and human agency all along" (1985:225).

We would add here not only that the dimensions of class struggle and agency have local manifestations but that they may be apparent only from a local perspective.

84. The extent of theoretical and cross-cultural understanding on this issue, which has come largely from the political economy turn in anthropology, is apparent from the following examples: Hedley (1979 [Canada]), Kahn (1980 [Indonesia]), Vincent (1982 [Uganda]), Holmes (1983 [Italy]), Roseberry (1983 [Venezuela]), Trouillot (1987 [Dominica]), Gavin Smith (1990 [Peru]); and, of course, the lengthy discussions on domestic commodity production in the *Journal of Peasant Society*. For an analytical, critical, and historical review of this material, see Roseberry (1988).

85. Akenson (1972:2).

86. There are long-standing agencies through which this dominant history has been transmitted: the schools, the church, the media, and political organizations. These not only existed at the time the history was being formulated but they also contributed to its formulation. Moreover, although these institutional interpretations often articulated with some local experience, they also were made to articulate with it—and to interpret it—by powerful, local agents who represented these interests—teachers, priests, intelligentsia, and political leaders. Shanklin presumably came across the essence of this dominant history when she encountered the "COBO response"—the fact that the notion of "centuries of British oppression" was used continually by people in Donegal to explain what was disliked, disapproved of, or not completely understood (1985:24).

87. This distinction between insider and outsider has been expressed in numerous ways by anthropologists at different times. The dichotomies of emic-etic, other-self, native anthropologist are examples. More recently, the separation of "voices" or the use of "history" as against "historicity" has reflected this distinction.

88. Yet there have been numerous studies that analyzed the processes of Irish agrarian reform using nationally based, aggregated statistics, economic data, and legal frameworks. For examples, see Solow (1971) and Kolbert and O'Brien (1975).

89. For example, Crotty's excellent, deconstructionist analysis of the history of Irish agriculture (1966) could tell us little about what might have happpened in Thomastown; nor could it do more than suggest very broad issues that might help us in our efforts to analyze agrarian history as it was experienced in Thomastown. Mainly it was a study of national trends—using aggregated (statistical) national patterns—and of official policies and politics in agriculture. As such, it provided us with the fact of a particular state policy, for example, and we could then try to ascertain if it had had any impact in the Thomastown area. Beyond that, this "history of Irish agriculture" had little meaning or applicability to our own efforts to do agrarian history.

90. Lyons (1973:219).

91. For Irish examples of this approach, see Connell (1962), Gibbon and Curtin (1978), and Breen (1982a).

92. For local analyses of marriage patterns in Ireland, see Birdwell-Pheasant (this volume), Symes (1972), Smyth (1975), and Breen (1984b).

93. In a 1981 review of Irish historiography, Ó Tuathaigh noted: "In Irish political history the most encouraging development of the past decade has been the shift in emphasis from, in Theo Hoppen's phrase, 'national politics to local realities.' " He cited Hoppen's work on electoral history as an excellent example of the genre (1981:88, 90). In the preface to his book published several years later, Hoppen indeed noted that he had been struck by the fact that the "more the detailed workings of individual political communities in Ireland were examined, the more striking and important seemed the gap between local realities and the rhetoric of national politics. Such communities, whether individual in the geographical or the social sense, often maintained a style of politics only intermittently in step with the stated aims and methods of the movement generally held to have dominated Irish history in the nineteenth century" (1984:vii–viii).

That said, Hoppen's analysis departed dramatically from what a historical anthropologist would call a local focus. He used aggregated data for counties (e.g., pp. 348–49 on agrarian outrages) or the nation (e.g., pp. 412 and 413 on the occupational and ethnic backgrounds of policemen and British soldiers; or p. 436 on rates of urbanization). His analysis moved over the entire country, both north and south. His analytical categories aggregated large numbers of "landlords," "laborers," and "farmers" from diverse areas and there was no in-depth analysis of a "localized place."

These observations are not to detract from Hoppen's excellent study. They simply illustrate the very different notion of "locality" that has characterized contemporary Irish historiography (e.g., L. Kennedy 1983; O'Shea 1983; Donnelly 1975; Feingold 1984; Boyle 1988) as compared with historical anthropology.

94. A telling example of the difficulties that this can raise occurred at an Irish Studies Conference in 1988. Gulliver presented some of his "unusual" findings concerning Thomastown's shopkeepers (see Gulliver's essay, this volume). A historian in the audience argued that it was because he had gone to the "wrong" place: if Gulliver had chosen a larger place or a "better" place, he would have found what historians had been telling him was there! A more promising outlook is Ó Gráda's discussion on the "incidence and ideology" of the famine. He stated: "Shattering dangerous myths about the past is the historian's social responsibility. In Ireland, where popular history is an odd brew of myth and reality, there is plenty for him to do" (1988:79). For historical anthropologists, of course, "odd brews" themselves constitute fertile ground for research.

95. Sabean (1990:10).

96. Cohen (1982, 1987).

97. Parman (1990).
98. Ennew (1980).
99. Parman (1990:13).
100. Donham (1990:141).
101. Silverman's analysis includes, at different times, the Thomastown area, the nontidal portion of the Nore River, the entire length (tidal and nontidal) of the river, all the nontidal regions of the watershed to incorporate the rivers Barrow and Suir, and the entire watershed system—both tidal and nontidal.
102. Examples of this textual strategy from historical ethnography have included Blok (1974), Schneider and Schneider (1976), Silverman (1980), Verdery (1983), Lamphere (1987), Peletz (1988), and Rosenberg (1988).
103. Examples have included Comaroff (1985), Bloch (1986), Sider (1986), and Newbury (1988).
104. For example, Inden (1976), Netting (1981), and Sabean (1990).
105. These formed the basis for Silverman's 1980 study of micropolitics between 1902 and 1970 in a Guyanese East Indian, rice-farming village.
106. This was the case in Santa María del Monte, a village studied by Behar (1986) using, for the most part, village-based records.
107. We found numerous documents—generated both in the private (e.g., shop accounts, farm records) and the public domains (e.g., estate maps, minutes of local organizations, correspondence)—in the hands of Thomastown people. It was our continued residence there and our ongoing assurances that we were interested in any and all "old papers" (and that we would always return them!) that often induced people to bring these documents to us or to to tell us about them.
108. Gulliver (1989) described both the fruitfulness of, and the methods for, linking archival research with fieldwork. Rosenberg noted of her work in France: "This system of moving back and forth between the village and the archives was both a source of inspiration and a check on flights of fancy. Grounding ethnography in history and history in ethnography provided me with a sense of what was plausible and what far-fetched in both fields" (1988:xiv).
109. Rogers added that there have been recent examples of historians interested in how (e.g., Davis 1987) and that this was a new approach. However, Rogers believed that the general distinction between anthropology and history remained: that the former has tended to ask how, whereas the latter has tended to ask why.
110. Behar (1986:12).
111. Behar (1986:13).
112. Behar (1986:13, 14).
113. Some other examples have included Cole and Wolf (1974), Schneider and Schneider (1976), Kottak (1980) and Frykman and Löfgren (1987).
114. Sahlins (1985:144).
115. Lamphere (1987:329).

116. Thompson (1972:43).

117. Thompson (1972:45–46).

118. The complex relation between meaning, abstractness, and applicability is apparent in these three examples. *Lineage* has a precise meaning and has generated great debate as to its applicability to any context whatsoever. The concept of a "political game" has been accepted almost as a metaphor, and apart from questions as to its paradigmatic implications, it has been used—without stimulating debate—in numerous cross-cultural instances. As to *power,* it has often been used, but there has been no agreement about what it means and it has been among the most problemmatic concepts that anthropologists have dared to use. Rogers recently suggested (personal communication, February 1991) that Thompson was against "crude" conceptual applications, not all applications. Nevertheless, it seems to us that not only have historians been wary of such applications (Cohn 1987c:66) but the problem also remains as to what constitutes "crude."

119. Cohn noted a similar phenomemon: "In working with judicial records for a local region in India, I felt hampered by not knowing the people I was dealing with, except from what was in the record. Simple questions with regard to the litigants, the lawyers, the judge and the witnesses, about their ages, their social and economic statuses, and their formal and informal relations to each other, could be answered only if the same individuals appeared in other cases or if other materials were available which gave information about them. Such questions can often be quickly answered in the field, but not in the library" (1987a:7).

120. Peletz (1988).

121. Rogers also asked if the temporal boundaries were the result of major breaks in Irish history that had caused the anthropologists to begin in the nineteenth century. This suggestion seemed less plausible to the anthropologists—both from their reading of Irish historical materials and from their experiences in their local places. Much depended on what they had been studying. For example, both Birdwell-Pheasant (given her concern with kinship) and Vincent (with her interest in the Poor Law and state building) had found that the famine of 1845–49 was an important marker. For others, this had not been the case and there was no agreement on the "major breaks." See our earlier discussion on temporality in Thomastown at pages 5–6.

122. Rosenberg (1988:58–71).

123. Netting (1981, chapter 4).

124. Lison-Tolosana (1983:7—originally published 1966).

125. Rosaldo continued: "Thus the early period of Rumyad history can be understood only through close attention to the observation of Ilongot historical consciousness" (1980:247).

126. We use Europe here because it contains the archival centers of the empires from which anthropologists have mainly come, in which they have mainly worked and whose documents they have mainly used. It is likely, however, that the archives from the centers of non–European empires—such

as those in China, Japan, Russia, Turkey, and India—also contain data of excellent quality. However, apart from Inden (1976) on Bengal, and Robert Smith (1972) and Nakane (1972) on Japanese family history, we are unaware of historical anthropologists who have dug deeply into these. Presumably we have simply missed them. Ohnuki-Tierney's (1990b) material on Japan appears to have been based on secondary sources, although this is not entirely clear.

127. An example was Silverblatt's (1987) study of the transformations in Andean culture and women's roles in the light of the Spanish conquest. This was an *early period* and an *early conquest*. Therefore, there were *archival remains,* albeit somewhat sparse and largely from the conquerors. However, using a *broad spatial area,* Silverblatt was able to move into the realm of *social relations* as well as into the *cultural domain* to try for an analysis that was located simultaneously in *political economy* and *culture change*.

128. For example, Fernandez (1990) used archival materials from rural Spain for a symbolic analysis of the "contest" over enclosure and change over two centuries. The available documentation might have allowed him to do more of a narrative or political economy type of analysis. Presumably he chose not to do so.

129. Primary documents, held by public bodies in Ireland, are simultaneously rich and patchy. Much was destroyed when the archives were burned during the Civil War in 1922. This has led to the oft-cited rationalization that "it was better to have a nation without an archive than an archive without a nation." Perhaps as compensation, Irish land records are far superior to any in England. Given the popular interest in local history, there have been several guides to holdings, such as Nolan (1982).

130. Surprisingly perhaps, many nineteenth-century materials are richer than twentieth-century ones. To take an important example: there were no government commissions after 1922 that published testimentary evidence from local witnesses as there were before Independence.

131. Ecologically, areas of intensive tillage counterposed areas of pastoral economies. Culturally, areas varied in the extent to which old Gaelic naming patterns had declined. Settlement patterns also varied—nucleated settlements had grown up around churches, castles, and mills; agglomerated settlements were farm based and kin based, usually around a head tenant farmer, his partners, and their laborers; and dispersed settlements were a third type, more difficult to find because of a shortage of data.

132. Birdwell-Pheasant elsewhere explained why she, and perhaps other anthropologists, "got into history. We do it in order to do better anthropology, because many of the socio-cultural-politico-economic processes that we are so intrigued with describing and explaining are processes that do not occur merely within a lifetime or over a generation, or even between two generations. They are (often stochastic) processes of multiple generations, the collective and collaborative product of long sequences of lifetimes. There are, indeed, cycles and patterns that can be discerned *only* within historical time

that are just as real as individual life cycles and patterns. . . . Unless we do history, then, we are like biologists who study flowers and leaves and seeds and pollen as distinct entities rather than as parts of a complex . . . ecosystem" (personal communication, March 14, 1991).

133. For example, Ohnuki-Tierney (1990b) and Fernandez (1990). A recent example of the controversy that may be engendered can be found in *Current Anthropology* (June 1990). It concerned Spencer's critique of Kapferer's analysis of cultural continuity and nationalist ideology in Sri Lanka.

134. The category of so-called shops in Thomastown has faded into artisanal enterprises in which tradespeople have sold their goods over a counter (e.g., shoemaker, tailor). The boundary also has been blurred by persons who have sold their services without a fixed place—for example, masons, insurance agents, electrical contractors. Thus, the term *shopkeeper* has been used in Thomastown, sometimes but not always, for some tailors and shoemakers; for a particular electrical contractor but not others; and occasionally, for the insurance agent but never for the mason. The term *shop* also has been used, by some people but not all, to cover the premises of so-called hucksters. Thus, insiders' usages have been extremely complex. They have varied according to the particular context and the person speaking.

135. The problems of applying concepts to the past have of course emerged in the most statistical of all historical endeavors—family history. For example, distinguishing *household* from *family* and from *domestic group* has proved difficult, as has distinguishing *kin* from *servant* (e.g., Netting et al. 1984; Sieder and Mitterauer 1983). Insider categories have proved as difficult to apply as ousider ones. Such difficulties have prompted Hammel, for example, to an extreme position of emphasizing outsider usage alone: "The more strictly that analyses of different data bases adhere to a particular scheme of analytic categories, the more likely those analyses are to be comparable with one another and the less likely they are to adhere closely either to the appropriate folk categories or to actual behaviour in the societies concerned" (1984:30). Many anthropologists would not accept that procedure. However, it does point to the problems that certainly have been ignored in Irish historical studies.

136. In Irish studies, it is only the stem family concept that has prompted efforts at concise definition. What Gulliver's study shows is that such an exercise is required in other areas as well.

137. For example, Kottak (1983) and Heiberg (1989).

138. For example, Silverman (1980) and Hansen (1989).

139. For example, Hammel (1978).

140. The term *litany* is appropriate here, for it is easier said than done. Yet how or whether to do it constitutes the essential anthropological problem today. See n. 149.

141. Even Comaroff (1985), for example—with *power* in her title—did not list it in her index.

142. Rogers added that, since Foucault ("language as power"), there has been a tendency among historians to pull in "noninstrumental usages" as well.

143. Of course there have been exceptions, particularly among Marxist anthropologists for whom the nature and cross-cultural applicability of "class" has been a central theoretical issue (e.g., Donham 1990; Smith 1990). However, the centrality of *power* was often not the main concern while the shortfall between sophisticated, theoretical constructs and messier empirical data has remained a problem.

144. For example, Vincent pointed to the American culture history school— of Mintz and Wolf, and their concern with "actual history"—in contrast with Steward's concern with "national integration" and modernization. Other examples of the confrontation between the two models were also given: Fallers (1967) as against Saul and Woods (1971) and applied anthropology as against action anthropology.

145. Roseberry (1988:170).

146. The existence and persistence of noncapitalist features have often been explained in terms of the functions that they performed for an overarching capitalism (Roseberry 1988:170).

147. Carol Smith (1985:194).

148. Wolf (1990).

149. Roseberry (1988:173). Roseberry stated: "A logical and historical separation of the 'local' and the 'larger context' . . . is no longer tenable." Instead, "anthropological subjects should be situated at the intersections of local and global histories." In saying this, Roseberry probably echoed a general feeling in the discipline today. Fortunately, though, he added that "this is a statement of a problem rather than a conclusion." Indeed, we would argue that it is *the* problem. It is an aspect of the "dilemma of levels, layers, and local termini" that we discuss earlier in this essay (pp. 25). However, there is a danger that Roseberry's statement about what is untenable will become a litany with which to criticize efforts in historical anthropology. For if our tribulations in Thomastown have done one thing, it has been to teach us that it is far easier to talk about history than to do it. It also has taught us that the previously mentioned dilemma is central.

150. Rosenhaft (1987:103).

151. For example, Sider (1986).

152. Rosenhaft (1987:105).

153. Hobsbawm (1980:7).

154. For example, in a somewhat negative review of Price's book, *Alabi's World* (1990), Hobsbawm contrasted "Richard Price's views about how history should be written and those of more traditional historians and anthropologists" (1990:46). That is, a historian divided anthropology—part went with history and part went awry—all without reference to the ways in which anthropologists themselves have carried on their internal dialogues and conflicts.

155. Ohnuki-Tierny (1990:2).

156. Tilly (1978:213). He added: "The portion of anthropology with which French and francophile historians have worked most effectively is only a small part of the field, and in some regards a backwater. Furthermore, the influence of historical work—including that of the *Annales*—on anthropological practice has been slight."

157. Cohn noted that "doubts are raised by eminent historians about the fruitfulness of closer working relationships with anthropologists." He cited Stone, Thompson, and Le Roy Ladurie. "What has been questioned is the appropriateness for the study of the European past of the theories, models, and methods which were developed by anthropologists in order to understand and interpret the non-European worlds" (1987c:66).

158. Indeed, textual analysis, as represented by Clifford and Marcus, for example (1984), is ahistorical.

159. For example, see Worden (1991).

160. As used by Turner (1957) and discussed by Van Velsen (1967).

161. Sahlins (1981:5).

162. Wolf (1990:591).

163. That the occasional historian has done fieldwork (Ohnuki-Tierney 1990a:2) is largely irrelevant. Most have not, nor have they been expected to. In contrast, almost always, anthropologists have been required to do so—both as a rite of passage and to collect/produce data. The different kinds of data and "comprehension" that have resulted were examined by Cohn (1987b:47–49).

164. Ortner (1984:159).

165. Ortner (1984:159).

166. Roseberry (1988:179).

167. Wolf (1990:594).

# II

## APPROACHING THE

## PAST USING

## IRISH ETHNOGRAPHY

# 2

# A Political Orchestration of the Irish
# Famine: County Fermanagh, May 1847

■

## JOAN VINCENT

Six men sat in a room in the Town Hall overlooking Enniskillen High Street on May 4, 1847.[1] Their board meeting had begun at 2 o'clock, and it was now approaching dusk. Only a month before, they and twenty-six others, all leading citizens of County Fermanagh, had been elected to serve as guardians of the Enniskillen Poor Law Union, along with ten appointed by the lord lieutenant of Ireland. The earl of Enniskillen was nominally its chairman; Edward Archdall and Abraham Nixon were its vice-chairmen.

This essay attempts, through the analysis of one incident, to suggest the structural relationships, and the constraints inherent in them, that helped shape the consciousness and response to famine of Fermanagh's Anglo-Irish ancien régime; its small farmers, cottiers, and laboring poor; and its emergent entrepreneurial bourgeoisie. Implicitly, it argues that their actions in response to the crisis of Black '47 can only be understood if they are placed in a somewhat different context from that usually adopted to explain the causes and outcome of the Great Irish Famine. Those most frequently proposed by political economists and nationalist historians rest on either the nature of the subsistence economy in Ireland on the eve of the famine or the political domination of Ireland by England. In this essay, three broader sets of relationship are suggested: the legislative nexus in which a new Poor Law was transplanted (with few modifications) from Westminster to Ireland; the setting of the British Empire, which provided a pervasive form of political consciousness for all classes in County Fermanagh, whether through familial, military, or economic connections; and finally, the process of monetization, which, as a national and global phenomenon, unevenly affected the population of this small, peripheral western Irish county.

The essay itself is divided into five parts. First, the events of May 4, 1847, at the union workhouse in Enniskillen, the country town of Fermanagh, are narrated; Christian moral discourse is portrayed under stress. The political culture that developed in rural Fermanagh in response to recurrent dearth is then outlined; by 1847 a potato truck system is seen to be its essential feature. The third section describes the crisis in the new administrative system of relief introduced into Fermanagh on the eve of the famine; imposed by the Westminster government, it undercut both the existing political economy and its cultural expression. The essay then returns to the events at the Enniskillen workhouse on May 4, 1847, and provides an analysis of those admitted to the workhouse on that day, relating this to the structural relationships outlined. Finally, this hegemonic moment in the faminization process in Fermanagh is linked with the abortive Irish revolution of 1848.

## A Meeting of the Board of Guardians, May 4, 1847

From October 1846 through April 1847, on average only eight board members attended the fortnightly meetings of the Enniskillen Poor Law Union in County Fermanagh. Attendance on May 4 was the lowest on record. Present on that day were only two of its thirty elected guardians: John Grey Vesey Porter, son of the Rector of Kilskeery, who had purchased the Manor of Carrick a few years earlier; and William Dane, member of a family of land agents for the earl of Belmore, elected for Enniskillen Town. Four appointed and ex officio guardians attended on May 4: Richard Hall, magistrate and landowner, and Captain Edward Archdall of Magheraboy, in command of the Fermanagh Yeomanry, were appointed guardians; Drs. Frith and Collum attended ex officio as the union's medical officers. The young John Grey Vesey Porter was in the chair. The board meeting was held in the Town Hall because fever had raged for the past several weeks in the workhouse itself. The routine business of the board was conducted over considerable noise from the yard, where a soup kitchen had been set up for the crowd waiting below. All hoped to be found eligible for admission to the workhouse for what was called indoor relief.

While the poor waited below, the guardians worked their way through the meticulous bureaucratic routine of the agenda prescribed by the new Irish Poor Law. As soon as the minutes of the previous meeting had been read and approved, the clerk produced the register. Here were recorded details of paupers admitted to the workhouse the previous week. Admission numbers marched down the left-hand side of the unwieldy ledger, followed by categorical details about each man, woman, and child, itemized less to satisfy the needs of workhouse management than to appease the hunger for statistics of the commissioners in Dublin: name, age, sex, townland of residence, electoral division, religion, condition on admission, date of admission. A right-hand column recorded the date on which the pauper left the workhouse since it was assumed that short-term relief of their distress would enable those admitted to return to their homes and families in a comparatively short time. Increasingly, this column registered deaths almost as often as the discharge of paupers. The register was examined and authenticated, signed by the chairman, and countersigned by the clerk.

The Treasurer's Book of receipts and payments was then produced and the day's entry again signed by the chairman. On May 4, 1847, it was not a reassuring document. Three lines could sum its content:

Treasure received Nil
Paid during the week £20.0.0
Outstanding balance against the Guardians £1200.6.9

A resolution was passed: yet another appeal to the government in Westminster to come to the rescue of the institution it had established against the wishes and judgment of those Fermanagh residents now obliged to run it.[2] Porter, as chairman, proposed that yet another representation be made to the Poor Law Commissioners about the strained resources of the union:

We owe about £4,000 to contractors besides £1,200 to Government. Our house is full of paupers and our hospitals are full of fever patients and numbers are sent away who apply for admission. Our weekly expenses can hardly be met by the sums brought in by our collectors and if the Government will not lend us £3,000–£4,000 as applied for

three weeks ago we will be unable either to pay our just debts or keep
our house open.

So overwhelming was their sense of irredeemable debt that the
guardians brought to a decision a matter long left hanging: what to
do about collectors who, despite their tenders and contracts, had not
produced the funds called for by the Poor Law rates. Reluctantly,
they ordered that summons be issued against the rate collectors and
their guarantors. All knew why the collectors had been unable to
bring in the money. The rate had been bearable in the early days of
the Poor Law system, when harvests had been good and farmers
could count on a steady income—days when they had been able to
employ several servants and laborers and when they had found it
profitable to let out portions of their land in conacre (corn-acre). But
that was 1838. Deflation had begun to set in for some of the smaller
yeoman farmers in October 1843 and had worsened thereafter. By
1847 money was in short supply.

In the uncertain economic climate of 1847, few were persuaded
that supporting the poor through a workhouse system was either
necessary or desirable. The Irish Poor Relief Act of 1838 had given all
but the very smallest of the tenant farming class the right to vote as
ratepayers for Poor Law guardians, and the more substantial (and the
more political) among them also gained the right to run for election
to their local board. Yet in Fermanagh, where so many of the gentry
were resident and retained an interest in the working of the system,
many of their tenants considered finding money for rates to support
the destitute a residual consideration compared with saving funds to
enable them to emigrate or, at best, maintaining their own families
on the land. Small farmers who chose to stay and see it through,
discharging workers to cut labor costs, were hardly prepared to see
their savings expended on keeping the self-same individuals in the
workhouse. A petition had, indeed, been circulated calling for a
county meeting to protest the recent rise in Poor Law rates. The
government that had thrust union with Great Britain on Fermanagh,
it was believed, had a responsibility to feed its poor. It did so in
England; why not, then, in Scotland and Ireland?

None of the six guardians sitting around the table on May 4 had
paid their poor rates for the past four months. This was not because
they did not care about the distress; their very appearance on the
board denied that. It was simply that, as heirs to opposition against
the union of 1800 that had placed the affairs of Fermanagh in the
hands of Westminster politicians, and critically sensitive to every

reluctant or vindictive move of its present government headed by the Whig John Russell, they did not conceive the Poor Law rates to be the best way of solving the problem of the county's poor. The begrudging, penny-paring actions of Charles Trevelyan at the Treasury were utterly alien to them. How characteristic, indeed, that the British had placed famine relief efforts under Treasury control.[3]

For far longer than many Anglo-Irish landlords who sought to improve their estates along the lines advocated by the leading political economists of the day (which might include enclosures of land and evictions of tenants), Fermanagh's conservative ancien régime had viewed the problem of the poor as the problem of the master. What had by 1847 become a trite cliché on everyone's lips—that the property of Ireland was responsible for the poverty of Ireland—was for them not recrimination but an accepted canon of landlord morality. The privileges and rights they enjoyed—although fewer than in previous decades—rested on paternalism, patronage, and public opinion. Yet placed in a situation not of their own making, obliged to supplicate the British cabinet in Westminster, they were unable to act as free and responsible men. Private charity and public disbursement they could and did engage in; the management of bureaucratic social welfare, much of which they felt was neither in their best interest nor in that of those who depended on them, was a different matter. Thus, in the administration of the government relief measures imposed on them, they formulated their own petty resistances.[4] Among them were the actions of the Enniskillen guardians in May 1847.

Christian Morality Under Stress

The week before, in the face of rising mortality in the workhouse, a most dreadful proposition had been put before the board. An elected guardian from Enniskillen town, Stewart Betty (one of the most conscientious of the elected townsmen, more scrupulous in his attendance than any other), had proposed that, to save expense, a new type of coffin—a slip coffin, as it was called—should be purchased. The idea of the slip coffin, with its mechanical spring and false base, was a hard one for the guardians to accept. Less than a week after he had made the suggestion, Betty was struck down by fever as if in moral retribution. In the debate on the issue, John Fee, an elected guardian from Castle Coole, where he was a neighbor of the young earl of Belmore, had stripped off the transparency of calling the contraption a coffin.

JOHN FEE: "Is it to bury them without coffins at all?"
STEWART BETTY: "Yes—to keep down expense."

At this point the clerk of the union, Paul Dane, observed that if the principle of using a slip coffin were adopted, not one but twelve or fourteen coffins should be made; otherwise, the cot on which they were carried from the workhouse to the burial ground would be grossly overworked.

JOHN FEE: "I think the county would spurn the idea."
STEWART BETTY: "We are not the first to adopt it—other unions have done it."

The clerk, however, knew how narrowly such a decision had been reached elsewhere. "At Mohill," he reminded them, "twenty-seven guardians were present and it was carried by a majority of one."

At this point, Captain William Corry, younger brother of the earl of Belmore, also an elected guardian, would have none of it, calling the very idea of a slip coffin shameful. Dr. Ovenden thereupon moved that the paupers should, indeed, have proper coffins; the thing should be done decently.

Since Betty's original concern had been with rising costs (he saw the slip coffin as an alternative to no coffins at all), Richard Hall again reminded his fellow guardians of the county's financial straits. "You talk as if we had money to 'do the thing decently.' " After a lengthy weighing of cost and morality, the item was postponed, to be taken up again on May 4.

The average cost of burying the dead was £10 to £12 a week, and Hall again suggested that it would be more economical to follow the example of certain other unions and purchase a slip coffin. The discussion then turned to whether the families of paupers could be asked to pay for coffins. The clerk told the board of the "astonishing" number of persons in the workhouse who had fathers or other relatives "doing well for themselves" in Scotland. Post Office money orders to the amount of £70 had been sent to workhouse inmates in one week alone by their friends and relatives in Scotland. There was apparently no discussion of what this meant for women who had to claim to be "deserted" to gain admission to the workhouse with their "part" (i.e., single-parent) families. Most likely, the guardians recognized remittances as a characteristic feature of the declining economy in which so many "breadwinners" were seasonal migrants to the English and Scottish mainlands. Hall immediately suggested that these funds be secured by the workhouse, but Edward Rogers, an elected guardian from the Ely division and a solicitor, pointed out that this was not legally possible.

If some of Fermanagh's Anglican gentry found the idea of the slip coffin objectionable, so did some of the general public. The editor of the *Impartial Reporter,* William Trimble, a vocal representative of emergent Presbyterian, urban middle-class principles and interests, found it not simply un-Christian but also unbusinesslike. He proffered advice:

> When our Guardians meet tomorrow, a most awful responsibility rests on them. We say economise in every way that humanity will dictate. Let the public never again hear of an enormous quantity of clothing being lost, and allowed to engender disease for want of washing etc., let no more provisions be lost by neglect; but oh! forbid it, shades of our forefathers! that in Fermanagh—moral, Christian Fermanagh—men, women, and children, should be buried without coffins.[5]

By May 1847 the very technology of a Christian burial, let alone its spirituality, was fast receding out of bounds for the guardians. Eyewitnesses spoke of the "shameless, indecent, and dangerous piling of the dead paupers in the new ground. Heaps are raised like double ditches, and sometimes numbers are left all night uncovered, until the pit be filled."[6]

Knowledge of all this must have lain heavily on the minds of the six guardians on May 4, but no further discussion of slip coffins took place; no adjournment until a larger and more representative collection of guardians be gathered; no vote taken. Instead the six men around the table deflected the moral issue onto those who specialized in such matters, instructing the union's three chaplains to be assiduous in their attendance at all funerals, so that all paupers might receive decent Christian burial. Timber and tools for making more coffins were to be made available forthwith.

The guardians had reached the point on the agenda calling for consideration of miscellaneous proposals and resolutions, but on this occasion, there were none. The hour was late but regulations required that, at the very end of their day's business, they examine the paupers seeking admission. As the distress had increased, so the business of running the workhouse had become more and more extenuated, the guardians sitting on into candlelight before this part of their routine even began. The desolate poor waited below. All had come from villages and townlands within walking distance of the workhouse. But this so-called walking distance was the journey of some eighteen or twenty miles that might be made by the healthy laborer in clement weather. Many of those massed in the courtyard of the Town Hall on May 4 had set out the day before in order to cover the distance.

There had been times when the charity of the guardians had outweighed the edicts of the commissioners in Dublin and their Treasury masters in London: they had provided food and a night by the fireside for those they had been obliged to deny admission for not meeting the specifications of the law. Setting up a soup kitchen in the yard below had eased the suffering somewhat, but the crowding together of so many of the destitute, as conditions worsened day by day and fever became more widespread, was a matter of concern. With the shadow of death so close to so many of those seeking admission, the six guardians sought to shortcircuit the process for any "labouring under fever or the prominitory symptoms thereof." Thus, they resolved on May 4 that instead of waiting in the courtyard to be interrogated by the guardians as to their status and condition, persons sick with fever should go directly to the workhouse master and, on the recommendation of a guardian and the medical attendant, be received as a matter of course.

The number and clamor of the paupers had grown throughout the afternoon as the debate and paper shuffling dragged on. Word was taken up to the board that some two hundred persons waited below. The hour was late and the guardians began to consider whether the lengthy process of discriminating among the many to find the deserving and eligible few might be set aside on this occasion. Some, they were told, were "parts of families," which it was against the law to assist. As a justice of the peace, Richard Hall maintained that, regardless of the pressing circumstances, their admission would be against the law. Debate ensued. He reminded his colleagues that they were the elected representatives of the county's ratepayers, *required* to turn away those not eligible, whereupon Dr. Frith, observing (perhaps sardonically) that it was *only* two hundred who waited below, appealed "in the name of God," that all be admitted indiscriminately. Seconded by William Dane, Hall called for a motion to be put that all who waited should be admitted. It was defeated.

Then the unexpected happened. Finding the door ajar, some of the waiting crowd began to push their way in. Their implosion filled the chamber, bringing the proceedings to a halt. Some guardians called out for the constabulary to be sent for; some called for the meeting to be adjourned. Others, with great difficulty, succeeded in clearing the small room. A journalist from the *Impartial Reporter* reported the scene:

Children appeared to be dying in the act of endeavoring to extract sustenance from the dried up breast of their parents, others more mature in years were propped up by some relative or acquaintance who was fast hastening to a similar state of weakness. The general appearance was truly sickening. An endeavour was made to enter the names when, some fearing they might be excluded, another rush was made and put *hors de combat* the guardians at the board. The horrors of the black hole of Calcutta were endured for them for a time—they rushed to the window and gasped for breath. [7]

Any choice they might have fast receding, the guardians announced that all should be admitted—indiscriminately—and Paul Dane began the task, late as it was, of recording admissions. The ledger entries stretched on for twenty-six large pages, the elegant and informed handwriting of the clerk being replaced after a while by the scrawl of an unknown scribe, poor of spelling and ignorant of townland names and locations. Gaps appeared in the columns. Protestant applicants were recorded as Roman Catholic, males as females; the names of townlands outside the union's legal boundaries were set down. Gender, religion, age of each pauper in turn were carefully recorded as if it were, indeed, a routine day at the workhouse. At last the task was finished. According to the official register, not 200 but 351 men, women, and children were admitted to the Enniskillen workhouse on May 4, 1847.

This sequence of events in Enniskillen on May 4, 1847, brought to an end the first phase of the faminization process in Fermanagh. The Benthamite goals of English administrative law had been achieved: the routinization of Irish local government had been substituted for an indigenous political cultural mode of coping with dearth—a process that, for rich and poor alike, replaced an asymmetrical exchange relationship, which was to some extent personal, with a faceless, alien bureaucracy. The moment was laden with conflict: the petty resistances of paternalistic landlords to the anonymity of the administrative machine; the clash within Christian morality of principle and practicality; the contradictions of new, opportunistic, entrepreneurial, urban jobbery coexisting with county traditions of family patronage. Above all, there was the crisis of an agrarian economy transformed by capitalist political and economic development. Their interrelationships—arguably in the context of legal impositions, militarism, empire, and monetization (or lack of it)—were encapsulated and politically orchestrated in this hegemonic moment of the faminization process.

## The Ancien Régime and the Culture of Dearth

The guardians who met in the Town Hall on May 4 and who, in despair of any other course of action, had admitted, against the law's intent, 351 clamoring paupers, had all been born in Ireland, most in Fermanagh itself.[8] They were members of a ruling class, an ancien régime, that kept abreast of public affairs and expressed an ideology that maintained public service to be the counterpoint of privilege. Their educations and their accents may have been acquired at Trinity College Dublin, Oxford, or Cambridge but, above all else, they were Anglo-Irish or Scots-Irish men of property whose estates and businesses lay within the county. As resident landlords or professional younger sons from gentry families, they knew their tenants and their clients and they understood the convoluted ties among tenants, cottiers, subtenants, and laborers on which their own security and well-being rested.[9]

The gentry shared, through a variety of political and economic links, a weblike culture of dearth produced and reproduced over the generations in the Fermanagh countryside. They were part and parcel of demands and expectations integumental to the ideology of social life for the population at large. All, in varying degrees according to class and religious persuasion, shared a calendar of social gatherings, some religious and some connected with rites of passage, patterns, pilgrimages, harvest festivals, commemorative feasts and celebrations, military parades and band performances, the dramaturgy of the Assizes, hilltop bonfires, horse racing and faction fighting, rotating markets, the consumption of illicit poteen, conacre, "Ulster Custom," and the like.

Fermanagh's peasantry had suffered harvest failures in 1728, 1739, 1740, 1741, 1757, 1770, 1773, 1775, 1800, 1807, 1821–22, 1830–31, 1832, 1834, 1835, and 1836–37. On each occasion, the culture of dearth had been sufficient to avert starvation. When famine struck in 1846, most of the county's landlords set in motion the procedures they and their forebears had engaged in for the past century. They set up local relief committees and organized private charity. Gale days were postponed and, in some cases, rents reduced.

The case should not be overstated. Both the marquess of Ely and the earl of Enniskillen appear to have left the county for long periods during the famine, and there is little on the record about their agents that is good. The dowager duchess of Ely remained throughout, residing on the estate close to the shores of lower Lough Erne and doing a great deal for the tenantry. But conditions were bad in the western mountainous regions on both estates, where many evictions and roadside deaths were reported.[10] The humane cultural ethos of the time was part constructed and part publicized by the fiery Presbyterian editor of the *Impartial Reporter,* whose weekly columns identified and listed, praised and criticized the actions of estate owners toward those living on their land.

As in earlier crises, however, the greatest relative costs of poor relief were borne mainly by compassionate small farmers and neighbors. Yeoman and tenant farmers, clerics and priests, artisans and small shopkeepers recognized their moral obligations to neighbors in need—locality and the spirit of place being of the essence. In all this, the political economy of the big house, with its accumulation and distribution of money, was critical to the well-being of the laboring classes, artisans, and shopkeepers alike. The *Impartial Reporter* frequently noted how much at the best of times the gentry were missed during the London season. Maria Edgeworth's novel *The Absentee,* set in nearby County Longford, brings out the irony of the very poor and the very rich in Ireland passing each other en route to England, both pursuing their respective seasonal rounds.

Later it was said that it was not one harvest failure but a series of bad harvests that brought Ireland to the brink of famine disaster but only one harvest had as yet failed in May 1847 and other causes must be sought for the collapse of the timeworn, rural safety net in Fermanagh. Elsewhere in Europe, elsewhere even in Scotland and Ulster, the potato blight had struck without the grim repercussions suffered within the western Irish economy. It is necessary, therefore, to be more specific about what it was exactly that failed.

## The Potato-Truck System

The culture of dearth evolved around a somewhat peculiar system of asymmetrical economic exchange that had come into being with the decline of rural industry in Fermanagh toward the end of the eighteenth century. This rested on what was then called a "truck system," in which labor was exchanged for land on which was grown a crop of potatoes sufficient for a family's annual subsistence. Called conacre (corn-acre) in Ireland, this agricultural custom may well have been one of the earliest seeds of capitalism introduced to Fermanagh by the Plantation of 1610. Over time and in different locations, it had undergone considerable modification, and this in part accounts for and reflects the severity of the faminization process in different localities throughout the county.

A contemporary account describes the custom in general as follows:

> The farmer engages his labourers from year to year, giving them land to produce their potato crop and seed when necessary, charging in almost every instance, a rent much beyond his own; and if a cottage be included, frequently in a similar ratio. Against this, he credits the labourer's work, keeping strict account of days and half-days, as the weather permits labour, and once a year—perhaps in some instances twice, the account is settled and the balance either way struck. Thus the "truck system" in its worst form exists in Ireland.[11]

Fermanagh tenant farmers were, indeed, doubly fortunate that agricultural laborers were prepared to accept this form of payment. On the one hand, they were provided with adequate supplies of spade labor when they needed it at the mere cost of giving what were virtually squatters' rights to the subtenants of subtenants. On the other hand, given the lack of money in circulation in 1838, conacre was, as Lord Clements put it, the "only species of remuneration which their employers can at present afford to give."[12] Yet the practice of conacre clearly contributed to the growth of an underclass—what a contemporary, John Bright, was a few years later to call the *residuum*.

In the long run the practice of conacre added to the weakness of noblesse oblige in the face of the famine crisis. Ties between landlords and tenants were personal, but landlords' links with the subtenants of the subtenants of their tenants had become tenuous in the extreme. It was from this cottier and squatter class that many of those seeking admission to the workhouse came. Beyond the reach of patron, family, employer, or "friends"—and increasingly so as the small tenant farmers who could afford to emigrated—this underclass remained remote even from local officialdom (the constable or parish clerk). In many cases, it was an alarmed citizen, coming across their fallen bodies by the roadside, particularly at the edges of towns, who facilitated their passage to the workhouse.

For although money provided the idiom of the conacre transaction (and might have been spent on market goods when the potato crop failed), the reality of coin rarely entered into conacre. The laborers, Clements noted, bargained for conacre in money but, "not having a six pence in the world, the farmers allow them, 'from charity,' to work out the rent in labour; and the *nominal* rent is worked out in *nominal* wages."[13] Credit and debt accounts were kept, but the balance was rarely settled in money. Usually, as Clements made clear, further debts were accumulated. The laborer would then be obliged, "necessarily obliged, to resort to mendicancy; or, what is much more common, he sends his wife and children to beg, till his fresh crop of conacre is ripe; while he, poor fellow, continues to work up the old score . . . at work every fine day of the year."[14] Conacre thus bound for months, even for years, on end, the same poor families to the same small tenant farmers within the neighborhood. The potato-trucking system was the critical component in the interdependency of laboring poor, tenant farmer, and landlord within a shared culture of dearth. It was pervasive, at least from 1780 to the 1840s, because dearth was pervasive.

The reciprocal entitlements involved in conacre rested on the significance of place to all the actors in the economic transaction, but to none was it more critical than the laborer obliged to migrate seasonally for the mainland harvests. Belonging to a locality alone made them credit worthy.

> What may be called their permanent industrial residence [is] preserved with greater tenacity . . . than any privilege which the mere written law can give. As soon as the harvest is over, they return, not only to the parish, but to the same corner of the parish, and the very townland which they have left [because] as long as they are candidates for support from agriculture in Ireland, their only chance of obtaining it is in the immediate neighbourhood where they are known. [Thus] arrangements for hiring, and labour, are generally made only among parties who are perfectly well acquainted, and who are probably born in the same corner of the same parish . . . a man would not leave his 'friends' if he could avoid it . . . those who do so are looked upon with distrust and dislike, and find it particularly difficult to obtain any regular work elsewhere.[15]

Conacre, as a form of customary law, was not the same throughout Fermanagh. Responses to a government inquiry into the condition of the poor in 1836 suggested the greater use of money in Tyrkennedy to the east of Lough Erne than in the west. In most areas, however, the county suffered a money-starved economy, and laboring men were obliged to work elsewhere for at least part of the agricultural year. For this reason, conacre conditions in Fermanagh, and problems of famine relief, were closely related to changes in agricultural conditions in England (particularly in the north) and changes in the Poor Laws of both England and Ireland.

## The Administration of Relief

It was never intended that the Poor Law Act imposed on Ireland in 1838 cope with famine relief. The Act required that the whole of Ireland be divided into unions, three or four to a county, based upon market towns that could be reached in a day on foot. At the hub of each union lay the House of Industry. The unions cut across "old and inconvenient" county and baronial divisions; they also divided large estates. The significance of place and the historically rooted ties among townland populations gave way to "tidiness" and considerations of efficiency, time, and work discipline. This brought home in no un-certain manner the landlord's loss of control over his tenants; in Fermanagh, an appeal made by Sir Arthur Cole, M.P. that his tenan-try not be divided between two unions was denied by the Poor Law Commissioners. The control and redesign of space was, of course, a major component in the imposition of the new political and cultural authority.

The setting up of the unions within their new boundaries was accompanied by the framing of electoral divisions, so that ideally guardians might be local representatives. It was assumed for Ireland as a whole that few resident landlords would be involved and that agents would represent landlord interests. It was anticipated that most of those engaging in union management would be merchants and professional men in the small market towns where the workhouses were located. None of these conditions prevailed in Fermanagh.

Enniskillen had been a closed borough until 1832, its corporation made up entirely of rent payers to the town's proprietor, the earl of Enniskillen. Its Poor Law politics tended to be more radical than those of rural tenants closely bound to the ultra-Tory, Fermanagh landed class. Leading townsmen were Presbyterian for the most part and much more sympathetic to the changes in political economy and administration on which the Irish Poor Law rested. An ideology of individual entrepreneurship, along with new forms of direct and indirect social intervention, blended well with their lowland Scottish historical traditions. In the circumstances, the involvement of Angli-can gentry in workhouse management (such as young Porter and the appointed guardians) was by no means detrimental to the well-being of the poor. Moments of overt hostility at the Enniskillen Union board meetings were often symptomatic of rising conflict between the landed class and a more urban, radical, capitalist interest.[16] Famine relief thus momentarily and precariously framed not only the agrarian revolution reflected in the famine but a civil revolution—politely projected—after which Fermanagh was never quite the same again.

Not only were the Poor Law Commissioners English, but so were the assistant commissioners who periodically inspected the unions. The commissioners, who were based in Dublin, were responsible to the English Poor Law Commission in Somerset House in London, and throughout the famine years, the system was notorious for the length of time it took for any decisions to be reached and for any executive action to be carried out. Isolated within this middle tier of the state bureaucracy, and at several removes from the seat of power, the guardians were severely limited when it came to direct action. In most cases, throughout Ireland, the middlemen bureaucrats who manned the boards had never known differently. In Fermanagh, the resident peers and gentry chafed against the bit, perhaps winning small victories, but losing ground in the long run.

It is difficult to convey the frustration that engulfed those undertaking the relief of the poor during the famine, a frustration that became increasingly perverse as the seasons passed. Wheelbarrows could not be made locally because specifications had to be followed and these had not arrived from Dublin. Record-keeping forms had to be ordered and paid for by the union itself, regardless of its lack of funds for essential foodstuffs. Inspections enforced the most minute details of diet and space allocation, regardless of overcrowding in hospital wards. Aggregated statistics had to be submitted at regular intervals to the commissioners in Dublin, thence to be forwarded to Westminster—signifiers of bureaucratic efficiency but a drain on the resources of the local agents obliged to spend time on them.

## Poor Relief Under Stress

Throughout the 1830s, political economists and government administrators had debated the fringe indicators between dearth and famine, but rarely did they bring their own persuasive philosophies and actions into the equation. The Fermanagh gentry saw quite clearly, however, that parliamentary and bureaucratic intervention both aborted and inadequately replaced their own local participation in the political economy of relief.

At first, the landlords and small farmers had taken all the usual measures to relieve distress, beginning to intervene in the local economy, as was customarily expected of them as early as October 1846. Rents were lowered; gale days were postponed; kindling was made available from Home Farm copses; root crops and new seeds were imported at the initiative of the landlord to be sold at cost. Much was done to encourage alternative subsistence crops to the potato. In some cases this smacked of social control measures such as Bentham would have delighted in, the seed being made available to "good" tenants who paid their rents. With the establishment of Poor Law Unions, many had been appointed ex officio guardians, as we have seen, and most had arranged for their political clients to be elected to office as well.

As the situation worsened, the gentry attempted to take more into their own hands. In advance of government authorization, soup kitchens were set up, with neighboring estates competing in the nutritional value of their recipes (printed in the *Impartial Reporter*) and the efficiency of their services. Wives and daughters organized "industrial" relief in the form of work bees and organized charities. Their husbands and sons sought ways of making the county's needs known to relief agencies in England, Canada, and the United States, engaging in detailed correspondence and arranging for the distribution of any goods received.

Even less formally, the gentry and professional men began to mobilize personal networks of kin and affines in Scotland, in England, and on the Continent; "old boy" networks; and clientalist ties throughout the Empire—with varying success.[17] Because Enniskillen was a major garrison town, many of rural Fermanagh's "surplus sons" served in British and Irish regiments in India, and their aid was solicited by those with military connections. Everything was done to counter an impression that existed in their personal outside worlds that, although other Irishmen suffered, Fermanagh was famine-free.

The admission register of the Enniskillen House of Industry told the story. During the first six years of its existence, between September 1840 and October 1846, the House of Industry had functioned smoothly, more or less in keeping with George Nicholls's design, paid for by the raising of Poor Law rates among the landowners and tenant farmers of the county. Even in mid-October 1846, at the onset of the long, hard winter, the workhouse was only half full. Designed to hold six hundred adults and four hundred children, at the close of the week ending October 17, it housed some 180 adults and 223 children. The union had been solvent right up until the end of December 1846. A rate had been struck of £2,987, and all but £125 had been collected. Ominously, though, only £7 had been collected in the last three months of the year. By the time the guardians met on May

4, the workhouse, built to accommodate one thousand paupers, held approximately twelve hundred.

Of the 1,211 inmates, the able-bodied numbered only 112, of whom 90 were women and 22 men. Of the total accommodated, 464 were children under fifteen years of age. The most severe overcrowding was in the workhouse hospital, which was built to house 60 patients but held 488 men, women, and children on May 1, 1847. Of these, 177 were diagnosed as fever patients. In the previous months the figure had soared even higher, but mortality had thinned the ranks. Charged to the electoral divisions, the constant rise in expenditure on coffins reflected the worsening situation.

The death rate mounted slowly. By mid-October there had been eleven deaths; by mid-November there were sixteen more; and another thirty-four occurred by the end of the year. Over sixty deaths in the last three months of 1846 alone—during a period when the harvest had been gathered and husbands, brothers, and sons had returned from seasonal work in England—was an ominous sign. Although over half were of men and women over the age of sixty and attributable in part to the harshness of the winter itself, an increasingly large proportion was younger.

For the poor in normal times, the workhouse was a place to go to die, when one was old or sick and had no family, friends, or neighbors to offer support. The climbing statistics reflected the end of dearth-alleviating remittances and the sharing of family food. Some of the old were left behind, abandoned by kin (frustrated tenants and ambitious servants in particular) who were able to emigrate. Others among them chose to remain in Fermanagh—keeping the family name on the farm—believing that matters would again improve as they had so often seen them do within their lifetimes.

Had the epidemiology of famine been better understood, the guardians would have read greater significance into the rising number of young men and women, one-sixth of the total, who had died during the closing months of the old year. Families that had known increasing distress throughout the hungry months of the summer faced the onset of starvation as the blight struck their potato fields. In their huddled poverty or flight from the countryside, in workhouse, soup kitchen, or roadwork gang, fortunate as they thought themselves to be, they were additionally exposed and vulnerable to the "famine fever" that attacked the county at the turn of the year. By the end of March 1847, 355 paupers had died in Enniskillen workhouse. This was three times as many as had died in the entire nine years since it had been built. Of these most were struck down by fever.

## The May 4 Admissions

Who, then, were the 351 men, women, and children admitted to the Enniskillen workhouse on May 4, 1847? Ironically, as in their daily existence in more favorable times, the destitute poor were grossly underestimated. Not "some two hundred" but 351 were admitted to the workhouse on May 4, 1847. The journalist's impression of women with babies at their breasts and small children clinging to their skirts was, however, true to the general character of the waiting crowd. Children did, indeed, outnumber adults; there were 163 men and women and 188 children.[18]

In the best of times, when a culture of dearth prevailed, a largely female world of the aged and the orphaned, the deserted and the bereft, the idiot and the infirm, was transported by a largely male world to the workhouse. But as the dearth economy steadily faltered, with the adverse conditions of the postwar Irish economy and new restrictions on seasonal movement to England, more men and young persons began to seek relief, necessarily within Fermanagh itself. Of the 351, only 27 were over fifty years of age, and of these 16 died within days or weeks of admission. Nine were women and 18 men.

In all, of the adults admitted on May 4, 67 were male and 96 female; of the children, 101 were male and 87 female. Most of the "family" clusters admitted were made up of mothers with three or four children, although in a few cases a father had a similar "family" in tow. Few "complete" families (i.e., mother, father, and children) were admitted on that evening. This may have reflected the relict conacre-family characteristic of rural Fermanagh in May, or it may have reflected an increasing number of "desertions."

The political, economic, and class structure of the localities[19] to which individuals belonged was reflected in the composition of the population admitted on May 4, 1847.[20] Apart from fever, the factors that, in different places and at different times, most often accounted for families and individuals having recourse to workhouse relief were evictions by landlords, desertion or death of a "breadwinner," and the large-scale emigration of family members. By May 1847, a politically paradoxical phase had been reached in the spread of the famine. The blight had hit first and hardest at the low-lying fields of Protestant small farmers (tenants of colonizers of the best lands since the seventeenth century); only then did it reach the small plots of those who had been driven into the mountains.

By May 4, the mountain townlands, largely Catholic, frequently dissident, and customarily almost wholly reliant on conacre and seasonal migrant labor, were also at risk. Thus, by May 1847, the two localities that contributed more applicants than any others were Laragh, a lowland farming area close to Enniskillen on the west of Upper Lough Erne from which many small farmers had emigrated to Canada, and Tempo, a mountainous locality bordering County Tyrone in the east, where a largely Catholic population had survived since Plantation times. Roman Catholics (255) outnumbered Protestants (94) by a ratio of nearly three to one among those admitted on May 4. (Religion was not stated in two instances.)

The extremity in which those admitted found themselves is evidenced by the mortality among them. Of the 351 admitted, 111 had died within three months. During the evening and night of May 4, a fourteen-year-old boy from Laragh, a father and his two children (all Catholics from Tempo), and a Protestant mother and her three children from Tempo, all died. These eight early deaths reflected certain regularities: a tendency for deaths to occur among all the members of one family; deaths of both Protestants and Catholics; a greater number of deaths among children than adults.

During the rest of May, all the members of five more families admitted on May 4 died, four of them from Tempo. Four were Magoverns from one mountain townland, Glen.[21] The fifth family, a mother and two children, came from the vicinity of Enniskillen town. Along with these families (comprising six adults and twenty children), twenty-seven more deaths occurred among those admitted on May 4: seventeen men, three women, four boys, and three girls. Six of the men and two of the women were more than fifty years old. As the famine progressed (its aftermath lasting until 1855 in Fermanagh), fewer of the elderly survived to be admitted. In June, deaths from among the 351 were fewer: eleven men, five women, eleven boys, and six girls (a total of thirty-three). In July they were fewer still: four men, one woman, three boys, and two girls (a total of ten). Starvation and fever deaths among the cohort appeared to be at an end. In all, out of the 351 admitted on May 4, 104 (two out of every seven) had died within three months.[22]

For Ireland as a whole, the famine almost doubled the death rate for all ages: task work on relief put males at greater risk; smallpox affected the young indiscriminately; cholera attacked the old. Yet the economic historian Cormac Ó Gráda has noted in his recent study

*The Great Irish Famine* a tendency among Irish historians to downplay famine mortality. Fermanagh's recorded population declined by one-fifth between the censuses of 1841 and 1851, and (as my larger study shows) high mortality continued in the county until 1856. It must be stressed once again at this point that this essay deals only with work-house mortality in one specific phase of the faminization process. The larger study from which these findings are abstracted suggests how the responses of gentry, farmer, and cottier, within the imposed legal and bureaucratic restraints on famine relief, led to considerable varia-tion in the timing, location, and alleviation of suffering. It also argues that these various outcomes must be placed within changing fields of compassion (and dismissiveness) outside of Ireland itself.

## Conclusion

The bureaucratic response to the events of May 4, emanating from Dublin, was to instruct that no more paupers be admitted until the number of inmates fell to one thousand—the number for which the workhouse had been designed in 1840. The guardians did not obey. Indeed, the Enniskillen guardians thereafter engaged in a running battle with the bureaucrats in Dublin and London, somehow escaping the fate of neighboring Lowtherstown Union, which was closed down for failure to comply with Poor Law regulations. It seems reasonable to believe that the chairmanship of the earl of Enniskillen, nominal as it was, might well have been responsible for the union's survival.[23]

For the bourgeoisie and gentry of Fermanagh, May 4 was a real-ization of their worst fears. They had from the beginning opposed the extension of the Poor Law to Ireland, fully appreciating that its purpose was not to mitigate the condition of the poor in Ireland but to prevent them from going to England. The new English Poor Law had been in place, violently contested, for over eight years. Impover-ished Irish migrants were being returned to Belfast and Drogheda; a safety valve on the conacre-trucking system was steadily eroded. Hostilities and violence grew between the English and the "undeserv-ing" Irish poor, and the massive participation of the Irish in the Chartist movement did little to endear them to the English middle classes and Parliament.

Fermanagh's ultra-Tory representatives in the House of Com-mons, along with the vast majority of Irish members, had spoken and voted against the extension of the Poor Law to Ireland. They had not held mass protest meetings on the eve of its implementation in 1838, as had members of their class in surrounding counties, but had instead organized more permanent and more insidious forms of opposition to the intrusion of the English bureaucracy with its utilitarian Benthamite principles. Calls for the repeal of the union and the revitalization of the Orange Order swept through Fermanagh, concurrently uniting and dividing those middle-class Catholics and Protestants who had invested their futures in Ireland. A very large number chose to emigrate.

The Fermanagh gentry contributed not simply to the enormous relief effort required in 1847 but critically to attacking the famine's underlying cause—the domination of Ireland's economy, bureaucracy, and political interests by the newly emergent, decision-making British bourgeoisie. Their attack took the form of scathing critiques, published privately and openly in the local newspapers, pamphlets on political and moral economy, and above all, efforts to persuade the City of London to extend the railway system into Fermanagh. All made clear that at the root of the disastrous economy lay a lack of money in circulation in the country and problems, not of the land, but of the laboring poor.

The revolutions of 1848 swept by the bushfires of nationalism throughout Europe led to conflagration in Ireland too. Since history tends to be written by victors, the abortive Irish struggle has come down in the annals of historians under the derisive title of "The Cabbage Patch War." A great deal has been made of the personal weaknesses of its leaders; the rhetoric of their martyrdom at state trials; their transportation and subsequent obscurity. Yet the triumphal return of the body of Terence Bellew Macmanus from California by train across the United States and then on carriage cart across from Cork to be buried in Dublin, quickly became a founding legend of the Irish Republican Brotherhood.

A less-well-known history places Macmanus in Tempo (his birthplace), as a cadet of a prominent Catholic aristocratic family, and as a prominent Young Irelander engaged in shipping arms from Liverpool to Dublin on the eve of the revolution. It was the drift toward violence that alienated a Fermanagh Protestant sympathizer with the Young Ireland cause—the Rev. John Grey Porter of Kilskeery, father of the chairman of the guardians on May 4. The involvement of these two men in the same place, at the same time, and surely known to each other suggests the argument toward which this essay is moving. The politics of the famine in Fermanagh must not be seen simply as part of an English stratagem to remove the threat of Irish attachments to European Catholic nations, to develop the British economy at the expense of the Irish, or to weaken the hold of the Anglo-Irish gentry in favor of an urban bourgeoisie in self-interested sympathy with Bentham and Chadwick's centralizing reforms. Rather, the politics of the Irish Famine requires the orchestration of the politics of Fermanagh's gentry, bourgeoisie, peasantry, and laboring poor—and these involved not only compliance with and suffering under the new bureaucratic edicts but resistance to British overrule and the seizing of new opportunities. Interests were clearly contradictory, but the essential question was one of power; and in this struggle, the reluctance of the Anglo-Irish landlords to cede control to English bureaucrats and their puppets was of no small account.

The costs of the famine in Fermanagh were borne by the laboring poor, the small farmers, and the gentry, Protestant and Catholic alike. Their integral structures and their interdependencies were weakened by the imposed alien management of the famine. Within another generation (i.e., by 1870), it was clear that a new Irish economy had engendered a new Irish society in Fermanagh. By 1901, a youth in a remote Boho mountain townland responded to a census inquiry into his occupation with one simple word—*capitalist*.[24]

## NOTES

1. The account that follows is based on records at the Public Record Office Northern Ireland (PRONI), including BG14/A/2 Minute Book of the Enniskillen Board of Guardians; BG14/G/1 Indoor Register (Workhouse Register); BG14/DD/1 Abstracts of Accounts; BG14/O/13 Returns of Officers, 1844–1948; BG14/CA/1 Ledger, February 1841–September 1847; BG14/O/6 Railway Materials; BG14/O12 one small box of correspondence and circulars of the Poor Law commissioners; Board of Guardians Elections; and BG14/K.A./1 Return of Deaths. Specific sources will not be cited here but may be found in my *Culture and Politics of the Irish Famine. County Fermanagh 1836–1856*. For a discussion of the place of this analysis within Irish ethnography in the historic mode, see Vincent (1990).

2. The extension of the Poor Law Act to Ireland in 1838 had been opposed by Fermanagh members of the House of Commons, all three of whom were ultra-Tories. In the light of his subsequent career, it seems likely that young Porter, chairing the Mayo Board meeting, would have been one of the few Whigs in the county to accept the workhouse system of relief with a modicum of grace.

3. The increasing power of the Treasury in nineteenth-century Britain is discussed in Corrigan and Sayer (1985:121).

4. Ironically, it was their foot-dragging response to initial instructions of

the Poor Law Commissioners that led to a belief that Fermanagh did not suffer from the famine. Charles Trevelyan's supposedly authoritative article on the Irish crisis in the *Edinburgh Review* drew on returns made to the castle up to August 10, 1846. According to these, it had not been necessary to set up a relief committee in Fermanagh. The first such committee was, in fact, established there the following month. This erroneous belief not only colored official reactions to famine in Ulster at the time, leading the commissioners to minimize conditions in the west of the province, but also was to be found in modern authoritative accounts of the Irish famine.

5. *Impartial Reporter,* May 1, 1847.

6. *Impartial Reporter,* May 15, 1847.

7. *Impartial Reporter,* May 8, 1847.

8. This is important for evaluating the actions of the Fermanagh gentry both as guardians and as landlords. Fermanagh was unique in Ireland (in 1847 as now) for its Church of Ireland, or Anglican Protestant, majority. The remaining thirty-one counties had either Roman Catholic or Presbyterian majorities. None of the six largest landowners, and only a few of the smaller gentry, were absentee. Many landlord and tenant families, Protestant as well as Catholic, had been present in the county for at least ten generations.

9. Fermanagh was remarkably free of the violence connected with Ribbonism or the Molly Maguires in the period immediately before the famine, in spite of horrendous incidents in the neighboring counties of Leitrim and Cavan. Agrarian outrages were limited to the earl of Enniskillen's estate in the extreme south of the county and to mountainous regions in the Ely estate in the west. Faction fighting was both sectarian and local, and at the same time and in the same localities, Captain Rock posters called on tenants—Protestants and Catholics—to unite against unfair landlords. Land agents were attacked in a few places, and corn mills were destroyed in others.

10. Something of the complexity of the faminization process in different parts of the county can be appreciated when it is realized that much of this mountainous region fell under the jurisdiction of the Ballyshannon Union in County Donegal. It might be argued that the marquess of Ely was less concerned for the welfare of those on his estate than other Fermanagh landlords who tried to renegotiate boundaries. It must also be recalled, however, that for some of the time, members of Fermanagh's ancien régime (the marquess of Ely and the earls of Enniskillen and Belmore, in particular) were away from home, engaged on service to the empire, as governors-general, for example, in Cape Province, New South Wales, or the Caribbean. The roles of family members then became critical in famine relief.

11. Clements (1838:77–78).

12. Clements (1838:78).

13. Clements (1838:106). Emphasis added.

14. Clements (1838:106).

15. Clements (1838:126–29).

16. This struggle between a largely Scottish Presbyterian bourgeoisie and

an Anglican landed gentry can be traced back to 1689 and the Glorious Revolution, as I tried to show in Vincent (1987). As dissenters, Presbyterians shared legal disabilities with Roman Catholics in both England and Ireland.

17. It cannot be overemphasized how much the imperial setting was taken for granted in Fermanagh. In 1849, when the Westminster government proposed to impose a rate-in-aid on the more prosperous regions of Ireland, Ulster landlords claimed that Ireland was "an integral part of the United Kingdom, and that Ulster has no relations with Connaught which are not equally shared by any other division of the British Empire" (quoted in Ó Gráda 1988:115).

18. According to the regulations, "children" were those under fifteen years of age on the day of their admission. Children's diets (rations) were smaller than those provided for adults and some children declared themselves older than they truly were.

19. Intensive fieldwork was carried out in Fermanagh in 1973–74 and 1982–83. Genealogical data were collected and reconstructed for four localities, adopting what I have called the "patch method of inquiry" (Vincent 1977). Two of these, Lisbellaw and Boho, were in the Enniskillen Union. Lisbellaw lay within Porter's Manor of Carrick; the townlands around Boho belonged to several estates.

20. From Boho, one widower and three single-parent families were admitted on May 4. One Catholic family was made up of the father with three children; another of the mother and four children under the age of ten. The remaining family was Protestant and consisted of the mother and five children. Of the sixteen admitted, seven died before June 20, leaving two sets of orphans. From Lisbellaw, nineteen paupers were admitted on May 4, all but five of whom were Protestants. Of three single-parent families, two were headed by males. Five "single" persons were also admitted: three men, one woman, and a child. Five died on the day they were admitted; the remainder survived the famine.

21. The families were made up of a mother with seven children; a mother with four children; a mother with five children; and a mother and father with one child. Only two Magovern households were still to be found in Glen when a valuation of tenements was carried out in 1863.

22. I have, as yet, found nothing in the Enniskillen records relating to the care and disposal of orphans, although there is excellent documentation from the Lisnaskea Union in southeastern Fermanagh. On the subject in general see McClaughlin (1987).

23. Unlike the Enniskillen Union under the nominal patronage of the earl of Enniskillen, and the Lisnaskea Union closely managed by the earl of Erne, the Lowtherstown Union prided itself upon its classlessness. Its guardians were constantly at odds with the Poor Law Commissioners, who eventually discharged them from their duties.

24. Manuscript Census, County Fermanagh, 1901. Public Record Office, Dublin.

## 3

# From Fisher to Poacher: Public Right and Private Property in the Salmon Fisheries of the River Nore in the Nineteenth Century

■

### MARILYN SILVERMAN

In 1802, the rivers of southern County Kilkenny were "celebrated for their salmon" and the "fishing . . . [was] free by custom to the inhabitants of the shores."[1] Over the next eighty years, on the upper waters of these rivers, the rights of private property gradually encroached upon and finally criminalized these rights of custom. The process was complex—woven out of an uneven interaction of numerous factors working sometimes together, sometimes in opposition. State policy, parliamentary legislation, case law, market exigencies, administrative priorities, and class and private interests were all relevant in varying ways at different times. The process also was fueled by the interaction of class segments that came out of the various and often opposing interests in the salmon fisheries themselves.

In this essay, I describe the encroachment process as it evolved on the upper river Nore in an area called Thomastown[2]—a locality comprised of landowners, mill owners, shopkeepers, tenant farmers, and laborers.[3] Some members of each class, but certainly not all, were interested in salmon fishing. Interested parties also pursued or advocated different types of fishing. The permutations were as follows:

| Type of Fishing | Land-owners | Millers | Farmers | Shop-keepers | Laborers |
|---|---|---|---|---|---|
| Weirs, fixed nets | x | x | x | | |
| Angling (rod fishing) | x | x | x | x | x |
| Cots and snap nets[4] | | | | | x |

There also were some from all classes who had no direct interest in the salmon fisheries but who occasionally entered the fishing arena in pursuit of other interests. Thus, classes seldom "marched into battle as solid phalanxes."[5] Instead, alliances across classes—based on interests in fishing or a lack thereof, and based on different modes of fishing—comprised part of the local and regional dynamic through which the process of encroachment wound its uneven but inexorable way in the context of a century increasingly dedicated to the rights of private property.

## The Declining Salmon Fisheries: 1800–31

Although the right to fish was "free by custom," for generations the fishing itself had not been free from legislative controls. It is important to note, though, that such controls never had been linked to the ownership or occupation of any kind of property. There were acts against destroying salmon fry,[6] fishing in the closed season,[7] and working weirs if they interfered with navigation.[8] Barony constables supposedly enforced these laws,[9] but on the Nore, in 1802, salmon fry were destroyed by mill weirs, "cots . . . fish . . . whenever they please" and salmon were caught "out of season, at illegal times, and in illegal ways."[10] As a result, the "quantity of salmon has . . . very much decreased within the last forty years" and "little is done to prevent the fishery from rapidly declining."[11]

In the first quarter of the nineteenth century, the declining salmon fisheries had become a "general complaint" in the United Kingdom.[12] Several parliamentary committees investigated, and one of them pessimistically concluded in 1825 that the decline would continue "more rapidly, unless effectual measures be resorted to for their preservation."[13]

The conditions on the upper, freshwater Nore at that time were described before one such committee by C. H. B. Clarke, a Kilkenny M.P. He observed that the salmon fisheries had "decreased considerably" because weirs had been erected on the inland, upper waters by "parties" who did not have any grant to do so.[14] He allowed that there were gaps (fish passes) in such weirs, according to law, but either they were placed in inappropriate places or else "every means is taken to frighten the fish from passing through." In short, the law existed, but "there are means taken to secure its evasion." He added that the "proprietors of mill weirs observe the law more correctly than those of the private weirs."[15]

Clarke's testimony distinguished several inland interests: mill owners, landed proprietors who held fishing weirs, and the gentry, like himself, with no discernible interest in fishing but with a concern for the law and the cost of salmon for the table.[16] Shortly thereafter, in 1829, "gentlemen interested in the protection of the Fishery of River Nore" subscribed to a fund to hire a fisheries inspector,[17] who over the next few years brought suits against those whose weirs did not "comply with the Act of Parliament now in force on the subject"[18] and who, in 1831, charged several Thomastown laborers for snap net fishing in the closed season.[19]

By 1831, then, all the fishing interests were distinguishable, as was the fact that Thomastown had both "uncommon poachers" as well as "common" ones.[20] Local poaching, however, did not explain the decrease of salmon on the inland Nore. Instead, it is necessary to look to the regional context—to the tidal waters and the estuary downriver from the Thomastown area.

## The Regional Context and the Uncommon Poachers

Patrick Magee, secretary of St. Peter's Society, a fishermen's association in New Ross, described how "since 1809, . . . some English and Scotchmen came over, and erected at Passage"—in the estuary—"Scotch weirs where the entrance to our rivers is very narrow; their fishery became very profitable, at the expense of . . . our tide and fresh water . . . fishery."[21] Earlier, in the estuary and tidal waters,

> gentlemen fished in cots; . . . our harbour's mouth was . . . fished legally by sea fishermen with drift nets; . . . there was abundance for all. . . . The cot fishermen had no objections to the small . . . weirs when fished by a gentleman for . . . his house, as each weir gave employment to one man, although they were contrary to the law, until they commenced . . . extending them into the rivers, and . . . setting them to tenants who fished them at all seasons.[22]

The law in all this, said Magee to an 1835 Parliamentary Inquiry, "appears . . . to protect . . . fishermen from the encroachment of the gentlemen and weir owners; but . . . these laws remained a dead letter for the last century; the gentlemen and magistrates who should have enforced them, became weir owners, and in receipt of great revenues therefrom, allowed the fishermen . . . to dwindle away into . . . poverty."[23]

Meanwhile, on the inland Nore, conditions also had worsened. By 1834, a fisheries inspector no longer was hired by private subscription and a petition "from the fishermen . . . on the Rivers Barrow and Nore, signed by about 1,000 persons complain[ed] of great distress."[24] According to Cornelius Maxwell,[25] a witness at the 1835 Inquiry: "Salmon are taken . . . with every description of net; . . . still-nets and stop-nets, which are illegal, are used on all the weirs. . . . Since the net and trap became of general use, the Salmon have decreased at least fifty-fold."[26] Those responsible for this were "powerful and influential individuals" who had "usurped" rights of fishing on the inland Nore—a river on which "there are no private rights of fishing." Maxwell cited two "landed proprietors," Tighe and Davis, who "claim a patent right of fishing with still-nets on their weirs; but might with them is right—they have no legal claim."[27]

Neither Magee, when referring to the tidal waters and estuary, nor Maxwell, when describing the inland waters, saw common poaching as relevant; the problem lay with the proprietors. They both also observed that voluntary subscriptions from the gentry were too erratic "to protect the salmon fishery, and to prosecute the weirs on the Nore." This failure, according to Magee, "induced us to try the only means left, that of forming a society."[28] This was St. Peter's Society; and "protection" meant a concerted attack on the tidal weirs. "Those weirs . . . became so destructive that by . . . 1830 our salmon fishery was reduced from about 500 to 20 nets, when we discovered many old Acts . . . in force against those weirs. . . . We commenced prosecuting and taking them down."[29]

Magee explained how a solicitor "gave a great deal of his time . . . to the fishermen, gratis. . . . At the last assizes of Kilkenny, he proceeded against weirs on the river Nore." Yet although the "parties pleaded guilty, . . . the weirs are kept standing, and fishing."[30] The Society also sent a stream of "papers and petitions" to the Waterford M.P. regarding "their rights as fishermen."[31] But the ineffectiveness of subscriptions, the courts, and petitions led to violent action. A proprietor in the Waterford estuary (near Passage) had "erected a weir . . . in . . . 1830, which proved most lucrative, and employed a great many hands. This weir was destroyed by a mob [in] . . . 1834, from the interior of the country."[32] Again, in 1837 and 1839, cotmen tore down "weirs that had been lately re-erected."[33]

## Region and Class: 1832–42

Magee's testimony suggests that a crisis in the tidal area and estuary occurred in the mid-1830s with a breakdown of the normative constraints surrounding the use of weirs or fixed nets: proprietors leased them to tenants who fished all year round, thus depriving the cot and drift net fishermen of their livelihoods. At about the same time, on the inland waters, Maxwell's testimony suggests that weirs, some illegal, with illegal nets, had come to dominate, and potentially destroy, the freshwater salmon fishery.

In this context, a regional, class-based coalition was mobilized as St. Peter's Society. It was formed "at a meeting of the fishermen of the rivers Barrow and Nore, assembled at Ross, 1st November 1835," and it clearly was a cotmen's association. The fees were very low and the monthly meetings were "never at a public-house." It also was panregional: watchmen were appointed for locations all along the river—tidal and nontidal.[34]

As a class-based, regional coalition, St. Peter's Society opposed the gentry-owned fixed nets and weirs—in the estuary, the tidal waters, and inland. In yet another part of the wider region, along the fresh water portion of the river Suir, which also emptied into the Waterford estuary, another society was founded "for the protection of the salmon."[35] It was founded in "about . . . 1835 or 1836" by the gentry, although "some few humble persons contributed who fished upon the river." They raised £200 to appoint water bailiffs to protect the breeding fish in winter,[36] they "induced the millers to give up" their "illegal practice,"[37] and they caused a "great many of the Scotch weirs" in the tidal areas to be legally prostrated.[38]

Despite a shared opposition to the tidal weirs, this Suir coalition differed significantly from the one along the Nore. The reason lay in the oppositional context in which each Society functioned, and this derived from the particular fishing conditions on the upper reaches of each river. On the inland Nore were six "stone weirs" based on titles granted in the sixteenth century.[39] Four were in Thomastown parish and two were a few miles south. The inland Suir had only one stone weir. Most landed proprietors along the upper river Nore also were weir owners; this was not the case on the Suir. As a result, the Suir

Preservation Society was made up of all inland proprietors in coalition against Scotch nets in the tidal waters and, in their own locality, against recalcitrant millers and cotmen who fished out of season. These were inland gentry who, in the words of one, aimed "to protect the *property* of those who are proprietors of the river."[40]

Along the Nore, it was cot fishermen from both tidal and inland localities who allied as St. Peter's Society and who challenged both the coastal fixed nets and the inland weirs. In this effort, they were aided by a Society to Protect the Fisheries of the River Nore. It too had been founded in 1835, but its members were inland proprietors of whom only "gentlemen (not being weir-owners)" were appointed to its Committee.[41] This committee immediately sent "circulars . . . to . . . millers, requesting their co-operation" and laid charges "immediately against the proprietors of all illegal weirs."[42] The inland owners on the Nore thus were divided while the cotmen were united into a regional coalition.

Water bailiffs were hired by both of the societies on the Nore, and by 1837, there was an impressive list of inland gentry[43] who had been had up at Thomastown Petty Sessions for weir violations.[44] A year later, the earl of Carrick was again charged, and in 1840, the bailiffs again prosecuted three local owners.[45] As a result, Carrick's weir had to be "reconstructed" in a way "agreeable to the provision of the Act"[46] and the brewer, Anthony Nugent—lessee of Dangan weir owned by Sydenham Davis—had to remove an "illegality in the queen's gap and . . . tail-spur."[47] In addition, a farmer who leased both farm and weir in Dysart was fined because the queen's gap was too narrow; a second charge was dismissed after he altered the "tail spurs to conform" with the Act.[48]

Although these prosecutions had forced weir owners to spend money on alterations, they had little effect. For weir owners kept "constructing fresh and illegal obstructions for the take . . . of . . . fish"[49]—a fact reflected in the prosecutions reported in early 1842. The farmer, Carrick, and Nugent all were had up again.[50] Prosecution costs accumulated. In 1841, the waterkeepers wrote that a "heavy debt has been incurred . . . which we are unable to pay."[51] This was because convictions did not mean that costs were recovered. When Lady Carrick appealed her second conviction, not only was her fine lowered but she was released from paying court costs.[52] The reports show, then, that the battle was unremitting. They also show that another cross-class alliance operated at the time—that of the bourgeoisie and the cotmen.[53] In 1840, the waterkeepers wrote to the *Kilkenny Moderator* requesting that "gentlemen, particularly the Fish-

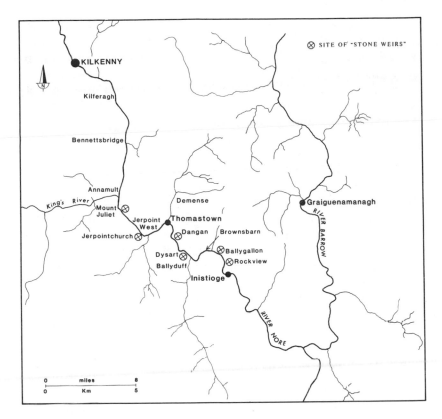

*Figure 3.1.* Localities and Stone Weirs along the Inland Nore River

ery Committee, . . . send in subscriptions to Peter Smithwick, esq., to enable them to prostrate" several new, illegal weirs.[54] Smithwick was a large brewery owner in Kilkenny city. In asking for subscriptions a year later, the waterkeepers described the editor of the *Kilkenny Moderator* as a "gentleman who feels an interest in the preservation of the river Nore."[55] The antiweir interests were linked with the urban-based, county bourgeoisie—a fact already apparent from the evidence given by Maxwell, the editor of the *Kilkenny Journal,* to the 1835 Parliamentary Inquiry.

That a similar alliance operated in the Thomastown area emerges from a lengthy dispute between 1836 and 1841. An 1841 petition "from the inhabitants of Thomastown" claimed that there had been a "communication with the sea for the last 500 years by means of the navigable Nore" but that, in 1836, a local proprietor, Sydenham Davis, had built a wall across the river "thereby putting an end to navigation." Davis "was brought before the petty sessions and agreed to remove the wall but later refused to do so." Then, "in the summer of 1838, one of the petitioners removed the wall himself at which Mr. Davis rebuilt it stronger than before." According to the petitioners, they were then "advised to proceed on an act of parliament of Henry VIII . . . by a memorial to the sheriff of the county."[56] They did this, but also "brought [Davis] before the petty sessions again. . . . The bench refused to intervene"[57] but reiterated that the "sheriff should be applied to . . . as it was without doubt that the wall was illegal."[58] That the sheriff had then refused to act precipitated the petition. In response, Dublin Castle confirmed the sheriff's responsibility, adding that he "is liable to a penalty if he refuses."[59]

This response was sent to a local flour miller. Indeed, all those named in the records of the dispute were local bourgeoisie[60] who, in fact, represented, as the petition claimed, "all shades of political and religious opinion."[61] They shared, however, a concern for the commerce of the town, and hence local navigation, and a distaste for the way in which Davis, sovereign of Thomastown Corporation, managed local affairs.[62] In this they were allied with local laborers who, as the petition stated, were undergoing "great hardship" because of the "flooding and . . . unemployment . . . attributable to the obstruction of navigation."[63]

These converging interests linked into the concerns of local cotmen who took over the dispute in late 1841. The waterkeepers brought a case—this time before the Kilkenny Petty Sessions as a breach of the fishery laws. In his evidence, waterkeeper Edward Bryan said that the length of the weir's spur wall interfered with the fish: "out of every 100 . . . going up the river not more than 50 . . . could escape . . . Mr. Davis' trap." Both Bryan and a laborer testified that the weir, although "taken down in . . . 1837" as ordered by the Thomastown bench, had "been built up again." Another witness said that Davis was continually building up the wall: the spur wall was ten yards shorter a year before. In contrast, a laborer for the defense testified that he "never saw a shorter weir than Mr. Davis'." On cross-examination, the witness admitted that he was "in the employment of Mr. Nugent," Davis's tenant. Davis's solicitor then "addressed the bench . . . and contended that the magistrates had no power to interfere with the private property of Mr. Davis." The prosecution countered with the "hope that the magistrates would protect public right in opposition to individual interest." Instead, the magistrates decided "to consult the law officers of the Crown."[64] The case finally "was decided in favour of Bryan. . . . Davis then appealed at the Quarter Sessions but the conviction was affirmed."[65]

Laborers had given evidence both for and against Davis; they therefore were linked into both the pro- and antiweir factions. Bryan, in his testimony, had said that he was a "fisherman" but also a "butcher by trade. . . . Five years ago I commenced prosecuting persons under the fishery act; pure love of justice makes me do so."[66] This irony suggests the intensity of conflict between the so-called public right as against private interest. For in his testimony, Bryan also insisted that none of the local weirs was properly or legally constructed. For him the opposition of proprietors and their weirs was everywhere and unending.

By 1842, two features were central. On the one hand, it was a "golden age" for fishermen. The class-based alliance and the antiweir gentry had ensured, according to Magee, that "by 1840 our rivers were open to the free passage of the salmon; the fishery increased 100 per cent by our perseverence."[67] On the other hand, it was a continuous effort to keep the inland weirs "fair" and the tidal Scotch weirs leveled.

## The Declining Salmon Fisheries: The Entry of the State in 1842

Salmon are species that migrate. The "most productive fisheries" were in the lower reaches of rivers, whereas it was landowners in the upper reaches who had to protect the breeding salmon, the spawning grounds, and the salmon fry.[68] Because the upper landowners had little "pecuniary interest in the fisheries," they were "indifferent to poaching, and unwilling to co-operate, either in purse or in person, towards its abatement."[69] For the members of the 1835 Parliamentary Inquiry, the solution was simple: "Poaching in Ireland, though in part attributable to the circumstances and habits of the peasantry, is principally encouraged by the absence of an efficient Police; and this again is referable to the peculiar nature of the property, and the conflict of interests which that occasions."[70] The state therefore had to ensure that upper proprietors received a fair share of salmon; the policing of the so-called peasantry would improve as a result. The upper propriety was to be coopted; the peasantry was to be coerced.

The mechanism was provided by a new Act (5th and 6th Vict. c. 105 and 106), which replaced all earlier legislation. Within the ideological context set out by the 1835 Inquiry, it had three ambitious but somewhat contradictory aims: to increase productivity, to allow everyone to fish, and to preserve the stocks.[71] Two aspects were crucial. First, to ensure supplies[72] and to mollify the lower proprietors, this 1842 Act legalized Scotch nets and "fixed engines" under certain conditions—such as whether the proprietor had exercised this right in the two decades prior to the Act. However, before 1842, the vast majority of weirs and fixed nets in the estuary were illegal—as St. Peter's Society had discovered. The 1842 Act legalized them.

Second, to coopt upper proprietors to improve preservation, the Act recognized the primacy of private property ("a several fishery") in inland waters; but it also recognized the public's right to fish ("a common of piscary"). Chapter 106, section 65

> enacted, That in the Inland and Freshwater portions of Rivers and Lakes in *Ireland* no Person, save the Owner of a several fishery within the Limits thereof, shall, . . . fish with . . . Net . . . unless in Cases when a general public Right of Fishing for Salmon with such Nets, in the Nature of a Common of Piscary, has been enjoyed for a Space of Twenty Years next before the passing of this Act.

Two problems were created. First, it was assumed that private and public rights could coexist on a daily basis. Second, the meaning of *inland* was unclear. *Murcott v. Carter* (1768)[73] distinguished navigable from nonnavigable waters and the kinds of fishing rights in each: "In rivers not navigable the proprietors of the land have the right of fishery on their respective sides; and it generally extends at *filium medium aquae*. But in navigable rivers . . . the fishery is common. It is *prime facie* in the king, and is public."[74]

Fisheries in navigable waters were public; in nonnavigable waters, they were private. The 1842 Act added the prescription that navigable/public waters were tidal and nonnavigable/private waters were nontidal, inland waters. However, the river Nore where it flowed through Thomastown created a difficulty: it was inland yet navigable. Its anomalous character was exacerbated because the rivers Nore, Barrow, and Suir had been designated "royal rivers" in 28 Henry VIII, c.22. They seemingly belonged to the Crown and thence to the public. The legal situation was summarized by a Q.C. and a fisheries expert two decades later: "There may . . . exist a public right of fishing in an inland water where the tide does not ebb and flow; and such is assumed to be the law in the Fishery Acts. . . . The public, however, cannot, except in such a royal river, claim the right of fishing. It exists in the owners of the adjoining lands."[75]

Until 1868, the navigable but inland, royal Nore and an Act that recognized public rights on private property formed the context for fishing and conflict in the Thomastown area.

### 1842–63: Irreconcilable Conflicts and the Evolution of Fisheries Policy

It was explicitly stated that the aims of the 1842 Act were to be realized without state intervention and that the "maintenance of the law was now with the public or with parties interested."[76] Some of the parties acted immediately. Within eight weeks, a notice of meeting was published "for carrying into effect the provisions of the New Fishery Bill."[77] The meeting was held in Kilkenny city with Major Izod, a proprietor, in the chair. After announcing that there now would be a "greater abundance of fish," he called for subscriptions "to defray the expenses of . . . prosecutions and . . . water bailiffs." Resolutions were passed to appoint a Fisheries Committee; to inspect weirs on the Nore, Suir, Barrow, and King's rivers; and to give "general support for the new . . . Act." Edward Bryan again was appointed bailiff.[78]

The closed time fixed by the Act came into effect in August 1844, but "it was not . . . generally observed." Even in 1845, it "has been but very partially observed."[79] Indeed, reports of fishery cases at the Thomastown Petty Sessions only began in late 1844. These had changed, however. Few weir owners were charged. Instead, it was fishmongers who were summonsed for possessing salmon in the closed season as well as one cot crew and one fisherman. The Act, and the gentry's response, were altering the nature of control.

This certainly was true as fisheries policy evolved over the next decade and as laissez-faire policies dissolved before irreconcilable conflicts that, although predating the Act, were aggravated by it. First, the Act required a 124–day closed season. It immediately became policy to make it uniform everywhere so as to ease enforcement.[80] However, coastal interests wanted a "lengthened autumn fishery," whereas inland interests wanted the "fishing before the month of February" and had "no objection to the autumn fishing being cut short."[81] The intrinsic conflict between upper and lower proprietors was exacerbated by a fixed closed time that was to be both uniform and enforced.

Second, class conflict became overt. The new fishing associations were "composed chiefly of . . . proprietors, . . . and their efforts . . . against offences . . . caused many of the poorer order to be convicted . . . and thus created an impression, an erroneous one certainly, that the law was one for the advantage of the rich, and an additional source of coercion on the poor."[82]

Third, the Act aimed to ensure a supply of fish to the public. It therefore legalized a technology (fixed nets) that encroached on the public fishery in tidal waters.[83] Moreover, "under the assumed protection of . . . the Act, weirs have . . . continued . . . or . . . have been erected either in ignorance or evasion of the law, from both of which serious disputes have arisen."[84] Conflict over types of fishing—"fixed engines" against "moveable engines" (drift nets, snap nets, and rods)—was exacerbated.

The Waterford estuary was an important arena. Before the Act, "very few" fixed nets remained; by the spring of 1843, "all the weirs sprang up again."[85] A panregional coalition arose again in response. The drift net fishermen at Passage "sought the aid" of the Suir Preservation Society, as did the "cotmen . . . of the Nore, Barrow and Suir." The Society prosecuted the owners of the fixed nets for fishing in closed time. They were fined £5 but continued fishing. Shortly after, the secretary of the Society came to Waterford to find the "bridge lined with police, the military and the magistrates all out, a descent of cotmen having been threatened." The last "were dissuaded from going to prostrate the weirs" and the Society, with the fisheries commissioners, jointly charged the owners with using illegal nets. The bench on the Wexford side of the estuary indicted them; the Waterford magistrates at both the Petty and the Quarter Sessions refused to do so. "The peace of the whole country was at stake" as two thousand fishermen[86] then took the "law into their own hands and openly prostrated the weirs."[87]

With the gentry blatantly breaking the law, the fishermen's "riots" in the Waterford estuary, and, more generally, the endless complaints and objections raised by competing interests,[88] the commissioners increasingly had to intervene. First, in Waterford over subsequent years, the Crown indicted many persons criminally who were tried by juries at the assizes. However, the Act only allowed legal action against a particular fixed net or weir, and as fast as convictions were obtained and the weirs prostrated, the gentry reerected them—under a tenant's name, for example. The Crown then had to, and did, begin the legal process again.[89]

Second, funds for enforcement were a problem. Not only were voluntary subscriptions insufficient[90] but upper proprietors paid while lower proprietors fished.[91] This produced a "hostile feeling."[92] Third, more enforcement was needed in any case. The commissioners recommended that the Constabulary Act be amended to allow the police to act in fishery offenses.[93] Soon after, a new Act (7th and 8th Vict. c. 108) did precisely that.[94]

In late 1844, a Fisheries Commission Inquiry into the closed season called two Thomastown area witnesses.[95] Major Izod, chair of the 1842 meeting of Kilkenny gentry,[96] observed that angling had been good before the 1842 Act, whereas after, the old obstructions remained, the closed season was not observed, attempts at protection had failed, and they had "got no assistance from those fishing in the tideway and estuary."[97] The fishery was declining. Izod, representing "the River Nore Fishery Association," asked that the closed season run from October 1 to March 1,

The second witness was Edward Bryan. He presented a very different picture. "At one time, in 1843, there were eighteen or nineteen water bailiffs on the Nore and its tributaries." It therefore was a "very valuable year" for a "man could well support his family by snap net fishing." There also was no "weir entirely across the river . . . nor any weir . . . that has not a Queen's gap." According to Bryan, then, there were no obstructions or poaching. Neither was there conflict over the varying modes of fishing: "there is no hindrance to angling, nor do any disputes take place in reference to fishing."[98]

Izod complained about a lack of enforcement; Bryan saw nothing to enforce. Either way, Thomastown people seemingly were free to fish as they wished. However, the two interpretations of local conditions suggest that the interests of gentry anglers were diverging from those of inland cotmen. A memorial signed by 108 Nore fishermen, which duplicated precisely one sent in by 74 Barrow fishermen, made this clear. The cotmen requested a different closed season (August 30 to January 31) from that requested by Major Izod.

The cotmen's request also differed, as they pointed out, from the estuary cotmen, who wished "to leave September open."[99] The interests of freshwater cotmen thus had begun to link inland localities at the same time that they caused a divergence from tidal cotmen. However, the inland cotmen's final request still allied them with cotmen everywhere and with all upper proprietors: "That the Board will not neglect the prosecution of the illegal and unjust Scotch weirs."[100]

By 1845, the commissioners noted a "decided . . . improvement in the commercial value of the Irish Fisheries" because of "individual enterprise," an expanding English market, "improved modes of capture," and the "construction of railways."[101] In this expansionary context, the commissioners retained the principle of a uniform "close season";[102] in so doing, they finally set one priority as paramount: to ensure a "maximum . . . productiveness . . of food." This meant that "commercial value . . . and not . . . private or local . . . interests" was central and that functional specialization was essential. Thus, the coastal and tidal fisheries were the "entire of the commercially valuable . . . fisheries," whereas the "fresh-water parts" were the "natural nurseries" that had to be regulated.[103]

This view received considerable fillip with the failure of the potato crop. That the fisheries had not provided an alternate food supply "established . . . the necessity for . . . developing . . . the fisheries . . . as a source of industry and trade, and consequently of food."[104] Initially, this was stymied because the years of distress had caused the inland fisheries to "suffer severely"[105] as a result of an "almost total neglect of . . . the close season, and of . . . the breeding fish and fry."[106] Illegal stake nets fished at all times; mill owners had nets attached "to their . . . premises; . . . whilst . . . persons of the better order . . . deliberately . . . angle[d] . . . notwithstanding the law." Either there was little enforcement or "merely nominal fines were imposed by the Magistrates. Under such circumstances, . . . little obedience could be expected from the other classes."[107] In Thomastown between 1846 and 1851, only one breach of the Fisheries Act was reported: the constabulary charged two fishermen with using an illegal net.[108]

Into the fray came financial and administrative change: 11 and 12 Vict. c.92 allowed funds for protection "to be raised . . . by a licence duty on the . . . instruments used for taking salmon."[109] Ireland was divided into seventeen Fisheries Districts. In each, a board of conservators was to be elected "by the . . . persons paying licence duty."[110] Each board was to enforce the Fisheries Act and to pass bylaws if needed, subject to the approval of the commissioners. The principle was that "local duties should be performed by local parties."[111]

Thomastown became part of Waterford District, an area of thirty-four hundred square miles[112] comprising the tidal and inland portions of the rivers Nore, Barrow, and Suir along with the Waterford estuary and coastline.[113] Its new board inherited the problem of proliferating, illegal stake nets in the estuary and the fact that these were "highly conducive to the supply of good fish to the market."[114] It inherited the various interest groups that were demanding changes to the closed season. It also was given the principle that it "must be guided solely by the . . . dispassionate consideration of what is good or bad for the fisheries, as regards their permanent productiveness to the public."[115]

Over the next two years, the law was "rarely . . . obeyed and never fully enforced [and] . . . all the old complaints [were] repeated."[116] The commissioners, however, continued to believe "the law, if faithfully observed, sufficient"; for then the "proprietors in the upper waters and anglers generally . . . would obtain a sufficient share of fish . . . to enlist their co-operation in close-time."[117] Yet the license duties remained "insufficient . . . for ample protection"[118] and, on many boards, the gentry predominated and so "evade[d] prosecution for illegal practices."[119]

Despite this, a "decided improvement . . . in the salmon fisheries" began[120]—accompanied by "greater co-operation" as interested parties allowed each other a "fair participation."[121] Such "participation" included only proprietors, however; and this had serious implications. For the abolition of nets on the inland waters (and, therefore, of cotmen) now was mooted. The commissioners presented the idea as a "general public good" that would "sacrifice only . . . a few." They argued that "there . . . never can be, commercially considered, much value in fresh water net fishings" and that "far more remunerative results would follow by letting the right of angling only."[122]

No action was taken at the time, but a new idea had emerged: the inland fisheries, not the inland fish, could be commoditized. This idea was reflected in the fact that the "exclusive fishing right upon the Mount Juliet property" was being "let for profit" annually to the "best bidder."[123] In addition, this idea was becoming associated with a new ideological construct. An 1853 newspaper editorial noted that "complaints" as to the scarcity of fish "are of late . . . most numerous" in the Nore. This was because "poaching is and has been . . . permitted."[124] Although "people pay for licences . . . willingly . . . as there was . . . hope for a better protection; . . . all the profits, to say nothing of the sport . . . are enjoyed by the unlicensed."[125] In other words, by removing the fish, the unlicensed removed the sport. In so doing, they lowered the value of the fishery. Moreover, although there were few prosecutions, "it is notorious that from one end of the river Nore to the other there are innumerable cot-owners whose sole occupation is the netting of . . . salmon."[126] For the editor of this gentry newspaper, cot fishing and unlicensed fishing (poaching) had become synonomous; and it lowered the value of a commodity—the inland fisheries.

The rhetoric subsided, but the number of prosecutions in Thomastown increased. There had been one in 1851, none in 1852 or 1853, and one in 1854. In 1855, there were five; and in 1856, three. None were weir violations. These prosecutions, in number and class bias, occurred in the context of an overall Irish fishery that "was steadily progressing. The quantity of fish captured has increased, and the value has become much enhanced by . . . steam communication." The "commercial importance" of the salmon fisheries was reflected in the "prices recently obtained for the rights of fishing," which also was "evidence of the position which such property now holds in the market for profitable investment of capital."[127] By 1860, two-thirds of the salmon catch was exported; and "with such demand and no possibility of an over supply," the commissioners happily declared that the interests of private property and public rights were "really identical."[128]

However, the "fishing season of 1860 was not so productive." The commissioners concluded that there were too many fixed nets "in the tidal portions" and that the rivers were "too closely fished." Apparently, the "high price of salmon . . . [had] induced many persons in the estuaries, and on the coast" to erect engines "within the last five years."[129] Ironically, the increasing prices had made salmon "a luxury" for "the wealthy." This, in turn, "stimulated . . . owners to procure fish for such profitable disposal."[130] Upper proprietors renewed complaints that the privilege of fixed nets had become "an abuse" and that the fixed engines were overfishing and evading the closed times. The commissioners forecast that if the "price of salmon in the market continue as high as at present, the further increase of such modes of capture may be expected." They suggested that "measures . . . be adopted to control this improvident system of fishing" in order to "secure the . . . largest supply of food at a moderate price."[131] They also recommended, again, that inland netting be banned. This suggestion previously had been made to mollify upper proprietors; now it was to alleviate declining stocks.[132]

Within two years, in 1863, the crisis was otherwise contained. The 26th and 27th Vict. c.114 proscribed any new fixed nets and set up special commissioners to investigate all fixed engines that, if found "in contravention of the common . . . [or] statute law," were to be prostrated.[133] By 1865, the commissioners had investigated 204 fixed nets and found that the "Act of 1842 was universally abused."[134] The nets were leveled. In their report, the commissioners announced that a "revolution has, in the past fifteen months, been effected in the modes of capture."[135] They also noted that "fishery property has much increased in value" as a result.[136]

### 1842–63: Class and Faction in the Salmon Fisheries

In 1861, there were complaints that illegal fishing in both the closed and open season by cotmen and anglers was rampant on the inland Nore and that more bailiffs were needed "who will do their duty without favour or affection to any person."[137] Clearly, enforcement was light at the time as bailiffs colluded, as local interest was minimal, and as the inland Nore fisheries were not yet of great economic value. Certainly there were few poaching charges before 1862.[138] This probably reflected the inability of the gentry to maintain subscriptions and, later, the concern of the conservators with policing mainly the tidal fisheries.[139]

In 1855 and 1856, however, there were the first reports that certain local owners were trying to assert the primacy of private right in Thomastown. Two proprietors, Davis and Marsh, each charged cot crews for fishing in their several fisheries without permission.[140] Despite "a crowded court" for the Davis case, "as all the cot fishers were interested," few details were reported.[141] Apparently, there were also no repercussions from these cases; certainly the owners did not repeat the charges. Probably this was because the more general trend at the time remained that of collusion between classes and of alliances across class lines. What form did this take?

First, proprietor-cotman conflict was constrained. Proprietors made up the Waterford board. At an 1856 meeting, one of the conservators opposed the raising of license fees because the "cotmen were not able to pay the small sum asked of them now." The chair, Thomas Elliott J.P., added: "The gentlemen who have weirs are the persons opposed

. . . to the only class who live by fishing; . . . it was . . . the strength of wealth against the poor man."[142]

Gentry "protection" of cotmen clearly derived out of the conflict between gentlemen weir owners and gentlemen anglers. It was enhanced by lines of collusion which followed personal connections. Elliott admitted to paying personally the license fees for several cotmen. When a laborer on the Carrick estate "was convicted for fishing . . . at Mount Juliet," the earl wrote "to say he did not wish [him] to be dealt with severely."[143]

Such gentry protection extended also from a paternalistic ideology. When the police brought a possession charge against the mother of Martin Murphy ("the notoriously frequent transgressor of the Fishery Laws"), the magistrates, "in consequence of the woman's poverty, decided that she would be sufficiently punished by the forfeiture of the fish" and a nominal fine.[144]

At the same time, of course, gentry protection necessarily was fragile—not only because it was based on a division among the gentry but also because the cotmen generally were seen by all gentlemen as natural poachers. When a conservator, at the previously mentioned meeting of the Waterford Board, asked Elliott "if he would reduce the licences if the cotmen gave up their cots during the close season," Elliott agreed.[145]

Second, there were alliances between the laboring fishermen and members of the Thomastown bourgeoisie. An example is provided by the relations between the cotmen and two flour millers, Pilsworth and Innes. The millraces for each of their mills were located in such a way that any alteration of either's weir affected the other's water power. In 1853, Pilsworth charged that two cotmen, Hutchinson and Kelly, "did . . . maliciously break down" his weir. Another cotman, Dawson, deposed that he "was looking for a fish in the mill race and saw Hutchinson and Kelly in an Innes boat at the weir; saw Hutchinson pull a stone off the weir at about the middle part." In yet another deposition, cotman Harry Colleton stated that "Mr. Pilsworth did not raise the weir even to its ancient height." Several months later, Innes sued Pilsworth for £2,000 "for doing great injury by diverting the course of the water that supplies his mill" by carrying out repairs to weir and millrace.[146] As this action reached the assizes, Innes was charged at the Petty Sessions "for allowing a net to be set on the Queen's gap of his mill-weir." The "two respectable witnesses" against him were two cotmen who apparently "found" the net in the gap.[147]

Clearly, the fishermen were aligned with particular millers; therefore, they were divided among themselves. This was reflected in other reported disputes. In 1844, a cotman charged another with "assault and threatening language over fishing." The witnesses for both were cotmen.[148] Similarly, when "the . . . fishmonger of no small notoriety"[149] was charged by a wealthy brewer for "threatening language and assault," witnesses for and against were fishermen.[150] Such cases, however, do not mean that class conflict was not also manifested. Cotmen at the time were charged with offenses against water bailiffs, the constabulary and the bourgeoisie.[151] However, such conflicts were neither pervasive nor exhaustive. It is important to understand that they occurred later in the period, when controls were increasing.

That factionalism and interclass alliances dominated the local arena is shown also in the diverse occupations of those charged with fishing offenses after 1851. Many were millworkers. Others were artisans: a shoemaker and two blacksmiths. Still others were lumpen—known because they occasionally were charged with rabbit poaching. However, among the offenders between 1851 and 1863 were men from other classes. The son of a hotelier was twice charged, as were several small corn millers, a publican, and a small farmer. None of these were cotmen.

After the 1842 Act, then, a broad alliance of antitidal weir interests typified the region while factionalism and interclass collusion marked the local arena. However, as the market for salmon and salmon fisheries expanded along with the conflicts engendered by such expansion, the varying and often opposing interests in the salmon fisheries changed in tandem. First, the public became increasingly involved, and in the latter years, when "fishery cases were entered for hearing . . . they seemed to excite some public interest."[152] Second, through legislation and its administrative agencies, the state was increasingly active. All this was accompanied by a gradual divergence of former allies. The panregional alliance called St. Peter's Society disappeared as the interests of inland cotmen diverged from the tidal ones over the timing of the closed season. In the inland fishery, the common opposition of some proprietors and all cotmen to coastal nets and inland weirs was dissolving into an angling (gentry) as opposed to a netting interest (laborers). What would happen when the common enemy of all these interests—the tidal nets and weirs— was removed?

## The 1863 Act and the Final Days of Public Right

The 1863 Act not only "revolutionized" the capture of salmon but increased the number that reached the upper waters.[153] More fish produced more fishermen. In Waterford District between 1853 and 1865, the number of cots increased sixfold and the number of cotmen went up twelvefold.[154] In the latter year, "in the Waterford estuary and Barrow river, . . . the demand for cots was so great . . . last spring that the builders could not supply it."[155]

Although the increase mainly was in tidal waters, the fresh water expansion probably was proportional. Moreover, with the removal of the weir-owning, gentry segment, Thomastown cotmen now faced a unified landowning class. Each was quickly mobilized. As the *Kilkenny Moderator*'s editor noted: "The clearing away of the obstructions . . . will but provide a larger quantity of salmon to fall . . . into the nets of the many cot-fishers between Thomastown and our city who habitually act in the most illegal manner."[156]

The editor was somewhat consoled by Section 24 of the new Act that banned fresh water netting every night between 8 P.M. and 6 A.M. To prohibit an activity, however, raised the problem of enforcement. "From . . . previous experience," the editor was not optimistic and suggested a remedy: "the thorough proscription on the use of cots . . . for any purpose whatsoever." Yet the new restriction was better than nothing. "If the gentry . . . will but . . . act energetically, much may be done for the protection of salmon from illegal means of destruction and for the increase of the fish in our rivers for legitimate sport and profit."[157]

For the cotmen, the best fishing—indeed, the only fishing—was at night.[158] The annual closed time was tolerable because it coincided with the time of year when salmon were of poor quality—often inedible and virtually unsalable. The weekly closed time (from Saturday night to Monday morning) that had been introduced in 1842 was very inconvenient. The new nightly closed time, however, was a restriction that limited drastically the public's ability and right to net on the upper waters. Because it coincided with a larger number of cotmen and an intensified gentry opposition that was determined to take advantage of the increasing rentability of its fisheries, conflict along class lines necessarily escalated. This was reflected in proprietors' renewed organizational efforts, in the cases before the Petty Sessions, in the interest that the public now expressed in these cases, in a new rhetoric of opposition, and in a new cohesion among cotmen.

Two days after the *Moderator*'s editorial, a "conference of the gentry . . . interested in the local fisheries" discussed the "new Act [and] the protection of the rivers from illegal fishing."[159] The meeting was attended by land/fisheries owners, by local weir owners, by members of the Suir Protection Society and of the Barrow Protection Society, and by a "number of fishermen from the locality" who "evinced a lively interest in the proceedings." At the start, the chair announced that "cot fishing in the fresh waters . . . was virtually done away with, as . . . it was useless to draw a net in clear daylight." Therefore, the object of the new Suir, Nore, and Barrow Protection Association was "to maintain the interests of the fresh water proprietors." Only Mulhalum Marum, an M.P. and a member of the Irish Party, mentioned other rights: cotmen would "benefit" from the Society's actions because they then could "have the fishing of the river at a reasonable rent from the owners of the several fisheries"![160]

The Petty Sessions soon reflected the proprietors' outlook, their new organization, and the fact that productive cot fishing now was poaching. First, no charges were laid against inland weirs. By 1865, all such weirs had their specifications fixed, and violations involving the structure of weirs seemingly occurred less frequently as a result.[161] Interestingly, no charges were laid against owners for fishing their weirs in the closed time. Second, charges against cotmen, and the number of crews charged—including crews from Bennettsbridge and Inistioge caught fishing in Thomastown waters—increased. That the enforcing agents—bailiffs and constabulary—were able to catch more crews more often was because there were more agents, more crews, and more activities that now were offenses. The scale of conflict escalated in tandem—as reflected in the *Moderator*'s numerous and graphic descriptions of "exciting chases after salmon poachers." Disguised cotmen were trailed on land and river by the head constable and groups of police and bailiffs who crept for hours along riverbanks in the middle of the night. Such exceptional commitment, planning, and effort by a large and diverse body of enforcement agents show clearly that the organization and scale of conflict had intensified. Interestingly, the cotmen refrained from any violence against the police. They were reported only as attempting to flee, never as attacking their attackers.

As the scale escalated, so did public interest and local rhetoric. At one Petty Sessions, the "court-house, on being . . . open, was immediately filled, the interest being, doubtless, to hear the result of a fishery case." A cotman, summonsed for "aiding . . . a party who had been illegally fishing," announced "that the next time he met the police at the river, or that they gave him any trouble, he would throw them into the water."[162]

A common consciousness among cotmen also overcame, gradually, the former factionalism. A cot crew was charged with fishing at night because a "squabble between two fishing crews" had "caused

. . . one of those crews to go to the head constable and say they were ready to prosecute the defendants." However, when the "head constable . . . had the case brought before the bench, . . . nothing could be elicited from these witnesses."[163]

The growing solidarity among cotmen was associated with confrontations between gentry and fishermen. A cotman charged John Greene, a weir owner, with angling in the closed season.[164] The watched became the watchers. Interpersonal violence began to correspond to class. A cotman was prosecuted by the police for assaulting a watcher, who, out of fear or sympathy, only "reluctantly" gave evidence.[165] In 1866, a cotman assaulted a publican,[166] and in 1867, two assault cases involved cotmen (a father and son) against housing middlemen.[167] During this same period, there was only one reported assault among the cotmen themselves.

It is not possible to know which of these conflicts were structural or idiosyncratic and perhaps the result of alcohol.[168] Yet by this time, the cotmen were demarcated as a distinct "category." George Bryan[169] stopped in Bennettsbridge on his way to address Thomastown's parliamentary electors and, "in reply to . . . fishermen, . . . promised that from henceforth he will have no one prosecuted for trespass on his property whilst engaged in fishing."[170]

In 1866, the Waterford Board passed a bylaw to "prohibit net fishing in fresh waters of the river Nore." That it did not cover the Barrow and Suir makes it clear that the Board was responding to pressures specifically from Nore owners. The bylaw went to the Fishery Commissioners for approval.[171] It was refused. The reasons were not given.[172] In any case, a judicial route was being pursued by the Barrow Fishery Protection Society, which already had received legal advice "as to the illegality of . . . cots in fishing in fresh water. . . . Owners of property along the . . . Nore . . . [are] preparing to assert their rights in accordance with that opinion. A notice has . . . been . . . posted . . . by . . . Francis Marsh Esq., forbidding . . . fishing . . . with cots, under penalty of a criminal prosecution."[173]

## 1868: Profits, Private Property, and Public Rights

Part of the proprietors' difficulty in "controlling" their fisheries stemmed from the cotmen's "right" to fish—a right legislated in the 1842 Act and subsequently supported by some legal experts. For example, a member of the Oxford circuit stated before a Select Committee in 1849 that "to whatever extent a navigable river goes, I hold

that it is a common fishery for the inhabitants." The chairman queried: "Even above the tidal portion?" "As long as it is navigable,"
replied the member.[174]

The public right to fish on inland, navigable waters ended on
January 20, 1868, with the case of *Murphy v. Ryan*.[175] Cotmen on the
Barrow had been found guilty of "trespass" on the "Plaintiff's close
. . . and [of] fishing therein." In the appeal, the defense "averred that
the close . . . from time immemorial has been part of . . . a royal
river . . . and . . . a public and navigable river . . . in which every
subject . . . had . . . the liberty . . . of fishing." The bench upheld
the plaintiff: "a 'navigable' river must be a tidal river, in which the
sea ebbs and flows."

> The designation "royal" does not, more than the description of navi-
> gable, . . . indicate a river of which the fishing is in the public. . . .
> The defence . . . relies on . . . an allegation of a custom that the public
> should have a *profit à prendre* in the soil, which, according to our view,
> is private property. . . . It is quite settled that such a custom cannot
> legally exist. . . . A right of way upon the land; . . . upon the water—
> all these rights may be established by usage because they are mere
> easements. . . . But no usage can establish a right to take a profit in
> another's soil; . . . and such a profit would be the taking of fish.

### 1868–71: Uncertain Law and the Personalization of Conflict

Immediately "Lord Carrick informed the fishermen that . . . cot-
fishing, except in tidal waters or by the owner of a several fishery,
was illegal."[176] This was not, as it turned out, correct. Instead, the
precise implications of *Murphy v. Ryan* remained unclear; as a result,
conflicts in the inland fisheries became highly confrontational and
personal.

At the first Petty Sessions of the open season, the courthouse was
filled with spectators very early—"it being . . . known that a number
of fishermen were summoned for fishing in the fresh water . . . with
cots and nets." Six cases were brought by water bailiffs against both
Bennettsbridge and Thomastown crews. All were found guilty. One
of the crews appealed to the next Quarter Sessions.[177] In the interim,
confusion was generated when a Lough Erne fishery case established
that the public had a right to fish in a navigable lake.[178] It was added
to when, at the Thomastown appeal, the defense cited the 1842 Act.
An elderly Thomastown resident "deposed that he knew the men to

have fished in that part of the Nore for more than 46 years, without hindrance."[179] The decision was held over.

Probably as a result, subsequent fishing prosecutions at the Petty Sessions did not include any charges of fishing in a private fishery. People waited; and other poaching offenses were heard in a volatile oppositional context. One fisherman, "when before the court, wilfully insulted the Justices" and "was sent to the county gaol for seven days." Another "was also imprisoned in the bridewell until the magistrates rose, for contempt of court, and wilfully insulting the Justices."[180]

By the Petty Sessions of May 1869, some unrecorded legal opinion probably encouraged a flurry of charges against cotmen for fishing in a several fishery. These were laid, however, not by bailiffs but by proprietors. The results further confused the legal situation when a subsequent appeal overturned a conviction because "the lands adjoining the fishery was not the property of Mr. Marsh, as they were tenanted."[181]

It is significant that only two proprietors—Marsh and Hunt—were responsible for these new cases. Neither lived in the Thomastown area yet both owned highly rentable fisheries there. This suggests that for a proprietor to bring a suit in his own name was the equivalent of a personal confrontation; and most proprietors seemed unwilling to do this. The nature of this dynamic is apparent in the following letter: "I beg you will correct a report that appeared in the *Moderator* . . . wherein Harry Innes . . . figures as respondent and Richard Hutchinson as appellant. Harry Innes never prosecuted any person for fishing in the river with rod and line, the prosecution . . . was instituted by a bailiff named . . . Read."[182] It had become important that the appropriate responsibility was properly assigned, even as to the particular bailiff.

Meanwhile, the law remained unclear. In early 1870, Marsh charged two crews with "entering" his several fishery. In one case, the cotmen were nominally fined.[183] In the other, the action was dismissed "without prejudice."[184] This uncertainty reached into the higher echelons of the fisheries administration. In a case brought soon after by the bailiffs, the cotmen admitted to fishing in the several fishery but "said they had the public right as far back as memory could reach." A magistrate "read [the] opinion of the law adviser, by which the bench were necessitated to fine them." The sympathetic reporter added: "This question has been before Petty Sessions, Civil Bill and Superior Courts for several years, and if the prosecutors succeed it will prevent these poor people fishing altogether, and probably drive them into the workhouse."[185]

In January 1871, an appeal at the Thomastown Quarter Sessions clarified the situation. Four cotmen admitted to fishing in a several fishery, claiming that they had "fished uninterruptedly for the last fifty or sixty years." The chairman noted this, adding that "in the recent case of *Murphy v. Ryan,* it was decided that no . . . right could be acquired by the *public* in rivers above the tidal flow. . . . To this decision, no exception can be taken." However, he added that this "was a decision by a civil court in reference to civil rights" and that, in the 1842 Act, the "Legislature can hardly . . . have been ignorant of the general law, in reference to the rights which could be claimed by the public by custom." Therefore, "what was meant" by the Act that allowed a "general right of fishing with such nets *in the nature of a common piscary"* if these "had been enjoyed for twenty years before the passing of this act"?

> It appears to me that the Legislature intended . . . that when such a public right, or perhaps more strictly speaking, "privilege" had been enjoyed or tolerated, for 20 years, the proprietors of the river banks . . . [must] . . . assert their legal civil rights by the civil remedies . . . but that the public were not . . . to be handed over . . . to the administrators of the criminal law.[186]

The Thomastown cotmen, having lost the "right" to fish, had regained the "privilege" of doing so, as long as the proprietor of the fishery did not resort to the civil courts to enforce exclusive rights to his private property. Ironically, it was privatization beyond what owners would have desired.

## 1871–84: The "Privilege" of Cot Fishing

The new privilege had major implications in the Thomastown area. It intensified the personalization process and, within the decade, it had factionalized the Thomastown gentry while simultaneously transforming the cotmen into a political force. A landowner now was required to lay his own charges. This personal involvement was associated with an increase in the potential for violence. A bailiff was caught in possession of an unlicensed gun, and another summonsed two cotmen, each of whom had, on different occasions, "threatened to drown him."[187] In court, the bailiff refused to testify: he "swore that he was afraid the defendants would do him some corporal injury."[188] The violence and the accumulated animosities between bailiffs and cotmen were accompanied by an increasingly involved public. Ascertaining the truth in fishing cases became a severe problem as perjury became a common way of building a case both for the prosecution and for the defense.[189] A bailiff swore that he saw particular defendants fish at a particular place and time; the defendants swore otherwise, as did several witnesses.[190]

In all this, only two proprietors tried to exercise exclusive rights over their fisheries. Marsh was one. The other was Thomas Doran—lessee of the Hunt weir at Jerpoint, conservator, employer of private water bailiffs, and "uncommon poacher." Over the years, a feudlike conflict came to link him and the cotmen. In the earliest record, in 1868, the "court house was pretty well filled by fishermen" to hear the case brought by William Murphy, cotman, against Doran and his bailiff for cross-fishing in the closed season.[191] Doran was fined. The next recorded encounter was in 1872, when two conservators inspected Doran's weir. They brought along a local cotman named Dawson "to point out the defects." Doran later charged Dawson with trespass. Dawson presumably had reported the weir in the first instance! The trespass charge was dismissed, as was a charge brought by Doran's son that Dawson had used threatening language.[192] Several months later, Doran was again charged with illegally altering his weir. An inspector ordered it realtered.[193] The cotmen clearly were watching Doran; on occasion, they probably framed him. A hotelier was charged with possession after Doran's son had stated, during the weir inquiry, that he saw fresh salmon in her hotel. The defense solicitor asked Doran junior "if he knew what kippered salmon" was. He did not. The solicitor informed the bench that Mrs. Bishop bought a large amount of salmon for the hotel during the open season and pickled it for the winter. The case was dismissed, but a month later, Mrs. Bishop was charged by William Murphy, now a water bailiff, with buying salmon in closed time. Murphy stated that "to defray the expense of this prosecution," he had "borrowed from Mr. Doran."[194] This case too was dismissed.[195] Two months later, again on Murphy's evidence, the "most respectable inhabitants of Thomastown" were had up for buying salmon out of season.[196] The first case was dismissed and the conservators hurriedly withdrew the others: "They had been brought entirely on a statement made to Mr. Doran, a Conservator," by William Murphy.[197] Murphy was fired. He probably only had been hired to inform; but had he also been put up to it by the cotmen, to get at Doran?

More generally, these kinds of prosecutions show that the conservators were unable to catch the cotmen poaching. Their own
comments at a Thomastown Division meeting confirm this: the water
bailiffs were "of no earthly use," the constabulary was indifferent,
and money from license fees went to Waterford, not to local enforcement.[198] They also had their own squabbles over how many bailiffs
to appoint or where to locate them. A major problem was where to
hold the next meeting![199]

By the mid-1870s, there clearly was little enforcement on the
Nore. Indeed, there were no fishery cases at the Petty Sessions. Yet
"salmon was never so plenty."[200] Prices too were good and the
cotmen did well.[201] Still, there was concern. The *Moderator* began to
provide weekly reports on the state of the fisheries and the poaching.
Presumably also, because so little had been gained from its judicial
and enforcement efforts, the "interested gentry" renewed the conflict
in the political arena: the Waterford Board again passed a bylaw
prohibiting nets on the inland Nore, and proprietors sent a memorial
to the Fishery Inspectors in support.

In March 1875, the Inspectors held an inquiry to decide whether to
pass the bylaw.[202] The reported evidence shows clearly that the interests of the fisheries administration had altered radically since 1863.
Then, a weir-owning gentry had concertedly and illegally opposed
the commissioners. By 1875, an officialdom that once had defended
the "humble fishers" now viewed cot fishing as an anathema and the
bylaw as a way to ensure that the fish went to market and the fisheries
to proprietors.[203]

The testimony also shows the depth of antagonism toward cot
fishing. The "memorial . . . from certain owners and occupiers"
insisted that the "river was continually . . . poached." A proprietor
*cum* conservator testified that the "illegal fishing is awful . . . between
Kilkenny and Inistioge; . . . they fish at night with cots constantly;
the weekly closed season is not observed."[204] Several police then
described "poachers" they had seen but failed to catch, often because
dogs were trained to "give the alarm." Although the cotmen's solicitor insisted that such testimony "proved no illegal fishing," the chair,
Major Hayes, countered that they had "proved the next thing to it.
Men do not go out at night in cots for their amusement."

The precise structure of the opposition to cot fishing came from
the cross-examination of a Captain Forster, lessee of a house and
fishery in Annamult, north of Thomastown: "no one has a right to
intrude on private property; his private water has been intruded on;
. . . has advocated putting down cot-fishing; . . . has written a letter

in the paper; . . . Mr. Tighe has not endorsed his opinion nor Lord Carrick."[205] Clearly, Forster had been trying to mobilize the gentry, and not all had joined him. Those who did shared two characteristics: they were either nonresidents (Marsh and Hunt) or outsiders who had rented a house and fishing (Doran and Forster). In contrast, such resident proprietors as Tighe and Carrick, the latter of whom was no supporter of cotmen, had not signed the memorial. Very likely, as residents, they wished to avoid the public confrontations that came from opposition.[206] They also may have wished to avoid the likes of Doran and Forster themselves.

To chairman Hayes, cotmen were "violators of the law." His opinion of Thomastown society was equally disparaging: "The more they encouraged gentlemen to settle amongst them the better."[207] In this he clearly misunderstood local class relations and sentiment in the salmon fishery. First, outsiders and absentees, concerned with sport and rents, respectively, were not necessarily part of local gentry society. Second, a Kilkenny fish buyer gave insight into the shop-keepers' position. He "can't answer that cotmen keep the close season," nor could he say that the fish he bought was "caught legally."[208]

Third were the millers. In 1869, 32 Vict. c.9 specified the lattices and bars that had to be attached to mills to aid salmon migrations.[209] The commissioners began immediate enforcement. At Innes's mill, "short work they made of it. Trial, conviction . . . and order" for works to be done "occupied just ten minutes. . . . A public meeting of the Nore millers is fixed for next week, to protest against future action of the Commissioners."[210] More generally, the millers were wary of fisheries officials, and their "dislike of . . . anything which may . . . remotely affect their water power is well-known."[211] They also had personal ties to the cotmen, many of whom were their workers. Ultimately, "poaching [is] carried on at the mills and weirs . . . owing to the protection which the . . . mill-grounds afford."[212] An arch inside Pilsworth's mill, where a sluice could be closed and salmon trapped, was a "celebrated place."[213]

Fourth, the absentees and outsiders were separated from farmers by an ideological twist made explicit in a letter to the *Moderator* from William Deady—a large farmer, corn mill owner, and Poor Law guardian. Deady objected to the "tone" of an earlier letter that "infer[red] that cot-fishing is illegal altogether."

> As is demonstrated by the Ulster tenant right, what is law but custom perpetuated legally? which in this case is tacitly admitted by having a

special licence yearly granted for this very mode of taking fish. The idea of likening it to poaching is extremely puerile. . . . In the interest of fair play I have written, I may say, against myself, being a rod-fisher.[214]

The rights of cotmen had become part of a broad, nationalist sentiment. In late 1875, a returned emigré was charged by the police for "fishing with a Tasmanian . . . net." The *Moderator* commented that "during his absence [he] seems to have imbibed little respect for British law."[215] That fishing regulations were British was not unimportant at the time. Nor was the *Moderator*'s idyllic description of the lessee of Dangan Lodge, who "generously distributes" the salmon caught with his rod "among the gentlemen . . . in Thomastown, in the true spirit of a sportsman."[216] In contrast, local sentiment necessarily defended the cotmen's right to a livelihood—even if the more cynical were to trace such sentiment to the ever-present concern of the propertied classes with poor rates. Said Deady: "Cotmen cannot be . . . compelled to relinquish . . . the means of providing their daily bread . . . unless it can be positively shown that they are . . . injurious . . . to the increase of salmon."[217]

Clearly, there was great interest in, and sentiment associated with, the fisheries. The *Moderator* gave weekly reports on conditions, catches, and prices.[218] Fishing seemingly was uninterrupted—by bailiffs or "blow-ins." There were few Petty Sessions cases, although there was an occasional report of a chase.[219] In this context, the *Moderator* began to foster a crisis climate: in the "three great centres of poaching on the river, Instioge, Thomastown and Bennettsbridge" was an "evil" that required an "organised system of repression."[220] Poaching interfered with rentability: "other rivers make good incomes from foreign anglers and there is no reason why the people of the Nore can't do the same."[221] Throughout, the coalition of cotmen stayed firm—despite countervailing pressures.

> Accounts from Thomastown that paradise of poachers show an unusual state. . . . A feud . . . among the poachers . . . has led to a spate of informing . . . which will probably result in . . . fishing cases at next Petty Sessions. If advantage . . . is to be taken it must be done quickly for it will not last and the poachers will . . . turn against the common enemy . . . again.[222]

The cases did not materialize. Instead, the cotmen took the offensive and sent a memorial to Colonel Tighe "signed by upwards of 100 fishermen . . . urging him to discontinue his sweep net fishing . . . as it impeded the progress of the salmon up the river."[223] A week later, however, the cotmen were on the defensive: the bylaw prohibiting nets on the inland Nore had passed.[224] "From Thomastown, where the main strength of the netting interest lie, . . . a petition is being organised to the Lord Lieutenant." Patrick Martin, M.P., was asked "to fight, on behalf of the fishermen's interests."[225] Four months later, "the net debate" still was "in the hands of the Lord Lieutenant."[226] It is not known what pressures were brought, or by whom, but a month later, a "meeting of the fishermen from Thomastown and Bennettsbridge and farmers with ground on the rivers banks was held at Bennettsbridge. . . . A vote of thanks was passed to all those around the county who had supported the cot men in their successful action against the by-law."[227]

If the farmers came out in support, the gentry bench in Thomastown preserved an impeccable fairness. A fisherman was charged with obstructing the bailiffs in their duty. A bailiff swore that "he saw a crew fishing on the river" and when he moved closer, the "defendant met him, and asked him in a loud voice so that the men on the river could hear him 'Who the d_____l are you at all?' and then struck a match . . . to give notice to the men fishing." In the chair was James Blake—a small, resident Catholic landlord. Like him, two of the other magistrates held no fishery; the fourth magistrate was Tighe's agent at Inistioge. Blake's response to the bailiff's evidence was that "there was no law to prevent a man from lighting a match on the bank of the river. The suggestion . . . was perfectly ridiculous." The case was dismissed.[228]

The paucity of reported cases and the charges of obstruction show that the bailiffs and constabulary were unable to lay poaching charges. With watch dogs and colleagues, cotmen were difficult to catch. Equally, there probably were few informers. This means that the cotmen—as fishermen—had the support of local people and—as poachers—they probably had the tacit approval of most. In the preceding Petty Sessions trial, they were not blindly opposed by their "natural enemy"—quite the opposite. For despite the efforts of the *Moderator* and those who supported its sentiments (e.g., Doran, Hayes, and Forster), most segments of local society (as represented by farmer Deady, the millers, the Thomastown bench, and the Kilkenny fish dealer) were unwilling to sacrifice the cotmen to increase the profits of absentee landlords and the sport of foreign gentlemen. In any case, as the fish dealer pointed out, he never asked whether the fish was legal or not. With heavy demand and high prices in the export market, locals depended on the cotmen to supply local needs. Indeed, the cotmen wisely kept that market well stocked—judging by the quantities that Mrs. Bishop pickled in her hotel.

In late 1877, Marsh again entered the fray with two civil suits against cot crews for fishing on his property: "It is our right to the several fishery . . . that we are here to protect," said his solicitor.[229] Within a few months, the "feud of water bailiffs against cotmen [reached] a new stage of development." Two cotmen, interrupted one night by bailiffs, threw stones. A bailiff "fired his revolver . . . which brought [the] cotmen to the bank, armed with paddles and threatening . . . vengeance." The bailiffs retired.[230] At the Petty Sessions, the illegal fishing charge was dismissed, but all were ordered to the Assizes.[231] There the bailiff said that he had not fired at the fishermen; the fishermen said they had only thrown small stones. All were ordered "to stand on their own recognizances."[232]

This event was allowed to tail off, but the conflict again spilled onto the streets. On the evidence of two cotmen, the police charged Doran's bailiff, now "an old man," who maintained that the case "was got up . . . through spite." It was dismissed. As he left the court, he "was attacked . . . by a crowd of fishermen and their wives."[233] The violence escalated. Two cotmen were wounded—shot by a water bailiff. The cotmen were charged with assault. At the Assizes, the bailiff said that he fired only when the fishermen beat him with a paddle after he was thrown into the water. In stark contrast, the cotmen said that when they came near the bailiff's cot, he simply struck his cot against theirs and fired his pistol. The jury refused to convict despite instructions to do so from the bench: "they believed the cot men assaulted [the bailiff] to prevent him firing on them."[234] At the next Petty Sessions, the cotmen were up for illegal fishing. The defense asked that "their worships . . . consider the hardships" to which the men and their "families had been subjected." The bench, however, already "had decided to inflict no penalty."[235]

The bailiff had made enemies, and the lines were fixed. The bailiff charged a cotman with calling him a "perjurer on the public streets,"[236] and after a fisherman had apparently threatened him, he pulled his revolver. He was summonsed by the cotman.[237] The women entered the conflict. After a bailiff prosecuted a woman for possession, he later charged her with using abusive language because "four times subsequent to the case . . . she met him within the precincts of the court and called him a perjurer."[238]

Yet the central issue of private property did not abate. Davis's heirs in Dangan lived outside the parish and let the house and fishery.

They brought two cases in 1880 against cotmen for fishing without permission. Davis's solicitor, Mr. Boyd, said that if the defendants would not repeat the offense, Davis would accept a nominal penalty. For the fishermen were "tenants of Mr. Davis's and he does not wish to deal harshly with them."[239] In any case, "if they had only asked . . . to fish for two or three days in the week he would have granted it."

Davis clearly was concerned not with the cotmen's right to net but with establishing exclusive rights to his property. In turn, James Kelly, the cotman who led the defense, admitted to fishing "because we had a perfect legal right" to do so. The magistrates disagreed. At Kelly's request they then inflicted a penalty sufficient to carry the right to an appeal.

The defendants faced a second charge. Kelly announced that "if we have no right to fish there [Davis] has no right either ( . . . laughter)." He then agreed not to fish in Davis's fishery until the appeal was heard. A third case ended the same way, after which the following occurred:

> COLLETON: Well, we won't fish there—until it is dark (loud laughter).
> MR. BOYD: Now, I shall prove the case against you, and I shall ask the magistrates to inflict the full penalty.
> COLLETON: Very well, Mr. Boyd, sure we are all monied men (renewed laughter), and this is a good season.[240]

At the Quarter Sessions, Kelly's solicitor argued "that common usage" allowed them to fish and that, in any case, they were fishing on Mr. Greene's side of the river. The latter argument clearly removed the defense from that of "common right." The bailiff simply insisted that the cotmen had fished on Davis's side and the conviction was affirmed. Boyd said that "if the fishermen promised not to go there in the future, Mr. Davis would be happy with a nominal penalty." The cotmen did so and thus they conceded the principle set in *Murphy v. Ryan* (1868).[241] However, a new feature was apparent in the proceedings: cotmen were playing to an audience. It was an audience that was both inside and outside the courthouse theater. At a Thomastown Land League meeting, Mulhalum Marum, M.P., presented a posture different from that in 1863 when before the gentry. "Did not the fishermen of Thomastown know that they were begrudged even the fish that sported in these waters?"[242] Similarly, the nationalist *Journal* commented that, because of the "greed . . . for property, . . . the right of fishing hitherto enjoyed by the cotmen

. . . is . . . challenged. It is a hard case that the humble descendants of fishers who trolled in these waters when vespers were sung in Jerpoint, before the abbey lands had been parcelled out to Hanoverian rabble, should be banished now. Even the water-bailiffs say that their hardship is a great one."[243] Indeed, "one of the fishermen who was in the affray" with the bailiffs was granted outdoor relief by the guardians. The chair noted: "There was no doubt but that there was a great distress existing among them."[244] In contrast, the commissioners noted the "valuable rod fisheries for which large rents are obtained"[245] and Bassett's 1884 Guide reported that Thomastown had "splendid salmon and trout fishing."

For the cotmen, the only option was to poach. When caught, they sometimes got off or had the penalty reduced because of a technicality.[246] The major tactic, though, was evasion. Alibis became central. A case was dismissed after a woman swore that a fisherman was "in her house, 'beastly drunk' . . . on the night of the alleged occurrence."[247] It also was still possible to torment Doran and he was charged with more weir violations.[248] Symbolic resistence, too, was possible. Two cotmen were fined for "obstructing Mr. William Percival of Dangan Cottage while he was legally fishing . . . by paddling a cot across his line."[249]

## 1884: A Privilege Criminalized and Poaching Institutionalized

In 1884, four cotmen were summoned at the Thomastown Petty Sessions by the head water bailiff for entering a several fishery. Convicted, they appealed to the Quarter Sessions. An outsider named Greenwood "proved that he . . . rented [Brownsbarn] house and garden, and the right of fishing and shooting from . . . the owner." He said that he had written "to the Conservators to prevent the cotmen from fishing." The cotmen's solicitor maintained that the bailiff had no right to institute the proceedings. The conviction was confirmed. On appeal to the Queen's Bench, the court held that: "It is clearly settled . . . that use by the public.. . no matter how long, will not confer a right to take fish in inland waters. . . . An action by a riparian proprietor . . . must succeed. . . . Why . . . should the owner be put to the necessity of bringing civil action against trespassers?"[250]

The new order was confirmed immediately. Bailiffs brought two cases against cotmen for fishing in Marsh's several fishery. They were convicted and did not appeal.[251] In 1899, a witness before a parliamentary commission noted: "On the Nore, . . . there are a band of fishermen at nearly every town from the tidal water upwards who, perhaps, pay a pound . . . to the proprietors of one bank, and so get permission to net; . . . once they get leave on 100 or 200 yards . . . they take opportunities of . . . poaching for miles."[252] The land Acts gradually transferred ownership of the land to tenant farmers, along with the several fisheries. Because most farmers had little use for fishing rights, they rented the fishing to the cotmen, who, as was their custom, continued to net at night all along the inland Nore.

## Conclusion: The Past, Local Studies, and Historical Process

In this paper, I have analyzed a process through which the rights of private property gradually encroached upon and finally eliminated customary rights. Although many of the issues surrounding customary rights are well studied in social history and in legal anthropology, the subject has received little attention in the Irish context where the historical and anthropological research agenda derives from other traditions and interests. *Anthropological analyses of the Irish past,* then, can broaden the research agenda for both historians and anthropologists in Ireland.

Equally, *ethnographies of the past* can complement the work of social historians. There are no studies of inland salmon fishermen in the British Isles and few references to the role of salmon in local political economies.[253] Thomastown's cotmen were "discovered" only in the course of collecting archival materials on the locality. Thus, because ethnographers often bump into the so-called people without history,[254] ethnographies of the past can expand the subject matter of social history. They also can add insights into subjects traditionally investigated by social historians. For example, poaching, as a social and cultural means of protest, is often analyzed as a fixed response to set conditions. However, historical ethnography can show how it also has been a slowly evolving cultural and social form, how it is a product of adaptation as well as protest, and how it results from negotiation as well as coercion.

Finally, cumulative processes may have a hidden trajectory that only *local, historical analyses* can uncover. In this paper, I have shown how changing interclass and intraclass relations at the local level directly affected and reflected an encroachment process that derived largely from an international political economy. That the conclusion was inevitable, in other words, is clear to us only in hindsight; it must be remembered that participants at the time had no such knowledge. As a result, their actions and reactions had a contextual logic that in turn partly explains how the unevenness was created in the first instance. It is this unevenness and indeterminacy that local historical analysis can uncover. In so doing, it allows for better understanding the dialectical relations between local and national, locality and region, class and segment, individual action and class formation, and material interest and ideology.

## NOTES

1. Tighe 1802:149–50.
2. A total of slightly more than two years of field and archival research was carried out in the Republic of Ireland at different times between 1980 and 1989. It was variously supported by the Social Sciences and Humanities Research Council of Canada (SSHRC); the Faculty of Arts, York University; and the Wenner-Gren Foundation for Anthropological Research, New York.
3. The population of Thomastown "town" in 1841 was 2,350. For the Catholic parish of Thomastown it was 7,410.
4. A cot was a canoelike boat made locally by carpenters. It held two men. A salmon fishing crew was made up of two cots and four men. In each cot was a paddler and a netman. The two cots moved along the river with the snap net held by the netmen between the two cots, sweeping the bottom of the river. When a salmon hit the net, the netmen pulled it in. Only one salmon was caught at a time.
5. This was Lee's critique of many studies in the Irish context that have used a class analysis (1981b:179).
6. Salmon fry are the young salmon swimming downriver to the ocean. The Acts protecting them were 2 George I. c.21; 17 and 18 George III. c.19; 10 Charles I. sess. 3, c.14; and 12 George I. c.7 (Tighe 1802:152).
7. The closed time was legislated by 31 George II. c.13. However, it was "extended on the Nore, as it is said by custom" (Tighe 1802:152).
8. Using the 28 Henry VIII. c.22, the sheriff could prostrate such weirs, and the "5 Geo II. cap 11. provides against their re-construction when legally prostrated" (Tighe 1802:153).
9. According to 26 George III. c.50.
10. Tighe (1802:152).
11. Tighe (1802:151, 153).
12. IUP 1824 [427] vii, p. 145. This also is briefly referred to by MacLeod (1968:115), who cited Sir Walter Scott from 1828.
13. IUP 1825 [173] v, p. 285.
14. IUP 1825 [393] v, pp. 458–59.
15. IUP 1825 [393] v, p. 459.
16. As evidence for the decline of the fisheries, Clarke said that "salmon

used to sell in the town of Kilkenny for twopence a pound, and now, I believe, it will be found very difficult to be got for tenpence a pound" (IUP 1825 [393] v, p. 459).

17. *Kilkenny Moderator,* June 27, 1829.

18. *Kilkenny Moderator,* July 31, 1830.

19. *Kilkenny Moderator,* January 19, 1831.

20. This is a distinction made by Hay (1975:213) to play on the prejudices of the eighteenth century landed classes who "execrated the 'common poacher' " in a context in which members of the gentry also were poaching.

21. IUP 1849 [536] xiii, p. 549.

22. IUP 1849 [536] xiii, pp. 555–56.

23. IUP 1837 [82] xxii, p. 558.

24. *Kilkenny Journal,* March 19, 1834.

25. Maxwell was the owner-editor of the *Kilkenny Journal and Leinster Commercial and Literary Advertiser,* a newspaper that followed a nationalist line at the time (Kenealy 1978).

26. IUP 1837 [82] xxii, pp. 555–56.

27. IUP 1837 [82] xxii, p. 555.

28. IUP 1837 [82] xxii, p. 558.

29. IUP 1849 [536] xiii, p. 555.

30. IUP 1837 [82] xxii, p. 558.

31. IUP 1849 [536] xiii, p. 578.

32. IUP 1837 [82] xxii, p. 548.

33. *Kilkenny Moderator,* September 6, 1837. The *Kilkenny Moderator* reported other such actions on June 14, 1837, and July 20, 1839.

34. IUP 1849 [536] xiii, p. 553. Despite this emphasis on protection, one unhappy witness before the 1835 commission said, "I cannot learn that they do much in the way of protecting; . . . their object appears to be rather to subscribe to prosecute the stake-net proprietors, under the 10th Charles I. c.14" (IUP 1837 [82] xii, p. 551).

35. IUP 1849 [536] xiii, p. 270.

36. IUP 1849 [536] xiii, pp. 270–71.

37. The millers' interests were fairly straightforward. They did not want any interference with their water power, mill races, or machinery. When pressed to give up illegal fishing, they probably did so simply to avoid prosecution and the possibility of subsequent interference.

38. IUP 1849 [536] xiii, p. 179.

39. Went (1955).

40. Italics theirs. *Kilkenny Moderator,* November 14, 1838.

41. *Kilkenny Moderator,* February 25, 1835.

42. *Kilkenny Journal,* February 28, 1835.

43. The list included names that were to recur again: the earl of Carrick, Sydenham Davis, Hugh Greene, Edward Hunt, John Nixon, Anthony Nugent, and William F. Tighe.

44. There were several ways a weir could violate the law. It could be

illegal altogether in that it was not held by a legitimate grant or charter. Or its "queen's/king's gap," which allowed salmon a fair chance of passing through, could be too small or blocked. It could be extended too far into the river. There could be spurs or abutments built onto the weir to which illegal nets could be attached. Finally, nets or traps may have been set on the weir.

45. *Kilkenny Journal,* September 19, 1838.

46. *Kilkenny Moderator,* January 18, 1840.

47. *Kilkenny Moderator,* April 29, 1840.

48. *Kilkenny Moderator,* April 29, 1840.

49. *Kilkenny Moderator,* August 4, 1841.

50. *Kilkenny Moderator,* March 26, 1842; *Kilkenny Moderator,* April 13, 1842.

51. Letter to the editor, *Kilkenny Moderator,* August 4, 1841.

52. *Kilkenny Moderator,* April 13, 1842.

53. There is little information on the cotmen in this early period. At the inquiry into the "condition of the poorer classes," local cotmen were described as laborers. The proportion who were full-time fishermen was never addressed (H.C. 1836 xxxi. Supplement to Appendix D, pp. 71–72).

54. *Kilkenny Moderator,* July 29, 1840.

55. *Kilkenny Moderator,* August 4, 1841.

56. It is not known who gave the advice to "proceed on an act of parliament," but it was the strategy of St. Peter's Society at the time.

57. *Kilkenny Journal,* March 10, 1841.

58. *Kilkenny Journal,* February 17, 1841.

59. *Kilkenny Journal,* March 10, 1841.

60. It was a bank manager (William Clifford) and a flour miller (William Bull) who "went about removing the wall" before Davis withdrew permission in 1836 (*Kilkenny Journal,* February 17, 1841). It was the parish priest (Rev. James Ryan), a Petty Sessions clerk (Edward Hutchinson), and William Clifford who brought the case against Davis in which the bench refused to intervene. (*Kilkenny Journal,* March 10, 1841). It was Harry Innes, the flour miller, who received the response from Dublin Castle.

61. *Kilkenny Journal,* March 10, 1841.

62. Silverman and Gulliver (1986:129–34).

63. *Kilkenny Journal,* March 10, 1841.

64. *Kilkenny Moderator,* August 21, 1841.

65. *Kilkenny Moderator,* November 10, 1841.

66. *Kilkenny Moderator,* August 21, 1841.

67. IUP 1849 [536] xiii, p. 549.

68. The commissioners did not explain why the lower fisheries were most productive because it seemed self-evident to them at the time. It probably was because more salmon were caught there, because it was closer to the export markets, and because saltwater salmon were considered of superior quality and commanded a higher price.

69. IUP 1837 [82] xxii, p. 490.

70. IUP 1837 [82] xxii, p. 490.

71. IUP 1843 [224] xxviii, p. 20.

72. The weirs and fixed nets were seen as the most efficient technologies (IUP 1837 [82] xxii, p. 548).

73. 4 Bur 2162. Cited in *Murphy v. Ryan, The Irish Reports* (Common Law Series) 1867.

74. Longfield (1863:10).

75. Longfield (1863:211).

76. IUP 1843 [224] xxviii, p. 21.

77. *Kilkenny Moderator,* October 15, 1842.

78. *Kilkenny Moderator,* October 26, 1842.

79. IUP 1846 [713] xxii p. 184.

80. IUP 1844 [502] xxx p. 36.

81. IUP 1844 [502] xxx p. 36.

82. IUP 1843 [224] xxviii, p. 21.

83. This was because fixed engines could only be set up by landowners who held land along the banks. Yet it had long been established that where a "river ebbs and flows and is an arm of the sea, then it is common to all" (1837 [82] xii, p. 561). It therefore was argued that, in the tidal waters, the 1842 Act "handed over to the landlords the rights which were then vested in the public" (1849 [536] xii, p. 547).

84. IUP 1844 [502] xxx, p. 37.

85. IUP 1849 [536] xiii, pp. 271–72.

86. IUP 1849 [536] xiii, pp. 271–72.

87. IUP 1844 [502] xxx, p. 37.

88. IUP 1844 [502] xxx, p. 36.

89. IUP 1849 [536] xiii, pp. 177–79.

90. IUP 1844 [502] xxx, pp. 37–38.

91. IUP 1843 [224] xxviii, p. 21.

92. IUP 1845 [320] xxvi, p. 217.

93. IUP 1844 [502] xxx, p. 38.

94. IUP 1845 [320] xxvi, p. 219. Increasing involvement by the commissioners was made simpler because nonfishing, propertied interests were not necessarily sympathetic to fisheries owners. For example, as rate payers, landed interests refused to pay compensation "for malicious injury done to fishing weirs now legally held." They were supported by the higher courts which "ruled . . . that these kind of weirs were not recognised as legal at the time of passing the Grand Jury Act" (IUP 1844 [502] xxx, p. 38).

95. IUP 1846 [713] xxii, pp. 255–56.

96. *Kilkenny Moderator,* October 26, 1842.

97. IUP 1846 [713] xxii, pp. 255–56.

98. IUP 1846 [713] xxii, pp. 256–57.

99. IUP 1846 [713] xxii, pp. 244–45.

100. IUP 1846 [713] xxii, pp. 244–45.

101. IUP 1845 [320] xxvi, pp. 211–13.

102. IUP 1846 [713] xxii, p. 186.

103. IUP 1846 [713] xxii, p. 186.

104. IUP 1847–48 [983] xxxvii, p. 240.

105. IUP 1847–48 [983] xxxvii, p. 240.

106. IUP 1847–48 [983] xxxvii, p. 243.

107. IUP 1849 [1098] xxiii, p. 494.

108. *Kilkenny Moderator,* September 30, 1846.

109. IUP 1849 [1098] xxiii, p. 495.

110. IUP 1849 [1098] xxiii, p. 495.

111. IUP 1849 [1098] xxiii, p. 493.

112. IUP 1846 [713] xxii, p. 199.

113. IUP 1849 [1098] xxii, p. 713.

114. IUP 1849 [1098] xxii, p. 496.

115. IUP 1849 [1098] xxiii, pp. 496–97.

116. IUP 1851 [1414] xxv, p. 71.

117. IUP 1851 [1414] xxv, p. 72.

118. IUP 1851 [1414] xxv, p. 239.

119. IUP 1851 [1414] xxv, p. 240.

120. IUP 1854 [1819] xx, p. 179.

121. IUP 1854 [1819] xx, p. 167.

122. IUP 1856 [ 21] xix, p. 39.

123. *Kilkenny Moderator,* February 10, 1849, and February 13, 1850. This was the earl of Carrick's property.

124. The editor complained that the water bailiffs were of little use; nor was he "aware of any . . . vigilance" on the part of the constabulary (*Kilkenny Moderator,* April 20, 1853).

125. *Kilkenny Moderator,* April 20, 1853.

126. *Kilkenny Moderator,* April 20, 1853.

127. IUP 1857 [2272, sess. 2] xviii, p. 28.

128. IUP 1860 [2727] xxxiv, p. 671.

129. IUP 1861 [2862] xxiii, p. 31.

130. IUP 1861 [2862] xxiii, p. 31.

131. IUP 1861 [2862] xxiii, p. 31.

132. IUP 1861 [2862] xxiii, p. 34.

133. IUP 1864 [3256] xxxi, pp. 33–34. Complaints no longer had to be made against each net individually. Instead, the special commissioners were empowered to investigate the legal title of all existing nets. By 1865, all legal nets and weirs were known and recorded as such. New nets could not be raised. Moreover, if a net had been declared illegal, prostrated, and then reerected, the commissioners could level it again without recourse to additional legal action.

134. IUP 1865 [3420] xxviii, p. 436. Among the weirs found illegal was one held by W. F. Tighe, Inistioge. It was "abated as injurious to navigation" (IUP 1864 [3256] xxxi, p. 45).

135. IUP 1865 [3420] xxviii, p. 433.

136. IUP 1865 [3420] xxviii, p. 433.

137. *Kilkenny Moderator*, February 9, 1861.

138. In 1857, there were four reported cases of illegal fishing in the Thomastown area. For 1858 and 1859, two cases were reported in each year; in 1860, there was none; in 1861, there was one; and in 1862, there was none.

139. In 1866, the commissioners reported that the Waterford Board spent too much of its funds on the lower waters, and they suggested a more balanced allocation (IUP 1866 [3608] xxviii, pp. 370–71).

140. Davis's land/fishery was in Dangan townland; Marsh's was in Jerpoint West.

141. In the Davis case it was reported that the bench adjourned to consult the law officers (*Kilkenny Moderator*, April 7, 1855). There was no follow-up report. In the Marsh case it simply was reported that the "parties were severally fined . . . and the nets . . . forfeited" (*Kilkenny Moderator*, May 14, 1856). I have no idea if or why the outcome of the cases differed.

142. *Kilkenny Moderator*, November 15, 1856.

143. *Kilkenny Moderator*, July 15, 1863.

144. *Kilkenny Moderator*, March 8, 1845.

145. *Kilkenny Moderator*, November 15, 1856.

146. The sources for these two cases are in personal papers, Thomastown.

147. *Kilkenny Moderator*, August 12, 1854.

148. *Kilkenny Moderator*, April 24, 1844.

149. *Kilkenny Moderator*, February 14, 1857.

150. *Kilkenny Moderator*, April 24, 1844.

151. For example, a water bailiff summonsed a fisherman for "using threatening and abusive language towards him" (*Kilkenny Moderator*, September 10, 1859), as did a constable (*Kilkenny Moderator*, December 8, 1860). The stationmaster summonsed the "notorious fishmonger" for the same offense and the fishmonger cross-summonsed the stationmaster (*Kilkenny Moderator*, April 6, 1861). Or, during a fracas in a pub, a cotman broke a window and then assaulted the constable who had been called in. The cotman's brother also was charged for obstructing the police officer who was "conveying his brother to the barracks" (*Kilkenny Moderator*, October 10, 1863).

152. *Kilkenny Moderator*, May 9, 1863.

153. IUP 1865 [34] xxviii, p. 433.

154. In 1853, 118 snap-net (cot) licenses were sold; in 1865, 374 were sold (IUP 1854 [1819] xx, p.193; IUP 1866 [3608] xxviii, p.392).

155. IUP 1866 [3608] xxviii, p.358.

156. *Kilkenny Moderator*, October 21, 1863.

157. *Kilkenny Moderator*, October 21, 1863.

158. Salmon hide from the light of day in deep, inaccessible pools. They also can see and hence avoid a net in daylight.

159. *Kilkenny Moderator*, October 24, 1863.

160. *Kilkenny Moderator*, October 28, 1863.

161. The special commissioners set up by the 1863 Act to investigate the

tidal stake nets also investigated the titles of the inland stone weirs. All in the Thomastown area were found legal and their proportions, gaps, and so on were specified and could not be altered (IUP 1867–68 [4056] xix, p. 685).

162. *Kilkenny Moderator*, March 5, 1864.

163. *Kilkenny Moderator*, April 6, 1864.

164. *Kilkenny Moderator*, May 6, 1865.

165. *Kilkenny Moderator*, August 12, 1865.

166. *Kilkenny Journal*, August 11, 1866. Several related suits and counter-suits for abuse and assault ensued between the publican and the cotman—and both their kin (*Kilkenny Journal* and *Kilkenny Moderator*, September 8, 1866).

167. It was not uncommon for middlemen to control urban housing; generally, they also were artisans (*Kilkenny Moderator*, November 13, 1867).

168. Alcohol use among cotmen was heavy. For example, a "fisherman . . . attempting self-destruction whilst in a state of intoxication" was saved by the efforts of several police and cotmen (*Kilkenny Moderator*, July 7, 1866).

169. A landlord with some of his holdings in the Thomastown area, none of which adjoined the Nore. His seat was at Jenkinstown, County Kilkenny.

170. *Kilkenny Moderator*, July 19, 1865.

171. IUP 1866 [3608] xxvii, p. 394; IUP 1867 [3826] xviii, p. 33.

172. IUP 1867–68 [4056] xix, p. 653.

173. *Kilkenny Moderator*, March 24, 1866.

174. IUP 1849 [536] xiii, p. 361.

175. *The Irish Reports (Common Law Series)* 1867:143–55. The case was argued in early 1867 before the Court of Common Pleas.

176. He did so from the bench at the next Thomastown Petty Sessions (*Kilkenny Journal*, February 8, 1868).

177. *Kilkenny Moderator*, April 11, 1868. The cotmen together seemingly decided to take only one case forward, possibly on their solicitor's advice.

178. *Kilkenny Moderator*, June 6, 1868.

179. *Kilkenny Moderator*, October 21, 1868.

180. *Kilkenny Moderator*, April 10, 1869.

181. *Kilkenny Journal*, June 30, 1869.

182. *Kilkenny Moderator*, October 27, 1869. The letter was written by Edward Hutchinson, the Clerk of the Petty Sessions, about his son Richard. Innes was the flour miller. All were Protestant.

183. *Kilkenny Moderator*, July 7, 1870.

184. *Kilkenny Moderator*, August 6, 1870.

185. *Kilkenny Journal*, October 8, 1870.

186. *Kilkenny Journal*, January 14, 1871.

187. *Kilkenny Moderator*, March 11, 1871.

188. *Kilkenny Moderator*, May 15, 1872.

189. At a Petty Sessions, for example, the Resident Magistrate "spoke at some length, on the nature of an oath—the invoking the name of God . . . to witness the telling the truth; and he exhorted all to remember what . . . it involved (*Kilkenny Moderator*, March 11, 1871).

190. *Kilkenny Journal,* June 8, 1872.

191. *Kilkenny Moderator,* May 9, 1868; June 6, 1868.

192. *Kilkenny Journal,* June 8, 1872.

193. *Kilkenny Moderator,* October 5, 1872; *Kilkenny Moderator,* March 26, 1873.

194. *Kilkenny Journal,* December 7, 1872.

195. *Kilkenny Moderator,* January 18, 1873.

196. *Kilkenny Journal,* March 8, 1873.

197. *Kilkenny Moderator,* March 8, 1873.

198. *Kilkenny Moderator,* February 7, 1874.

199. *Kilkenny Moderator,* February 6, 1875.

200. *Kilkenny Moderator,* February 28, 1874.

201. Salmon fetched about 1s. a pound (*Kilkenny Moderator,* March 25, 1874).

202. *Kilkenny Moderator,* March 12, 1875.

203. IUP 1873 [c.758] xix, p. 644; IUP 1874 [c.980] xii, p. 601; IUP 1876 [c.1467] xvi, p. 582; IUP 1877 [c. 1703] xxiv, p. 391.

204. The cotmen seemingly took part from the audience. At one point, the chair "checked the fishermen for some ugly remarks which they were occasionally volunteering" and their solicitor "told the fishermen" that he "would give up the case, if it was not left in [his] hands."

205. *Kilkenny Moderator,* March 12, 1875.

206. For example, a fisherman loudly interjected during Forster's evidence that "Captain Forster poached himself . . . but there is no one to summon him" (*Kilkenny Moderator,* March 12, 1875).

207. *Kilkenny Moderator,* March 12, 1875.

208. *Kilkenny Moderator,* March 12, 1875.

209. IUP 1870 [c.225] xiv.

210. *Kilkenny Moderator,* October 27, 1869.

211. IUP 1866 [3608] xxvii, pp. 374–75.

212. IUP 1867 [3826] xviii, p. 41.

213. HC 1901 [Cd. 448] xii, p. 139.

214. *Kilkenny Moderator,* May 15, 1875.

215. *Kilkenny Moderator,* October 2, 1875.

216. *Kilkenny Moderator,* April 21, 1875.

217. This was part of his letter to the *Kilkenny Moderator,* May 15, 1875. This sentiment also was expressed when the cotmen's solicitor, in cross-examining Forster, accused him of doing "all in his power to take bread out of their mouths." Interestingly, chairman Hayes objected strenuously to this wording. Hayes added that a "gentleman is bound to protect his own property when he takes a house and land."

218. *Kilkenny Moderator,* March 17, 31; April 28; May 19; June 9; July 21, 28; August 11, 1875.

219. For example, *Kilkenny Moderator,* April 21; August 18, 1875.

220. *Kilkenny Moderator,* August 11, 1875.

221. *Kilkenny Moderator,* May 3, 1876.

222. *Kilkenny Moderator,* June 23, 1876.

223. *Kilkenny Moderator,* July 13, 1876.

224. *Kilkenny Moderator,* July 22, 1876.

225. *Kilkenny Moderator,* November 22, 1876.

226. *Kilkenny Moderator,* March 7, 1877.

227. *Kilkenny Moderator,* April 21, 1877.

228. *Kilkenny Moderator,* June 9, 1877.

229. *Kilkenny Moderator,* November 10, 1877.

230. *Kilkenny Moderator,* June 8, 1878.

231. *Kilkenny Journal,* July 3, 1878.

232. *Kilkenny Journal,* July 17, 1878.

233. *Kilkenny Moderator,* May 10, 1879.

234. *Kilkenny Journal,* July 12, 1879.

235. *Kilkenny Journal,* August 6, 1879.

236. *Kilkenny Moderator,* September 6, 1879.

237. *Kilkenny Journal,* October 8, 1879.

238. *Kilkenny Journal,* April 7, 1880.

239. Davis held urban property and a great deal of laborers' housing.

240. *Kilkenny Moderator,* March 6, 1880. This case is described in more detail in Silverman and Gulliver 1986, pp. 213–16.

241. *Kilkenny Journal,* April 17, 1880.

242. *Kilkenny Moderator,* December 1, 1880.

243. *Kilkenny Journal,* February 11, 1880.

244. *Kilkenny Journal,* May 29, 1880.

245. IUP 1881 [c.2871] xxiii, p. 431.

246. For example, an appeal to the Quarter Sessions that the penalty for an offence "did not encompass the forfeiture of the gear" resulted in the conviction being quashed (*Kilkenny Journal,* June 25, 1881).

247. *Kilkenny Moderator,* September 5, 1883.

248. *Kilkenny Moderator,* May 3, 1882.

249. *Kilkenny Moderator,* May 10, 1884.

250. *Reg. [Morrissey] v. Justices of Kilkenny, Law Reports (Ireland),* vol. 14, 1884:349–52.

251. *Kilkenny Moderator,* May 10, 1884.

252. HC 1901 [Cd. 448] xii, p. 137.

253. The few examples include Bartrip (1985) and Macleod (1968), who in fact were mainly concerned with the development of law and public policy.

254. Wolf (1982).

4

# The Languages of Belief: Nineteenth-Century Religious Discourse in Southwest Donegal[1]

■

## LAWRENCE J. TAYLOR

*Different Voices: Competing Religious Narratives*

There was a protestant [*gallta*—literally, "foreign"] woman in Glen who was inhospitable toward the locals [*gaedhil*—literally, "the Gaels"] who were going on Columcille's *turas* [local pilgrimage to a holy well]. The cairns [piles of stones which marked the pilgrimage route] were on a piece of her land, and she went and broke every bit of bottle and glass she could find and threw it on the cairns, to prevent the Gaels who would be doing the pilgrimage from crossing her piece of earth. She fell sick. When she was dying, she was barking the whole time until she died as if she were a dog.[2]

This short narrative was one of hundreds of legends gathered in the 1930s and 1940s from men and women then in their seventies and eighties living in southwest Donegal. Many of the stories related individual and social dramas with religious themes and actors—saints, holy wells, and powerful priests. All such figures or places displayed power, by punishing of enemies, as in the preceding case, or by rewarding the believer with a cure. Gathered by a native-born folklorist and now stored in the National Folklore Archive, this corpus of texts constitutes a rare and potentially fertile resource for a historical ethnography of the region in the late nineteenth century. The collection may also represent a larger opportunity: to assess some features of the role of language in local religious life generally and, thus, to shed anthropological light on questions concerning the historical sociology of religion. In this respect, as we will see later, the region in question stands as an attractive case study for what might be called an anthropologically oriented, Weberian treatment of the changing face of Catholicism—for the role of competing discourses in the growth of church domination is critical if little understood. The problem is what to make of such stories, how to contextualize and interpret them, and how to weigh their social and cultural impact.

We can begin by noting that stories, like the one about the well, were not the only religious narratives to be heard in that time and place. In mid- or late nineteenth-century west Donegal, the mainly bilingual Catholic population could read and/or hear an interesting variety of texts. Consider the following two extracts, the first from an issue of *Duffy's Fireside Magazine* and the second from a sermon book of the Redemptorist missionaries.

> Twas a calm evening in summer. A peasant went forth to a sequestered wood, to perform his devotions at a shrine of the Virgin Mary. He knelt before an altar, on which there was an effigy of our Lady, and ornamented with those simple charms which artless piety is wont so happily to suggest. Then in the depth of solitude, he chaunted [sic] a hymn of love, and offered to the Queen of Heaven the outpourings of a devoted soul. Near the shrine there was a river, whose gentle murmurs seemed to harmonize with the peasant's song. The moments sped swiftly as he prayed. Tears fell from his eyes, but they were joyous tears, emanating from the heart, that peerless fountain of eternal love. The glowing sunbeam was on the wane, and the peasant, revolving past memories, and inspired with hopeful visions of the future, sank into a dreamy reverie.[3]

> What voice of God is this? Is it the voice of the Eternal Judge, who sentences you to be thrown into the abyss of hell, thus to depart from him for evermore? No! It is the voice of your merciful Saviour, who visits you today, who invites you to make your peace with him—who offers you the great, extraordinary, rare grace of a mission—"Come," he says, "depart not from me—Come to me." Before the commencement of the Mass you witnessed the opening ceremony "This is the acceptable time."[4]

These three pieces—folk story, sermon (see appendix 4.1), and magazine piece (introduction to a poem, see appendix 4.2)—suggest something of the range of religious voices and imagery available in

Irish and English to the inhabitants of western Ireland by the middle to late nineteenth century. The very coexistence of these quite disparate voices and idioms demands that we listen to them as the people did, not according to the pristine and artificial isolation of our own intellectual categories, but in concert—however disharmonious. Clearly, the proper context of even the "traditional" folk story extended beyond the confines of any narrowly defined "peasant" social world and language to include a complex network of associations and contending constructions of reality that characterized (though certainly not uniquely) Donegal in the last quarter of the nineteenth century. My intention here is to explore that diversity in an effort to discern something of the complex character of popular Catholicism in that particularly interesting, transitional period in Irish history—when the renewed vigorous intrusion of the institutional church coincided with other important social and economic changes discussed later. In the process, light might also be shed on two issues of more general interest: first, the role of discourse in structuring religious experience in complex societies; and second, the ways in which anthropological interpretations of discourse can be useful to historiography and the theoretical problems of historical sociology. Here the term *discourse* is meant to suggest a *language* in Foucault's sense, which both constitutes a particular reality by talking about it and disallows other, competing discourses.[5] I am arguing that the three texts cited earlier may each have represented a competing discourse within the realm of Irish Catholicism in the late nineteenth century. Viewed in this way, these and other narratives may have represented a discursive struggle between competing forms of power.

## The Power of Religious Narrative

Anthropology—particularly in Europe—has paid far less attention to religious words per se than to religious action. Although there are many studies of "folk religion" in the ethnography of European Catholicism, the emphasis has been on ritual, a bias reinforced not only by anthropological leanings rooted in Durkheim but by explicit or implicit comparisons with Protestants—where the "text" may purport to replace the rite. After all, anthropologists, like many other Western intellectuals, have tended to view religion rationally from the Protestant perspective forged during the Reformation. According to this received wisdom, Catholicism consists mainly of ritual magic, and Protestantism, particularly in its more "purified" forms, is characterized by reasoned speech and a focus on the Biblical text. It is no wonder that in turning to their own continent, ethnographers sought out colorful rites in Catholic Europe. Consequently, even though some progress has been made in noting and analyzing Protestant ritual, Catholic discourse has been routinely undervalued.[6] Folklorists may have done more with narrative texts in particular, but in Ireland, texts have been used mainly as raw material for typological classification or as expressive evidence of a general worldview.[7] Yet a consideration of any late-nineteenth-century (or indeed, twentieth-century) European Catholic population—no matter how "folksy"—reveals not only that religious discourse (which typically survives in narrative texts) figured importantly in daily life but that, as our own case shows, folk stories were not the only sort of religious narrative encountered.

Thus, there is reason to develop an approach—at once historical and anthropological—to interpreting religious narratives and, more generally, the discourse in which such narratives played a critical role. Although European historians and anthropologists have worked out some of their most creative borrowing in the analysis of symbolism and systems of thought and meaning, in Ireland there has so far been little sign of this sort of reciprocity.[8] Where historians of Irish religion have turned to anthropology, it has been to the somewhat outmoded functionalist concepts of magic developed by Malinowski and Radcliffe Brown explaining local heterodoxies as simply responses to basic needs or community relations.[9] Although such observations have not been without merit, they did not constitute a great advance over the doctrine of "survivals." This reluctance to incorporate more recent anthropological approaches in Irish historiography has been in marked contrast to the interaction between historians and anthropologists working on such topics in France or Italy, where the cross-fertilization has been extraordinarily productive.[10] From this interdisciplinary field, a dynamic model of religious culture has been evolving, one attentive to the ways in which the generation of rituals, devotional forms, and discourse create both meaning and power.

This interdisciplinary approach has obvious relevance for the history and ethnography of Irish Catholicism, where the interactive relation between local religious practice and "official," institutionally generated forms of devotion has been both complex and vital to any understanding of local experience. Some of the complexity has been revealed by focusing on "religious occasions" (as I have done elsewhere),[11] such as a mission, pilgrimage, or healing mass. Several such occasions (e.g., missions) could play a particularly crucial role in introducing or promoting new ways of being religious by symbolically and dramatically acting out and depicting the central beliefs, attitudes, and emotional stances. At the same time, however, locals themselves appropriated such occasions, revealing in their own accounts of missions, for example (as we shall see later), a different sort of religious experience from that intended by the missionaries. I have called this subcultural diversity of religious perspectives "fields of religious experience," by which I mean to indicate a loosely bounded "interpretive community" with a generally shared understanding of religious meaning.[12] That is, at any religious occasion there will be individuals in attendance representing more than one field of religious experience. In mid- to late nineteenth-century Donegal, we can usefully distinguish at least two distinctive "fields" in this sense: a "chthonic," or earth-oriented, religiosity of most of the peasantry and a "civil" Catholicism primarily associated with the middle class. Yet it was not simply a question of folk versus official religion, for new fields could begin among various groups of locals (witness apparitions or, more currently, charismatic Catholicism) or particular branches of the clergy.[13] The difference among fields of religious experience is indicated by the variation in religious texts with which this paper is concerned. However, these narratives are not being presented here merely as passive expressions and hence evidence of subcultural religious differences. Rather, I am claiming that such texts may have played a crucial and active role in creating and maintaining the distinctive perspective of such fields of religious experience.

Religious discourse takes different forms in the different fields (it can be formal and informal, written and oral), but in all fields narrative has a privileged role. If we consider discourse to mean a way of talking about and hence seeing the world (or some section of it) that depends on a range of critical words, oppositions, and so on, then narratives, or stories, are perhaps the most affective, and hence effective, expression of any discourse. Beliefs and knowledge are often, and certainly most strongly, embodied in the form of stories. Aside from whatever deep structures or unconscious repressions they might express (or secrete), narratives about human or anthropomorphic subjects command attention through their ability to make abstractions concrete and to provide opportunities for identification. None of the self-conscious creators of discourse—states, churches, and professions—have been slow to realize this. Thus, narratives may represent competing cultural and social realities and occasionally regimes seeking (consciously or not) hegemony. In those cases, two sorts of narration have been critical. First, there are the stories that vivify the institution or regime and its worldview: stories about saints, revolutions, or even prototypical psychological cases that are the Freudian equivalent of the exempla. Second, there are the stories one learns to tell oneself and others about oneself: the selective self-narration of autobiography. The true internalization of a discursive worldview is both achieved and expressed in the relation (aloud or not) of the incidents, experiences, and emotions of one's own life in the terms provided by the discourse. This process is perhaps clearest in the cases of something like conversion, when the reorganization of experience into a new order is striking; but that is only a more extreme version of the role of narratives in what anthropologists have broadly called *enculturation*.

Religion offers particularly striking examples of these powers of narrative. In religious stories the general human interest in plot is much heightened by the possible inclusion of elements of wonder and promises of power. This was true not only of the folk story with which we began but of all three of our texts, in each of which something of the potential functions of religious narrative was evinced. That is, they all not only portrayed a religious world but, in at least two cases—the folk story and the sermon—they asked the listener to enter that world, to put himself or herself in the story. Although such narratives, as our opening examples illustrate, can be very different in form as well as content and thus have, by virtue of their differences, distinctive inherent characteristics, they all share properties that gave narratives a particular cultural force. An understanding of the role of religious discourse in late nineteenth-century Irish Catholicism requires an appreciation of both the peculiar and general characteristics of these narratives. Such texts, however, can hardly be understood apart from the situations and occasions of their use, so I will begin with a sketch of the social context and then turn to the power and meaning of the texts.

## The Audience: Changing Social Context

Several changes, hardly unique to southwest Donegal, took place through the middle decades of the nineteenth century. All were potentially crucial to the production and consumption of religious (and other sorts of) discourse. Three transformations were particularly relevant: first, a change in the number and composition of social classes; second, a shift in the settlement pattern; and third, an increased presence of external institutions and of the culture they promoted.

The rise—with the aid of landlords—of an indigenous Catholic merchant class began with the depression after the Napoleonic Wars; by the 1870s, the market towns of the region—Carrick and Ardara—essentially had achieved their present appearance.[14] These towns, though hardly imposing even by rural European standards, did come to constitute a significantly new kind of social space that both housed and symbolized the new class. The petty bourgeoisie were not the only users of the town. Clearly, that class always represented a minority of those to be found on the streets or, more important for our concerns, in the pubs, which were licensed during the 1870s and which slowly replaced or at least supplemented the home and the rural "shebeen" as the principal sites of social drinking. The local peasants who came to the towns, whether on market days or more frequently, were of course the main clientele of the pubs and thus found themselves drawn into social interaction and especially communication not just with other peasants coming in from other directions, but with publicans.[15] In this emerging social world, these publicans, like the millers of whom Ginzburg wrote, served a crucial function as perhaps the most important mediators and interpreters of local information.[16]

The home circumstances of those peasants had also changed. The old *clachan*,[17] a nucleated hamlet settlement pattern with a rundale field system, had been reorganized by improving landlords in the 1840s. These small clusters were replaced with the contemporary social geography of more "dispersed" and hence isolated homesteads. The rise of the town and pub thus coincided with a reduction in at least some aspects of communality in the countryside.

Finally, the development of physical and social closeness in town and increasing isolation in the countryside was accompanied by the simultaneous penetration of two institutions from the outside world. The Catholic church accelerated a process it had begun earlier, the building of chapels capable of housing the entire parish and thus providing a crucial symbol of and stage for introducing a new religious discourse. At least equally significant was the proliferation of national schools, spreading the English language and a form of civility that echoed the rhetoric of the church.

It is clear that these transformations each contributed importantly to the production and consumption of the various forms of religious discourse we have discerned. However, addressing the questions of *who* read and/or heard, *how* they understood the disparate forms, and *what* was the historical impact of such texts, is not so simple.

Two sorts of evidence strongly suggest that such texts exerted a powerful influence on local religious experience. Historically, the transition in religious behavior that Larkin called the "devotional revolution"—the process whereby Roman devotions and regular church attendance became the Irish norm by the middle of the nineteenth century—was accompanied by what contemporaries described as powerfully and emotionally received parish missions.[18] Moreover, the impact of the sermons was evidenced in the folk reaction—stories about the miraculous occurrences at missions—to be found in the folklore archives. There was also, however, my own ethnographic experience of the role and power of narratives in this part of Ireland (though I doubt it is peculiar in that respect). I saw what was left of formal storytelling, but it was the general attention awarded narrative in whatever form and situation that I found most striking. An anecdote, when told well, riveted the audience in house or pub, and the Victorian tendency to commit written verse or story to memory was still an attribute of the older locals. They told me of the yet more vital role of narrative in the world of their parents, and historical descriptions as well as the volume of stories in the folklore archives convinced me that they were right. Finally, there is the logical possibility that narratives played an exaggerated role in Irish Catholicism, which, for reasons of local religious tradition as well as English suppression, was relatively weak in iconography and ritual pomp.

It is tempting, and to a limited extent justified, simply to interpret the form and function of the texts from the perspective of class relations. The folk story was a peasant cultural form from this perspective, the magazine piece a distinctly middle-class expression, and the sermon a text consciously contrived to domesticate the "wild Irish" peasantry—part of what might be called the church's "civilizing process"—or better, "civilizing offensive."[19]

If both the classes and texts are considered in isolation from one another, this reading is convincing. But in southwest Donegal, and probably in any other region, the picture was a bit more complicated. The relatively few members of the local middle class hardly lived in a totally distinct social and cultural milieu, though, as we shall see, discourse may have played an important role in building a class culture. Moreover, although presumably such periodicals as *Duffy's Fireside Magazine* would have enjoyed only limited circulation in this region in the mid- or even late nineteenth century, the contents of that and other urban-oriented periodicals might very well have found their way to a wider audience through the relation of narratives or opinions, in whatever emended form, to nonreaders, especially by such crucial mediators as publicans, priests, and schoolteachers. In the other direction, however, the flow was fairly certain and important. That is, folk religious narratives were well known and, from my experience, not often belittled by the more middle-class inhabitants of the region. As for the mission sermon, it is certain that nearly everybody was subjected several times during his or her life to such performances, and the actual texts are available.

Individuals thus participated in more than one discursive world; but that is not to say they were not pulled in particular directions. Further, the texts themselves, as we shall see, reveal an interesting interaction among discourses and the social/cultural worlds for which they stood. They appropriated and transformed one another. Thus, they did not amount to evolutionary layers, although they entered the fray at different historical points. Rather, they contended and borrowed and persisted through adaptation as long as some semblance of the social formation that generated them continued. Let me turn to this complex relation between religious discourse and society by taking up the texts one at a time.

### Charismatic Landscape: The Folk Narrative

The folk narrative told the story of Protestant interference with a local pilgrimage and the divine retribution that followed. Columcille's *turas,* like the vast majority of local religious pilgrimages in Ireland, required the devotee to follow a prescribed route through local terrain, stopping for "stations" (obligatory prayers) at any number of sacred spots, but culminating at a natural spring, or holy well, marked in this case by a cairn: a great pile of stones brought by pilgrims. Like many local religious narratives, it was a legend of power and exemplary of several genres suggested by one or another feature: holy well stories, saints' stories, Catholic versus Protestant stories, place-name explanation narratives.

It may immediately strike the reader that the holy well story is composed of structural and possibly historical elements. On the structural side, depending on your theoretical bent, you might penetrate to various depths of primordiality: from shared Indo-European folklore motifs to universal human themes of divine power, to the symbolic expression of the basic structure of either the human mind

(Lévi-Strauss) or personality (Freud). Yet there may also have been a particular, historical side to this story. In fact, the pilgrimage in question did cross a number of what were Protestant holdings on its way to the well. A woman of one of these farms might have interfered with the pilgrimage, and certainly such a woman would have died, perhaps soon after (although the story does not claim it), and perhaps horribly.

The historicity of such stories is yet clearer in other cases. In fact, I first became interested in the relation such narratives bear to historical processes and events through my serendipitous discovery of a collection of estate agent's letters discussing, among other things, the eviction of the parish priest from his small holding in 1876. I was subsequently taken to the home of a ninety-one-year-old woman who recited in Gaelic the folk version of the event at which her own father had been present. Considering the data contained in the letters and other contemporary sources, I concluded that the folk version, which included a number of miraculous feats on the part of the priest, was probably not strictly accurate. Yet the folk version was interesting not just as an example of locally garbled history but as an indication of the way locals appropriated events to form an ideology that to some extent both defined and framed their perception of local reality.[20]

In terms of events, the preceding example well illustrates the possible form such a relationship may take. Following Turner, I would argue that there is a dialectical relation between social dramas like that of the priest's eviction and the stories told about them.[21] The priest, as familiar as anyone with the prerequisites of symbolic confrontation, may well have constructed the event in a culturally meaningful way. By doing so he provoked a narrative, but the narrative that was eventually formed selectively appropriated the event. Finally, insofar as these stories provide an ideological framework that influences behavior, they may act as both models of and models for history.

But why are some events more culturally interesting than others? If a corpus of stories helps sustain a particular interpretive framework—a cultural ideology or field of religious experience—it must do so in the face of "real" experience. Sometimes events conform well enough to such cultural expectations that they can be taken up into the narrative structure with only appropriate embellishment, as in the case of the priest versus the agent. However, a historical experience may be important and deeply felt, but either because it takes the form of process rather than event or because other cultural forces are powerful enough to repress its direct representation, narrative has difficulty laying hold of it. In such cases, other events, even infrequent and apparently (to the disinterested observer) undramatic ones, may be cast in an important narrative role because they can be made to carry a certain symbolic weight. The folk narratives I shall consider here can be understood from this perspective; they have sustained a particular field of religious experience through such direct and indirect appropriations of historical events and processes.

To understand this dialectic between narratives and historical experience we need to take a long—however schematic—view of the process. In particular, I want to focus on the subject of the story I began with, holy wells, whose devotions and stories throw a particularly illuminating light on the history of Irish Catholicism.

The respective fates of holy well devotions illustrate the differences between the paths taken by continental and Irish Catholicism. As Brown demonstrated, the cult of saints in early Christian Europe made the graves and relics of saints, and the shrines associated with them, the sites of pilgrimage.[22] Since these shrines were controlled by the bishops, such devotions served to strengthen episcopal domination. In Ireland there seems to have been less use of relics in early saint cults; rather, their devotion was concentrated on holy wells associated with miraculous acts during their lives. Particularly along the western seaboard of Ireland, such wells were unassociated with bishops or other centralizing religious regimes. Instead, they were associated with eremitic monastic communities (and later, their ruins) on wild moor, mountain, and island. Geographically and politically, they celebrated the power of the periphery, not the center. Their liminality was an appropriate expression of the dangerous power that was present there, for it was at such locations that one also met, and to some extent still meets, fairies and ghosts. This early monastic form, unlike the continental cult centers described by Brown, reinforced rather than challenged existing notions of a metaphorically parallel, powerful world to which one might get access at liminal points of time and space.

What of continuing devotions at holy wells? Most historical accounts have referred to the "patterns": festivities on particular days—sometimes an associated saint's day, but not always—when any number of people gathered to "do the stations," proceeding around the well or from one pile of stones to another, saying so many *aves* and *paters* on the way. According to numerous contemporary accounts from the twelfth through the nineteenth and even twentieth centuries, these patterns were occasions of postdevotional heavy drinking, faction fights, and sexual liaisons. However, when and where Ireland

became home to a more Romanized religious regime (beginning with
the Vatican-supported Anglo-Normans), the clergy, or various members of it, attempted to limit or eliminate such practices, but apparently with relatively little success before the mid-nineteenth-century
famine. After that point, however, such liminal chaos was successfully attacked and the patterns were either terminated altogether or
domesticated.[23] The priest then could lead the people through the
passive rounds, after which they went peacefully home. Indeed, many
clergy so successfully coopted and tamed such devotions that by the
twentieth century, clerics began to revive defunct pilgrimages in
order to reinvigorate what could now be perceived as quaint "local
custom."

Does that mean, however, that the "folk field of religious experience," based as it was, to some extent, on well devotions, was also
successfully domesticated, and liminal conceptions of power replaced
by vertical ones mediated by priest and saint? To some extent the
answer is yes, and the process was well named by historian Larkin
the "devotional revolution."[24] Yet the evidence of discourse reveals
ways in which such change was mitigated. For the stories about wells
shed a different sort of light on both the character of the religious
experience involved in the devotional exercises—what it meant or
means to the people—and the people's reaction to the drastic changes
brought about so recently by clerical domination—the devotional
revolution mentioned earlier. To what extent, we can ask, did the
discourse of well stories keep alive an older field of religious experience that emphasized not the vertical relations of Roman devotional
structures but the parallel world of natural power mediated by liminality?

One genre of stories concerned the origins of wells, which were
not in fact always associated with saints. In Donegal, for example,
the Well of the Holy Women (*Tobar na mBan Naomh*) and Doon Well
(*Tobar an Duine*), the latter having a very active devotion, were not
connected by tradition to any particular saint, nor was there a single
clear origin story.[25] For most wells, however, legends did account for
their origins in the acts of, predominantly, early Celtic saints whose
lives were set in a kind of prehistorical dreamtime when and where
they wandered through the landscape destroying dragons and the like
and not always acting as paragons of virtue. Rather, they were capri-
cious, powerful creatures whose power was demonstrated in stories
as alternately damning or blessing. As far as the wells were concerned, they, like other features of the landscape, were marked by
some gesture of the saint, such as a fallen tear or a staff striking a

rock. These saints, and their wells, were autochthonic. They were the relations of chiefs whose genealogies could be traced backed to the hero-gods of Gaelic mythology. As for the "stranger converter saint," Patrick, his legends and associated places converted him as well into part of the immovable landscape. In short, all early Irish saints were autochthonic ancestors.

Unlike legends about the origins of wells, stories concerning the actual power of wells were set in "real time" and sometimes involved named individuals firmly placed in the recent historical landscape. The power of wells was displayed in such narratives in two ways: curing and punishing.

I frequently heard curing narratives that often took an anecdotal form. A typical variant was the following:

> Oh there's great curing in that well. There was a woman brought her daughter to that well once and nothing could cure the child. She was that sick, and couldn't walk at all. She had brought her to all the wells, even Doon Well down in the North there, and nothing did any good for her. Anyway her mother brought her here to *tobar na mban naomh* and she spent the night by the well, and her mother took her away in the morning and she was cured. And by god, she stayed that way because she lived to a great age and she used come here to visit over the years—we all knew her as an old woman—and it wasn't long ago that she died.[26]

Such stories served to demonstrate the primary power of the wells and to justify and encourage their continued use. Interestingly, they rarely, if ever, mentioned the saint other than to denote the well; rather, the well was pictured as powerful in itself. Curing was not achieved through intercession but through proper contact with the liminal power accessible at such holy places. However, it is neither helpful nor accurate to distinguish this sort of devotion as magical versus a more religious saint-mediated curing. Both may involve "automatic" power and both may consider the moral state of the individual as relevant to the efficacy of the act.

Another class of narratives did not take the story form but simply described significant aspects of the well. They may have been included in the performance, preceding actual legends about the well's powerful achievements, or they may have been offered in response to inquiry from the listener. Such narratives often spoke of the presence in the well of an apparently immortal fish—a trout or a salmon—that may have appeared to the devotee. This manifestation may have been a sign of either imminent cure or death, of the viewer or someone connected to him or her. Not only was this fish unconnected to the saint but its appearance once again manifested the well's liminal position and power—a power that might have been dangerous as well as helpful: it was a window into the other world and hence potentially divinatory or oracular.

The other narrative type was the sort with which we began, which presented the power of the well in another light, as a potentially destructive force vis-à-vis its enemies. There were many stories on this theme, all of them involving Protestant interference with holy well devotions. Either they took the form of our first legend, wherein a landlord or landholder tried to prevent access to the well, or they portrayed a scoffing Protestant who attempted to demonstrate the powerlessness of the well. A recurring version of the latter theme had a Protestant putting his foot into the well to demonstrate its ordinariness. He was unable to remove his foot until aided by a priest, and then—in some variants—only with a promise of conversion.

In all these stories the central opposition is of Gael (local Irish Catholic) versus Gall (Protestant interloper—literally, foreigner). The pitting of the autochthonic forces embodied in the well against the intrusive foreigners is not in itself surprising. It is interesting, however, that the clergy themselves, who were, after all, the more persistent and concerned enemies of at least the earlier forms of well devotion, were not depicted in any tales as enemies of the well. Indeed, anticlerical folklore has been conspicuous by its relative absence in Ireland—when compared especially to the Mediterranean region. I suggest that the nineteenth-century campaigns of the clergy were successful, not only in stamping out liminal behavior but in repressing expressions of sexuality and hostility toward itself. As a result, the only way the alternate, essentially non-church-oriented religiosity of well devotion could be sustained by locals was through a symbolic sublimation that replaced one intrusive enemy—priests—with another—Protestant foreigners.[27]

In fact, the folk field of religious experience, to which this well discourse contributed, included an appropriation of the clergy itself in the popular narratives about—and indeed continuing devotion to—drunken priests.[28] In the many accounts concerning the power of alcoholic priests, junior members of the clergy—typically curates rather than parish priests—were opposed both conceptually and politically to the controlling authority of the institutional church. Like the early saints, they were depicted wandering through nature, curing and cursing as capriciously as any shaman—and sometimes directing people to wells for help with their ailments: clearly liminal types.

These stories constituted another sort of sublimation, where repressed religiosity and probably sexuality could be talked about in appropriately disguised form.

Taken together, the discourse embodied in the narratives discussed here managed to sustain what we have called a folk field of religious experience, based on notions of the opposition of nature and culture and of liminal access to autochthonic power. Various historical experiences of domination, by both Protestant foreigners and the institutional Catholic church, each of which attempted in its own way to reorient native *mentalité,* were, by means of such discourse, appropriated as actors in these primeval dramas. Finally, the degree to which such stories and other, more informal exchanges have continued to structure the experience of well devotion was shown through their continued use. The formal *turas* (holy well pilgrimage) may not have attracted very many people, and they tended to speak of it just as the church would have wished them to, as a penance. Yet many individuals have continued to seek cures at holy wells, leaving in reciprocal exchange for their favors items ranging from rags to coins to broken religious objects. The reputation of these wells has risen and fallen, and people have sought them across local boundaries if they heard stories of their power. In no case that I know of was the reputation of a particular well strongly linked with current devotion to the associated saint; nor was the well's power in any way linked to or dependent on its geographic proximity, or iconographic relation, to any institutional church. If anything, the decaying ruins of the eremitic monastery, near which such wells may be located, lent further strength and poignancy to their oppositional distance from the typically late nineteenth-century churches located in the center of towns. All this suggests that the Weberian process of church domination did not succeed in desacralizing or disenchanting the Irish landscape. Indeed, the surviving charismatic character of that landscape suggests a further emendation to Weber's theory of the loci of such power.

### *"What Voice of God Is This?"*: *The Redemptorist Sermon*

The dialectical relation between rival discourses and the fields of religious experience they articulated is particularly clear in a consideration of the missions. I have elsewhere considered the history and ethnography of Redemptorist parish missions in Ireland.[29] However, some sense of the general historic role and ritual structure of the mission is necessary to interpret this text.

The mission arose as a religious form in the Counter-Reformation, which saw a general reorganization of devotion and domination in the Catholic church. Just as they recognized the need to missionize the newly discovered "savages," various church orders understood that such techniques could prove effective in "converting" European folk as well. The parish mission, as developed by the Jesuits and refined by the Redemptorists, brought Mediterranean ritual pomp together with a structured sermon series. The sermons in effect laid out a whole cosmology and put the listener into it. In contrast to the folk, autochthonic idiom, this new discourse pictured a vertical world—heaven above, hell yawning below, and the church and its sacraments as the only means to attain the former and avoid the latter. Moreover, the performance quality of the mission, with its high theatrics and thunderous presentation, reinforced the verticality of the vision. The listener was dominated and certainly experienced that domination emotionally as well as conceptually.

Given this aspect of the missions, it is interesting to note their role when they finally arrived in mid-nineteenth- rather than seventeenth- or eighteenth-century Ireland. Although the devotional world they expressed was already to some extent established in other, typically urban regions of Ireland, contemporary descriptions of the missions in the west indicated their utter novelty there.[30] To judge by contemporary accounts from the 1840s and 1850s, the first Irish missions were extraordinary events, with the emotional character of a conversion experience. Later missions were more regular affairs, however, and one could not be "born again" every few years. Yet when contrasted with ordinary religious life, even the regularly scheduled missions of the late nineteenth century had the aura of the unusual and perhaps extraordinary event. This power, although generated in a religious context, was increasingly used in the social control of the peasants and laboring classes. Reconciliation of "faction fighters," an early focus, gave way to an unremitting assault on the evils of drink and such social occasions as would promote its use and other improprieties.[31] Thus, the mission played an important role in the church's "civilizing offensive."[32] In that regard, we need to make an important distinction between the persons and discourses of, respectively, parish priest and Redemptorist missionary. The parish priest might well have represented a role model of civility for the aspiring rural middle classes, as Inglis maintained, and thus his speech could have served as a model of proper religious language for that class.[33] In contrast, the

Redemptorist's dramatic manifestation of power and authority was far more distancing. Most of the congregants were hardly encouraged to see the missionary as a model of anything they could hope to emulate; his language condemned, and if the sermon narrative drew the listener in, she or he was made abject before the powerful God/ missionary.

The textual qualities of the sermon, especially when considered in light of their performance quality, are both powerful and strikingly different from those of the folk story.[34] We should begin, however, by asking to what extent such a sermon was heard as a narrative by the people of late nineteenth-century Donegal. The Redemptorists, like other preachers, had frequent recourse to narrative exempla to illustrate an argument. As performed and heard, however, the opening sermon of the mission also had less obvious, but arguably compelling, narrative qualities. The task of this opening sermon was to narrate the mission itself, to draw attention to the dramatic structure of the event—indeed to make it "an event." What is crucial is the quality of time, and that is the theme of the sermon—the "acceptable time." The mission was portrayed as a potentially transforming experience, an event in the story of your life and the life of your community. This was, of course, the literal truth. Parish missions lasted for at least two weeks and, in rural hinterlands, were certainly events in all senses of the word. Moreover, the sermons that stretched over the time were a series of dramatically linked texts that told the story of salvation and how to achieve it. Thus, to the degree that it succeeded, the sermon promised to be its own story, to narrate itself and the lives of the parishioners. This made the listener, of course, a character in the story. What the missioner hoped and called for was a self-narration, a conversion story that, if told at some future date, would make of the mission the climax, the critical moment in the plot.

For the listeners, there were of course other things going on in and around this text. Like the folk narrative, it was concerned with describing the characteristics of supernatural power and representing the ways in which that power was mediated. Thus, it portrayed holy space as well as holy time, but in the sermon, that space was decidedly vertical rather than horizontal. Heaven was above and hell below, as the listener would be reminded throughout the mission. Moreover, mediation was to be found not in the landscape but in the church, in the sacraments, and in the person of the missioner himself. If the mission was an "acceptable time," it was also an "acceptable place." Finally, this verticality was communicated not only through the content of the sermons but in the performance. In a sort of reverse Durkheimian way, the mission sermon helped produce and reproduce a social mirror of the sacred universe it described. That is, the missioner demonstrated priesthood as domination and, more generally, the overwhelming cultural power of the encroaching institutional world. In the process, of course, the specific language of the sermon, a particularly inflamed and Roman version of institutional church discourse, was empowered—including such key notions as heaven, hell, purgatory, sin, grace, penance, and so on. By all accounts, this performance quality, as well as the texts themselves, made mission sermons very different from ordinary Sunday homilies.

It is also worth noting that if the form of the mission was novel in places like nineteenth-century Donegal, the "master sermon" was not. Charles McGlinchy, of the then Irish-speaking Inishowen peninsula in the north of the county, remembered his father (b. 1810) reciting from the sermons of Father Gallagher.[35] These eighteenth-century Irish language sermons by a noted bishop of Raphoe (Donegal's diocese) were apparently available in printed editions through the ensuing century and were well known to the literate peasantry of that diocese. The Redemptorists—whether they knew it or not—were following in that tradition, for unlike several local priests, they missionized in Irish not in English and were probably more powerfully heard as a result.

What, in fact, did the local populace hear? Direct light can be shed on "listeners' response" by turning to the people at whom the sermons were directed. Something of their impact on the "folk" is conveyed by the stories that have found their way into the National Folklore Archives. There are only a handful of catalogued "mission stories," most of them collected from elderly men and women in the 1930s, relating stories of the missions of their youth or that of their parents. These short narratives stressed the forceful, and fearful, power of the occasion. Several spoke of miracles, such as keeping candles lit in high winds and, in maritime communities, bringing fish into local waters. The conversion of an especially inveterate sinner may also have been related, typically involving the renunciation of drink. What is clear in such instances, however, is that the stories described the transformations as magical as much as moral.

Indeed, *pace* Weber, in all these tales there is a noticeable lack of separation between ethical-behavioral transformations and so-called magical power. For the Redemptorists, the general confession was the point of the mission. But the folk memory appropriated the event in a different way, in which power and extraordinary penance were described in the typical vocabulary of the transforming religious experience. The mission was treated as a liminal, powerful, and penitential event on the order of, for example, a pilgrimage to a holy site like Station Island in Lough Derg.[36] These interpretations, it must be noted, would still have done nothing to detract from the efficacy of clerical domination. They would, however, have had the unintended consequences of possibly reinforcing the very world they sought to undermine—what we might call the folk or chthonic field of religious experience.

### "A Chaunt of Love . . .": "The Peasant at the Shrine"

Clearly, the experience of reading the *Duffy's* piece (see appendix 4.2) was different in every possible way from hearing either of the other two texts. One can imagine—unfortunately, only imagine—the shopkeeper, who was financially most likely to receive this periodical, sitting in his or her parlor with a copy of *Duffy's* or some other piece of popular literary culture. The social interaction, unless the piece was read aloud, would have been between the reader and the text, a civilized act in a civilized setting. In such circumstances, the act of reading may well have made for the individual a crucial connection between the class culture and notions of petit bourgeois civility, on the one hand, and religiosity, on the other.

The Victorian act of reading such literature, of course, would have been matched by the civility in the content of the magazine extract and of the poem that it introduced and that continued in a similar vein. Such a text would have worked very differently from both the other narratives in that the reader was not in this case being asked to put him or herself into the story. The probably middle-class reader of this rather standard piece of Victorian sentimentality (in its Catholic guise) was hardly expected to identify with the peasant at the shrine. Indeed, the effect was more likely distancing: even though represented as a fellow Catholic, the peasant as "folk" was clearly "other." The identification was instead with the writer—the fellow middle-class sentimentalist—and in that way the impact of this text was likely to be very different indeed from the Redemptorist sermon. Of course it was aimed at a different audience. Although the sermon served the "civilizing offensive" by seeking to domesticate the savage peasant through control and domination, the poem may have contributed to Elias's "civilizing process" by providing an example of language and thought for emulation.[37]

Although such a discourse of peasant otherness might have merely reinforced the thoroughly bourgeois self-image of a city dweller, there is some irony in the possibility of such newly minted, middle-class merchants as would have been found in the west contemplating such a depiction of their first cousins. If they did, however, it probably contributed to the growth of a rural class consciousness among the new petit bourgeois of that area. In the experience of reading *Duffy's* magazine, one identified oneself as a "reader" and, by virtue of that activity, a participant in a particular cultural community. One may also have learned to see the "peasant" (formerly a neighbor or relation) as the sort of person one "read" about, the sort of person who lived in stories of this sort (unlike in folk stories, where the listener was asked to identify with the subject).

At the same time, the text sentimentalized religion in general (see appendix 4.2), and in that sense it would have directly affected the reader's own religious worldview. The field of religious experience presented in the text involved an interesting twist relative to that field represented in the folk story about Columcille's well. The *Duffy's* piece too placed a "peasant at a well" or rural shrine—accurate enough location of a significant point of mediation with the divine—but the piece associated the shrine with Mary, who then enters into the story. Although Mary was a familiar enough personage in the chthonic field of religious experience, the folk image of Mary was quite different, at least as evidenced in folk narratives. O'Laoghaire described the "homely and intimate fashion in which the Bardic poets spoke of Mary" and the easy familiarity of peasant prayer to the Mother of God.[38] If Mary was familiar and addressable through prayer, however, she was (and has continued to be) not much localized in that idiom and not nearly so woven into the landscape as the Irish saints, even though in several of the folk narratives she accompanied those saints (Brigid in particular) in their wanderings through mythic dreamtime. The magazine piece, on the other hand, depicted an altogether different cosmos: a characteristically Victorian religious blend of the homely and the powerful—in that most useful of all versions—Mary. Where Protestantism prevented such direct Marian expression, as in English and American popular religious discourse, *Mother* was used in place of Mary, and rather than a holy shrine in the forest, one would have read about the Mother's grave.

In common with the folk narrative, however, this magazine piece may seem, from our perspective, to empower the landscape: mediation happened in the forest—already in short enough supply in nineteenth-century Ireland—and nature apparently triumphed over culture. Yet if placed in the context of general Victorian discourse, this text can be read neither as an instance of Romantic rebellion against cultural authority (in this case, as embodied in the institutional church) nor as a return to a folk perspective on natural power. Rather, the sentimental otherness of scene and character might have served the role of complementary opposition. Such a piece preserved and domesticated its subject in harmless textual form; it no more challenged bourgeois civility and church-centered religion than Victorian depictions of female sanctity and influence challenged male authority. Indeed, one can go one interpretive step further in this direction by noting the seductive role of this discourse in the general church campaign ongoing through the century to tame holy well "excesses." I say seductive because reconstructions of experience through narrative may have acted on the listener or reader very differently, and arguably more effectively, from condemnations of peasant abuses. Here discourse joins that ancient Christian strategy of reconsecrating rather than destroying the "pagan" shrine. In Bede's time, Saint Augustine tried to redefine Anglo-Saxon notions of divinity by putting Christ on their altars. At various points in later Catholic history, Mary served the same function, in these cases replacing localized with generalized devotions.[39]


## Conclusions: Meaning and Power in Religious Discourse

This essay has explored the contribution that competing religious discourses may have made to the creation and maintenance of "fields of religious experience" in late nineteenth-century Donegal. I use the term *explore* advisedly, for the interpretation of such sources as are treated here—particularly at this point in the state of the evidence— can only contribute suggestively to our understanding of crucial but complex cultural relations. Nevertheless, I argue strongly that the excursion through such sources is very much worth the trip. First, it is clear to any ethnographer or historian working in Ireland that narrative discourse has had a generally important role in expressing and thus defining the way the surrounding world has been perceived. This is clear in a consideration, for example, of the use of "historical" narratives in Northern Ireland. Second, those who have worked in the area of Irish religiosity will also acknowledge the prevalence of such narrative structures in that realm of experience.

Given these observations, it should be profitable to examine the possibility that specific types of religious narrative played particular roles in defining different, and in some cases competing, ways of being religious—what I have called fields of religious experience. Insofar as these different fields often shared a number of religious occasions (e.g., Sunday Mass, Redemptorist Mission, even holy well pilgrimage), their distinctiveness may have rested on their respective ways of talking about such events.

The three narrative segments explored here—the folk story, the magazine piece, and the Redemptorist sermon—do not represent an exhaustive catalogue of distinctive, religious narrative types. They do, however, suggest both the range of religious discourse available in one corner of late nineteenth-century Ireland and the ways in which such forms may have contributed to different fields of religious experience. We are inevitably struck by the differences in language, imagery, and notions of the supernatural. Yet their differences are, of course, meaningful only to the extent that there are similarities among them. All three described where holiness was, how to get at it, and what mediated between people and that world. Thus, they were about the power—what we can call religious power—that resided in particular points of time and/or space. Each text described this mediation differently and, in the course of telling the story, empowered a kind of language to the extent that it succeeded in both describing and, as an aspect of performance, re-creating the miraculous.

Insofar as they are distinctive, these discursively constituted realms can be designated as different fields of religious experience. The folk story issued from what we may call a chthonic, folk field and, given the fact that such narratives were in the late nineteenth and early twentieth centuries (and when I was in the field, still were to a much reduced degree) regularly told and heard in a variety of circumstances, we can presume that they constituted (or were important elements in) a religious discourse that sustained the understanding of the supernatural world that we have discussed in this paper. That religious cosmology may well have enjoyed further moral significance as a metaphoric representation of the human world. Yet it is also clear that in the period to which these stories can be certainly dated—the middle to late nineteenth century—they were not the only sort of religious language encountered by the Catholics of southwest Donegal, or in the rural west of Ireland generally. Another sort of Catholic discourse was embodied in both written and oral texts available to the inhabitants of even such peripheral areas. These texts included sermons delivered in the churches by local and visiting clerics, collections of such sermons by renowned individuals such as Bishop Gallagher in Donegal (an early Gaelic language sermonizer) and Father Burke everywhere (including the Irish American community).[40] There were also those religious texts that reached that local world via devotional pamphlets, books, and popular magazines. All these may be said to have expressed another field of religious experience, a kind of "civil Catholicism" whose supernatural verticality replaced chthonic horizontality.

A consideration and comparison of these texts has allowed me to penetrate, at least to some depth, into the respective religious universes they both described and, to an important extent, generated. The exercise also points up the social and even political potentialities in such texts and the experiences they sought to capture and create: the relation between meaning and power. To the extent that these texts and fields were linked to social formations, both texts and formations may have competed. Especially in periods of rapid social change, the ability of particular narrative forms to make sense of experience is tested, even as new narrative forms are being introduced that resonate with new social realities. This is clear in comparing the narratives we have been exploring here. The folk narrative responded to changing circumstances by sustaining a basic view of power and mediation through incorporating new characters and situations into its story. At the same time, the church's participation in an increasingly vertical world—in terms of class as well as supernatural relations—was expressed in a different sort of narrative: the sermon. For particular individuals, one narrative form may have been more consonant with their experience of power, and if the other language or idiom lost for them its ability to represent the world in this way, it would have been drained of its potency. Thus, the contest was not only between beliefs and devotional forms but between the voices and languages that described and, in a sense, created them. Moreover, since these voices were embodied in particular individuals, groups, settings, and occasions, these too competed through the texts for cultural authority and, as a corollary, for social power.

Thus, the "civil Catholicism," which the other two texts expressed and to some extent helped bring about, involved social as well as supernatural verticality—that is, a new set of class relations. The sermon achieved this by taming and controlling the peasantry; the magazine piece achieved it by contributing to a distanced bourgeois culture and identity. This social task was accomplished, or at least attempted, through the emotional power of religious narrative. The texts performed their functions differently; each had its own form and logic. Thus, the folk stories sought to create a sense of place through powerful imagery of magical intervention. The teller and the listener stood in an egalitarian relation to one another, a relation both created and expressed by an act of communication that did not much privilege the speaker. For the narrator did not put her/himself in a mediatory position relative to divine power—although s/he may have accrued a certain status as mediator of the tradition and hence emblem of the "traditional community." The other forms of discourse explored here were very different in that they both issued from human authority in a more direct and concrete way and represented the speaker or writer (whether person or institution) as all-knowing, in contact with God or Godlike himself. Between the two—the sermon and the magazine piece—there are, however, obvious and great differences. The missioner "instructed" and so used the language of argument. The magazine piece, on the other hand—to use the nineteenth-century idiom—"influenced." In the terms of that central Victorian binary opposition, the sermon was masculine whereas the magazine piece was feminine.

Yet, as we saw, none of the fields or those who dwelt in them have been passive; thus, the competition among them has been complex. In each one, certain elements occurring in the others were appropriated, transformed, and interpreted. Events and experiences were thereby placed within a master narrative whose purpose was to assert the dominance of one way of seeing over another. But to overpower another discourse, each narrative to some extent reproduced it, thus possibly sustaining the enemy with new life. This is clear, for example, in the competing narrative versions of the mission. Thus, we find not an evolutionary layer cake but a dialogical relation between conflicting social and cultural formations—wherein religious discourse, for reasons of its somewhat special historical potency, played an especially vital role. Here is a perfect instance of the mutual reinforcement of meaning and power.

APPENDIX 4.1
REDEMPTORIST SERMON

Today if you hear the voice of the Lord harden not your hearts.

Ps. 94

## Introduction

What voice of God is this? Is it the voice of the Eternal Judge, who sentences you to be thrown into the abyss of hell, thus to depart from him for evermore? No! It is the voice of your merciful Saviour, who visits you today, who invites you to make your peace with him—who offers you the great, extraordinary, rare grace of a mission—"Come" he says "depart not from me—Come to me."

Before the commencement of the Mass you witnessed the opening ceremony[.] This is the acceptable time . . . Jesus Christ hanging on the cross was by your parish priest carried to the entrance of the church to meet us, his ambassadors, as it were—to invite us, to preach the glad tidings of salvation to his people, we kissed the crucifix—we took it and carried it to the altar—"Benedictus Dominus Deus Israel" we sang "Blessed . . . Israel," because he . . . working the redemption of . . . the salvation from our enemies and from the hands of all that hate us. That we may . . . him without fear, in holiness and justice before him all our days (Is. 52.70) O' how beautiful are the feet of him that brings no good tidings and that preacheth peace, of him that showeth forth good, that preacheth salvation, that saith to Sion Thy God shall reign. Yes—Your God shall reign from this day forward—He shall reign in the parish—He shall reign in your family—He shall reign in your hearts—This is the object, this the End of the mission and of our coming: to establish, to confirm, to consolidate, to perfect the reign of God among you. Blessed be the Lord God—If a mission is to succeed well and for this we all are looking forward—If a mission is to be to the glory of God and to the salvation of many in Israel, three parties must work hand in hand—stand side by side, linked heart to heart, must make common cause of this work:

    I. God, who gives you the grace of the mission
   II. The missionaries who preach the mission
  III. The people i.e. you, who get the mission

Therefore, today if you hear the voice of the Lord, "harden not your hearts." Ps. 94 This is the acceptable time—spread it abroad—tell it to everyone and everywhere—on the house tops—in the streets at home—A mission is nothing less than a second Redemption on a small scale—What is a mission? A mission is a divine message, a divine calling—an invitation from on High—Every good gift and every good thing comes from on High, the Father of Lights—For Christ we are ambassadors—The end which God has in view when giving to a parish the grace of a mission is nothing else than the total conversion of the parish—not only the conversion of this or that man or woman, but the conversion of all and each one of us—to extirpate vice and sin—to plant—to plant virtue among the people of the parish—"There is a time to plant says the Holy Ghost and a time to pluck up; a time to build and a time to destroy."

Those who are living in vice and sin are called upon and will be enabled to give up their evil life—those who are slothful, lukewarm, on the point of being cast away from God altogether must take up their first fervour—those who are good and perfect must become better and more perfect still. If the vice of drunkenness prevails in the parish, this vice must be rooted out during the mission—The impurity, sloth neglect of the sacraments and of Holy Mass is to be found in the parish—These must be given up—If people are separated from each other by hatred spite envy jealousy the mission intends to reconcile them—priests and people—one heart and one soul—all—husband and wife, children and parents—In a word God intends to renew the spirit, the face of the whole parish—A great work indeed; a work, which can be done but by God himself—A mission—as I have described it just now—is not a new invention—Missions are as old as the world as old as the church of God—and nowadays missions are so necessary, as useful, as important as they were in times past—There is always something either public or secret which must be amended—God has always been accustomed to send at certain times men, called missionaries, to people, whom he loves, in order to revive their religious spirit—Such missionaries were the prophets of old, Noe, Moses Isaias—Jeremias, Jonas—Noe, whilst building the ark, preached to the people repentance. He gave a mission to them which lasted one hundred years. Jonas the prophet was sent to Ninive—"the Ninivetes could not distinguish the right hand from the left" —"Forty days yet" he cried "and Ninive shall be destroyed" He gave a mission to them—His words sank deep into the hearts of the Ninivetes—At the preaching of Jonas they all did penance in sackcloth and ashes, from the king on the throne down to the beast in the stable—all had been instruments of sin and stumbling blocks—Such a missionary—yea, the greatest, the best, the sublimest of all was our dear Lord, Himself—God who spoke to us at sundry times and in divers manners—in times past through the prophets to our fathers—spoke to us in these days through his own Son Jesus Christ—For three full long weary years he gave a mission to the people of Palestine—"do penance he said, change your life, return to God, for the kingdom of Heaven is at hand,"—And Our Lord after having finished his own mission the work for which he was chosen and sent, chose and sent his apostles, his representatives, to continue his own mission—"Go ye . . ." Again in the course of time God raised special men up for the same purpose—filled them with his own spirit, endowed them with a special lustre of sanctity and of learning—fitted them out and sent them to rescue whole countries and nations from eternal ruin—drawing them out of the abyss of infidelity and immorality—Such men of God were St. Benedict, St. Bernard, St. Francis, St. Dominic, St. . . . . St. Vincent de Paul, and last yet not least of all St. Alphonsus de Ligouri—They walked and worked in the spirit of Elias—And these saints gathered around them disciples—companions according to their own spirit—They founded religious orders, the chief end of which is nothing else, but to continue the work of Jesus Christ, the redemption of mankind—And these orders—these men—this work—have been blessed and approved of, are protected, empowered and highly favoured by the Popes and the Bishops of the Cath. Church—At present God has sent to you the sons of St. Alphonsus, The Redemptorist Fathers, to preach the glad tidings of salvation to preach peace and to offer you pardon. II Cor. 5:20 We are, therefore, as St. Paul says, ambassadors for Christ—God as it were exhorting you by us—For Christ, we beseech you, be ye reconciled to God—Behold now is the acceptable time—behold now is the day of salvation—During the acceptable time of the mission—during these days of salvation, God will shower his graces upon you—The dew of ordinary graces which are at hand at other times, become heavy showers of rain during the mission—There will be no lack or want on the part of God nor will there be any lack or want on our part.

II

The second party which must work for the success of the mission are the missionary fathers—We, too poor feeble men as we are must take a great share in the work Now what is our work? As I have said already, a mission is the continuation of the work of Christ Himself: a second redemption on a small scale—Thus the same as Christ did during his public life we are going to do during the next week. First of all Our Lord preached to the people, to them that were sitting in darkness, in ignorance, in the shadow of death. A light sprang up, the light of the gospel—Thousands flocked to him—followed him even into the desert—to listen to his sermons—And the banks of the river Jordan re-echoed with the voice of the divine missionary—He instructed them about God—their last end—He showed them the way of salvation—the enormity of sin—the obstacles of the way to heaven—So do we—We shall preach to you the same Gospel—the Gospel of Christ—We do not preach a Gospel different from what you have heard and learnt already. This would be heresy—If an angel Came down from heaven to preach another gospel, let him be accursed—do not listen to him—Turn your back upon him—We preach Christ and him crucified I Cor. To the Jews a stumbling block, to the Gentiles foolishness, but to them that are called, to you, brethren—Christ is the power of God and the wisdom of God—We shall preach to you all you must know and do in a short time, and in clear simple language, so that your faith and the knowledge of your faith will be revived and increased in a few weeks. Again Our Lord prayed much for the people, whom, to save he had come down from heaven—Without prayer, without earnest and fervent prayer our preaching will not move you—It will be like sounding brass—It will reach your ear perhaps, but will not penetrate the depth of your hearts—Thus we too shall pray for you and with you throughout the mission—in morning—during Holy Mass—during our work—in the evening esp. we shall offer up the Rosary and after the sermon we shall say together 5 Paters and Aves for the conversion of sinners at the tolling of the bell.—Moreover Our Lord did not only stir the people up—did not only show them the enormity of sin and the abyss of hell as a natural consequence of sin—but he showed them the abyss of his mercy also—He forgave the sins of the people—He conversed with sinners—He led them back to God.—This mission was a mission of mercy—salvation—"I am not come to destroy.". . . . . . Oh! how kind, how merciful was our dear Lord to poor sinners, who with a contrite heart emplored his pardon—The woman caught in the very act of adultery was not rejected or condemmed, but pardoned by him—How mercifully did he treat St. Peter and Matthew, that poor outcast, Mary Magdalene and the very thief hanging on a gibbet—We too shall do the same—follow his example—We are not come to throw you into despair, nor to reject and condemn you—We are among you—to help—to pardon—to save you—There is no sin however great—no crime however enormous which cannot be pardoned during this mission. If your sins were as red as crimson—they will be washed as white as wool, and if they were as numberless as the stars in the sky—they will be blotted out, all without exception, provided you approach us with a contrite and humble heart and the firm will to amend your life—story of Mary Magdalen—story of the woman who died in the chapel—And our Lord fed the people with miraculous bread. He fed them even with his own flesh and blood—He sacrificed himself for the remission of their sins—So shall we do—

The Holy sacrifice of the Mass will be celebrated every day from early in the morning till a late hour.—The Blood and Body of Christ will be offered up for your salvation, yea, all who are anxious and prepared will be nourished day by day with the body of Christ in Holy Communion.—The whole parish—All and each one of you are invited—And as for ourselves we are ready—if necessary—to lay down our very lives—for your salvation—We shall not spare ourselves—We shall work for you—as you soon will see—from early in the morning till late at night—ready to receive everyone—and the poorest—the most miserable of all will be our most cherished children—If we give preference it is to the poor, the abandoned sinners and thus we hope to make ourselves useful instruments in the hand of God—And we rest convinced that the mission will be crowned with the happiest success, if the third party co-operates with God and the missionary fathers.

III

This third party are you my d. br. You, too must do something—and even much during the mission—You must avail yourselves of the grace of the mission—You must come to the mission—You must come regularly, fervently from the very beginning—throughout all the mission—up to the last, morning and evening—If you ask me how many sermons must I hear I must answer—all—How many instructions—all if possible. You must come to the mission in the right spirit—i.e.—in the spirit of repentance—Not because the weather is fine—not because you like to listen to this or that preacher—Not because you meet some friends on the occasion—But because you want the mission—because you are anxious to be instructed—roused and stirred up—anxious to learn to know God and your duties better and to love God more and more—If you do not come to the mission or if you take it carelessly—If you come only when you like and stay away when you please then you will forfeit many a great grace, and to some the mission will be fearful judgment—At the end of the mission God will pronounce a fearful . . . instead of a blessing on such obstinate, reckless people as receive the grace of the mission in vain—In the course of time God sent missionaries to many people and parishes—those who availed themselves of the mission secured their eternal salvation—those who rejected that grace prepared for themselves a more fearful hell than they would have experienced if they had not got mission—This was the case with the people of

Israel—Israel got a three years mission, preached by the Son of God Himself—a better missionary than whom cannot be found either in heaven or on earth—What was the result? Was Israel converted at the end of Christ's mission? No! Israel was obstinate—A few it is true clung to Christ—Yet the nation as such nailed him to the cross—See! this was the result of his mission—The murder of the Son of God— Why? What was the reason—Here is the reason—They did not avail themselves of his mission and did not approach him in the right spirit and thus it came to pass that they got blinder day by day—At the end they would not be converted:— "Jerusalem, Jerusalem. . . . " This will probably be the case of everyone of you, who do not come to the mission—After a time and perhaps ere long—even before the mission is brought to a close—the way to peace and happiness—the grace of conversion will be hidden from your eyes—will be out of your reach—You will have outrun the mercy of God—and then such a reckless man or woman will open his or her eyes—when it is too late—when there is no chance anymore of repentance—in the flames of hell—story—To many this mission will be the last chance and the last extraordinary grace to save their souls—a grace which is offered only every 4 or 5 years is a rare grace—If they do not take advantage of this grace they will die in their sins. The last straw breaks the horse's back—So it is with sin and the neglect and abuse of sin—in the lifetime of St. Alphonsus, a man, who was given to drink and neglected his duty was called upon to come to the mission—What did he answer to the invitation? Being in a public house at the time he took a glass filled with drink "This is my mission" he said raising the glass to empty it—But it never touched his lips—Before he could put it to his lips he dropped down dead—Where was he going at that time? Not to the mission, but to hell forever—(the man in Coatbridge)—Today if you hear the merciful invitation of God—harden not your hearts. Now is the acceptable time, now is the day of salvation—Receive not this grace in vain, but avail yourselves of it as much as you can—Who avails himself of the mission?—Who will profit by it? Who will make a good mission. Mark well! it is . . .

APPENDIX 4.2
THE PEASANT AT THE SHRINE

Twas a calm evening in summer. A peasant went forth to a sequestered wood, to perform his devotions at a shrine of the Virgin Mary.

From *Duffy's Fireside Magazine* 5, no. 3 (1853), Dublin.

He knelt before an altar, on which there was an effigy of our Lady, and ornamented with those simple charms which artless piety is wont so happily to suggest. Then, in the depth of solitude, he chanted a hymn of love, and offered to the Queen of Heaven the outpourings of a devoted soul. Near the shrine there was a river, whose gentle murmurs seemed to harmonize with the peasant's song. The moments sped swiftly as he prayed. Tears fell from his eyes, but they were joyous tears, emanating from the heart, that peerless fountain of eternal love. The glowing sunbeam was on the wane, and the peasant, revolving past memories, and inspired with hopeful visions of the future, sank into a dreamy reverie.

The legend relates, that a spirit, attracted by his song, and captivated by the beaming smiles that played about his lips, solicited him to dwell in the land of spirits beneath the river's bed. Indignant, he scorned the proposal, and swooned away. At midnight it was discovered that his soul, no longer fettered by earthly ties, had winged its flight to the home of everlasting peace. The foresters say that heavenly music is often heard swelling on the breeze, and sometimes at the still hour of midnight, the Virgin comes in glory to keep watch over the peasant's tomb:

> Far on a green and mossy glade the Virgin's altar stood,
> And around it waved the countless trees of a deep and lonely wood;
> Hard by, a noble river roll'd down its sparkling sand,
> And sunbeams dance upon its wave like nymphs of fairyland.
>
> The passing breeze played calmly o'er the water's crystal sheen,
> And murmured soft, sweet melodies to heaven's Virgin Queen;
> The wide-spread boughs of the forest trees were mirror'd deep below,
> And brightly shone their trembling leaves in the evening's golden glow.
>
> Vases of wild, but holy flow'rs, from mountain, stream, and dale,
> Of roses fair, and violets bright, and lilies of the vale,
> Bloom'd sweetly on the altar of her who reigns on high,
> And their odours wafted fragrance to the clear and tranquil sky.
>
> A censer fil'd with sweetest gums was swinging there the while,
> And a taper shed its chast'ning light, pure as an angel's smile.
> The ev'ning sun was sinking fast beneath the torrent's rill,
> While his parting smiles, o'er the mountain's brow, wax'd faint and
>     fainter still.
>
> A peasant knelt on the woodland sward, with tearful eyes and dim,
> Pouring to heaven a gladsome strain—'twas Mary's ev'ning hymn:
> "No wealth," he sigh'd, "is mine to give—no gems to deck thy shrine,
> But this heart, my sole, sole treasure, is thine—for ever thine."

Bright visions of the happy world flash'd o'er his raptur'd breast,
And he long'd to soar to those blissful climes where the weary are at
    rest;
Still, as the thrilling song he breath'd died faintly through the wood,
Its echoes wak'd the river spirits that slumber'd 'neath the flood.

Now, as he gaz'd on the Virgin's form, nor thought of else beside,
A spirit, gliding o'er the wave, sprang forth from the streaming tide:
In tones of mell'd music, straight it whisper'd words of love,
But the peasant still pray'd fondly, for his thoughts were far above.

"Come to my home," the phantom cried,
Beneath the roar of the deep, deep tide;
Follow me—follow thy spirit-guide.

"Chaplets of coral I'll wreathe for thee,
And the rolling river thy shrine shall be;
Child of earth, then follow me.

"I'll sing thee a sweet, a heavenly air,
Nor trouble shall dim thine eyes, nor care,
But joys the purest shall greet thee there!

"Soft music of waters shall glad thine ear,
Sounds which spirits alone may hear,
More sweet than the lov'd song of childhood's year!

"Pearls the choicest will grace thy throne,
Supreme thou'lt rule 'neath the dashing foam;
Come then oh! come, to my spirit home."

When the peasant heard those silv'ry tones, a frown rose on his brow;
Fainting he shrank from the phantom's clasp—his heart was Mary's
    now!
When the chilling breeze of midnight blew coldly o'er the deep,
The woodmen found him smiling in a calm and breathless sleep.

The song of the river spirit, by that wood is heard no more,
But Mary's hymn still echoes, bounding softly from the shore;
And oft on a summer's midnight, when moonbeams light the wave,
The Virgin, cloth'd in fairest robes, leans o'er the peasant's grave.

F. K. P.

## NOTES

1. The field and archival research on which this article is mainly based
was conducted from July 1986 through July 1987 and in the summer of 1989.
It was made possible by a fellowship from the U.S. National Endowment
for the Humanities and a research grant from Lafayette College. This article

is part of a more general study of local religious life (for a book in progress), based on participant observation and extensive interviews in the area, as well as archival research particularly in the Redemptorist Library, the National Library, and the National Folklore Archive, both in Dublin. My work on religion follows from a long-standing research interest in the area that began with several months fieldwork in 1973, further fieldwork through most of 1976, and occasional return visits. Other aspects of local history and ethnography are treated in Taylor (1980a, 1980b, 1981, 1985, 1987). This paper has profited greatly from the comments, suggestions, and assistance of the participants at the Conference on Anthropology and History held in 1989 and from Maeve Hickey Taylor, Seamus Ó Catháin, Father Brendan McConvery CssR, Howard Schneiderman, Pat Donoghue, and the editors of this volume.

2. *Roinn Béaloideas* V.142.

3. "The Peasant at the Shrine," F.K.P 1853.

4. From "Mission Sermons," undated (likely the last decades of nineteenth century). Notebook of the Redemptorist Order, Marianella House, Dublin.

5. Foucault (1972:21–71).

6. On the ritual orientation of folk religious studies in Europe see, for example, Badone (1990) and Christian (1972).

7. For classificatory studies see Ó Súilleabhain (1951); for more interpretive studies see Glassie (1983) and Ó Healái (1974–76, 1977).

8. Rather, it has been in the area of social structure and organization that most mutual interaction has taken place.

9. See, for example, Connolly (1982).

10. See, for example, among historians, the works of Davis, Brown, Ginzburg, Sabean, and Burke and among anthropologists, those of Christian, Schneider, and Bax.

11. See Taylor (1989a, 1989b, 1990a, 1990b).

12. Taylor (1990b) has the fullest treatment of the concept of fields of religious experience.

13. See Bax (1987).

14. See Taylor (1980b).

15. In fact, the absence of a significant group of landless laborers in such communities made them very different from towns in other regions of Ireland. For a most marked contrast see Silverman and Gulliver (1986) and Silverman, this volume.

16. Ginzburg (1980).

17. See Buchanan (1970) and Taylor (1980a).

18. Larkin (1972).

19. See Elias (1978, 1982) and Inglis (1987).

20. See Taylor (1985).

21. Turner (1982:72f).

22. Brown, Peter (1981).

23. After the famine, a decreased population, especially among the poor-

est classes, allowed for a much higher priest/parishioner ratio and hence more effective social control of a population much more likely to acquiesce.

24. Larkin (1972).

25. See Logan (1980). My knowledge of both wells is based on fieldwork in the region.

26. Author's field notes.

27. See Taylor (1985, 1990a) on the theme of replacing the clergy as the enemy with Protestants.

28. See Taylor (1990a).

29. See Taylor (1989a).

30. See Whelan (1988b).

31. Faction fights were a commonly reported feature of rural Irish life involving ritualized battles between local groups. Early mission records reveal an interest in such matters.

32. Verrips (1987).

33. Inglis (1987).

34. An extract was given at page 143. A fuller text is given in appendix 4.1.

35. McGlinchey (1986).

36. Lough Derg is a small lake in County Donegal, near the Fermanagh border; Station Island is in the middle of the lake. Penitential pilgrims have been going there for centuries. Currently, about thirty thousand per year come and stay for three days of fasting and sleepless rounds of prayer.

37. See Elias (1978, 1982) and Inglis (1987).

38. O'Laoghaire (1982).

39. See Christian (1981) for a discussion of "localized versus generalized devotions."

40. Bishop Gallagher's sermons were published in Irish toward the end of the eighteenth century and reprinted at intervals through the nineteenth century. Father Thomas Burke's sermons, delivered in Ireland and America, were famous through the period and available in many editions.

5

# Shopkeepers and Farmers in South Kilkenny, 1840–1981

■

## P. H. GULLIVER

In this essay I examine the relations between shopkeepers and farmers during the nineteenth and twentieth centuries in one locality in south-eastern Ireland. My focus, however, is principally upon the shopkeepers. In particular, I take two propositions—two notions that seem to have been fairly commonly accepted about the history of rural Ireland—concerning the connections between these two occupational categories of people. One proposition is that shopkeepers have been largely recruited from farm families and they and their children have tended to marry into farm families.[1] As a result, it has been held, shopkeepers and farmers have been closely linked by kinship and have had, and still have, mutually dependent and supportive relationships with each other that excluded other members of rural society. The second proposition is that shopkeepers have been men of influence and local leaders in public affairs, in part because of those close linkages and by virtue of their entrepreneurial experience but also as they have pursued their own interests and as a result of pressures from local people.[2] Both propositions have come principally from historical studies in western counties, although they also occur in folk cultural models.

My present intent is to examine these propositions by reference to detailed information at a local level in order to see how far they have been applicable there and with what reservations and modifications. The locale of inquiry is Thomastown in County Kilkenny, some ten miles south of the city of Kilkenny.

The archival records used for this purpose relate to the period 1840–1981. They include registers of marriages and baptisms (and genealogies constructed from them), county newspapers, minute books of the Thomastown Board of Guardians and Rural District Council, surviving wills and deeds, land and property records, and commercial directories. In addition, I use shop, farm, and family histories, together with some family papers and shop account books and a variety of information garnered from living people through open-ended interviews, participant observation, and general ethnographic inquiry in the locality. The quantity and validity of information are, of course, poorest for the earlier decades of the period, but it is reasonably dependable, although often incomplete, at least from 1870 onward.[3] Unfortunately, it has been impossible to discover some of the kinds of archival data much used by historians: estate records, letters, diaries, travelers' accounts, and official local inquiries. Thus, it is impossible to augment my skeletal outline with the observations of participants in earlier times in the particular activities described in this essay. This major lacuna, important enough in itself, is particularly distressing to an anthropologist accustomed to the availability of rich information at the local level.

Thomastown was founded in the twelfth century as a defensive and trading center. Since at least the eighteenth century, the "town" has comprised a cluster of short streets bisected by the river Nore. There have been no administrative or other boundaries around the town: it gradually faded out along approach and side roads. Its approximate population was about 2,350 in 1841; it gradually decreased to about 770 in 1936 and thereafter increased to about 1,300 by 1981. Somewhat larger numbers of people lived within a radius of four or five miles. These included farmers (some 200 in 1841, about 100 in 1981) and skilled, unskilled, and clerical workers and their families. Together with "town" residents, they were the main customers for the shops that have been concentrated, among residences and workshops, in the central part of the town. However, some specialist shops, such as those selling hardware, farmers' supplies, specialty goods, and pharmaceuticals, attracted customers from greater distances. Thomastown has been a railway town since 1848 and was the center of a Poor Law Union and later, of a Rural District, which it remained until 1926. Petty and Quarter Sessions were held in the courthouse in preindependence times. Thereafter, there was a district court.

In 1846, there were forty-one shops, excluding tiny huckster shops but including retail establishments, pubs, and shops where artisan-proprietors worked and sold their goods directly to the public. In 1911, there were thirty-nine shops. Thereafter, although earlier artisans' shops (e.g., bootmakers, saddlers) disappeared, being unable to compete with imported factory-made goods, the total number of shops slowly increased with the introduction of new retail establishments. In 1981 there were forty-five shops. Only a few shops, tiny and ephemeral, have been located outside the town, and the last of these closed by the 1960s.

Local opinion in the 1980s was that Thomastown's shops "were always small" in comparison with some of the larger establishments in Kilkenny and Waterford. At the turn of the century, for example, a prosperous pub-grocery occupied a space of some fifteen by twenty feet; another long-established but less prosperous pub measured eight by six feet, including the bar. Although two larger, supermarket-type shops were begun in the early 1970s, most shops have remained small. Pubs and groceries have predominated, but there have always been draperies, bakeries, butcheries, and shops selling hardware and building and agricultural supplies. Twentieth-century additions have been newsagents, chemists, and businesses dealing in electrical goods and in the automobile trade (petrol, spares, repairs, cars). Thomastown's shops have been able to supply almost all the requirements of the local population. Even in 1981, in response to a survey questionnaire, people expressed strong preference for these shops for most purposes, although about two-thirds of all households had a car, which gave them access to more numerous shops in the cities of Kilkenny and Waterford.

## The Family Origins of Shopkeepers: Paternal Linkages

In considering the linkages and relations between shopkeepers and farmers, it is convenient to look first at family origins. Thus, it is possible to see to what extent shopkeepers have come from farm families, bearing a natal kinship linkage between farm and shop.

In the following account, for convenience and simplicity, I distinguish between "larger" and "smaller" shops by reference to size of business and apparent profitability. This assessment is crude and impressionistic, but it allows me to suggest some pertinent generalizations while avoiding the implication that all businesses and their proprietors have been alike in socioeconomic characteristics. The term *shopkeeper* can only be roughly descriptive of occupation and should not indicate a solidary class.[4]

Family origins can be indicated by the occupations of the fathers of shopkeepers, using simple occupational categories of shopkeeper, farmer, artisan, and laborer. Table 5.1 gives data on all "smaller" and "larger" proprietors (but excluding ephemeral hucksters) for four selected years from 1884 to 1981.[5] The largest category of proprietors throughout the period comprised sons and daughters of shopkeepers—falling from about two-thirds to one-half of the totals over the hundred-year period (ignoring the small categories of unknown and other occupations). This is scarcely surprising in view of the strong normative and practical emphasis on inheritance.[6] The second-largest category of shopkeepers came from farm families: rising slightly during the period from one-quarter of the total in 1884. They have been concentrated, although not exclusively, in the larger shops. The large majority of them, in shops of all sizes, were complete newcomers to shopkeeping when they began in business (i.e., they had not inherited from a previous proprietor, although one or two in each of the years were heirs [typically matrilaterally] to going concerns). A third category of proprietors comprised children of artisans or laborers, mainly but not exclusively in the smaller shops. In total, they increased from one-eighth to about one-fifth of all proprietors during the period. Thus, there is a general pattern in which the proportions of shopkeepers coming from farm, artisan, and laborer families increased a little, while those from shop families correspondingly decreased. Sons and daughters of farmers have been numerically significant, particularly in the larger shops, but they were not nearly a majority.

Despite the local emphasis on inheritance, at least a half of all shops in each selected year did not pass to the heirs of the preceding proprietors. Either there were no children or other acceptable kin to inherit and continue the business or existing children did not do so because of commitment to other careers or refusal to become shopkeepers. Moreover, it has been even less common for a shop to persist into a third generation or more—about one in seven during the nineteenth century, increasing to about one in five in this century. Yet since 1884 at least, failure to inherit has not resulted in a reduction in the number of active businesses for more than a brief period. This has meant that

Table 5.1

The Family Origins of Shopkeepers

Occupations of Fathers of All Shop Proprietors in Selected Years

| Father's occupation | 1884 | 1911 | | 1945 | | 1981 | |
|---|---|---|---|---|---|---|---|
| | All | Small | Large | Small | Large | Small | Large |
| Shopkeeper | 19 | 2 | 15 | 7 | 14 | 8 | 13 |
| Farmer | 8 | 1 | 8 | 3 | 9 | 4 | 9 |
| Artisan | 1 | 2 | 2 | 3 | 1 | 2 | 1 |
| Laborer | 3 | 4 | 2 | 1 | 0 | 2 | 5 |
| Other | 3 | 0 | 0 | 2 | 0 | 0 | 1 |
| Unknown | 3 | 3 | 0 | 0 | 1 | 0 | 0 |
| Subtotals | | 12 | 27 | 16 | 25 | 19 | 26 |
| Totals | 37 | 39 | | 41 | | 45 | |

In all tables (1) proprietors of the very smallest ("huckster") shops are excluded; (2) shopkeepers in business in a particular year began as proprietors at various times in the preceding twenty years or more.

there has been a continuous supply of noninheriting newcomers who either purchased existing businesses or began new shops in converted or constructed premises.

Table 5.2 gives data on the family origins of these new recruits (noninheriting newcomers) to shopkeeping. Here the pattern is less clear. Children (mainly sons) of farmers have consistently comprised the largest category through the years, but they were never a majority. The cases of unknown origin in the earlier years may have obscured these results. However, research experience strongly suggests that farmers' children have always been better remembered and recorded than others. Therefore, the figures for children with farm origins may well be correct enough, whereas those for children with artisanal and laboring origins may be too small.

The picture is clearer if we look only at new recruits to the larger shops: broadly speaking, rather more than half came from farm families. Conversely, fewer complete newcomers in the smaller shops have had farm origins. This in itself is to be expected, if only because of the greater availability of capital and credit to farmers' children. It may be added that virtually all the proprietors of the tiny ("huckster") shops were of laboring origin.[7] Nevertheless, in noting this pattern, it would be simplistic and misleading to conclude that all recruits to the larger shops came from farm families and remained successful in their businesses while recruits to smaller shops came from other families and continued on a small scale. The practical facts are that in each selected year—indeed, at all times since the 1840s, as far as is known—there were one or two smaller shopkeepers who had come from farm families; and there were two or three larger shopkeepers who originated in artisanal or laboring families and had been able to expand their businesses to a larger scale. In addition, there have always been a few noninheriting recruits from other shop families.

The sons (and occasionally daughters) of farmers who became shopkeepers were, of course, invariably not heirs to the parental farms. Farmers have acknowledged and, as far as possible, practiced parental responsibility to provide for noninheriting sons and daughters. While daughters were expected to marry, one possibility for a son has been to assist him to train as a shop assistant with the hope that in due course he would acquire a shop of his own. There have been other options, however—principally to assist a son to emigrate to find employment (typically to North America) or to assist him to acquire skills and thus entry to better-paid employment.[8]

Other sons remained as laborers on the farm or locally, and some

Table 5.2

Complete Newcomers to Shopkeeping

The Occupations of Fathers of Shop Proprietors Who Did Not Inherit Their Businesses

| Father's occupation | 1884 | | 1911 | | 1945 | | 1981 | |
|---|---|---|---|---|---|---|---|---|
| | Small | Large | Small | Large | Small | Large | Small | Large |
| Shopkeeper* | 1 | 0 | 1 | 2 | 2 | 5 | 4 | 4 |
| Farmer | 1 | 3 | 1 | 7 | 3 | 9 | 3 | 8 |
| Artisan | 0 | 1 | 1 | 2 | 2 | 1 | 0 | 1 |
| Laborer | 3 | 1 | 2 | 1 | 1 | 0 | 4 | 3 |
| Other | 0 | 1 | 0 | 1 | 2 | 0 | 0 | 0 |
| Unknown | 2 | 1 | 3 | 0 | 0 | 1 | 1 | 0 |
| Totals | 14 | | 21 | | 26 | | 28 | |

*In these cases the proprietors did not inherit their parents' shops but began new businesses.

were fortunate enough to obtain a farm by other inheritance or by marriage. Thus, the route to shopkeeping has been but one possibility, and although perfectly respectable, it has been the least favored in practice, perhaps because it required a larger financial commitment. Farmers have very seldom assisted more than one son to become a shopkeeper. Since 1840, the large majority of local farm families, on both larger and smaller farms, have never supplied a son to shopkeeping.

In brief, recruitment to shopkeeping from farm families has been continuously important—especially for the larger shops. However, there has always been a majority of proprietors, in both larger and smaller shops, who did not come from farms and who were not, therefore, directly linked in that way to farmers. Only a minority of local farmers have been so linked.

### Marital and Matrilateral Linkages Between Shopkeepers and Farmers

In addition to the linkages created between some shopkeepers and farmers as farmers' sons entered shopkeeping, a second kind of connection has been through marriage and the consequent creation of kinship ties. Among people in both occupational categories, the prevailing ideology has been one of farmer-shopkeeper endogamy in keeping with the continuing notion that people and their children in those two occupations have been approximately equal in social status and superior to artisans, laborers, and those in clerical and semi-professional occupations. Table 5.3 gives data on shopkeepers' marriages. The numbers are too small for more than tentative conclusions to be drawn. Although farmers' daughters have constituted the largest single category of shopkeepers' spouses—the strongest preference among shopkeepers—they were never a clear majority during the last hundred years or more. Adequate figures are unavailable for shopkeepers' marriages in the earlier years of the nineteenth century, but the indications are that they were much the same in proportion. Shopkeepers and their sons, therefore, seem consistently to have desired to marry a farmer's daughter. Such marriages brought in dowries that were valuable for business purposes and created potentially useful kinship links. Moreover, deliberately or not, those marriages substantiated shopkeepers' claims to status and equality with farmers.

The data in Table 5.3 also suggest that the overt rule of status-class

Table 5.3

Shopkeepers' Spouses

| Shopkeepers active in | Fathers of Spouses | | | | | Totals |
|---|---|---|---|---|---|---|
| | Shopkeeper | Farmer | Artisan | Laborer | Other | |
| 1884 | 9 | 12 | 2 | 3 | 1 | 27 |
| 1911 | 11 | 9 | 4 | 5 | 2 | 31 |
| 1945 | 5 | 16 | 3 | 2 | 5 | 31 |
| 1981 | 8 | 11 | 2 | 7 | 3 | 31 |

Spouses include either wives or husbands as relevant. Shopkeepers who were widow-heirs are included as spouses.

endogamy has been breached fairly frequently. Something like a fifth of all shopkeepers married daughters of artisans and laborers during the last one hundred years. In these cases, however, the shopkeepers were most usually themselves the sons of artisans or laborers; indeed, the proportion of apparently "unorthodox" marriages is similar to that of such shopkeepers. In part, this has been the result of the practical fact that most of these shopkeepers were already married to a woman of the lower status-class by the time they moved into shopkeeping. However, such a shopkeeper maintained kinship connections and general contacts with people of that lower status and was commonly considered to remain in that status despite his new occupation. Even the successful proprietor of this type, let alone the one whose business remained small, was unable to gain acceptance of equality from established shopkeepers and farmers; therefore, he and his sons did not—one might say, could not—marry their daughters. Mere success in business was scarcely enough, at least until the third generation; but like all shop businesses, relatively few of these persisted into a third generation.

The smaller shopkeeper with a farming or established shopkeeping background also sometimes married down, but more often, he or his son was able to maintain a semblance of status by marrying the daughter of a small farmer or a small shopkeeper to whom he was acceptable. In short, the practical rule of status endogamy referred, on the one hand, to medium and larger farmers and larger, established shopkeepers (particularly those who had farming origins) and, on the other hand, to laborers, artisans, and smaller shopkeepers.

So unusual and traumatic were breaches of this narrower rule that such cases were well remembered in the 1980s, even from times before elderly people were born. Where the breach involved the heir to a larger shop—or to a farm—it resulted in parental disinheritance of the wilful, errant son, even though sometimes he was later reinstated. It was less traumatic in the case of a noninheriting son, although nevertheless disapproved, and it often resulted in weakened kinship relations.

Matrilateral links have been more important than affinal ones in creating relations between shopkeepers and farmers. As a result of their fathers' marriages, about two-thirds of the larger shopkeepers in 1911, 1945, and 1981 had mothers who had come from farm families. These were either women married to farmers whose sons had moved into shopkeeping or women married to shopkeepers whose sons had inherited the retail business.[9] The proportions of smaller shopkeepers with matrilateral links to farmers were about one-third during the same period.

Given these data, what can be concluded about the kinship connections between shopkeepers and farmers? It is reasonable to say that, over the decades, a significant proportion of shopkeepers—and in particular, of larger shopkeepers—through birth and marriage have been connected with farmers by paternal, matrilateral, and affinal ties (and combinations of these ties). Moreover, within the limitations established by the rule of status endogamy, shopkeepers and farmers have been willing to acknowledge approximate equality of status and some commonality. These conclusions and their implications must, however, be treated cautiously

First, and most important, farmers in the locality outnumbered shopkeepers by a factor of at least six to one in the mid-nineteenth century, decreasing to about two to one in the last quarter of this century.[10] Therefore, alliances through marriage and subsequent kinship have been made *only* between some shopkeepers and a minority of farmers. That is to say, these linkages must not be emphasized too greatly, especially not for farmers.

Second, it has been rare for the heir to a larger farm to marry a shopkeeper's daughter; he has ordinarily and preferably married another farmer's daughter. This has consistently limited the number of farmers directly linked to shopkeepers. Moreover, both noninheriting sons of shopkeepers, some of whom married farmers' daughters, and noninheriting sons of larger farmers, some of whom married shopkeepers' daughters, generally migrated away, and thus kinship ties were attenuated or even virtually lost.

Third, linkages by marriage and kinship did not necessarily prescribe close cooperative relations. This must be emphasized if only because it has sometimes been assumed in the literature that a genealogical connection creates some more or less automatic relationship along with rights and obligations. Rather, such a linkage in Thomastown involved a propensity to friendship and mutual assistance that might or might not become important. A friendly and prosperous farmer kinsman could certainly have been valuable to a shopkeeper. For example, in some cases, the farmer agreed to act as surety when the shopkeeper required a loan from a wholesaler or other supplier of credit, and a few farmers themselves even advanced money. Yet this did not always happen, if only because not all farmers had the means. More generally, a shopkeeper was, through marriage, potentially brought into a local network of farmers. This not only validated his claim to status but gave him access to information and opportunities to gain influence. Again, however, this did not invariably work out in practice; in any case, farmers' networks were often quite localized, thus offering only limited potentialities for shopkeepers.

Fourth, although the more successful, established shopkeepers have increasingly become accepted as equal in status by larger farmers there has continued to be ambivalence, with reservations on both sides. Each has considered the other to be not quite the same, translating differences of lifestyle and diversity of interests into uncertainties of assessment. Thus, at least in the twentieth century, each has ascribed a slightly lower status to the other. Although this has not noticeably hindered marriages, it has limited—or expressed limits to—relations between shopkeepers and farmers.

Fifth, success in shopkeeping has not necessarily involved kinship links with farmers. This can be demonstrated by taking the half dozen largest and most prosperous shop businesses in each of the four selected years. Most of these businesses were owned and managed by the sons of shopkeepers who had inherited them from their parents and who had expanded both their retail and nonretail activities. Inheritance of a going concern was never, of course, an inevitable prescription for success, and many heirs merely kept the business going or saw it shrink. However, the absence of a farm family background or connection appears to have been no great obstacle to business achievement. In 1884 and in 1945, there were two farmer's sons among the most successful shopkeepers; there were none in 1911 and one in 1981. Moreover, business success was not necessarily accompanied by marriage to a farmer's daughter. Such marriages did not occur for four out of the six in 1911, for five in 1945, or for three in 1981. These men married mainly the daughters of shopkeepers or other businessmen. The sample is, of course, small but sufficient to make the point that major business success has not necessarily been associated with close linkages with farmers. I suggest, though I cannot prove, that such linkages were not thought necessary to business success per se and to the status it afforded.[11] Perhaps it was those who were rather less successful who sought to bolster their positions by linkages with farmers.

## Other Connections Between Shopkeepers and Farmers

Another connection between members of the two occupational categories came, formerly, from the employment by shopkeepers of farmers' sons as assistants. Until fairly recently, assistants were rarely employed in the smaller shops, so that such connections were not made with farmers. In contrast, larger shops have always had at least one assistant, and in the nineteenth century and until about 1960, most of these were farmers' sons. Not all were from local farms and did not, therefore, bring the potential of active relations between farmer and shopkeeper. As far as can now be discovered, taking a farmer's son as trainee or full assistant was not necessarily a business strategy to link the shopkeeper with the assistant's kin as customers.[12] It could scarcely have worked that way, if only because many came from a distance, beyond the range of regular customers; and assistants often did not stay for long before they moved to other employment or into their own shops. Account books from earlier in this century do not indicate any strong customer loyalty deriving from this sort of connection. Shopkeepers have explained that farmers' sons were employed because they were sufficiently available. Some farmers could afford to pay for a son's apprenticeship or to subsidize a son on a low wage; but artisans and laborers were unable to do that, even had their children been acceptable. Shopkeepers have also claimed that sons and daughters of farmers and shopkeepers were to be more trusted to do the work and not to divulge information about the business. In practice, it seems probable that in large part this was a distancing strategy against people of laboring status and a claim to equal status with farmers. Only the employees in unskilled work came from lower-status families: "porters," who did the heavy and cleaning jobs, and delivery men. That prejudice has only disappeared in the last decade or so; by 1981, virtually all shop assistants were wage-earning sons or daughters of artisans, laborers, and clerical workers or of the shopkeepers themselves. At the same time, farmers' sons no longer sought to become shop assistants: other than farming, these men had come to prefer training that led to skilled, semiprofessional employment.

Shopkeepers and farmers have always had different life-styles and economic interests. Few individuals have shifted from one category to the other or have belonged to both. Since at least the 1840s (but probably earlier) and until 1979, there was only a single case where a farmer became a shopkeeper in Thomastown: the heir to a small farm sold it and used the proceeds to purchase a pub. In 1979, a local, very large farmer purchased a shop (to provide for a young, noninheriting son), which he managed in addition to his farm; and in the same year another local farmer inherited a small pub from an unmarried, putative distant cousin. These latter cases seem unlikely to have set a precedent.

Similarly, the large majority of shopkeepers, including the largest and most prosperous, have consistently not seen farmland and farming as opportunities for the investment of profits and entrepreneurial expansion. This has been the case whether or not they themselves had come from farm families and irrespective of changes in land prices and the relative prosperity of farming. At any one time in the last 140 years, only two or three shopkeepers were also active farmers—that is, beyond the possession of a few "town acres" for a horse and a cow or two.[13] Only one shopkeeper in the present century purchased land as an investment for later resale and with no intention of farming. Earlier this century, but not in the nineteenth century or in the later twentieth century, one or two prosperous shopkeepers purchased farmland to provide for a son who would not inherit the shop business. Indeed, when occasionally a shopkeeper or his wife inherited a farm, the subsequent choice was to sell the shop and to take to full-time farming. In only one case did a shopkeeper continue his business after inheriting a farm.

Shopkeepers and farmers alike have considered the two occupations to be incompatible because they involved different life-styles and skills—and often distant locations—that were not easily combined. For the shopkeeper, it seems to have been easier and more attractive to invest and expand into another retail line, artisanal production, or the provision of services (i.e., into "urban" activities) than into farming. Additionally, both shopkeepers and farmers have often chosen to put their money into their children's education and careers and into small financial investments. Consequently, there has been little overlapping of economic activities and interests among the two groups and, in that sense, no development of commonality. Insofar as individual farmers were valued customers—and by no means were they all—their prosperity was important to shopkeepers. Conversely, the goodwill of shopkeepers was important to farmers who needed longer-term credit than was ordinarily available to other customers.

The evidence does not suggest marked importance on either count.

## Summary: Patterns of Recruitment and Marriage

There have been limited linkages and active relations between shop-keepers and farmers in the Thomastown locality. They have never been universal or necessarily strong. Insofar as they have been impor-tant, they have concerned mainly the larger shopkeepers. An obvious point, but too often neglected by local people and historians alike in their generalized statements and usage of the occupational labels, is that shopkeepers—and for that matter, farmers—have not constituted a solidary social class. I seek to take account of that by a crude dichotomy of "larger" and "smaller" shopkeepers. From this emerge some of the general patterns through the last 120 years or more. The connections between larger shopkeepers and farmers have not been absolute, but they have been distinctive. This has resulted from the fact that recruitment to shopkeeping from farm families has been predominantly in the larger businesses. Similarly, marriage and kin-ship connections and the employment of assistants have involved principally the larger shopkeepers. However, it is important to note that kinship relations between larger shopkeepers and farmers have not been invariably close in practice. Moreover, only a minority of local farmers, of whatever size, have been involved in these ways, and not all larger shopkeepers. Most smaller shopkeepers have had no formal linkages at all with farmers. Therefore, it is necessary to be cautious in generalizing and to avoid giving too great an emphasis to the significance of farmer-shopkeeper linkages and relations.

## Shopkeepers and Public Affairs, 1840–1922

In this and the following section, I examine the participation of Thomastown shopkeepers in public affairs and assess the significance of the connections between shopkeepers and farmers as they affected that participation. Let me begin by quoting the generalization of one social scientist that seems to express a fairly typical view of rural Ireland: "Shopkeepers and publicans were people who supported the Leagues with leadership . . . partly to further the interests of the rank and file, partly to further their own interests and partly because they were forced by circumstances and by the community."[14]Although this statement referred to the last quarter of the nineteenth century, the viewpoint has been widely applied in time and space. However, in the Thomastown area, in the nineteenth century and later, shopkeepers had little public influence and certainly were neither organizers nor leaders.

Thomastown shopkeepers were not members of official government bodies in the nineteenth century—baronial grand juries, magistracy, and after 1850, the Board of Guardians of the Poor Law Union. These bodies were dominated by local gentry until the early 1880s. By that time the Board of Guardians had effectively become the major local government authority over a region in which the population of Thomastown parish comprised about one-fifth. After 1881, members of the gentry held no Board offices and seldom even attended meetings. The board's offices and proceedings were thereafter monopolized by larger farmers. In 1883, about half of the elected members of the board farmed more than one hundred acres. Thomastown "town" (where shopkeepers were located) was divided between two electoral districts (local constituencies for the election of members). Each of these districts included extensive rural areas and, with a predominantly farmer electorate, consistently returned two farmers who, by informal arrangement, were unopposed candidates. Only in 1891 was the proprietor of a hardware shop elected, but perhaps more significantly, he was also the owner of a flourishing tannery and a small farm. When the new Rural District Council was first elected in 1899, a little over half of the councillors were farmers with more than one hundred acres and another quarter farmed more than fifty acres.[15] With an extended suffrage, two Thomastown shopkeepers were also elected and a third (the tanner) was temporarily coopted. Only one continued for long as a councillor, although he was joined by two others for a couple of years in 1908. Neither he nor they were prominent in council activities.

As elsewhere in rural Ireland, both the Board of Guardians (after the early 1880s) and the later Rural District Council were more than organs of local government. Each provided a public forum for expressing political and social opinion and was, therefore, of some importance as anti-Ascendancy sentiment, nationalist strength, and agitation increased. Moreover, as Feingold pointed out, the boards effectively provided training and experience in administrative and political operations.[16] Shopkeepers had little or no part in this, as demonstrated in both the minute books and local newspaper reports.

At the unofficial level of political action, a few shopkeepers in 1844 were briefly involved in local support of O'Connell's antiunion movement. In addition, about half supported a gentry initiative to restore cargo carrying on the river Nore to the old terminal in Thomastown—an unsuccessful attempt to stimulate commercial activity. Thereafter, as far as the records go, shopkeepers played only a minor part in famine relief actions or in other public activities. Parish priests secured more financial assistance for various ecclesiastical and charitable purposes from individual shopkeepers than they obtained from farmers; but shopkeepers were principally submitting to clerical pressure and accepting the opportunities to demonstrate their status by their public contributions. They were scarcely involved in the activities themselves.

As in Leinster generally, Thomastown was late in starting a branch of the Land League; it did not do so until the end of 1880. At the inaugural meeting, attended by political activists from all over southern Kilkenny County, a few shopkeepers were present, but none were reported as prominent. At only two of the subsequent meetings was a single shopkeeper reported as being present, and according to the newspaper accounts, he did not speak. In 1882, the founding meeting of the National League branch was chaired by a larger shopkeeper who also farmed some fifty acres. Nine farmers were the other participants. The same shopkeeper chaired the second meeting two months later, but after that the chair was taken by a farmer. He was apparently too conservative for the tastes of the radical farmers and received no overt support from other shopkeepers, although occasionally one or two attended subsequent meetings.

There seems little question that shopkeepers' participation was slight and that it did not involve them as organizers, let alone as leaders. It is clear that branch meetings were little concerned with local or urban issues that might have attracted shopkeeper interest. The consistent concern for nationalist, political, ideological expression, and the underlying demands for land reform did not engage the few shopkeeper attenders. As in the board of guardians, where local issues were prominent, in the National League branch larger farmers monopolized control and the expression of opinion.

Much the same pattern held for the local branch of the United Irish League (U.I.L.) after 1900. The only reported occasion when large numbers of shopkeepers attended a meeting of that branch was in 1902 after one of them had been evicted from his thirteen-acre pasture field on the edge of the town. The farmer majority expressed no more than nominal sympathy and proposed no action, being much more concerned with contemporary cases of evicted or allegedly mistreated farmers. As a result, the Town Tenants League was founded, and its first list of members included thirty-four shopkeepers (out of a total of thirty-nine at that time) and fourteen other town residents. The new organization achieved nothing concrete, other than the public expression of shopkeeper awareness of common interests and the need for mutual support. Most probably, no active support was offered by farmers and the U.I.L. For them the town tenants' organization may well have seemed an unnecessary diversion from the principal activist concerns: tenant-farmers' rights, tenant purchase of farms, and nationalism. The Town Tenants' League disappeared after a couple of years and shopkeepers continued in their passive role as some of the more generous contributors to the U.I.L. (although in the annual collections of 1905 and 1910, well over half gave nothing at all).

In 1906, three young, smaller shopkeepers were among the nine members of the provisional committee of the local Sinn Fein (radical nationalist) club, and another nine were reported at the meeting to select that committee. Those three continued to attend meetings regularly, and one later became president. However, as the club's activities merged with general nationalist endeavor, particularly after 1916, farmers again dominated. Meanwhile, the majority of shopkeepers, including the larger ones, quietly supported the Irish party (moderate constitutionalists) or were altogether apathetic. The evidence is slim, but archival and oral information indicate that, with only one or two exceptions, shopkeepers—prosperous or otherwise—remained quiescent during the years up to 1922. Nor were their sons any more active.

The poverty of mutuality between shopkeepers and farmers was evident also when, toward the end of the nineteenth century, the shopkeepers first began to attempt autonomous collective action in their own interests. In 1891, a Reading Room Association was begun in premises in a town street. Its officials were shopkeepers, as were almost all its members, and no farmers participated. The rooms provided a place for shopkeepers to meet for leisure activities and talk about common concerns. A formal meeting on the premises that year produced agreement to press for the arrangement of more frequent fairs and markets in the town. Farmers were not involved in this and seem not to have been consulted, although the markets were in agricultural produce. The expressed intention was further to develop the town as a commercial center. The effort was not immediately successful, although weekly butter markets began a few years later. Monthly livestock fairs began in 1906, with two shopkeepers as the secretaries of the administering committee—neither of whom had farming interests.

Again, in 1896, some of the larger shopkeepers in the Reading Room Association began collective action to induce the Board of Guardians to install street lighting in the town. This was strenuously opposed by the farmers on the Board, and by one or two other larger farmers who lived nearby, as being both expensive on the rates and unnecessary. Before the matter was settled (the costs to be met by urban ratepayers only) there were sharp warnings from farmers that they were not prepared to pay for the nonessential convenience of townspeople. This incident involved the display of divergent interests, and farmers publicly voiced their suspicions and opposition.

After this successful effort, shopkeepers mounted no further public collective action, though whether this was in deference to farmers' opposition is impossible to say. The Reading Room continued as a meeting place for town notables, although informants agreed that this effectively ceased during the War of Independence. The premises were given up in 1924.

Four conclusions are evident from this brief survey up to 1922. One is that some of the larger farmers in the area dominated public affairs in both official and unofficial arenas. Second, when shopkeepers did participate (and they never did so consistently), they were minor players. They were not men of influence or leaders. The third conclusion is that the farmer leaders and chief activists were almost entirely concerned with farmers' problems and with ideological support of nationalist issues: they were unsympathetic toward issues affecting urban residents, including shopkeepers. In contrast, shopkeepers, when active, were concerned with local, town affairs, and most showed little interest in farmers' issues or nationalist politics. Fourth, over the years neither farmers nor shopkeepers seem to have made much, if any, appeal to kinship links as a basis for mutual support and common action in public affairs.

This persistent detachment of Thomastown shopkeepers from national and local political activities and from farmers' interests and concerns contrasted with reports of heavy shopkeeper involvement and significant leadership in some other parts of Ireland. The most detailed analysis referred particularly to Connaught in the years up to and including the Land Wars. Clark concluded that, in that region, "townsmen constituted an important part of the challenging collectivity" against landlords and the Ascendancy that led to and engaged in the Land Wars. There, townsmen "were numerically over-represented . . . [and] often assumed leadership roles" in Land League branches.[17] Presumably, shopkeepers were the most numerous among these townsmen, since some members of the "small business class

. . . came to rival landowners and clergymen as wielders of local power and patronage."[18] Clark supported his assertions by describing two crucial ways in which shopkeepers became "socially integrated into rural society." First, shopkeepers and farmers were closely linked by many marriages and by the numbers of farmers' sons who became shopkeepers. Such linkages were intensified as the small Irish towns there became "appendages to the farming population."[19] Second, farmers were not only the principal customers of the urban shopkeepers but also the recipients of substantial credit such that shopkeeper-farmer relations often became patron–client ties. This meant not only that farmers were dependent on shopkeepers but that shopkeepers became dependent on farmers and therefore were obliged to support them in activist movements and to provide leadership.

A shopkeeper who joined the movement would therefore distinguish himself as a friend of the farmer. Those merchants and publicans who had particularly established themselves as local patrons could furnish political leadership to their clients as a way of compensating for the loss of the usual benefit they supplied. Or if they were still able to give credit, they could join the land movement to supplement the benefits they provided in an effort to increase their clients' indebtedness.[20]

Kennedy provided further evidence that suggested that Clark's conclusions were applicable beyond Connaught and continued to be relevant long after the Land Wars period. The evidence indicates that traders, unlike small farmers and agricultural laborers, enjoyed considerably more political power than their numbers in the population alone warranted. They were overrepresented on certain popularly elected bodies, from county councils to the parliamentary party, in the early twentieth century.[21]

Kennedy observed that this condition was not limited only to western counties and cited Wexford and southern Tipperary as examples. However, Kennedy also commented that the "situation was quite different" in Carlow and Westmeath, although he gave no details.[22] This may also have been true in nineteenth-century County Cork. In Donnelly's thorough study of that county, there was virtually no reference to any role that shopkeepers played in political movements.[23] Feingold discovered a total of five "townsmen" (possibly shopkeepers) in that county in 1886 who were officeholders in four south coast boards of guardians—scarcely a preponderance—whereas there were none at all in the cattle-grazing unions of Kanturk, Millstreet, and Mitchelstown.[24] Regional differences were also suggested by Kennedy's investigation of a sample of chairmen and

vice-chairmen of county councils in 1905.[25] On average, he found
that 27 percent of them "followed trading occupations"—a dispro-
portionately large number, with the highest proportions in Connaught and the lowest in Munster. Similarly, Fitzpatrick stated that
in County Clare during the 1910s, "among those who held or sought
political office, publicans and shopkeepers were probably the dominant group."[26] However, no data were provided to substantiate this.

Chubb's well-known findings contained no regional discrimination. He reported that "employers and managers (mainly small shopkeepers, publicans, owners of family businesses, and contractors)"
comprised 3.2 percent of the country's population in 1961 but 31
percent of county council members, 34 percent of Dail deputies, and
20 percent of cabinet ministers at about that time.[27] No doubt these
figures were correct, but they were simply gross statistics at the
national level, telling us nothing of the origins and bases of those
"employers and managers." Indeed, the figures obscured what we
would wish to know and understand: referring only to the national
level, they implied that shopkeepers and towns and rural areas were
all the same throughout the country, turning the reality of local and
regional variety into the simplified, misleading monolith of "Ireland."

Gibbon and Higgins gave a few examples of shopkeepers exercis-
ing political patronage and influence, although their typicality and
regional distribution are unclear.[28] Those authors were of the opinion
that "gombeenmen" (mainly larger shopkeepers?) shifted their strategy from a preindependence patronage (to secure the electoral positions of clients through whom business interests could be furthered)
to a "modern" combination of patronage and brokerage (to create
blocs by which the gombeenmen might secure electoral positions
themselves). In either case, gombeenmen were politically influential.

None of the preceding writers provided details of the particular
kinds of businessmen involved. Unduly vague terms, such as *small
business class, traders, employers* and *managers,* or *gombeenmen,* left open
the questions as to what sort of individuals (and in what contexts)
had been influential in public affairs (e.g., the largest retailers, perhaps, or those with multiple business interests, or those with an
enterprise that was economically dominant in a locality). Similarly,
there is very little information on the locations of their businesses—
whether they were in large or small towns or in towns in more
densely populated rural areas. Hoppen noted that shopkeepers had a
"significant influence within borough constituencies" (the larger towns)
in the middle of the nineteenth century.[29] In contrast, Kennedy commented, in a footnote, that "trader" representatives on the County

Council of Tipperary (South Riding) "in 1908 were based not only in such towns as Clonmel, Cashel and Cahir, but also in the tiny country villages of Bansha, Killenaule, and Limerick Junction."[30] Whether that was also the case at other times, there and in other counties, is unknown.

It could be suggested that my findings in Thomastown were the result of historical conditions different from those elsewhere; but this is unclear and there is good reason to think that comparable conditions held in some other parts of Ireland. In his pioneering study of local government in the second half of the nineteenth century, Feingold concluded that in "regions where the cattle graziers were numerically powerful (Munster and Leinster) they did not need the assistance of the shopkeepers" in their political endeavors.[31] However, to test Feingold's hypothesis and to seek explanation, further essential kinds of information are required. We need a sample of local areas—both larger and smaller towns—in various parts of the country during the past one hundred years or more. From this it should be possible to discover what kinds of businessmen, if any, and what other individuals were influential participants in public affairs—local, regional, and national—at different times. In this, account could be taken of important variables: governmental and other organizations, office holding, patronage, brokerage, and leadership.

In the absence of such information, I can only suggest a number of factors that together appear to have been related to the exiguous participation of Thomastown shopkeepers in public affairs. First, Thomastown has always been a small town, even by Irish standards. It is quite possible that politically active shopkeepers were chiefly located in larger towns, associated with more vibrant commercial and political activities, where a few shopkeepers were able to gain a greater prosperity and a wider prominence, less constrained by farmers' presence. As previously noted, there is exceedingly little information in this respect.

Second, Thomastown was not a new or rapidly expanding commercial center during the second half of the nineteenth century. It was already well established by the end of the eighteenth century as an inland port and as a retail, service, and small manufacturing center. The numbers of shops remained almost constant throughout the nineteenth century and well into the twentieth century, even as its flour milling and tannery industries expanded (albeit still fairly small) and there developed a small tourist trade connected with fishing and hunting.[32] In the period under study, there was a significant resident population of artisans and nonagricultural workers—landless and earning cash wages.[33] They were continuously major customers of the shops. In contrast to nineteenth-century Connaught and early-twentieth-century Tipperary, Thomastown shopkeepers may therefore have been less dependent on farmers' custom and more dependent on the local, urban-based wage workers. This suggests that Feingold's hypothesis may require broadening to include the structure of the whole local economy and not only the numbers of larger farmers.

Third, although there always were some half a dozen more prosperous shopkeepers, this was not a town dominated by one or two larger entrepreneurs. Possibly because of this, there was no record of any gombeenmen who became notable patrons of farmers, dispensers of favors and influence, and therefore overt or covert leaders.[34] Indeed, a crucial ingredient of such a role may well have been absent: the extensive credit provided to farmer-customers that not only gave considerable power to the shopkeepers but induced them to support anything that promised benefit to farmers. In Thomastown, throughout the period in review, there was an absence of evidence of (rather than positive evidence for) significant patron-client ties as a result of extensive credit. This too goes against a common assumption concerning the nineteenth century. Yet for Thomastown, neither archival information nor farm and shop family histories indicated acute credit crises, whereas such credit as there was appears to have been spread among many shopkeepers rather than being restricted to one or two.

Fourth, political activities in Thomastown were seldom intense. In the second half of the nineteenth century, most farmers seem to have been able to pay their rents more or less on time as they experienced the gradual, overall increase in agricultural prosperity. What activity there was prior to, during, and after the Land Wars or in the years up to 1922 was almost entirely monopolized by some of the larger farmers. This condition, of course, supports the hypothesis that where in Ireland there were numerous larger farmers, shopkeepers and other commercial entrepreneurs were excluded from, or at least limited in, political influence and leadership in preindependence times. This seems to apply to County Cork, although apparently not to southern Tipperary (if Kennedy is correct). The reverse hypothesis—many smaller and few larger farmers and so greater shopkeeper participation in public affairs—can be applied quite well to Connaught, Clare, and perhaps other western areas. Further testing of these hypotheses is called for.[35]

Fifth, as I have shown, kinship links between shopkeepers and farmers, though by no means negligible, were limited among the total of local farmers. They scarcely provided a firm basis for political cooperation, and in that sense they appear to have been unimportant. In any case, the majority of local farmers who were prominent in public activities up to 1922 were not so linked to shopkeepers. This goes some way in explaining why they showed little sympathy for the interests of shopkeepers and why they did so little to recruit shopkeeper support and advice. In the 1890s (and later, in the 1930s), when shopkeepers began to act collectively in local matters of commercial and urban interest, they in their turn showed little concern for farmers' interests. It may also be significant that over the years, few of the most prosperous shopkeepers had farm origins or were linked to farmers by marriage.[36]

It is uncertain if, in Thomastown, kinship linkages between shopkeepers and farmers were fewer and weaker than in some other parts of the country where shopkeepers' public participation has been reported as more active. More numerous and perhaps stronger kinship links seem to have existed in County Roscommon in the second half of the nineteenth century. Clark showed that 40 percent of "traders and business proprietors" were sons of farmers and almost two-thirds were married to daughters of farmers.[37] These proportions were higher than for Thomastown at the same period. The information just is not available for other areas.[38]

## Shopkeepers and Public Affairs After 1922

After 1922, farmers' participation in public affairs diminished considerably. The political context changed with the establishment of the Free State, of course; and by 1926, the Thomastown arena of local government disappeared with the abolition of the Rural District Council. Farmers seem to have lost their zeal when they successfully acquired secure possession of their farms. However, a local member of the Farmers' party was elected to the Kilkenny County Council in 1928 and farmer members of Fine Gael in 1945 and 1974. The other elected county councillors in the Thomastown constituency since 1922 have been members of the Labour party.[39]

Shopkeepers were no more active at the official level than they had been previously. Most of them, as well as most local farmers, favored Cumann na Gaedheal and Fine Gael parties, although a few became firm Fianna Fail supporters. No shopkeeper or shopkeeper's son was a candidate for election at county or national levels, and very few were at all active in local branches of the parties. More than one shopkeeper declared that politics and business did not mix: the strong implication was that political enthusiasms were bad for business, taking up a shopkeeper's time and energy and deterring customers of different political persuasion. However, one or two pubs became recognized as informal political party centers at election times.

At the local level, however, by about 1930, shopkeepers began to become active. The abolition of the Rural District Council left something of a vacancy that, in local views, was not adequately filled either by what was seen as the rather remote bureaucracy at the county council headquarters or by local county councillors. Gradually, the larger shopkeepers came together in an attempt to deal with local issues of concern to themselves and urban residents. At first this was done informally, with the support of the parish priest, through their majority membership of the executive committee of the Young Men's Catholic Association. They created and operated ad hoc committees to deal with savings, river flooding, and an annual festival. In 1936, shopkeepers' interests and actions were formalized by the founding of the Traders' Development Association. After two years, the association claimed thirty-one shopkeepers (out of a total of forty-one at the time) as subscribing members. The only other members were the priest, the local flour miller, and a teacher. The association was concerned wholly with local urban issues and was dominated by half a dozen of the larger shopkeepers. It was they who were the officials and who proposed actions and served as deputations to government officials and politicians. Local farmers did not participate in the association.

There were some successes in obtaining governmental action, but there were also many failures with unfulfilled promises and downright refusals. Local shopkeeper status and influence were poorly translated into power and achievement. Perforce, as it seemed to them, shopkeepers had to accept the roles of requesting and protesting to those who held power—bureaucrats and politicians—and with ineffective resources of their own. It seems fair to say that the successes occurred only when the powerholders were more or less ready to act, and the common failures occurred when they were unwilling or unable to act. As a result, the association grew less active, with its leading members disillusioned, and it disappeared altogether in 1953. A second attempt was made, in 1970, to coordinate shopkeeper interests and actions concerning local problems by founding a new association. On the whole, it was no more successful than its predecessor. Lack of confidence to be able to achieve much and an absence of shopkeeper unity were indicated by the fact that, up to 1981, only about half of all shopkeepers ever became members and fewer actually attended meetings regularly. Although one achievement was to collect valuable funds to assist in the creation of a community center in the town, the shopkeepers themselves did not participate in the endeavors of the Thomastown Community Council to promote local amenities.

A point of significance for the purposes of this essay is that these shopkeepers' associations were concerned not with rural issues and farmers' interests but with urban affairs, and largely those touching shopkeeper interests. In all this the lead was taken by the larger shopkeepers. These men did not act on behalf of all the people in the locality or of farmers in particular. However, they claimed special status, experience, and wisdom in choosing the relevant issues and recommending solutions, and in so doing, they expressed their own commonality and their distinction from other urban residents. Consciously or not, in effect, they also expressed their distinction from farmers.

## Conclusion

The intent in this essay has been to survey some of the characteristics of shopkeepers in a specific local-level context since about 1840. In particular, I have examined the connections between shopkeepers and farmers and the nature of shopkeepers' participation in public affairs. Some conclusions are possible insofar as the history of Thomastown is concerned. First, although new shopkeepers have been regularly recruited from farm families throughout the period in review, such recruits have never been a majority either of all shopkeepers or of noninheriting newcomers. Second, there have been only limited kinship linkages between shopkeepers and farmers; therefore, social relations and mutual support have not been strongly marked since the 1840s. Third, although links between larger shopkeepers and farmers have been more common, not all such shopkeepers were so linked, and then only a minority of farmers. Fourth, in the nineteenth century and up to 1922, shopkeepers exerted inconsiderable influence in public affairs, whether in official or unofficial activities. Some of the larger farmers were public leaders, spokesmen, organizers, and activists since about 1880. They and other farmers showed little concern for "urban" issues or the problems and interests of shopkeepers. Fifth, after 1922, farmers largely retired from public, activist participation. After a time, at the purely local level, shopkeepers organized themselves to promote their common interests—and to a lesser extent, "urban" interests generally. Not all shopkeepers participated, and only a few were at all active. The results of their action have been slight, as the larger shopkeepers—the organizational leaders—have been unable to convert their claim to superior status into effective influence.

Two other conclusions have arisen here that also run counter to common assumptions. One is that few successful shopkeepers have sought to invest in land or to become farmers; conversely, farmers have not sought to become shopkeepers. Second, there is an absence of evidence that farmers were ever heavily in debt to shopkeepers or that shopkeepers, as creditors, were able to influence farmers or were induced to support them.

All these conclusions refer, of course, only to Thomastown and its locality. Thomastown has been and remains a small town: the same conclusions might not be reached in a comparable study of a larger town in the same or another region. Nor is it assumed that, in any case, Thomastown has been typical of all smaller towns. It is not the purpose of a local-level study such as this social anthropological research in Thomastown to reach conclusions applicable to a whole region, let alone the whole of Ireland. On the other hand, local-level study can reveal—as it has in this particular case—results that run counter to some common generalizations. Such dissentient results call for reexamination of the generalizations in question and of the information on which they have been founded. The results for Thomastown may be singular and explicable in terms of some particular features of that context. Conversely, the generalizations themselves may need to be modified in some ways. Unfortunately, comparable local-level studies are scarcely available in this connection, and therefore it is not possible to suggest explanation in terms of, for example, regional variation, the size of town and its particular history, the size of farms, the number and variety of shopkeepers, the level of prosperity. However, it is most unlikely that Thomastown has been unique during a century and a half.

## NOTES

1. In the literature, Arensberg and Kimball (1940) were the leaders in putting forward this proposition. Later writers seem merely to have followed them without adducing new supporting evidence (e.g., Lee 1973:98, Peillon 1982:25, and Ó Gráda 1988:162). In contrast, however, Bax (1976:139) noted

that marriages between town and farm families were uncommon in "Patricksville."

2. This notion, often unexplored, has frequently occurred in the literature. A few examples are Brown (1981:26), Garvin (1981:83), Hoppen (1979:194, 1984:52ff, 472), and Lee (1973:98).

3. See Gulliver (1989).

4. Between 1840 and 1981 the vast majority of shopkeepers were men; only a small minority were spinsters or widows. Not only was it assumed in Thomastown that a widow only held the business in trust for the next generation but female shopkeepers—whether widows or spinsters—were not involved in public affairs. For these reasons the present analysis of kinship and public activities is carried out using a male-centered perspective, although the statistical data refer to all shopkeepers regardless of gender.

5. The following table gives some idea of the occupational structure of Thomastown. The figures are for male household heads in 1911 and 1981 in the electoral divisions (DEDs) of Thomastown and Jerpoint Church. Those DEDs, which included both the town and surrounding townlands, were smaller than the undefined area from which shop customers were drawn. The following figures only roughly indicate the distribution of occupations in the locality.

| 1911 | | 1981 |
| --- | --- | --- |
| 11.4% | Shopkeepers and business | 10.4% |
| 22.1% | Farmers and farmers' sons | 9.4% |
| 13.2% | Skilled workers | 26.6% |
| 42.7% | Semi- and unskilled workers | 31.0% |
| 3.6% | Clerical and semiprofessional | 15.0% |
| 7.0% | Other | 13.6% |

6. With a similar emphasis on inheritance throughout Ireland, no doubt there has everywhere been a comparable preponderance among shopkeepers of the sons and daughters of shopkeepers. Information is scanty indeed. For Ennis, County Clare, Arensberg and Kimball (1940:327) implied that some majority of shopkeepers in the 1930s had come from shop families, as heirs of parental businesses. No figures were given and the authors did not pursue the matter. They chose to concentrate on the minority recruitment process from farmer's son to shop apprentice to assistant to self-employed shopkeeper.

7. These tiny, ephemeral shops, as one elderly informant put it, "sold anything and everything but not much of anything." Usually occupying part of a room in a cottage, they were endeavors by poor, unemployed and often elderly individuals to earn a few pennies.

8. Assistance (e.g., fees and maintenance) to acquire skills has become more common in recent decades with the increase in facilities for specialized training and in job opportunities.

9. The proportion of two-thirds is subject to the reservation that, for 1911 and 1945, mothers' origins have been less well remembered than fathers' origins. There remain unknown or uncertain cases (one-fifth in 1945 and one-third in 1911) for which it is quite possible that more readily forgotten, nonfarming origins pertain. Thus, the actual proportions of mothers with farm origins were probably somewhat smaller. The large number of unknowns for 1884 and earlier preclude any useful conclusions for the nineteenth century.

10. It is difficult to give the numbers of relevant farmers. First, the area from which farmers have been customers is unclear. Second, there is the problem of defining *farmer* so as to exclude those (claiming that appellation) who only had "a bit of land" and whose livelihood came largely from another occupation. Moreover, although thirty to forty acres of moderately good land made a viable farm—and farmer—in earlier generations, this is no longer the case. As a crude approximation only, there were some two hundred farmers in 1849 and about one hundred in 1981.

11. The reasons for business success have been various, and no general, single explanation is apparent. Among the relevant factors are individual initiative, rejection of sufficing and a readiness to take risks, training and experience in business, the early discovery of a profitable new line or method of business, willingness to expand into other retail enterprise and into services, careful accounting and a sharpness in dealing, an enterprising spouse, and some good luck.

12. Contrary to the assertion of Arensberg and Kimball (1940:344).

13. Shopkeepers who were also active farmers had either inherited the farm along with the shop or purchased land.

14. Garvin (1981:83).

15. Similar proportions existed in 1913. Admittedly, crude acreage is a poor indicator of relative farmer prosperity where the agricultural quality of land varied a good deal. Nevertheless, the indications from these figures are suggestive enough for present purposes.

16. Feingold (1984:233–34).

17. Clark (1979:275, 300).

18. Clark (1979:128).

19. Clark (1979:135).

20. Clark (1979:267).

21. Kennedy (1983:368).

22. Kennedy (1983:369).

23. Donnelly (1975). Donnelly also stated that he did not think to inquire specifically about shopkeepers during his research (oral contribution to symposium, Annual Meeting of the American Committee for Irish Studies, University College, Dublin, June 1987). But had shopkeepers been prominent, this would surely not have escaped his notice.

24. Feingold (1984:216).

25. Kennedy (1983:358).

26. Fitzpatrick (1977:88).

27. Chubb (1982:95).

28. Gibbon and Higgins (1974).

29. Hoppen (1979:194).

30. Kennedy (1983:369).

31. Feingold (1984:226).

32. Thus, Thomastown (as perhaps other towns in eastern Ireland) did not share in the national increase in shop numbers in the second half of the nineteenth century (Cullen 1972:142). However, although shop numbers in Thomastown remained more or less constant, the ratio of local people (customers) per shop fell considerably as the population decreased by about two-thirds between 1841 and 1911.

33. See n. 5.

34. The term *gombeenman* does not occur in the records or in oral information in Thomastown.

35. See Feingold (1984:225–26) and Hoppen (1979:223).

36. See page 186.

37. Clark (1979:118–19).

38. Bax (1976:139) noted that marriages between town and farm families were uncommon in "Patricksville," County Cork in the 1960s. Taylor (1980b:72) stated that in southwestern Donegal in the nineteenth century "merchants tended to contract marriages with other merchant families in the same or nearby merchant community." No empirical data were given in either case.

39. The constituency for the county council elections has comprised an area of south-central Kilkenny that included two other small towns of about the same size and composition as Thomastown.

6

# The Early Twentieth-Century Irish Stem Family: A Case Study from County Kerry

■

DONNA BIRDWELL-PHEASANT

For at least a generation of social scientists now, rural Ireland has been portrayed as the land of stem families. The central authority for the characterization continues to be Arensberg and Kimball's 1930s study of a rural sector of County Clare in the west of Ireland. With the recent reissue of Arensberg's *Irish Countryman* making the material readily available to another generation, it is timely to review the case of the Irish stem family in historical perspective. This review of necessity encompasses not only the history of the family in Ireland but also, in some measure, the history of anthropology as well.

The Arensberg and Kimball study has been cited more than once as ahistorical.[1] Moored as it is to a functionalist view of society and culture, it invites such criticism. Indeed, the Ireland of Arensberg and Kimball often seems to float in a timeless void, isolated from the perturbations of modern history and disconnected from any meaningful cultural linkage with Ireland's Gaelic and British past.

Other analysts have tried to tie the image of the stem family in Ireland to certain quasi-historical or quasi-evolutionary processes. Connell spoke of the "diffusion" of such features as the match from one part of the country to another.[2] Brody and later Scheper-Hughes conjured up the process of "demoralization" to account for what they perceived to be a general decay of social process in the Irish country-side.[3] None of these analyses was linked any more solidly to Irish history than was that of Arensberg and Kimball.[4]

Much of Irish agrarian social and cultural history has been di-chotomized by the Great Famine of the mid-nineteenth century, pro-ducing a framework of "prefamine" and "postfamine" adaptations. Within this framework, Arensberg and Kimball's Ireland is part of the literature on "postfamine" adaptation.[5]

Although Arensberg and Kimball never used the term *stem family* in their major works on rural Ireland, the Irish case has become entrenched in the literature as a classic example of the stem family system.[6] The concept of the stem family belongs to a set of descrip-tive categories—with strong evolutionist and moral implications—credited to LePlay.[7] The contrast was with the "patriarchal family" in which all sons brought their wives into the family home, and the "unstable family," better known today as the "nuclear family," in which dispersal of all the children was the norm.[8] Somewhere be-tween these two extremes lay the stem family—one in which there was cross-generational continuity of households, as with the patriar-chal family, but in which most children were dispersed, as in the nuclear family. Only one child—usually a son—needed to marry within the parental household for the goal of continuity to be realized. For LePlay, the patriarchal family was archaic, whereas the nuclear family—unstable by definition—was an indication of modern decline. The paragon of virtue was the stem family household, which had evolved out of the patriarchal structure and subsequently disinte-grated to give rise to the nuclear form.

Segalen restated a definition of the stem family as a "recognized type of 'large family' " characterized as a "domestic group that gath-ered three generations under one roof: the father and mother, one of the married sons and his wife, and that couple's children. To these might be added other unmarried children and servants."[9] This was faithful to LePlay's definition of the stem family, which was summa-rized by Laslett as a system wherein the "parents married off and kept within the group only one of their children whom they nominated successor."[10]

The recent upsurge of comparative studies in European family history has raised additional questions about the description and inter-pretation of the stem family and, consequently, of the stem family's place—and Ireland's place—within the purview of European family history.[11] The Cambridge school, under the leadership of Laslett, made a case for the predominance of the nuclear family in most parts of Europe (but especially England) since at least the seventeenth century.[12] This challenged the notion that the nuclear family was unstable and, consequently, allowed it to emerge as morally more acceptable. Indeed, it was the stem family that was portrayed in the work of Segalen as the unstable form.[13]

Under LePlay's original family evolutionary scheme, then, Ireland appeared as a quaint survival in which the morally appealing stem family system was preserved. The Laslett doctrine suggested that the Irish stem family was but a deviation from the dominant (and stable) nuclear family type, probably due to some recent shifts in either demography or society.[14] These attempts to turn the morality of LePlay's scheme on its head did little to clarify the nature of the stem family itself. Quite the contrary, they raised grave questions about the true position of the stem family in European social history and about the criteria by means of which we are to identify stem families in Ireland or elsewhere. Is the stem family an evolutionary stage? Is it a mere deviation from a more stable nuclear family norm? Or is it something else?

Verdon, working from his own field study in Quebec, and incorporating data from other authentic cases of the stem family (he included the Basque country, the Alpine valley, and Ireland) isolated a set of common features characterizing the system. The features he identified included impartible inheritance, usually with delayed devolution (wherein the father is loath to part with the property until it becomes absolutely necessary) and/or conditional devolution (where the heir is specified at his marriage but does not assume control until his father's death); arranged marriages for heirs; and the absence of any strict rules for specifying which son will inherit the farm.[15]

As evinced in the Irish case, the stem family scenario has generally been held to entail the "inheritance of the farm by one son, the emigration of the rest, the dowry for the daughters, and the provision for the old people."[16] Stated in even stronger terms, it is the "custom of only two children per family being permitted to marry locally."[17]

This Irish model of the stem family, then, departs a bit in emphasis from the original theoretical concept. Verdon argued that, since impartible inheritance was found in so many areas of Europe where the stem family did not occur, impartible inheritance was a necessary, but not a sufficient, condition for the emergence of a stem family system.[18] Segalen, however, in her discussion of stem-type inheritance, noted that the transmission of the family patrimony to a single heir need not preclude either payment of some compensation to nonheirs, or the provision of other "children" with a "small dowry," or strategies by means of which younger sons are wed to farm heiresses.[19] Since the last may sometimes entail a dowry too, it is possible to argue that all the preceding compromise the "unitary" nature of the farm inheritance in that something is being extracted from the family patrimony to provide for children other than the stem heir. Laslett too noted that, "The others, *being given their shares of the inheritance,* went away to found their own households."[20] Fitzpatrick delved more thoroughly into Irish data and also concluded that strict unitary inheritance was not necessary: "Despite the common contrary assumption, the stem system is not inconsistent with modes of land disposal more complex than impartible inheritance. Provided that one choice holding is set aside for the preferred inheritor, the sale or distribution to others of further fields or houses need not disrupt the continuity of the household."[21]

We would do well to distinguish, then, between what we might call a rigid stem family model and a loose model. Under a rigid model—the model generally attributed to Arensberg and Kimball—the farm is passed on intact to a unique heir, a son who succeeds his father as head of household and farmer of record and whose marriage finances the dowering of one and only one sister. The other siblings of the heir are dispersed: they "travel." If we "loosen" this stem family model, then more offspring can receive an inheritance from the farm patrimony and marriage can be facilitated for more as well. Fitzpatrick's analysis of "preferential" inheritance is readily accommodated by such a loose model.[22]

There is a decided difference in emphasis in the two models. Under the rigid model, for example, the dispersal of the noninheriting offspring is seen as a positive goal, as indeed it is in the nuclear family system. Under the loose model, on the other hand, the dispersal of offspring is neutral or even negative, while the provision for offspring in addition to the main heir is seen as a positive goal. Unitary inheritance, furthermore, becomes "preferential" inheritance, allowing for a much greater degree of variability among cases.

It is easy to see how Arensberg and Kimball's functionalist community study lent itself so readily to adoption as a classic case of a stem family system. However, it should be emphasized that Arensberg and Kimball themselves never suggested the rigid stem model as the ideal model of farm succession in County Clare. In times past, Arensberg told us, "all the sons and daughters could hope to be provided for on the land." For the period of his study, he noted that "such a situation is still an ideal," although one seldom realized.[23] The ideal, then, was not the marriage of the one inheriting son and the one daughter with dowry and the dispersal of all the rest, but rather the favorable settlement of all offspring. A loose model was much closer to the ideal, as observed by Arensberg and Kimball, than a rigid model.

If the rigid model has not been an accurate "model *for*" behavior in agrarian rural Ireland, why has it become institutionalized in the literature? Perhaps its acceptance lay in its utility as a "model *of*" behavior—that is, its accuracy as a description of actual behavior in the countryside. Even though the Irish farmers may not have been striving to meet the criteria of the rigid stem model, we might observe a strong *statistical tendency* indicating inadvertent realization of its criteria.

Analyses of data that would allow us to test such a hypothesis remain inadequate in the literature to date. There has generally been more heat than light generated in debates such as that which occupied the pages of *Comparative Studies of Society and History* in 1983. Gibbon and Curtin initiated the debate in 1978 with a study that set out to demonstrate that adherence to a stem model (defined primarily by the presence of three-generation households) was highly variable, and that the main factor accounting for the variability was farm size and type of enterprise. Their data and analyses were subsequently criticized, although their hypothesis has never been effectively challenged.[24] Hannan found a rigid model of Irish peasant life reasonably accurate, although he hastened to point out that its "historical and regional specificity is quite marked."[25] Fitzpatrick, on the other hand, concluded that Irish adherence to a stem family pattern was "strikingly uniform," although he was only able to discover such uniformity by "loosening" the model to include limited partible inheritance.[26]

The remainder of this paper constitutes a test of the adequacy of the rigid stem family model as a "model of" rural agrarian Ireland, based on a longitudinal and historical data set reaching back into the late nineteenth century but focusing primarily on the early decades of the twentieth century. Factors signaling adherence to a rigid model are those that emphasize, on the one hand, the continuity of the family in the farm and, on the other hand, the dispersal of the noninheriting siblings. Specifically, I will look for evidence that farms were being passed on intact to a unique heir, a son who could keep the name on the land, thus ensuring a continuity of family identity. To ensure this continuity further, the son would marry. Continuity will also be indicated by the occurrence of households that, at the appropriate stage of development, consisted of three lineal generations. Finally, the dispersal of noninheriting siblings will be taken as evidence of adherence to a rigid stem model. By attending to these five features—unitary inheritance, son inheritance, heir marriage, the coresidence of three generations, and the dispersal of noninheriting siblings—I should be able to determine whether there is a good match between the rigid model of the Irish stem family and the behavior of early-twentieth-century Irish farm families in the field study area.

## Case Study: Ballyduff, County Kerry

In 1986, I went to Ireland to collect longitudinal data for the investigation of rural family systems.[27] The selection of field site was conducted with a careful eye to avoid the characteristically anthropological error of confusing poverty with traditionalism. Although I was looking for a site in the "traditional" west of Ireland, it had to be a place where it was feasible for people to make a decent living through farming. With the assistance of staff members of the Economic and Social Research Institute and An Foras Taluntais in Dublin, I was able to find a satisfactory site in northern County Kerry, centered on the small town of Ballyduff. All the land in the selected area is defined as capable of supporting at least fifty units of livestock per one hundred acres; about a third is capable of producing seventy to ninety units per one hundred acres; and another third is assessed as of such quality that ninety or more units of livestock could be grazed per one hundred acres.[28]

Ballyduff lies within a predominantly dairying region where two-thirds of the farms in the late 1960s were under fifty acres and 85 percent were no bigger than seventy-five acres.[29] Within the study district itself only nine farms in 1986 were over one hundred acres, of which two were over two hundred acres. Dairy farming predominated over any other agricultural pursuit and was strongly organized under the leadership of Kerry Co-op, a dairy farmers' cooperative with an aggressive marketing strategy. Kerry Co-op owned meatpacking plants and a milk products plant in addition to the usual facilities for the packaging and marketing of fresh milk. It maintained offices in the John Hancock Tower in Chicago.

Delivery time at the local collection point in Ballyduff afforded an opportunity to observe the range of dairy farmers in the area. Some brought their milk in shiny stainless steel bulk tanks; others had a few of the old-fashioned milk cans in a trailer pulled behind the car or tractor. A few still brought in their one or two cans of milk by donkey cart. A few more were such large producers that the Kerry

Co-op milk truck came to collect at the farm. Individual annual quotas, negotiated with Kerry Co-op in accord with current EEC policies, ranged from about two thousand gallons to over seventy thousand gallons.

County Kerry has been dominated by livestock, specifically dairy farming, in the region of the study district at least since the Great Famine. Records produced by the Ordinance Survey in 1841 reveal that most of the land in the study area was, at that time, devoted to the production of oats, potatoes, barley, and wheat, with only two townlands given over mostly to grazing. By 1851, however, arable use for the whole of County Kerry had declined to only 16 percent (nearly 101,000 acres) of all the farmed land in the county. Arable use declined further to only 9 percent (61,400 acres) in 1901. Tillage recovered somewhat by 1942, when it accounted for 16.7 percent of farmed land, or nearly 94,700 acres. Another decline then set in, so that by 1970, crops accounted for less than 6 percent (31,900 acres) of farmed land in the county. Since 1851, pasturage has never accounted for less than 450,000 acres of farmed land in County Kerry.[30]

The study district comprises twenty-six contiguous townlands and the town center of Ballyduff.[31] The composition of the study area was determined by a combination of historical and contemporary associations. In the past, the townlands were divided between the two parishes of Rattoo and Killury and were under the authority of three main landlords and several smaller ones. Today, all the townlands belong to the parish of Causeway. The study area does not correspond very well to present-day administrative divisions, as it includes townlands belonging to three District Electoral Divisions—Ardagh, Ballyduff, and Drommartin. The area does, however, correspond rather well to the present-day catchment area for the Ballyduff creamery, excluding only a handful of farmers who live on the other side of the Cashen River and who have been historically marginal to the Ballyduff interaction sphere. The frequency with which farmers must bring their milk to the central collection point makes this a reasonable basis for defining a "community" within a dispersed settlement region such as rural Ireland.

The baseline for the data set is furnished by the original census schedules of 1901 and 1911, which provided information on 1,660 individuals living in 293 households in 1901 and 1,613 individuals living in 279 households in 1911.[32] Background materials were provided by Small Area Population Printouts from the Office of the Census[33] and by Griffiths Valuation for 1852.[34] Additional data were collected from parish registries of births (2,723 entries) and marriages

212 DONNA BIRDWELL-PHEASANT

(711 entries) from 1900 onward, civil registries of deaths from 1900 through 1947 (884 entries), land registry records of land purchases and transfers (761 cases), and family histories from seventy-five personal interviews conducted with the help of a research assistant.[35] Each interview provided life course data on ten to seventy-four individuals.

The compiled data set comprises information on the life histories of 5,753 interrelated individuals of whom 638 have been identified as farmers and 2,099 as the offspring of farmers.[36] Of 348 discrete households present at any time from 1901 through 1911, 169 were farm households, 71 were laborers' and/or fishermen's households,[37] and 14 were headed by shopkeepers or publicans. There were also households of eleven coastguards, six military pensioners, four carpenters, four teachers, and four blacksmiths. There were three nurses, three gardeners, two landlords, two masons, and two creamery managers as well as a baker, doctor, tailor, bootmaker, dispensary keeper, dressmaker, relieving officer, harnessmaker, caretaker, land steward, coachman, and wool weaver. In an additional forty-one households, no productive occupation was entered for the head of household.

In this section, I rely primarily on data for three cohorts—Generation 1 (those born before 1840 and living at the time of the 1901 census), Generation 2 (those born 1840–1870), and Generation 3 (born 1870 to 1900). These cohorts are, of course, somewhat arbitrarily defined, but the thirty-year unit does correspond in general (or on average) to the length of the Irish generation, and the break points utilized enable me to make the most rational use of the 1901 and 1911 census data. Generation 3 is of special interest, as it includes most of those who would have been "in the farms" while Arensberg and Kimball were "in the field" in County Clare. Data are further broken down by sizes of farms—a "large farm" consists of forty or more acres; a "medium farm" of twenty to thirty-nine acres; and a "small" farm of fewer than twenty acres.[38] The distribution of farm sizes by generation is shown in table 6.1.

Table 6.1
Distribution of Farms by Size and Generation of Farmer

|  | Farm Size (in acres) | | | | | |
|---|---|---|---|---|---|---|
|  | 70+ | 40–69 | 30–39 | 20–29 | 10–19 | 10 |
| 1—Born before 1840 | 2.3% | 14.0% | 14.0% | 20.9% | 27.9% | 20.9% |
| 2—1840–70 | 9.7 | 20.4 | 13.6 | 15.5 | 18.4 | 22.3 |
| 3—1870–1900 | 9.2 | 16.0 | 18.5 | 17.6 | 16.8 | 21.8 |

Unitary Inheritance

Keeping the farm intact in the hands of the designated male heir consistently appears as an important element of the rigid stem model; it is one of the elements in terms of which the rigid model differs most significantly from a loose model. It is also taken to be a post-famine adaptation to the excesses of subdivision that contributed to the ravages of the famine.[39] Subdivision was, in fact, prohibited by Section 54 of the Land Act of 1903 and again by Section 4 of the Land Act of 1927.

In Ballyduff, the biggest farmers exhibited the greatest deviation from the "ideal" of unitary inheritance, and the smallest farmers adhered to it most rigorously (see table 6.2).[40] Among farmers holding fewer than ten acres, 95 percent of the farm transfers recorded entailed the passing on of the entire farm to a unique heir. It may be reasonably argued that small farmers adhered to this principle of unitary inheritance by default—the farm generally could not support more than one family.

Among the very largest farmers—those whose farms were larger than seventy acres—only 65 percent of farm transfers were unitary inheritances. Large farmers were more inclined than others to subdivide their farms, as well as more likely to inherit multiple farms. It may well be argued that it was the inheritance of more than one farm that placed some of these farmers into the "large" category. These farms often continued to be thought of as separate farms within the first generation and were thus more likely to be subdivided. On the other hand, the use of portions of the family farm as a lesser inheritance for nonstem heirs, or even as a dowry for a daughter, was more likely among larger farmers and contributed to the phenomenon of multiple inheritances: a son might inherit his home farm in addition

Table 6.2

Percent Distribution of Types of Farm Inheritance Among Farmers of Three Generations Born Before 1900, by Farm Size

|  | Large farmers | Medium farmers | Small farmers |
|---|---|---|---|
| Farm inherited intact | 73.7% | 86.1% | 91.5% |
| Farm subdivided | 12.3 | 8.3 | 0.0 |
| Farm acquired as joint inheritance | 7.0 | 5.6 | 5.6 |
| Multiple farms inherited | 7.0 | 0.0 | 2.8 |
|  | $N=57$ | $N=72$ | $N=71$ |

to a small farm or piece of land given, say, to his mother as a dowry, or perhaps to an unmarried uncle as an inheritance.

The incidence of joint inheritance—the practice of having two or more heirs for an undivided property—was rather evenly distributed across all sizes of farms. Joint tenancy, like subdivision, was a response to the desire to keep more than one child in the farm without formally dividing the holding. In 1852, joint tenancy was found among over a third of the landholders in four of the townlands in the Ballyduff study district, among 20–30 percent of landholders in four more townlands, and among at least 8 percent of landholders in an additional four townlands. Under joint tenancy, each farmer might well have his own house and some outbuildings, but there was no official division of the property. Records of the Ballyduff Land League for August 1881 sketched the plight of two brothers who "allowed their farms be sold by their landlord in Tralee. They were two farms but they held in common."[41]

The relative frequency of joint tenure or subdivision has largely depended on the changing attitudes of landlords and legislators.[42] Local efforts to comply with the demands of landlords while adhering to different values produced some complex cases. Land registry documents recorded instances of ownership as "tenant in common of an undivided moiety" or even cases where the individual was owner of "two undivided third parts" of a property.

Son Inheritance

The inheritance of the farm by a son, who can continue the family name upon the land, is generally taken to be an important component of the rigid stem family system.[43] Son inheritance appeared to be a strong preference in all farm classes within the Ballyduff data set (see table 6.3).

Success in transferring the farm to a son was greatest among those with the largest farms. Of those farmers whose property exceeded seventy acres, nearly 82 percent in Generations 1–3 successfully transferred the farm to a son. There was a distance of fifteen percentage points between these most successful farmers and the least successful (thirty to thirty-nine acres) farmers.

Another element that is often included as part of the Irish "rigid" stem family system is the eleventh-hour designation of which son is to inherit. Theoretically, this was done to keep other sons in suspense and thus dedicated to laboring for the father on the farm. Verdon

Table 6.3

Frequency of Son Inheritance and of Farmer Nonmarriage by Farm Size
for Three Generations

|  | Large farmers | Medium farmers | Small farmers |
| --- | --- | --- | --- |
| Farm inherited by son | 76.5% | 70.9% | 70.6% |
|  | (N=68) | (N=86) | (N=109) |
| Farmer nonmarriage | 9.0 | 7.1 | 6.3 |
|  | (N=67) | (N=84) | (N=111) |

made this tension-breeding element a centerpiece of his analysis of
the stem family system, stating clearly that "there are seldom any
strict rules of inheritance."[44] I found little evidence of such eleventh-
hour designation of heirs in Ballyduff for the period under analysis.
In a few cases, sons who returned home between the 1901 and 1911
censuses may have done so in anticipation of an inheritance that was
as yet undetermined. However, I also encountered in the census
records specific designation of still unmarried sons as "farmer's son"
while his brothers were designated as "farm laborers."[45]

It is noteworthy that in all my discussions with farmers in Ballyduff only one farmer volunteered to me the importance of keeping
the sons guessing about which one would inherit. This particular
farm had been signed over to the youngest son of four, who, at the
time of my study, remained unmarried at the age of thirty. His elder
brothers (ages thirty-three, thirty-six, and thirty-eight) had all emigrated, and two were already married. In some cases, attempts to
"keep them guessing" may not have had the desired result.

For those cases where the birth order position of the inheriting son
was known, nearly half the heirs were eldest sons. Considering the
fact that 66 percent of all farm families in Generations 1–3 had more
than two sons, this suggests the existence of some small degree of
bias favoring the eldest son as heir.[46] The Ballyduff data also suggest
that bias favoring the eldest son was strongest among the largest
farmers. The smallest farms, being marginally productive, tended to
turn the older children out to earn their own living long before the
old man was ready to pass on the inheritance.

A slight statistical bias favoring primogeniture may not constitute
anything that Verdon would agree to call a "strict rule of inheritance."[47] However, there are cultural factors that may be relevant
here. Within the Ballyduff area, there was a practice of naming the
eldest son after the paternal grandfather.[48] Although the local people
deny that there has been any conscious preference for passing the

farm to the son who bears the same name as his farmer grandfather, the "marking" of the preferred heir in this way is probably culturally significant. In eighty-five cases a farm was passed on to an individual with the same first name as the individual from whom it had been inherited.[49] This represents nearly 36 percent of the total cases in which first names of both individuals were known and in which both of the individuals were men. The regularity and significance of this practice in Irish history merits further study.

Despite the clear preference for a son as heir to the family farm, failure of son inheritance did not emerge as a strongly charged issue. In the extended data set for six cohorts (including those in the farms in 1986), 8 percent of known transfers had gone to a daughter, 3.5 percent to siblings, and 6.6 percent to a niece or nephew. Furthermore, 11.8 percent of landholders for the entire time period were women.[50] Female ownership ranged from a low of 5.4 percent in Generation 1 to a high of 14.9 percent in Generation 3. Women did not represent dead ends for the land: of seventy-six female landholders, only seven were unmarried. Furthermore, of the 285 farmers in my sample for whom both the donor and recipient of the farm were known, almost 17 percent either received their farm from a woman or passed it to a woman. One farmer shared with me his observation that, in general, the name changes on the land every three or four generations.

When inheritance had to resort to nephews and nieces, keeping the patronym on the land did not emerge as a high priority, although the heir did tend to be a consanguine more often than an affine of the farmer. For County Donegal, Shanklin reported a clear preference for a brother's son who had the same surname.[51] In Ballyduff, of forty cases involving niece or nephew inheritance, nineteen involved a brother's child and eighteen a sister's child; the remaining three heirs were nephews of unspecified kinship. Naming customs ensured that both brothers and sisters would have had a son named after the grandfather. Marriage customs may have biased selection in favor of the sisters having sons who lived near enough to be of some assistance to the bachelor or childless farmer.

A case study may best illustrate the hierarchy of values at work here. The case record begins with Seamus C. who held 9.0 acres in the townland of Ardoughter in 1852 (see figure 6.1). This was inherited by his son, Dermot, who became full owner of the property in 1922 under the Land Acts. Dermot C. had a son, Michael, who married out into a farm in a neighboring townland in 1911. He also had a foster daughter, Anne R., who married Seamus B. The C. farm

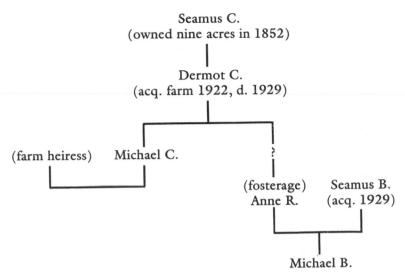

*Figure 6.1.* Farm Inheritance in the C. Family

in Ardoughter was deeded to Seamus B. in 1929, the same year that old man Dermot C. died. In this case, there was a son who could have inherited the property; but since he had already been well provided for elsewhere, the farm was passed to a foster daughter in her husband's name. This foster daughter was probably a granddaughter of Dermot C.[52] In this case, farmer C. ensured his son's welfare by allowing him to marry into a better farm than the one he had rights to inherit. Some things are more important than keeping the family name on the land. Keeping a family in the farm is perhaps of greater importance than keeping the farm in the family.

Taken separately, none of the categories of farm recipients other than sons contains a very large percentage of the total. Taken together, however, they account for over 18 percent of all transfers. It makes some difference whether they are to be treated as "successful" or "failed" farm transfers—"makeshifts," to use Arensberg's term.[53] The passage of the farm to someone other than a son in one generation did not appear to have had a significant negative impact on subsequent transfers. Of 142 individuals other than sons who received farms, fifty-nine heirs, or 41.5 percent, subsequently passed the farm to their own sons. Only 4.9 percent passed to strangers, usually through the mechanism of sale. This compares favorably with the 4.7 percent of inheriting sons who also subsequently passed their family farms to a stranger.

Heir Marriage

The next factor in the rigid stem family model is the necessity of marriage for the farm heir. Arensberg and Kimball were most emphatic about the importance of heir marriage: "Only through marriage does one attain full stature," they wrote, adding that failure to marry meant also "failure to provide for the dispersal and reformation of one's group" as well as "failure to maintain or establish the alliances making status among one's peers."[54]

In Ballyduff, all three categories of farmers were, in the cohorts under study, remarkably successful at contracting marriages. In each class, at least 90 percent of the farmers married. The highest figure was 96.6 percent, and this was for the smallest farmers (see Table 6.3). Whatever the rates of nonmarriage may have been in Ireland in general during this time period, the farmers in this relatively prosperous district were still managing to find spouses.[55]

When the heir did fail to marry, it did not constitute a practical problem in Ballyduff.[56] Of thirty-nine cases of unmarried farmers for whom complete data on farm transfers are available, six (15 percent) passed the farm to a brother's son, twelve (31 percent) to a sister's son, five (13 percent) to a brother, four (10 percent) to a sister, and six (15 percent) to other relatives. Only four (10 percent) passed the farm to unrelated individuals. Although the proportion of unmarried farmers who passed farms to strangers exceeded the average figure of about 5 percent, the regularity with which these bachelor farmers were able to pass the farm on to a relative is noteworthy. These are the farmers who are usually cast as "dead ends" in the classic "gloom-and-doom" ethnographies of rural Ireland.[57] In Ballyduff, almost 85 percent of all unmarried farmers were successful in keeping the farm in the family.

Although it was certainly preferred that the heir marry and produce a new generation in the farm, what really seems to have mattered most was that some member of the sibling set marry and reproduce locally. That at least ensured a supply of candidates as heir to the family farm. In the case of the M. family of Knoppoge, for example, three bachelor brothers held the farm jointly in the 1930s while two other brothers apparently emigrated. Two sisters, however, married into farms in neighboring townlands. When it came time for the farm to be passed on, a nephew from one of these marriages was selected.

Three Coresident Generations

The next criterion of the rigid stem family—the sine qua non in some analyses—is the prevalence of three-generation households. As has been well recognized in the literature, the three-generation form of the stem family household is but one phase in the family and household development cycle. Taking it as a starting point, it is easy to see that it would cease to exist with the death of the elderly grandparents and would not come into existence again until after one of the grandchildren married and had children. Thus, one cannot expect a very large proportion of households to exhibit the three-generational form even where it is customary for all households to pass through such a stage.

Laslett suggested that in a community in which formation of three-generational households was a regular part of the development cycle, "we should expect something between about 22 and 27 percent of all households, or perhaps even more, to have a generational depth of three or above," although he accepts Wrigley's lower figure of 15 percent as a reasonable minimum.[58] Fitzpatrick wisely advocated caution in utilizing any such "standard" figures, which would, at any rate, be applicable only to a large population or a sample whose claims to represent the appropriate universe could be statistically substantiated.[59] A case could be made for Ireland that a somewhat lower frequency would be consistent with a three-generation ideal. Where marriage is not entered into until the middle to late thirties (or beyond), the "old couple" often will not last many years after the birth of the first grandchild. Under such a regime, the three-generation structure can be very fleeting indeed.

Gibbon and Curtin found 12.2 percent of 295 households in their study of fifteen selected townlands to be three-generational.[60] Of these 295 households, 80 percent were headed by farmers. Fitzpatrick found three-generational households among 13.8 percent of the farming households in his 1901 sample and among 14.1 percent of the farming households in the 1911 sample.[61] In Ballyduff (see table 6.4), I found that among strong farmers (those employing one or more servants and/or controlling 40 acres or more) three lineal generations were present in 14.3 percent of households headed by individuals born before 1900. Among more modest farmers, 12.6 percent of the households were three-generational.[62]

In identifying these three-generational households, I followed

Table 6.4
Frequency of Coresidence by Three Generations,
by Occupational Class

|  | Strong farmers | Modest farmers | Nonagricultural labor | |
|---|---|---|---|---|
| Three lineal generations | 14.3% | 12.6% | 11.5% | 11.1% |
| Three total generations | 25.0 | 23.4 | 15.4 | 22.2 |

Fitzpatrick in counting only those where the three generations were linked in clear lineal descent—that is, grandparents, parents, and grandchildren. There were a number of other households, however, in which a grandchild or grandchildren were present who were not the offspring of a resident son or daughter. Such households were, I believe, correctly identified by Fitzpatrick as cases of fosterage—the custom of raising children in a household other than their natal one.[63] When these cases were added to the lineal three-generation households, the figures increased in an interesting fashion. Strong farmers reached the 25 percent mark and modest farmers reached 23.4 percent. This suggests that the three-generation household was an element of Irish culture transcending both class differences and the normal demographic limitations.[64]

## Dispersal of Siblings

In Ireland the question of dispersal of siblings from farm households generally translates, under the rigid model, into permanent emigration. Discussions of sibling dispersal sometimes reveal the covert assumption of the ethnographer that it is the natural tendency for children to want to leave home and for parents to want to "empty the nest" of all offspring, save the heir.[65] The fate of noninheriting sons and undowered daughters is treated casually or else ignored altogether. In the Arensberg and Kimball scenario, one son inherits, one daughter with a dowry marries into a farm, and the other children "must travel."[66]

Such permanent long-distance emigration was a historical rather than a cultural phenomenon.[67] As noted in the introductory remarks, the permanent dispersal of all noninheriting offspring was not the ideal, even in County Clare in the 1930s. Simple logic suggests that if only two children from each family settled locally over several generations, kinship networks could not be as dense as they are often observed to be. Hannan's 1979 study of 408 contemporary farm families, drawn from Ulster, Connaught, and the two westernmost counties of Munster, found that the farmers who were able to maintain strong local kin networks—that is, those who avoided excessive permanent emigration—were more successful as farmers.[68] Whether the strong kin networks are to be seen as a cause or a consequence of the strength of the farming enterprise is irrelevant. The fact that the two go together is the significant point.

The density of kinship networks in some townlands of Ballyduff clearly indicates that permanent universal emigration for nonheirs has not been very assiduously practiced. The families intermarried in different ways in each succeeding generation, resulting in a dense web of kinship. For example (see figure 6.2), in the townlands of Cloghane and Kilmore in 1852 there were, in the larger farms, two A. families (the heads of household were probably cousins), a D. family, and an H. family. By 1901 we find one A. son married to a D., and another D. daughter married to an H. In the second A. family, a foster daughter (there were no natural offspring) married a K. from the nearby townland of Clashmelcon. Two of their sons married H. women. Michael married Margaret H.; her brother Timothy married Michael's grandfather's cousin's granddaughter Hanora A., whose daughter Catherine married Michael's brother Patrick. In the H. family of 1901, two sons and two daughters ended up in local farms, with another son and two daughters also marrying locally. In the D. family, one son and three daughters ended up in local or regional farms. In the K. (originally A.) family, three sons married into or inherited local farms.

The dispersal of nonheirs was sometimes facilitated or encouraged by their being given some inheritance from the family estate. For the Ballyduff area, in only nine cases did instruments of land transfer include reference to payments being made to noninheriting siblings. Nearly four times as many instruments included provisos for such siblings' continued occupation of the family home "until marriage" or "until age 21" or "while he works on the land in a reasonable manner." Sometimes these "burdens" on land ownership included inhibitions prohibiting the owner from selling the property without the approval of siblings named in the instrument. This suggests that there was more often concern to provide for nondispersing (or late-dispersing) siblings than to "buy out" their interests and facilitate permanent dispersal.

Permanent emigration of all nonheirs must be seen as a short-term, self-terminating strategy pursued primarily by those farmers whose

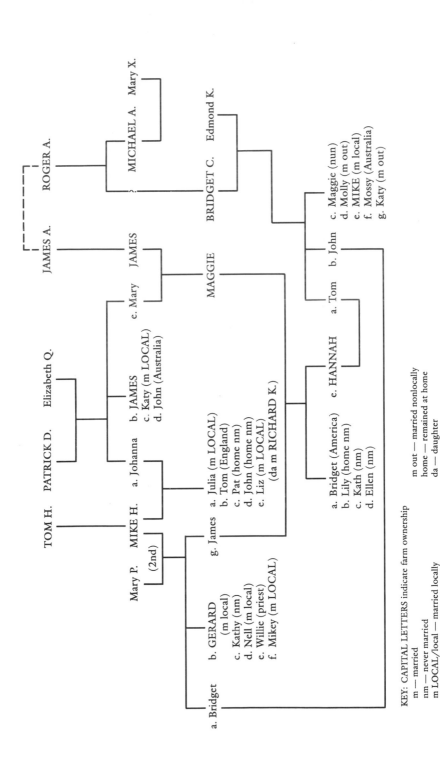

KEY: CAPITAL LETTERS indicate farm ownership

m — married                          m out — married nonlocally
nm — never married                   home — remained at home
m LOCAL/local — married locally      da — daughter

*Figure 6.2.* Density of Local Kinship Networks

Table 6.5
Indicators of Sibling Nondispersal, by Farm Size,
and for Three Generations

|  | Large farmers | Medium farmers | Small farmers |
|---|---|---|---|
| Sibling(s) remain at home, unmarried | 28.6% ($N=21$) | 36.0% ($N=25$) | 35.3% ($N=17$) |
| Sibling(s) marry and settle locally | 68.2 ($N=22$) | 65.7 ($N=35$) | 72.0 ($N=25$) |

Table 6.6
Siblings of Farmers Placed in Other Farms: Percent Distribution by Farm
Size for Three Generations

|  | Large farmers | Medium farmers | Small farmers |
|---|---|---|---|
| Sister married into farm | 89.5% ($N=19$) | 61.9% ($N=21$) | 64.3% ($N=14$) |
| Other sibling also in farm | 61.9 ($N-21$) | 46.4 ($N=28$) | 41.2 ($N-17$) |

farm enterprises were so marginal as to offer little future for heirs and
no future at all for siblings. The association of stem families with
both postfamine adaptations and "gloom-and-doom" ethnography is
no coincidence. Verdon stated: "In Ireland, it was at the very moment
when land pressures started to be relieved through mass emigration
that stem families first made their appearance."[69] Fitzpatrick, on the
other hand, saw "mass emigration" as an indicator of the decay of the
stem family.[70] Defined under the rigid model, the stem family emerges
as a paradoxical sort of phenomenon: almost as soon as the system is
well established enough to be clearly identifiable, it will also be
observed to be in decline.

For the cohorts under analysis in Ballyduff, fewer than half of
those identified in family history interviews as permanent emigrants
came from farming families. About a third of the farmers in this
study had one or more siblings who remained at home and never
married. More than two-thirds had siblings (other than the requisite
sister with dowry) who had married locally (see tables 6.5 and 6.6).

In some cases, additional houses were built on the family property
to accommodate nondispersing siblings. Sometimes the new house
was for the newly married heir while a parent continued to occupy
the old home with one or more as yet unmarried offspring.[71] In other
cases, the two houses accommodated siblings who held the farm

jointly. Between 1901 and 1910, such household fission produced ten new households in Ballyduff, and fifteen new households emerged as an apparent consequence of neolocal postmarital residence within the district. Neither of these phenomena is accounted for in the rigid stem model.

The incomplete dispersal of siblings in Ballyduff may again be due in part to the relative prosperity of agriculture. In other words, the severe form of sibling dispersal, in which one son inherits, one daughter marries into a farm, and everyone else is written out of the scene forever may be a consequence of economic distress. It seems clear that complete dispersal was not the guiding goal in Ballyduff. Rather, the preference was for the favorable placement of as many children as possible, including local settlement in many cases.

### Farm Size and Stem Factors

The rigid model of the stem family is unsatisfactory as either a "model for" or a "model of" behavior in the Irish countryside. Although the rigid model is more applicable to certain times and places than to others,[72] a loose stem model is more universally applicable and more conducive to instructive comparison and analysis.

Perhaps what has been most effectively demonstrated here is that the stem family model—whether in rigid or loose form—is not a unitary phenomenon but a confluence of variables that can in fact come together in a number of different ways. The distribution of these variables by farm class emerged as an important focus of this analysis.[73] There was a significant difference in the operation of the five factors discussed that depended on the size of the farm enterprise.

### Big Farmers

In general, big farmers were most likely to divide the farm, to inherit more than one farm, or to be involved in a joint tenure arrangement. Larger farmers also had a tendency, during the early decades of the twentieth century, to purchase additional farms for nonstem heirs under the favorable provisions of the Land Acts. This to some extent accounts for the greater numbers of large farmers who had a sibling other than the sister with a dowry in a farm.

The economic attractiveness and prestige of the large farm enterprise made this class of farmer most successful at transmitting the farm to a son—and this in spite of the somewhat higher rates of nonmarriage and slightly smaller-than-average completed family size. Large or "strong" farmers were also most successful at forming three-generation households, lineally or otherwise. This was not simply caused by the availability of a big house that would be more congenial to larger numbers or greater diversity of coresidents. These most affluent farmers could most readily have afforded the separate dwellings necessary to avoid such expansive households. The positive value associated with the three-generation household is most evident under such conditions of clear choice.

Large farmers were least likely to have coresident, unmarried siblings. Here again, it appears likely that their relative wealth made them more capable of financing the education or training that enabled such siblings to find a livelihood off the farm, whether their ultimate settlement was nearby or far away. Finally, their ability to hire servants and laborers made coresident siblings unimportant to the ongoing agricultural enterprise.

Although larger farmers may appear to have been more successful at sibling dispersal, their children in many cases remained strongly tapped into a vital family network. These largest farmers were the most successful at marrying a sister (and sometimes several of them) into a farm. The rather unremarkable statistic regarding other siblings who married locally (68 percent for large farmers, compared with 66 percent for medium-sized farmers and 72 percent for small farmers) masks the fact that, for large farmers, the reference region extended beyond that which was utilized for drawing the statistic. That is to say, the sons and daughters of large farmers married the sons and daughters of other large farmers and thus often drew from a wider region than did the small to medium-sized farmers. This was, furthermore, a self-reinforcing tendency—if you had relatives in another region, the likelihood that you would find a spouse from that region increased.

## Small Farmers

The smallest farmers were most successful at accomplishing unitary inheritance. However, as noted above, they generally had little alternative as the patrimony was simply too meager to support more than one family. They were, by contrast, least successful at finding a son to accept the place—and this in spite of the fact that they had the lowest incidence of nonmarriage, the lowest age at marriage, and the largest average completed family size. They were also least able to form three-generation households. However, they had the highest proportion of siblings married locally. There were, of course, more small farms than large farms and thus a larger pool of potential marriage partners available locally. The likelihood of local settlement was further increased by the fact that small farmers sometimes deigned to allow a younger son or daughter to marry the offspring of a tradesman, a laborer, or a fisherman.

Medium-Sized Farmers

With respect to most of the five criteria, medium-sized farmers truly fell "in between" the largest and smallest farmers. This supports the argument that these indicators are sensitive to the size and productivity of the farm enterprise.

On a few variables, however, the medium-sized farmers deviated from the pattern of continuous distribution. Specifically, they appeared less able than either large or small farmers to dower a sister into a farm, and they had fewer siblings who married locally than had either larger or smaller farmers. Both of these features may be due to the fact that medium farmers were, on the one hand, more sensitive to status than were the smaller farmers and were, thus, less willing for a child to marry a nonfarmer. On the other hand, they were less able to tap into the wider regional marriage pool that was available to the larger farmers. Taken together, this resulted in fewer potential marriage partners for medium farmers than were available for either large farmers or small farmers.

## Of Time and the Stem Family

When we abandon the rigid stem family model in favor of a loose model, our views of Irish rural history are transformed. Perhaps it is merely the salutary effects of abandoning a functionalist model and turning to look at Irish history as a force shaping social process through its effects on the lives of real people that makes the difference. The five variables comprising the stem model—unitary inheritance, son inheritance, heir marriage, the three-generation household, and sibling dispersal—have been affected differently by historical events and circumstances.

First of all, the requirement that the farm be passed on intact is not rooted in Irish culture; it arose historically from landlords' management strategies, legislative decisions, and economic exigency. "Rigid" stem ideals were reinforced by the triumph of freehold "ownership in fee simple" in the late nineteenth and early twentieth centuries and by laws in 1903 and 1907 prohibiting subdivision. Prior forms of tenure—especially under the ancient contract system[74] and to a lesser extent the various forms of Norman and English feudalism—were more flexible.[75] Moreover, despite the legal circumscriptions of 1903 and 1927, farmers continued to try to provide for as many children as possible, which they often did by settling more than the one sister with dowry into farms nearby as well as by carving off small portions of the family farm as a lesser inheritance. These parts and pieces were then redistributed in each generation. This historical aspect of the system emerges only with a longer time perspective than is customary among most anthropologists. Unitary inheritance, then, is a feature responsive to both economic and demographic factors and is not a cultural fixture.

Second, the patrilineal notion that a farm ought to go to a son and that, by whatever means, the patronym ought to remain upon the land, emerged only weakly in this study. In fact, the observations here are more consistent with an ambilineal, or cognatic, rather than a patrilineal conceptualization of the family.[76] To the extent that a son is the preferred heir, it is because the man is the primary farmer. However, the Irish understand clearly that a farm needs a woman as well as a man. Son inheritance, then, is a cultural factor unrelated to any rigidly patrilineal ideals. It turns pliant under demographic pressures.

Third, the provision that the inheriting son must marry has also been shown to be of variable importance. As long as someone in the sibling set married in order to provide an heir in the next generation, there seems to have been little sense of crisis. At the very least, it is erroneous and misleading to assume that bachelor farmers constitute "terminal families" or signal "family failure." In Ballyduff, they were well able to find an heir for the farm from within the family. Nonmarriage is a culturally acceptable option in Ireland, even for farmers. Demographic factors affecting the availability of spouses and economic factors affecting the attractiveness of farm life as opposed to other opportunities also have had their impact on the frequency of heir marriage.

Fourth, the three-generation household occurred with notable frequency among all farm classes of the rural district under study here, although it was most regularly achieved by those who could best afford it—that is, the most well-to-do farmers. The frequency with which the three-generation household was simulated by inclusion of grandchildren through fosterage is a strong indication of the cultural importance of the concept of three generations.[77] Of all the five factors under analysis here, this is probably the one most strongly embedded in Irish culture.

Finally, the dictate that noninheriting siblings "must travel" is not a cultural prescription with any historic depth; rather, it is an adaptation to economic marginality and absence of opportunities for livelihood in the countryside. Wherever possible, it is apparent that farmers tried to settle children locally or otherwise provide for their well-being without extruding them permanently from the extended family network.

Acceptance of the rigid stem family model has led many observers to write—sometimes eloquently—about the death of Irish culture[78] and the "eclipse of community" through demoralization,[79] or to emphasize the prevalence of "terminal families" and "family failure."[80] The "gloom-and-doom" ethos that has pervaded native Irish scholarship is itself a phenomenon worthy of examination.[81] The removal of a proportion of each successive generation from the countryside may appear tragic to those who are being removed (and it is they, invariably, who have done the analysis and writing). But this regular outflow of "surplus" population—which has varied from trickle to tidal wave, depending on time, place, and circumstance—has been part and parcel of the Irish family system for many generations. What is more fascinating than their predictable departure is the regularity with which their descendants still return to Ireland with a clear sense that they are somehow "going home."

What looks like failure under a strict interpretation of the rigid stem model is in fact the strength of the real system—its flexibility and resilience. The only real "failure" occurred when the farm and family nexus was finally broken—when the family died out and/or the farm passed to strangers. Of all the farm transitions for all generations in the Ballyduff study area on which I have the requisite data (484 cases), less than 3 percent were acquired from individuals of unknown identity and unlikely to be related. About 6 percent of the 484 farms were passed to strangers, usually by sale. This is a total of only twenty-five cases in which the farm-family nexus is known to have been broken over the entire eighty-five years of the study period, from 1901 to 1986.

The rigid stem family model has also perpetrated a view of the Irish as more concerned with the integrity of the enterprise (an eminently English characteristic) than with the livelihoods of the family. The change in emphasis here allows us to resolve the paradox observed by Hannan when he commented on the existence of "conflicting aims" within the system. He identified these as follows: "to pass on the family property (the patrimony) as a unit from one generation to another, while also providing for all the other children in the family."[82] If we accept that neither aim is an absolute, then we can see that they are not really in conflict because the long-term success of each depends upon the other. A more adequate statement of the ideal would be something like "preservation of the farm-family nexus" with the coequal values of the integrity of the farm and the integrity of the family being creatively balanced against one another in each successive generation.

In sum, I would argue that, although the manifest forms and processes of Irish farm families have certainly changed through the generations, the preservation of the farm-family nexus has been a consistent goal. Keeping the farm intact was never more important than providing for the children of the farm; however, providing for the children's children required caution against dividing up the farm too finely. Keeping the name on the land was an ideal that was easily relinquished when a sister's son seemed better fit to occupy the place. Ensuring a spouse and children for the farm heir was not of critical importance, provided that one or more of his siblings married and produced potential heirs. The three-generation household, although only briefly experienced in its true lineal form (and for many farmers never experienced at all due to demographic circumstances), was yet of such symbolic importance that customs allowing households to replicate such a form through fosterage survived well into the twentieth century. By this time, fosterage customs appear to have lost whatever practical adaptive value they may once have had. Fostered-in children often disrupted the labor-consumer balance and only rarely stepped in as substitute offspring to become heir to the place. Finally, dispersal of the siblings of the heir was the most highly variable of all the components of the stem model.

We have still failed to answer the question of why the rigid stem model became so entrenched in the literature and so readily equated with the Irish peasantry. The best explanation is that it fit our needs at a certain stage in the development of anthropology, when functionalist analysis and the "ethnographic present" were standard fare. Fortunately, our comprehension of change has now burst the bonds of such naive concepts as diffusion, unilinear evolution, and even acculturation, modernization, and development. Perhaps we can now confront history and process and the complexities of particular eth-nographic cases more effectively.

The stem family is neither an evolutionary stage nor a deviation from a nuclear-family norm; rather, it is an adaptive pattern that can emerge whenever and wherever economic and demographic circum-stances are right and the cultural setting is congenial. The variability that can be observed in the regions where the stem family has emerged can be tied to such circumstances and productively analyzed. Such analysis and comparison will be most useful if the various component features of the stem family system—unitary inheritance, son inheri-tance, heir marriage, three-generation households, and sibling disper-sal—are not assumed to co-occur but are treated instead as separate, though potentially interconnected, phenomena.

Simplistic typologies and classificatory schemes are useful at cer-tain stages of the development of scientific and historic understand-ing. In the case of the history of the family in Europe—and especially in Ireland—they have clearly outlived their usefulness. It is time to deconstruct the stem family model and release Irish rural history from the hold that the image of the stem family has too long held over it.

## NOTES

1. Gibbon (1973); Brody (1973); Hannan (1982).
2. Connell (1962).
3. Brody (1973); Scheper-Hughes (1979a).
4. This is not to suggest that historical awareness is totally lacking in all analyses of the Irish family. As counterexamples, note Gibbon's treatment of the "dissolution" process of the "middle peasantry" and O'Neill's analysis of "proletarianization" in the generations leading up to the Famine (Gibbon 1973; O'Neill 1984).
5. Shanklin (1985). Although stem families surely existed prior to the Famine, as documented for County Cavan by O'Neill (1984) and for Galway and Meath by Carney (1980), they increased in frequency and prominence after the Famine (Breen 1984a; Fitzpatrick 1982).
6. Arensberg (1937, 1988); Arensberg and Kimball (1940); Goldschmidt and Kunkel (1971); Verdon (1979).
7. LePlay (1871).
8. Laslett (1972:16–17).
9. Segalen (1986:18).
10. Laslett (1972:16); see also Gibbon and Curtin (1978:429).
11. Much of the substantive progress in analysis of the history of the European family has developed out of the seminal work of Hajnal (1965, 1982). Hajnal did not include stem family systems in the formulation of his

hypothesis, however, choosing to make general contrasts between simple family systems and complex family systems. Moreover, his hypothesis was primarily about family formation and especially marriage practices, topics that are not discussed in any detail in the present paper. Thus, although I acknowledge the importance of Hajnal's work and that of many Europeanist scholars who have followed (or disputed) his lead (see especially Alter 1991), readers will find no further mention of his work in this paper.

12. Laslett (1972:59–60).

13. Segalen (1986:31–37).

14. Laslett (1972:22).

15. Verdon (1979:95–96). Verdon also cited the generally tense nature of relationships within the family, specifically between father and son and between daughter-in-law and everybody else. Verdon's main point was that the stem family is part of a system in which the "limit of growth"—mainly the result of economic factors—is different from that of systems having either larger patriarchal families or smaller nuclear ones.

16. Fox (1978:99).

17. Kennedy (1973:151–52). For the record, the definition is qualified with "under stable agricultural conditions."

18. Verdon (1979:103). Jural regulation of inheritance and child dispersal in various parts of Europe has been discussed by Gaunt (1987), d'Argemir (1988), Douglass (1988b), and Kertzer and Brettell (1987).

19. Segalen (1986:19).

20. Laslett (1972:16); my emphasis.

21. Fitzpatrick (1983:366–67).

22. Fitzpatrick (1983).

23. Arensberg and Kimball (1940:77).

24. Fitzpatrick (1983); Varley (1983); Harris (1988).

25. Hannan (1982:153).

26. Fitzpatrick (1983:369).

27. Research was supported by a Fulbright Research Fellowship and an association with the Economic and Social Research Institute in Dublin. Further funding was supplied by National Science Foundation grant No. BNS–8606731 and grants from Lamar University, Beaumont.

28. Kerry County Committee of Agriculture (1972), end map.

29. County Kerry Committee of Agriculture (1972).

30. Kerry County Committee of Agriculture (1972:122).

31. The townlands included Ardcullen, Ardcullen Marsh, Ardoughter, Ayle, Ballyhorgan, Ballyhorgan Marsh, Benmore, Bishopscourt North, Bishopscourt South, Cloghane, Clooneagh, Derrico, Derrira Beg, Derrira More, Farranedmond, Kilmore, Knockananore, Knocknacree, Knoppoge North, Knoppoge South, Lacca East, Lacca West, Leagh, Leagh Marsh, Rahealy, and Rattoo.

32. This data source is unusually rich, as the researcher is allowed to examine the actual forms filled out by census takers for each household in

1901 and 1911. Data include family relationships, occupations, ages, marital status, education, fluency in Irish, and any disabilities, as well as information on houses and outbuildings. These census schedules are kept in the Public Records Office, Dublin.

33. On request, the Office of the Census will provide researchers with copies of aggregate census data for the specific area of his or her research. Some of these give detailed information by townland. More recent printouts include general information useful for interpreting the census categories.

34. Although the main intent of Griffiths Valuation was, of course, to provide a basis for taxation, it provides an important "snapshot" of heads of households at this particular point in time.

35. I would like to thank Ms. Clare O'Grady-Walshe for her able assistance and companionship in the completion of the field research. I am also very grateful for the assistance and support of the Ballyduff Historical and Archaeological Society, the Ballyduff Magazine Society and the Rattoo Heritage Society. In particular, I would thank Bertie O'Connor, Patsy McKenna, and Mossy Michael O'Connor.

36. Some may find it surprising that in a predominantly farming area such a small percentage (only 11 percent) of those born there would actually be classified as farmers. Consider that most of the thirty-four households in the town were not headed by farmers and that some of those in the rural areas also pursued other occupations, as enumerated later. Furthermore, in a given farm family, usually no more than two or three offspring in any generation (which might include from two to a dozen or more) would be farmers.

37. Along the Cashen River within the study area, fishing was a specialization but not a full-time occupation. Salmon fishing was the major source of revenue, and it was a highly seasonal activity. The rest of the year, the fishermen hired out as laborers or else emigrated temporarily to England. In the census records, fishermen were most often identified as laborers. Thus, it is a practical convenience to lump laborers and fishermen together as a single category.

38. The breakdown of farms into meaningful categorical groups is inevitably controversial. Arensberg and Kimball apparently used a breakdown of less than fifty acres (although they also mentioned thirty acres) as a small farm, fifty to one hundred acres as a medium-sized farm, and anything above one hundred acres as a large farm (1940:30); Arensberg (1988:49). Gibbon and Curtin defined small farms as being under ten acres, breaking the middle category into farms of ten to fifty acres in the "lower range" and fifty to one hundred acres in the "higher range." They also described their categories in terms of valuations, defining areas with a valuation of less that £4 per annum as "lower-valuation areas" and those with valuations of £4–15 per acre per annum as "higher-valuation areas" (1978:453). Fitzpatrick sought to combine these two measures of rural prosperity and poverty by using the valuation of the farms to create categories, while using different break points in the

different areas, depending on the average standards of farm prosperity and poverty prevalent in the region (1983:356). My categories reflect the "natural" breaks in the distribution of farm sizes in the Ballyduff area. I have not attempted to control for farm valuations.

39. Shanklin (1985:84). O'Neill (1984) provided a somewhat more thoughtful and comprehensive analysis.

40. In general, once the data were broken down by both farm size and cohort, the resulting sample sizes were too small to manipulate statistically.

41. National Library, Land League Records.

42. Ross (1986); Clark (1979).

43. Arensberg (1988:82); Shanklin (1985:86).

44. Verdon (1979:95–96); see also Harris (1988:421–22).

45. This observation raises some interesting questions regarding census takers and census forms. The census forms were designed, written, and printed in Dublin, and the categories did not always correspond very precisely to the "native categories" in the countryside. Marilyn Silverman reported that in Thomastown such cognitive dissonance does not emerge in the census records—there was a consistent designation of the head of household as "farmer" and each child as either "farmer's son" or "farmer's daughter" (personal communication). I suspect that the relative consistency or inconsistency of census categories and their application is a localized and probably highly variable phenomenon. Even within the Ballyduff area, the different "styles" of the several census takers can be detected.

46. Of some 750 sons born to farmers of Generations 1–3, only 264 were first sons. A random distribution of farms without regard to the birth-order position of the heir would result in some 35 percent of first sons inheriting, whereas in fact more than 45 percent of heirs were first sons.

47. Verdon (1979:96).

48. Breen (1982b:703).

49. I do not here include an additional two cases for which the same statement could be made, but in which both reference individuals were women!

50. I did not count widows as landholders; only women who were primary heirs as daughters, sisters, nieces, and so on, of the previous owner were counted here. This is not to belittle the fact that many farm widows truly became farmers in their own right nor to ignore their legal status as owners. It is done in recognition of the fact that widows are generally seen as holding the land "in trust" for the heir. A widow (or widower) merely "extends" the tenure of the deceased owner, delaying only temporarily the devolution to the heir within the next generation.

51. Shanklin (1985:86).

52. I was told that, in the past, daughters (and especially eldest daughters) often returned home to give birth to their first child, sometimes leaving the child to be raised by the grandparents in fosterage. This custom was corroborated by census data indicating the presence of grandchildren without their

parents as well as the absence of known living children from their parental household. In addition, birth records often indicated the place of birth as the mother's home townland rather than the townland of the parents' postmarital residence.

53. Arensberg (1988:91).

54. Arensberg and Kimball (1940:221).

55. Hannan noted that "by 1911 most demographic analysts had concluded that . . . a higher rate of celibacy and late age of marriage had become the main defining demographic feature of western Ireland" (1982:150).

56. In a recent study, Guinnane (1991) suggested that the late age at marriage and high rate of nonmarriage for Irish farmers was tied to the accessibility of alternative support mechanisms—specifically, continuing ties to siblings, the ease of securing "surrogate heirs," and certain provisions of the Poor Law.

57. Even Hannan, who generally took a more positive outlook on agrarian conditions, used the "percentage of all farmers who are over 55 and who have remained single" as a "measure of the level of failure of the small farmer class to reproduce itself on its own property" (1982:159–61).

58. Laslett (1972:58–59); Wrigley (1969:131–35). Demographic constraints on the statistical prevalence of the stem family also have been discussed in some detail by Douglass (1988) and by Kertzer (1989). Both acknowledged that cultural preferences could significantly mitigate the impact of demographic factors.

59. Fitzpatrick (1983:363).

60. Gibbon and Curtin (1978:438).

61. Fitzpatrick (1983:361).

62. The categories *strong farmer* and *modest farmer* reflect the shift to a different data set, one organized in terms of households rather than individuals. Since this data set relies primarily on the 1901 and 1911 census schedules, information on farm sizes is not as precise and cannot support the three-category scheme utilized for the individual-based data set.

63. Fitzpatrick (1983:360, note 47).

64. Hammel (1984:40) stated that "of the three factors that might affect proportions of households by type, an unambiguous and strictly followed cultural rule system has the greatest effect, followed by randomness, followed by actual differences in central demographic rates." This is a general, theoretical observation whose applicability to any given case can be affected by such things as the nature of demographic differences and the rigidity of cultural rule systems. His main point—and the one to be made here—is that the "relative weight of influences can be discussed."

65. Verdon (1979:98); Cole and Wolf (1974:200–1).

66. Arensberg (1988:82).

67. Fitzpatrick (1982:63–69); Hannan (1982:153).

68. Hannan (1979:97–98, 199).

69. Verdon (1979:98).

70. Fitzpatrick (1982:67).

71. In this case, the construction of the second house may also be seen as an attempt to avoid three-generation coresidence.

72. As Hannan noted, its "historical and regional specificity is quite marked" (1982:153).

73. This issue of class and occupational diversity in the actual incidence of stem family forms was productively addressed by d'Argemir (1988).

74. Outright ownership of land as personal property was not a feature of the ancient Irish system. Rather, as described in the *Senchus Mor* (1865), land was held on a contract basis through rights acquired by individuals as clan and family members. These matters are treated most fully in the "Corus Bescna" in vol. 3 of the *Senchus Mor* and in the tracts in vol. 4 dealing with Fine organization, succession to land, and tenancy.

75. Drudy (1982:198) observed that the Irish system is "too rigid to effect anything but modest structural improvements. In England and Wales, where almost half the farms are rented, structural change has been markedly greater. In Ireland, it must seem ironic that the predominance of owner occupation— a status sought so avidly for so long—may be one of the key obstacles to agrarian development."

76. Fox (1967:146ff). It is unfortunate that anthropology has appropriated the term *clan* as a technical term referring to kinship units constituted by unilineal descent. When used in reference to the Scots (Parman 1990:107–8) or the Irish (Fox 1978:69–70), *clan* refers to a kinship group based on cognatic descent.

77. The frequency with which laborers also produced three-generation households is worthy of a passing reference. However, since I find that this phenomenon was part of an entirely different pattern (Verdon 1979:91–92; O'Neill 1984:19, Birdwell-Pheasant 1986), I defer consideration to another paper.

78. Scheper-Hughes (1979a).

79. Brody (1973).

80. Symes (1972); Hannan (1982:158); Fitzpatrick (1983:364).

81. This concern is addressed by Gibbon (1973:485) and by Shanklin (1985:10–12). Examples of native scholarship of the "gloom-and-doom" genre include Healy's *The Death of an Irish Town* (1968) and O'Brien's pamphlet entitled "The Vanishing Irish: Nation of Bachelors and Spinsters" (1952).

82. Hannan (1979:70).

# 7

# Making the Documents of Conquest Speak: The Transformation of Property, Society, and Settlement in Seventeenth-Century Counties Tipperary and Kilkenny

## WILLIAM J. SMYTH

In a place called Clomantagh in the barony of Crannagh in north Kilkenny, a ruined castle and church stand beside a single farmstead. There are many such places in north Kilkenny. The local people say that there was once a village here that was destroyed by Cromwell. As it happens, Oliver Cromwell never marched through this part of Kilkenny, but the story of the destruction of the village still carries a central truth. It points to the radical transformation in property, society, and settlement structures in Ireland that followed on from the reconquest of Ireland by England in the early modern period. In particular, the story addresses the consequences of the Cromwellian plantation and settlement of Ireland after the "Civil War" of 1641–52.

Yet in the three baronies of Iverk, Knocktopher, and Ida in south Kilkenny (figure 7.1), a total of eighty-six nucleated farm villages have survived, many since at least the medieval period. As Burtchaell has pointed out, the survival of both the duke of Ormond as a leading landlord in this region and quite a number of the old lesser gentry as owners and middlemen provided political protection and patronage for such village communities.[1] Proximity to Waterford city and port meant that these commercially oriented farming villages were able to

sustain and to reproduce their social, economic, and settlement structures by transferring surplus sons and daughters into the commercial
life of the city and the surrounding towns, into the ranks of the clergy
or overseas to Newfoundland and elsewhere. Such communities also
were clearly sustained by cultural continuities in the shape of an early
resurgent Catholic church, a still vibrant oral and written tradition in
Irish, a strong commitment to the competitive and communal field
game of hurling and to other "archaic" features such as "abductions"
and local gentry control of forms of dress and hairstyles. This village
world of south Kilkenny was therefore one of much adaptability,
continuity, and durability.

These two scenarios—the seeming destruction of Clomantagh village and the survival of eighty-six farm villages—reveal the very
different experiences of people and the contrasting histories of settlements and communities at the two ends of a relatively small Irish
county. Moreover, the same county also reveals—as does its much
larger neighbor County Tipperary—other significant regional and
local variations in the social history and ethnography of its rural and
urban communities. It is in these contrasts and variations that my
central research interest lies: in the application of geographical strategies to an understanding of the transformation of Irish societies and
settlements since the seventeenth century. I have worked at the local
parish level, where it is possible to delineate transformations in landholding, settlement, and society from the early eighteenth century
onward.[2] Such work has revealed, however, a chasm between the
recognizably "modern" society of the 1750s and what prevailed before and immediately after the Cromwellian plantation of the mid-
seventeenth century. The elucidation of the nature of Irish settlement
and society in the pre-Cromwellian era is therefore a central concern
of mine. In addressing this question, I have worked and continue to
work at the regional level, focusing in particular on the counties of
Tipperary and Kilkenny but also on the other counties and regions of
Munster and south Leinster.[3] Equally, I have been concerned with
the reconstruction of the consequences of the Cromwellian settlement, both in the short term (say in the period from 1653 to 1660)
and in the longer term—for that poorly researched period in Irish
social history that stretches from around 1660 to 1730. In addressing
these issues, I also work at the island-wide level—seeking to identify
the essential regional and structural forces at work[4] while also recognizing that Ireland and its component regions and settlements have to
be continuously and increasingly located in, and integrated with, the
wider British and Atlantic European frameworks.[5]

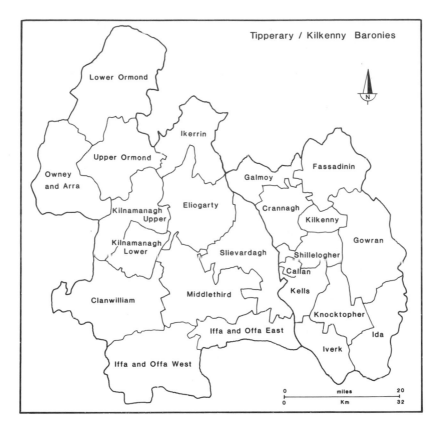

*Figure 7.1.* Baronies of Counties Kilkenny and Tipperary

The objective of this paper is one of reflection—to tell the story of the problems and pleasures of this research endeavor; to dissect and highlight the varying qualities and defects of the seventeenth-century documentary sources that are most relevant to the historical geographer; to emphasize the need for a continuing interaction between documentary, field, and "folk" research strategies; and, it is hoped, to reveal some of the general principles underlying, as well as the rich regional diversities that still characterize, the arrangement of property, society, and settlement in Ireland but more particularly Tipperary and Kilkenny. To provide a clearer focus for this discussion, it first is necessary to analyze the evidence available for elucidating the character and transformation of the settlement structures and to ascertain what this evidence tells us about the changing nature of Irish society in the seventeenth century.

## Interrogating the Source Materials

After three decades of significant economic development during which the island was gradually integrated into the wider Atlantic economy, Ireland's population in 1640 may have stood at around two million. By 1653, it was probably reduced to around 1.3 million—that is, by about one-third. A man close to all the action at this time, Sir William Petty, suggested a reduction in Ireland's population of that order [6] However, the precise nature of, and the regional variations in, these population transformations are unclear. What is clear is that the new radical Commonwealth government quickly set in motion a series of acts of settlement and a number of associated property surveys. Both the acts and surveys provided the framework (outside of the already planted areas) for the massive transfer and redistribution of property units to a new Protestant elite and for the consequent reconstruction of such properties in both town and countryside by a new energetic landlord class. At the end of the Commonwealth period and in part to ingratiate themselves with the soon-to-be restored Charles II, the Cromwellian members of the Commonwealth Convention in Ireland also agreed to the imposition of a poll tax that would partly defray the expenses of the large army that then garrisoned the island. Early in the reign of Charles II, and under the stimulus of the tireless Sir William Petty, the poll tax was replaced by a tax on all fireplaces—known subsequently as the hearth tax.

The conquest and settlement of Ireland in the mid-seventeenth century has therefore provided the historical geographer and anthro-

pologist with a wide range of survey and related materials that can
yield insight into the nature and reconstruction of society and settlement at this time. However, unlike nineteenth-century state documents, the reliability, comprehensiveness, and meaning of the seventeenth-century materials are still far from clear. To redistribute land
from the old owners to the new Cromwellians, a survey by local
juries in each barony in each of twenty-seven counties[7] was carried
out in 1654, giving a narrative description of each property, its relative location and estimated valuation, and occasionally, uneven and
often incidental details about land use, settlement, and leasing patterns. This survey has come to be known as the Civil Survey. Unfortunately, only fourteen of all or part of the county volumes of the
Civil Survey have survived. That for County Kilkenny, apart from
the city itself, has been lost. In contrast, the Civil Survey for County
Tipperary, edited with a superb introduction by Simington, is a rich,
deeply layered, and ambiguous document that, among other things,
reveals the ancient tenures, land measures, and territorial divisions of
each parish and barony in the county.[8] Indeed, insight into the strength
of local custom in the county comes from the fact that seven different
land measures were still used over the different baronies of the county
as late as 1640.

After the Civil Survey in 1654, all confiscated properties were
mapped at parish and barony scales, providing clear details of the lie
of property and denominational boundaries but again offering highly
uneven and ambiguous insights into the layout of settlement, roads,
and infrastructural items generally. This mapped survey, complete
with its terriers that give additional information in relation to property owners and settlements, came to be known as the Down Survey.[9] Again the survival rate of the parish maps of the Down Survey
varies within and between counties. For County Tipperary, parish
maps survive for five baronies; those for four baronies and two
Liberties of County Kilkenny survive. Additional insights can be
gained from the superimposition of the Down Survey maps on the
mid-nineteenth century, first-edition Ordnance Survey six-inch sheets
for Counties Tipperary and Kilkenny. These combined map sources
highlight many transformations between the mid-seventeenth and
mid-nineteenth centuries. Likewise, useful insights are provided by
the summary details that have survived of the Transplantation Certificates—that is, the censuslike materials required of the old elites as to
the family members, retainers, stock, and crops that they intended to
take with them in their exile to Connaught.[10]

The Books of Survey and Distribution also provide a most comprehensive list of properties: first, for the period immediately before and after the Cromwellian settlement; second, after the Williamite confiscations in the 1690s; and third, after the sale of the Forfeited Estates in 1703. These great post-Cromwellian ledger books list "the losers" on the left side of the ledger, the name of the townland and its acreage in the middle, and the names of the "winners" and their "successors" up to 1703 on the right side. These survive for all parishes, baronies, and counties in Ireland.[11] It is unlikely that any other country in Western Europe has equivalent state ledger books that detail the transfer, by 1703, of almost a whole country (86 percent) from old proprietors to a newly conquering elite. It may have been that political theorist Sir William Petty, who initiated this detailed accounting by the state of the status, size, and location of all Ireland's properties.

Sir William Petty was also instrumental in conserving for us the records of the 1660–61 poll taxes. Pender (and before him Hardinge) argued that these records with their "population" statistics constituted a census—hence, the title of Pender's edition of the manuscript returns still held by Petty's descendants—*A Census of Ireland c. 1659*.[12] This "census" appears to be the most comprehensive and most accessible of all the documents that have come down to us from the mid seventeenth century; yet it has received little attention—no doubt because it is generally perceived as an incomplete, highly flawed, and very ambiguous document. As figure 7.2 illustrates, the so-called census first itemized "Numbers of people" for each county, barony, parish or town, townland, or street. The second column, headed "Tituladoes names," listed persons holding titles of honor (whether lords, knights, esquires, or gentlemen) or titles of professional calling (whether mayors, aldermen, doctors, lawyers, or merchants). The final column distinguished the number of people classified as "English"/"English & Scots" as opposed to the "Irish." At the end of each baronial entry, the returns also identified the "principal Irish" family names for each barony. However, the survival rate of the returns has varied. No returns have survived for all of five counties and for large parts of two other counties. The returns for four towns and quite a number of individual parishes are missing in County Tipperary, but the Kilkenny materials look very reliable and quite complete.

To illustrate the difficulties, complexities, and potentials of the seventeenth-century documents, it is useful to look in particular at this so-called 1659 census. The problems of interpretation are manifold. There are problems about the dating, provenance, and nature of

| Parishes | Places | Numbs of People | Tituladoes Names | Eng | Irish |
|---|---|---|---|---|---|
| **Kilsallagh** and pt of the Parish of Castletowne | Ballingduny | 10 | | | 10 |
| | Parish of Castletowne | 9 | | | 9 |
| | Killsallagh | 33 | | | 33 |
| Sollohodbegg Parish & Kill | | 52 | | 2 | 50 |
| | Phillipstowne | 7 | | | 7 |
| | Getenstowne | 10 | | | 10 |
| | Ballychisteen | 6 | | | 6 |
| Religmory | Religmory | 63 | | 6 | 57 |
| (*folio* 74). | Clogbussell | 39 | | | 39 |
| | Ouldgrane | 42 | | | 42 |
| | Ballycloghy | 13 | | 2 | 11 |
| | AbbyeIshell | 11 | | 2 | 9 |
| | Beallourine | 18 | Nathaniell Lawrence gent | 4 | 14 |
| | Ballyvadey | 17 | | 2 | 15 |
| | Clogleagh | 10 | | | 10 |
| | Ballygriffen | 36 | George Clarke Esq Gyles Martin gent | 6 | 30 |
| | Parte of Religmory towne | 119 | | 20 | 99 |
| Killfeacle | Killfeacle | 41 | | | 41 |
| | Part of Ballynckedy | 4 | | 2 | 2 |
| | Granstowne | 8 | | | 8 |
| | Knockballinoe | 6 | | | 6 |
| | Dromleyney | 4 | | 1 | 3 |
| | Ballyglassin | 10 | | | 10 |
| (*folio* 75). | Killfeacle | 15 | | | 15 |
| | Bally McKeady | 28 | Jehhep Jegnys Esq | 4 | 24 |

Principall Irish Names [and] Their Numbs

Bryen, 30 ; Boorke, 48 ; Barry, 11 ; Butler, 11 ; Connor, 12 ; Commyne and Comane, 10 ; Cleary, 10 ; Carrane, 8 ; Daniell, 24 ; McDaniell, 11 ; Dwyer and O Dwyer, 24 ; McDonnogh, 15 ; English, 13 ; Fogurty, 7 ; Fahy, 7 ; Fitzgerrold, 9 ; Gerrold, 7 ; Hiffernane, 28 ; Hicky, 16 ; Hogane, 28 ; Kenedy, 16 ; Kearney, 8 ; McLoghlin, 11 ; Lonnergane, 9 ; Lynsy, 11 ; Murphy, 7 ; Meagher, 14 ; Magrath & McCrath, 17 ; Mullony, 9 ; Morissy, 7 ; McNemara, 7 ; Quirke and O Quirke, 19 ; Ryan, 77 ; Ryardane, 9 ; Shea and O Shea, 14 ; McShane, 15 ; McTeige, 26 ; Tobyn, 9 ; McThomas, 11 ; McWilliam, 17 ; Walsh. 19.

(*folio 74 verso*).   The Number of People in the Bary of Clanwilliam : Eng, 180 ; Irish, 2713 ; Totall Eng & Irish, 2893

*Figure 7.2.* A One-Page Example from the So-Called Census of Ireland, 1659

this source material as well as further problems of inference, reliability, and comprehensiveness.

The original manuscript volumes of the so-called 1659 census were discovered in 1864 by W. H. Hardinge among the papers of the direct descendants of Sir William Petty. The first confusion arises from the fact that Petty himself indexed the so-called census returns as part of his *Surveys of Ireland*.[13] This description clearly misled Hardinge, who ascribed the returns to the late 1650s and saw them as in some way complementary to, and consequential on, Petty's island-wide mapping of properties, townlands, and parishes in the Down Survey.[14] Pender, in his invaluable published edition of these returns, saw no need to depart from Hardinge's statement that "we are here dealing with a Census return (unfortunately incomplete) of the people of Ireland."[15]

However, Simington and Pilsworth consistently argued that the returns are not a full census but rather are summary abstracts of the poll tax returns of 1660. Simington's analysis of both the Poll Money Ordinances of 1660 (and 1661) and the machinery these provided for the collection of the poll tax confirmed that the poll tax records could provide a mass of data on the number, status (ethnic background), and dwelling places of people above the age of fifteen years.[16] These data could then be abstracted in the form presented by what Hardinge and Pender had labeled "census" returns. Simington also noted other manuscript evidence of the Irish revenue returns of the 1660s that clearly explain why there are missing returns in the so-called census for nine baronies of Meath as well as all of the counties of Cavan, Mayo, and Tyrone. These returns are missing because the poll tax details for these counties were not returned to the central exchequer and therefore could not have been abstracted by Petty and his clerks. The authorship of the format of the returns is highlighted by the use of the specific term *Titulado*—Petty's own very distinctive and somewhat ironic term for the gentry. The specific inclusion of details as to the number of "Irish" and "English/Scots" also suggest the hand of Petty, who had constantly sought this kind of ethnic data for Ireland for the year 1641, for 1653, and almost certainly for 1660–61.

Pilsworth supported Simington's arguments and confirmed the date of the returns as 1660 and not 1659.[17] He noted that the number of sheriffs and other notables returned in the so-called 1659 census actually held office for most of the year 1660. He also noted that clergymen, including bishops, were never returned in the list of "Tituladoes." They were never returned because all holders of ecclesiastical offices had been specifically exempted from the payment of a poll tax. Pilsworth concluded that "it seems to be proved convincingly that they (the 'Census' lists) do in fact represent the summarised form of the Poll-Tax Returns for 1660."

Additional evidence pointing to the poll tax origins of the "census" is provided by the returns for the city of Drogheda that were laid out according to the poll tax classes beginning with "gentlemen and their wives," followed by "yeomen," "labourers," and "soldiers and their wives." Similarly, the specific 1660 taxation categories of "foreigner" and "servant" occurred in the returns. Even if deficient by the order of 50–55 percent, the hearth money records of the mid-1660s (the records of the tax on hearths or fireplaces initiated in 1662 to replace the poll tax) also clearly, if indirectly, confirm that the poll tax is a partial list (i.e., of adults) and not a full census of all the population. Likewise, an analysis of surviving individual poll tax returns for three Tyrone parishes (1660) and for Clonmel (1661) confirm that the overall sex ratio in these poll tax returns is quite even and that, apart from children, and even allowing for early age of marriage, both single adult females and most single adult males who were not working as servants were excluded in these returns.[18] As a working hypothesis, it is suggested that a multiplier of 2.4 (2.5 if one assumes an island-wide underestimation of at least 10 percent) would be most applicable to all areas where the returns seem most reliable.

Simington and Pilsworth, therefore, were correct in seeing the returns as abstracts from the 1660 poll tax. Pender's reluctance to accept these arguments stemmed in part from his reliance on Hardinge's prior arguments. Pender did examine one of the surviving poll tax returns for County Tyrone—that of the parish of Termonmcgurk—but argued that this return bore not the slightest resemblance to what he called the "1659 census" returns. The original returns, he argued, had no listing of "Tituladoes," no division of inhabitants into English and Irish, and no listing of principal Irish or English names. However, it is clear that the "Tituladoes" (the highest taxpayers) could easily be identified from the original parish returns of the poll tax lists; it is equally clear that Irish and English family names could have been identified from the detailed listing of both Christian names and surnames. Pender's examination of the Poll-Money Ordinance of 1660 thus did not convince him that the returns he was editing and that he called the "1659 census" could emanate from this source. Pender clearly did not allow for either Petty's great organizational skills or his penetrating mind, which could plan for specific details regarding the gentry and the ethnic status of taxpayers to be abstracted from the original poll tax returns.

In conclusion, Pender and Hardinge's arguments must now be set aside. First, the central date for the so-called census is not 1659 but 1660. Second, the returns as published are not a census but an abstract of the adults taxed in the poll tax of 1660. Third, the surviving original poll tax parish records confirm that the full population can be estimated by using a multiplier of the order of 2.5. Fourth, returns clearly are missing for identifiable counties and baronies and for a not yet fully identified series of parishes within individual counties. Fifth, internal inconsistencies in the returns as between counties and baronies—although not a major issue—still need to be ironed out. In summary, the realization of the nature, provenance, and date of the returns allows the scholar to make careful yet powerful inferences about Irish settlement and society in the 1660s.

A final important source, although again highly uneven in quality and distribution, is the early returns of the hearth money taxes. In 1662, legislation for the taxation of each fireplace in the country was enacted, and as Dickson, Ó Gráda, and Daultrey have skillfully shown, these returns provide the most comprehensive guide to population levels and changes in Ireland between the 1690s and the first reliable census of 1821.[19] However, the earliest returns of the hearth monies, in the 1660s, are much less reliable and more difficult to interpret. They clearly only provided returns for about 50–55 percent of the total number of households in many counties. Also, their quality varied in these early years. In County Tipperary, for example, there is a great discrepancy between the very poor returns for 1665–66 and the much more reliable ones for 1666–67, although the latter may still be defective by around 40 percent.[20] Unfortunately, the actual returns for County Kilkenny have not survived, but the work of Ossory's great historian, Carrigan, has left us with useful manuscript details for the baronies of Ida, Knocktopher, Shillelogher, Kells, and Galmoy (see figure 7.1) and with selective materials for the remaining baronies.[21]

In summary, then, for a historical geographer concerned with data sources that are as areally comprehensive as possible, the seventeenth-century returns are very much a mixed bag. The poll tax offers many possibilities of interpretation but also many pitfalls. The Civil and Down Surveys are much less comprehensive spatially but have their own richness of detail with regard to properties and settlements. At the same time, such details are uneven and display strong variations in content not only between counties but also between different baronies in the same county. Nevertheless, these and the solid Books of Survey and Distribution provide essential data on changing property structures. Moreover, however sparse and uneven the early hearth money records are, they too help to flesh out elements of the social structure while also providing clues to levels of cultural assimilation, settlement composition, hierarchy, and a host of other issues. Finally, for Counties Tipperary and Kilkenny, the Ormond deeds are a special if still mainly untapped source for geographers and ethnographers.[22]

## Counties Tipperary and Kilkenny: The National and Regional Contexts

Using the poll tax returns of 1660–61 as to the distribution and density of population, figure 7.3 illustrates the relative location of the study area, Counties Tipperary and Kilkenny, within the island.[23] The area stretches from deep in the sparsely populated woodland-bogland complex of the midlands in Lower Ormond in County Tipperary to the densely populated lands outside the gates of the port city of Waterford that, for much of the late medieval period, was the second city of the island. A great range of environmental and locational conditions therefore characterizes this region: much bogland and wetland in Tipperary's northern and eastern margins—great stretches of hill and mountain country also in Tipperary in the Keeper Hill, Barnane, Galtee, and Knockmealdown complexes—and some of the richest land in Europe along the Nenagh and more particularly the Suir Valley and its tributary areas. In contrast, County Kilkenny has a more muted and more subtle landscape (figure 7.4). Its mountains, the so-called Walsh Mountains in the middle south, never rise higher than 294 meters. Elsewhere its gently rolling landscapes are interspersed by the hill country at Brandon and west of Graiguena-managh, by the extension of the Slieveardagh hills into the baronies of Crannagh and Galmoy to the northwest, and by the extensive carboniferous plateau country around Castlecomer to the northeast. Given the apparent ubiquity of these rolling landscapes, the dominant feature of Kilkenny is its central limestone plain drained by the Nore River and its tributaries that stretch from Ballyragget in the north to Ballyhale in the south and eastward from Callan to the more modern Goresbridge on the river Barrow. A second important lowland zone lies within the bend of the Suir to the south, which in turn narrows considerably between Waterford city and New Ross; and, as figures 7.3 and 7.4 emphasize, these port towns, especially Waterford, clearly exerted a strong influence on economic activities in the wider hinterland—as did the long-established inland river towns in Kilkenny and in south and east Tipperary.

A mixed economy prevailed throughout County Kilkenny, with cows and cattle occupying an important part in farming life. Its upland areas were much more geared to pastoral pursuits, as the distribution of *bawns* (walled enclosures for cattle and sheep) suggests. Likewise, the Ormond deeds now and again provide glimpses of the important role of cows, sheep, pigs, and even goats in local economies. There were strict rules at parish (and townland) level regarding the grazing of common grasslands and the impounding of stock in lieu of rent or the king's taxes. Such issues were a regular feature in the sheriff's accounts.[24] The seventeenth-century expansion of a commercial pastoral economy and the improvement in the landscape generally is also suggested by the imparking and enclosure of townlands adjacent to some towerhouses and mansions. Yet it is also clear that an open field tillage economy and the production of grain crops, especially of wheat and barley, was the dominant feature over most of lowland Kilkenny. In Hardinge's summary of the Transplantation Certificates, Kilkenny dominated the south and east of the island in the production of winter and spring grain crops: 41 percent of all winter wheat and 33 percent of all spring grains returned by the transplanting elites from the country as a whole emanated from County Kilkenny alone.[25] Ploughmen and harvesters were, therefore, key figures in the yearly cycle of most Kilkenny townlands. Grain crops were also central in the diet of the poor while providing a regular cause of conflicts between local farmers with regard to the hedges that bounded their tillage plots.

Contrasts with some of the best lands in County Tipperary are very sharp in this regard, for again the Transplantation Certificates reveal that one-third of all sheep returned by the island's old elites came from pastoral Tipperary—suggesting a level of sheep production in Tipperary twelve times the level of County Kilkenny. Yet southeast Tipperary also had a powerful grain production component. In contrast, the more sparsely populated region in the north and west of County Tipperary was much more emphatically "cow and small oats country."[26]

These economic patterns were underpinned by cultural forces with deep roots. Based on the returns of principal Irish families at the end of each barony in the so-called 1659 census, I have elsewhere explored the strength of medieval settlement by the Anglo-Normans in the southeast of Ireland (see figure 7.5).[27] Under the long-standing patronage of the Butler lordship and pivoting around the port city of

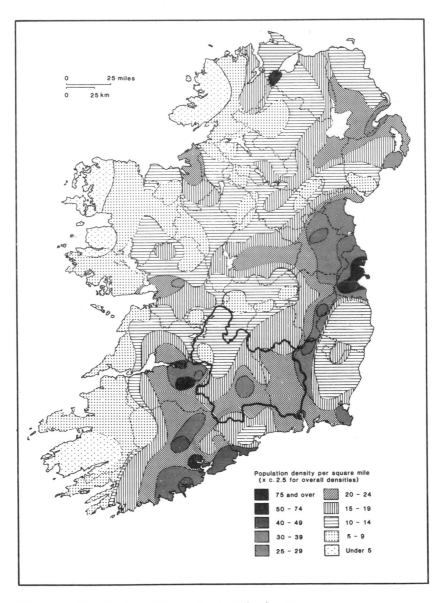

Population density per square mile
(x c. 2.5 for overall densities)

75 and over    20 - 24
50 - 74    15 - 19
40 - 49    10 - 14
30 - 39    5 - 9
25 - 29    Under 5

*Figure 7.3.* Distribution of Population in Ireland, 1660

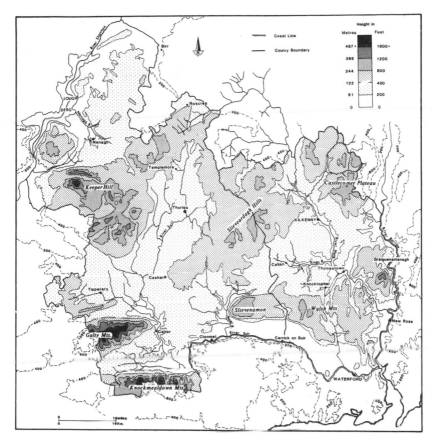

*Figure 7.4.* Counties Kilkenny and Tipperary: Location, Topography, and Main Settlements

Waterford, substantial rural communities and solid market towns had been developed by the settlers along the navigable rivers of the Suir, Nore and Barrow. North and northeast Kilkenny, however, still reflected long-standing pressures from the Gaelic midlands, whereas across the middle of Tipperary a buffer zone existed between the core area of Anglo-Norman culture in the southeast and the Gaelic territories of the north and west that bordered the Gaelic heartland of the Irish midlands.

Much has been written about the assimilation of the Normans to the Irish way of life in the later medieval period—especially in relation to their adoption of Irish language and literature and kinship and economic strategies. However, much that has been written has been rather one-sided.[28] Equally relevant was the assimilation of the Irish to the feudal norms of the Anglo-Normans—for, in essence, a hybrid culture had already emerged in this part of east Munster/south Leinster. The hearth money records, with their detailed evidence not only of surnames but also of Christian names, are helpful here in testing questions of assimilation. Apart from some isolated examples (as west of Cahir, where the first "nationalist" historian Geoffrey Keating lived ["I am of Old English descent but belong to the Irish tradition"]), the Christian names introduced by the Anglo-Normans in the medieval period remained in constant use among their descendants, the Old English, in the mid-seventeenth century. In contrast, figure 7.6 shows the adoption of medieval Christian names by many people of Gaelic-Irish descent, and we see, first, that the density of Norman settlement is faithfully reflected in the gradual dilution of Gaelic Christian naming patterns as we move from the northwest to the southeast of the county. Second, even the most Gaelic areas show significant attrition in naming patterns (reflecting, among other things, the earlier Norman cultural impact in these regions). Thus, on the one hand, the strength of "old style" (i.e., Gaelic Christian) naming patterns in exposed lordships like that of the O'Fogartys (in Eliogarty) illustrates the resistance of small but powerful Gaelic lordships to Anglo-Norman "incursions." On the other hand, in the feudalized parts of south and east Tipperary, Anglo-Norman cultural, political, and economic influences, as symbolized by changes in Christian names, have gone very deep indeed, breaking up the old territorial networks of the Gaelic families. Given the importance of Norman family names in Kilkenny, it is likely that a similar transformation in naming and cultural patterns had occurred over much of this county as well.

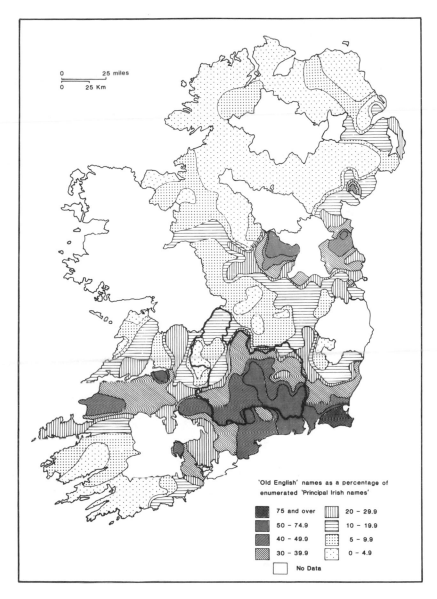

*Figure 7.5.* Distribution of Old English (Also Known as the Anglo-Normans) in 1660

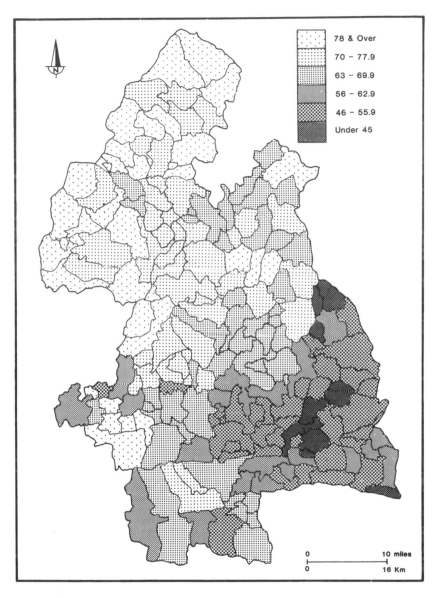

*Figure 7.6.* Distribution of Medieval Christian Names among the Gaelic
Population of County Tipperary, 1666–67

## The Property-Owning Matrix

Underpinning these population, economic, and cultural patterns was the property framework. The ownership and control of land was the central fulcrum of economic and political power in seventeenth-century Ireland. Property units also provided crucial territorial structures that shaped the location and character of most human activities. Using the Civil Survey for County Tipperary and the Book of Survey and Distribution (B.S.D.) for County Kilkenny, the landownership patterns for this region can be carefully mapped for c. 1640.

Figures 7.7–7.10 highlight a number of features relating to the distribution, shape, and size of the property units and the ethnic composition of their owners. In essence, these maps reveal three major cultural worlds. Both south and east Tipperary and practically all of County Kilkenny were dominated by individual property owners of Old English descent. In contrast, north and west Tipperary and the hill country generally was characterized by a hierarchy of Gaelic land units, shared by varying numbers of kin in complex partnership arrangements. Between these two major regions, in the buffer zones such as Clanwilliam, the territory of Ileigh, and Upper Ormond, "modernizing" Gaelic families and "hybrid" Old English commanded individual properties.

From the end of the high medieval period onward (i.e., from c. 1350), Counties Kilkenny and Tipperary had been dominated by the Butler families, headed by the earl of Ormond, who at different times had ruled from Nenagh, from Carrick-on-Suir and, most particularly, from Kilkenny city (figures 7.7 and 7.8). In effect, Tipperary and Kilkenny formed a single Butler lordship effectively administered as a single powerful unit of political and economic integration.[29] The Butlers were also the dominant landowners in the towns of Roscrea, Nenagh, Thurles, Cahir, Gowran, Inistioge, Knocktopher, and Callan. So first, the Butlers commanded the *core* areas of the region and the economy. Second, the Ormond Butlers of Kilkenny also controlled all the frontier territories of the county—lapping up to the county boundary in all cases except where the wide expanses of the lower Suir and Nore-Barrow river systems already formed a defensive barrier. In addition, the earl of Ormond virtually commanded the rich middle core of the county from Dunmore in the north to the former abbey lands of Jerpoint; he also commanded the strategic lines along each side of the navigable stretches of the Nore. Adding a further shield to the towns and better lands, the remaining Butler

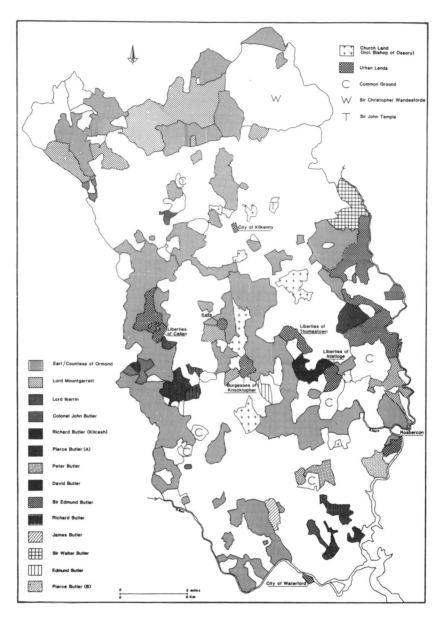

*Figure 7.7.* Butler Lands in County Tipperary

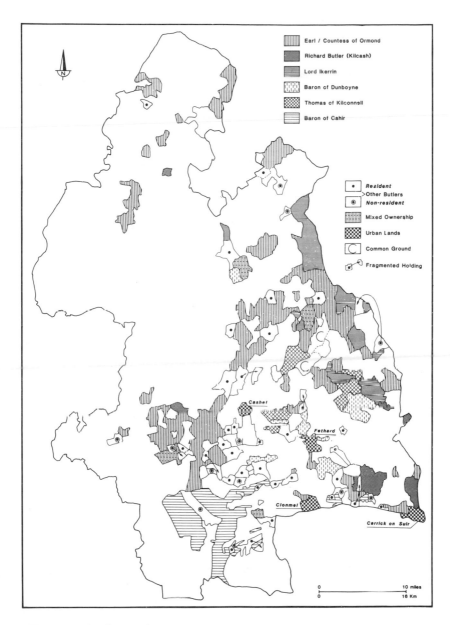

Legend:
- Earl / Countess of Ormond
- Richard Butler (Kilcash)
- Lord Ikerrin
- Baron of Dunboyne
- Thomas of Kilconnell
- Baron of Cahir

- • Resident
- > Other Butlers
- ⊙ Non-resident
- Mixed Ownership
- Urban Lands
- C Common Ground
- Fragmented Holding

Cashel

Fethard

Clonmel

Carrick on Suir

0      10 miles
0      16 Km

*Figure 7.8.* Butler Lands in County Kilkenny

families (including the powerful Lord Mountgarrett) controlled the fertile lands along the old strategic front to the Gaelic territories to the north—along with key Butler allies: the Graces to the northwest and the Purcells and Cantwells to the northeast. The head tenants on the individual Butler manors were for the most part lesser Butlers, members of other leading Old English landed families, or key members of Kilkenny city's professional and merchant classes.

The remainder of the rich central lowlands of County Kilkenny was owned either by key Anglo-Norman dynasties, such as the Shortalls, the St. Legers, and the Blanchfields—each commanding a long-established territorial domain—or by leading (but often *absentee*) merchant families of the city of Kilkenny, such as the Shees, the Archers, and the Archdeacons (figure 7.9). To the south, the complex hierarchical territories of the Walsh family ("the Lords of the Mountain") extended right across the county from Tybroughney in the west to near Rosbercon in the east. Key centers in this upland region were held by members of the extended kinship network of the Walshes. The remainder of the south was dominated by long-established landed families, such as the Forstalls, the Fitzgeralds, the Denns, and Gaules, whereas some descendants of the Waterford merchant families, such as the Strangs and the Grants, held the lands fringing the lower courses of the navigable rivers.

Kilkenny County, therefore, was a land of closely linked groups of long-resident proprietors, deeply rooted in their respective territories, with wide-ranging marriage and kinship linkages with adjacent families. Each ruled a local "fiefdom," with their estates, manors, and townlands often managed by members of the extended kin net. In turn, these property units provided the central fulcrums for the hierarchy of towns, villages, hamlets, and farms that typified this deeply humanized part of Ireland.

South and east Tipperary was similar in character to County Kilkenny except that its northwest facing borderlands—such as those of Galmoy and Fassadinin in Kilkenny—had long been exposed to military, economic, and demographic pressures from the adjacent Gaelic heartlands. However, as in County Kilkenny, the Butler administrative strategy throughout the late medieval period was to control and protect the Butler towns, and indeed all the towns of the southeast, in order to maintain the peaceful conditions necessary for commercial agricultural production, and good rents for the Butlers, in their hinterlands. This objective had been clearly achieved long before 1640. Meanwhile, the earls of Ormond, acting both in their own interest and in that of the crown, had gradually asserted military and political

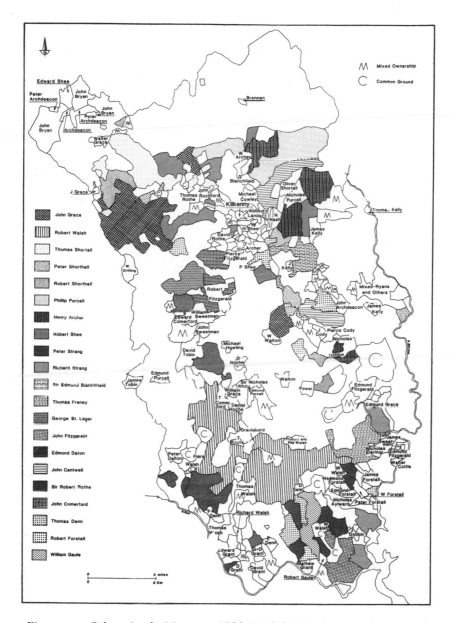

*Figure 7.9.* Other Anglo-Norman (Old English) Landowners in County Kilkenny

authority over the remainder of the county both by controlling the frontier towns of Nenagh and Roscrea and by planting key kinsmen (like Richard Butler of Kilcash) or key Kilkenny allies (such as the Graces and Cantwells) on former churchlands and other borderlands in the northern part of the county. Behind this long-standing Butler shield a solid array of individual Old English landowners ruled in the rest of the south and east of the county (figure 7.10b). Some occupied extensive estates either in the upland edges (such as the Tobin territory in the hill country north and east of Slievenamon and that of the Prendergasts at the foot of the Knockmealdowns and Comeraghs) or in the more exposed buffer lands (such as those of the Purcells to the north of Thurles). The majority of these Old English lords, however, occupied small (around one thousand acres), compact estates, each of which dominated its own tightly managed world. As in Kilkenny, some lands (e.g., near the county town of Clonmel and the episcopal capital of Cashel) were newly owned by Clonmel or Waterford merchants in this highly commercialized world that had long been exposed to market influences and that was characterized by clear cultural and economic innovations in the form of new mansions, enclosures, and such practices as haymaking.

The Gaelic lands of Kilkenny had almost disappeared by 1640, for in the previous sixty years, the vast patrimony of the O'Brennans of Fassadinin had been whittled down to a pathetic forty acres by the insidious penetration of the earl of Ormond and his Old English henchmen. The O'Brennan patrimony was finally obliterated by the creation of the great modern estate of the Wandesfordes centered on the old manorial keep of Castlecomer, soon to become a classic landlord-middleman town.[30] Only the Ryans, from their heartland in Idrone in Carlow, kept a residual if resilient foothold in the Leighlin parishes of east Kilkenny. In the extreme northwest, the Bryans (originally O'Byrne, but now clearly assimilated to the Old English order) manned the gap on the edge of the former woodlands and boglands of the Gaelic fastnesses to the north.

Figure 7.10a for north and west Tipperary tells a very different story. Here the Norman overlordship of the early medieval period appears to have been shrugged aside. The hill country of the Kilnamanagh, Keeper Hill, and Arra Mountain region was dominated by lineage-based groups of O'Dwyers, Ryans, O'Briens, Gleesons, and others, and much of the lowland territories of the two Ormond baronies was still held in complex partnership arrangements by branches of the O'Kennedy clans. However, throughout these Gaelic lands and underneath the property pattern, there was ongoing attrition, at both

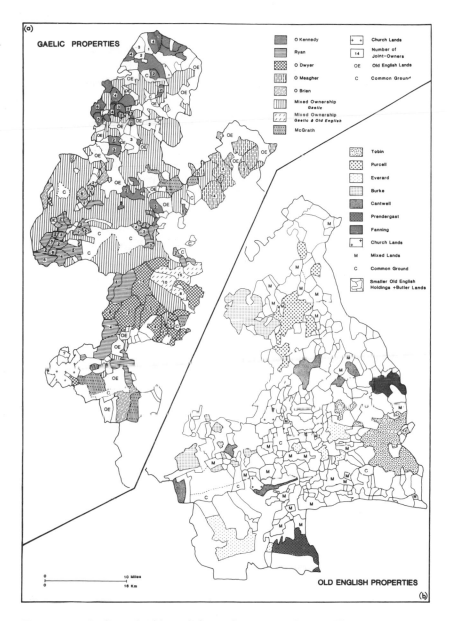

*Figure 7.10.* Gaelic and Old English Landowners in County Tipperary

the leasing and the mortgaging levels. Already by 1640 the still vast O'Kennedy lands had shrunk through acquisitions by mainly Old English (and some New English) purchasers, as had the low-lying Gaelic lands on all the edges of the hill country of Tipperary. Likewise, subtle intrusions took place at the leaseholding level. Overall, however, the Butler shield was, for the most part, to protect even these Gaelic lands from the full-blooded infiltration of the New English forces at work in much of the rest of Ireland at this time.

These ownership details are clearly essential to the study of social and settlement structures. However, the property maps do not reveal the conditions of life for the majority of the population, nor do they reveal for County Tipperary that alongside the names of Ryan, Butler, Burke, Hogan, Dwyer, and Kennedy, families bearing such nongentry surnames as Welsh/Brenagh, Donoghoe, Kelly, Connors, and Murphy were more conspicuous in the hearth money records than all the other landowning families. Likewise in Kilkenny, alongside the Butlers, Shortalls, St. Legers, and other Old English landowners, there were layers of Cahills, Hennessys, Phelans, Keeffes, Meaghers, Murphys, Brennans, Brophys, Carrolls, and Delaneys scattered throughout the townlands, villages, and towns.[31] The Gaelic substratum was very deep indeed in County Kilkenny.

We must therefore look to the occupation of the land and its settlement arrangements to catch a glimpse of the whole population, both gentry and nongentry. For example, the hearth money records for County Tipperary can be used to suggest other aspects of the geography of kinship and family structures. The relative distribution of patronymics as surnames reveals other subtle layers in the cultural geography of the region—highlighting the more closely knit, intimate, and kin-based cultures of Slievenamon, southwest Tipperary, the uplands of the northwest, and the adjacent lowlands of Owny and Arra, Upper Ormond, and Ikerrin.

## Settlement and Occupational Structures

Seventeenth-century documents were only incidentally concerned with issues of settlement or social structure. Reconstructing these patterns, therefore, involves a careful combing of what the Civil and Down Surveys have to offer combined with a retrospective use of what the 1660 poll tax and to some extent the early hearth money records suggest. The difficulties arise because settlement details from the Civil and Down Surveys are both uneven and fragmentary. Likewise, the rather better evidence from the 1660 poll tax and hearth money records has to be looked at very carefully at the detailed townland level. On the one hand, for example, in manorial centers such as Ardfinnan in Tipperary or Fertagh in County Kilkenny, population size may be exaggerated as such returns may also include (as the Civil Survey sometimes confirms) the populations of satellite hamlets and farms.[32] On the other hand, separate returns may exist for separate townlands, when in fact a settlement focus converged at the meeting place of these townlands. So, for example, in Borrisokane in Tipperary and Knocktopher in Kilkenny the returns depress the relative status of such centers in the settlement hierarchy.

Having compensated for these deficiencies insofar as they can be established, a relatively clear picture of the settlement hierarchy can be constructed from the 1660 poll tax return for both counties and for County Tipperary from the hearth money records of 1666–67. The superimposition of Down Survey maps on the mid-nineteenth-century Ordnance Survey six-inch maps is also helpful here—if only to highlight how often old settlement centers were buried under landlord demesnes created mainly in the eighteenth century. The juxtaposition of the seventeenth- and nineteenth-century maps also indicates the sharp contrast between evolved as distinct from planned landscapes and societies (i.e., between regions of greater continuity and the regions of deep transformation)—a fact that mirrors the deep divisions of Irish society that followed on from the Cromwellian settlement.

Figure 7.11 places the counties of Tipperary and Kilkenny in their regional and national contexts, underlining the relative distribution of townlands returning forty adults or more (i.e., townlands with a population of more than one hundred in 1660). County Tipperary reveals three distinct patterns in relation to population size. First, in the southeastern baronies, well over 20 percent of the total number of townlands had populations in excess of one hundred. This was the best and historically most secure land in the county, with a good communications network by road and river to Waterford port, a dense network of substantial market towns, and a compact "manorialized" property structure. The larger townland populations in this region were therefore strongly related to a mixed arable intensive economy where laborers, artisans, and other service classes underpinned a complex settlement and social hierarchy. South and east Tipperary were therefore on the edge of a wider belt characterized by high farming and a developed settlement and social hierarchy that had matured in a time of feudal centralization. A "manorial" village

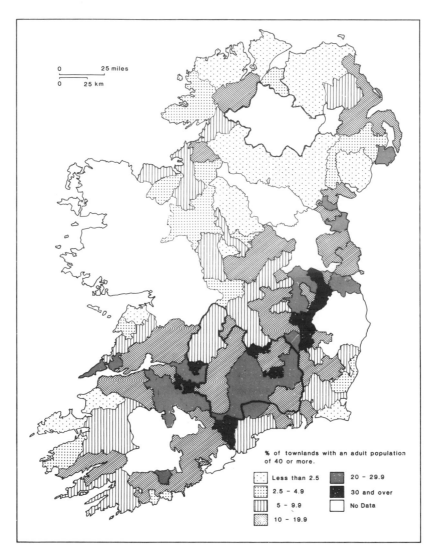

*Figure 7.11.* Distribution of Townlands with an Adult Population of Forty or More in 1660

economy, substantial farms, markets, mills, fairs, and towns were long-standing features of this society. The central heartland of County Kilkenny was also very much part of this kind of culture world.[33]

County Tipperary had a second important region of moderate population densities where 10–19 percent of townland populations exceeded one hundred and where over 40 percent exceeded fifty. This middle bandolier of settlement, running from Clanwilliam to northeast Ikerrin, was in a zone of mixed ecology, containing much good land but also some hill and bogland. It was a zone of both old and newly emerging towns where mixed farming, a mixed settlement structure, and a mixed ethnic heritage are evident. Some baronies in south and north Kilkenny, and indeed all the baronies bounding the dominant core of settlement in east Leinster along the Barrow and Liffey, were characterized by similar patterns of mixed settlement.

Third, at the other end (the north and west) of Tipperary in the lakeland-midland baronies of Owny and Arra and the two Ormonds, a weaker nucleated settlement pattern was evident in this region long dominated by Gaelic lords. This mosaic of lowland, bogland, woodland, and hills was on the margins of a commercialized economy in the seventeenth century—as it was in the nineteenth. Remoteness, the absence of an urban hierarchy, the fragmentation of landowning patterns, a more Gaelic cultural world, the dominance of a pastoral economy in what was often "small oats and cow country," and the scattering of a wide range of institutional foci (i e , churches, castles, and mills) among the *different* townlands within individual parishes— all had combined to make for a looser, more flexible, more dispersed, less stratified, and less populated settlement pattern. Under 10 percent of these denominations had populations in excess of one hundred. County Kilkenny had no such region in the mid-seventeenth century.

The nature of urban experiences can also be documented from the 1660 poll tax and the 1660s hearth taxes. The very different and more recent urban life of the north and west of Tipperary as compared with the rest of the county and all of Kilkenny clearly emerge here (figures 7.12 and 7.13). In addition, the evidence highlights the resilience of the "native" townspeople in all these southeastern towns, with the crucial exceptions of the county towns of Clonmel and Kilkenny, the episcopal capital of Cashel, and the garrison towns of Nenagh and Roscrea. A more hidden urban Ireland is thus revealed where the often walled, sometimes small but socially and morphologically complex borough towns of the south and east still retained an overwhelming proportion of the older stock of townspeople. Therefore, another lesson that emerges from the poll tax pages is that these old

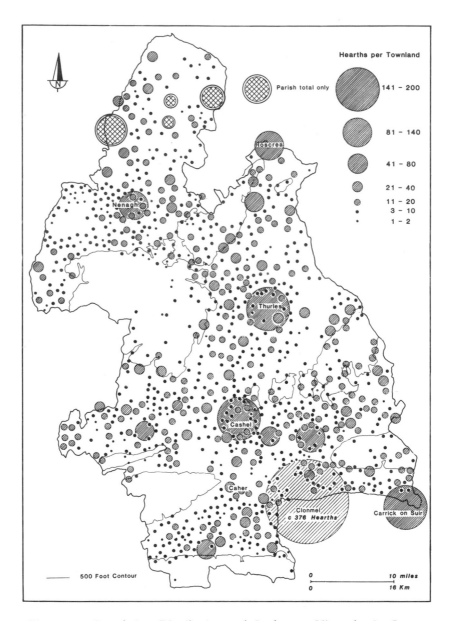

*Figure 7.12.* Population Distribution and Settlement Hierarchy in County Tipperary, 1660

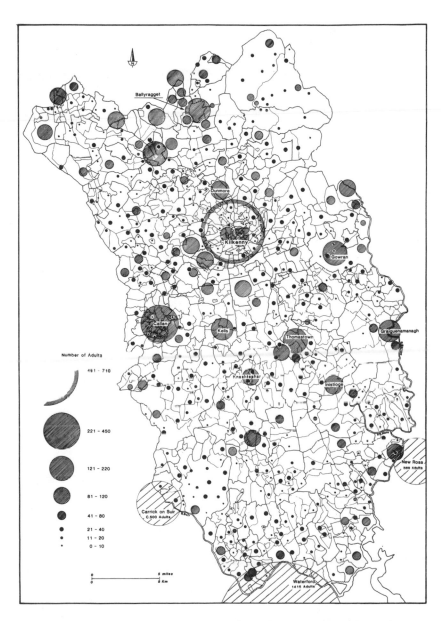

*Figure 7.13.* Population Distribution and Settlement Hierarchy in County Kilkenny, 1660

and battered towns had weathered the storms of the medieval period and were still in place to benefit from the upswing in the economy from the mid-fifteenth century onward. Clearly, these more elaborate and enduring urban societies helped to sustain the population densities and complex rural settlement hierarchies that are discussed later.

In both counties, it is clear from a comparison of the Civil Survey or Book of Survey and Distribution land units and the settled denominations returned on the poll tax and hearth money records that a sizable minority of the land units were not permanently settled. This was particularly the case in two very different kinds of regions. On the one hand, in the more Gaelic upland territories such as Owny and Arra, many of the individually distinguished upland grazing denominations were only seasonally used by inhabitants of more low-lying townlands. On the other hand, in the most feudalized and developed baronies in County Kilkenny, such as around the town of Kells and in the Liberties of Kilkenny city, many large fields and gardens were not permanently settled but were worked from a distance, belonging as they did to a wider territorial framework of "manorial," demesne, or burgess lands.

Overall, however, both Counties Kilkenny and Tipperary reveal a very high level of occupation of land units, as compared, for example, with more western counties, such as Clare and Roscommon, where less than half of all enumerated townlands were permanently settled in the mid-seventeenth century. Kilkenny, however, was even more closely settled and occupied than was Tipperary, for in such baronies as Iverk, Knocktopher, Kells, and Shillelogher, over 90 percent occupation of all enumerated land denominations was reached. Only Slievardagh in Tipperary matched this intensity of settlement. However, in Callan and Galmoy in Kilkenny County and Clanwilliam in Tipperary, up to 85 percent of all land units were settled, and most of the remaining baronies in both counties showed an occupation rate of around 70 percent. The overall impression, then, is of a well-settled, well-worked countryside characterized by a great range of landscape elements, an intimate network of field names, highways, lanes, crops, firm banks, dry or wet ditches, and sometimes quickset hedges—all itemized in rich detail by the inhabitants of Tipperary in their descriptions of the boundaries of each parish and barony.

Figures 7.12 and 7.13 provide a *detailed* picture of the settlement hierarchies in each county for the 1660s. An initial observation is that the towns of south and east Tipperary and Kilkenny occupied fulcrum positions in nurturing the rural settlement hierarchies in their vicinities. They were both the gathering points and the stimuli for the more intensive production of grain and cattle surpluses in their hinterlands. I shall return to the role of these larger central places later, but first the nature and variety of the rural settlement patterns must be addressed.

In Tipperary there was a fundamental contrast between two zones: 1) the more highly commercialized, mixed farming, individual property areas of the Suir valley and its tributaries, with their complex settlement hierarchies; and 2) the hilly, more wooded, more pastoral regions of the Knockmealdowns, Galtees, Glen of Aherlow, the hills of Kilnamanagh and Owny and Arra, and much of Upper Ormond, which formed one continuous line of smaller settlements all along the western half of Tipperary. Its more fragmented pastoral lands on the eastern borders also exhibited smaller population concentrations.

In County Kilkenny, 48.5 percent of the townlands returned in the poll tax contained nineteen adults or less; 36 percent had twenty to thirty-nine; and 21.5 percent contained forty or more. The baronies of Ida, Crannagh, and Knocktopher had population patterns closest to the county norm, albeit with a slight underrepresentation in townlands with more than forty adults. However, the richest core baronies of Kells, Gowran, and Shillelogher had a much more evenly balanced and more elaborate settlement hierarchy, with about a third of all settlements in each of the three categories. These were the baronies with the most mature and complex settlement hierarchies. They also were the baronies that contained a high density of solid, substantial towns—namely, Gowran, Graiguenamanagh, Thomastown, Inistioge, Kells, and Callan (see figure 7.12).

To the north of County Kilkenny, the baronies of Fassadinin and Galmoy were each relatively exceptional. Frontier Galmoy was dominated by settlements at the upper end of the spectrum (38.1 percent with over forty adults), and Fassadinin's middle-level settlements (twenty to thirty-nine adults) were well above the county average. Not surprisingly, the two baronies that were dominated by large cities (namely, the barony of Iverk and the Liberties of Kilkenny) were dominated in turn by the cities of Waterford and Kilkenny and had a much weaker settlement hierarchy: more than 70 percent of all denominations in these baronies contained less than nineteen adults. The settlement hierarchy in Iverk may have been further depressed by the proximity of the strong town of Carrick-on-Suir.

However interesting such summaries of regional variations are, they only provide a general picture of land occupation, settlement, and population structures; they say little about the detailed settlement arrangements and the organization of local society. Elsewhere I have detailed the range of evidence necessary to elicit the nature and variety of settlement structures in Tipperary.[34] That quite a number of even the smallest townland communities (i.e., those with less than nineteen adults or eight to ten hearths, or houses) were compact settlement clusters was strongly suggested by the Down Survey maps for Slievardagh and several other Tipperary baronies. Likewise, incidental yet widespread details in the Tipperary Civil Survey pointed to a similar conclusion. While allowing for a variety of uses for the term *village* at this period, there is much circumstantial evidence to suggest that the Tipperary jurors often were making a distinction between the "lands" of specified denominations/townlands and the actual settlements (i.e., "townes"/"villages") that served as focal points for the local community and that gave their names to the land denomination as well.

The cumulative evidence from a range of sources therefore suggests a variety of agglomerated settlement forms for widely different communities located in seven of the nine baronies within Tipperary County. Even in Owny and Arra, where dispersed settlements were the norm, some descriptions in the Civil Survey highlight a greater concentration of settlement within townlands that were also characterized by joint ownership and management of arable lands that remained undivided by permanent fences. I suggest that some of the smallest agglomerations comprised kin-based clusters. Others, as shown when the hearth money and Down Survey evidence are combined, had settlement arrangements associated with the management of a particular townland by a resident farmer-owner and his partners and laborers. Still others clearly involved a head tenant with a bigger house (i.e., taxed for two or more hearths) who managed a townland with a clustered settlement. However, the majority of smaller clustered settlements were probably associated with partnership farmers of "husbandman" status who worked the lands mainly for subsistence.

Dispersed farm settlement was generally associated with the more substantial thatched and stone houses of the Down and Civil Surveys than with the "straw cabbins." The former were especially conspicuous in the grazier/sheep-farming parishes of County Tipperary. The notion of the dispersal of population, however, needs to be examined at other scales. The degree of association between the fragmentation of ownership patterns in the north and west of Tipperary and the scattering of populations at the townland level, whatever the *form* of settlement within such townlands, is striking: the greater the fragmentation of property, the greater seems to be the scattering of the population. In Owny and Arra alone there were more than 250 landowners, as compared with, say, Slievardagh, a more feudalized and larger barony on the borders of County Kilkenny, which had only forty landowners. In the former, fragmented landowning patterns clearly allowed and encouraged a wide dispersal of farms over a large number of clearly distinguished townland units. In the latter, rather different processes were at work. Large, consolidated, privately owned estates in Slievardagh acted both to reduce the number of separate settlement units and to concentrate a much greater variety of resources, both human and material, at specific "manorial" centers of control (see figure 7.11).

Likewise, it is important to note the parallel dispersal of institutional foci in the more Irish areas as compared with their concentration in one head settlement in the more feudalized regions. Whatever the settlement patterns within the townlands of the northern and western parishes, the striking feature as compared with south and east Tipperary was the scattering of institutional centers—parish churches, castle strongholds, mills—between a large number of townlands within a single parish.

Nucleated settlements in County Tipperary can be confirmed more confidently as the population size of the townlands increases above the mark of twenty adults (around ten hearths, or households), and especially above the mark of forty adults (around twenty hearths, or households). The Down Survey, Civil Survey, other documentary sources (including descriptions of individual parishes of Tipperary in other seventeenth-century commentaries), aerial photography, and oral traditions all provide important clues to the forces making for greater nucleation in the middle, and especially in the upper, population levels. Here the two most critical elements associated with nucleated settlements were the presence of a landowner, with his towerhouse or castle (or, less often, a substantial stone house), and the parish center, with its church, graveyard, and glebeland. Where the landlord's castle and the parish church were combined together, in the one place and, indeed, when they were augmented by milling and other service functions, the forces for settlement concentration were very great indeed. For example, late-sixteenth-century Elizabethan fiants indicate that artisans formed an essential part of the village population. Thus, a number of Tipperary's "manorial" villages (i.e., Castlegrace, Newcastle, and Knocklofty) included not only yeoman farmers, husbandmen, and laborers but also horsemen, houndsmen, clerks, carpenters, butchers, tailors, weavers, harpers, and blacksmiths.[35] Indeed, the hearth money records provide further clues to nucleated settlements in their returns on the extra fireplaces of the blacksmith's forge. Of all forges enumerated in 1666–67, 86 percent were associated with townlands that had ten or more hearths (i.e., townlands with a population of at least fifty). Sixty percent were associated with townlands with twenty-five or more hearths (more than 125 people). The blacksmith, à la Oliver Goldsmith, was clearly an integral element in the village landscape. Finally, two other clues to nucleated settlement status in the hearth money records are the presence of ovens and a significant increase in the number of women householders paying hearth taxes. The latter were likely involved in service or huckster-trader functions in these larger villages.

To summarize the Tipperary evidence on social and settlement hierarchies in the countryside: three kinds of village nuclei can be identified—the parish church-centered village; the manorial-type village, where church and castle were located together; and the castle-village. Historically, Irish parish centers were powerful settlement foci and community anchors, and in spite of the dislocation of the Reformation in County Tipperary, as many as 55 percent of its parish centers still retained a significant nucleating role. Consequently, the great majority of such parish nuclei still comprised the largest settlements in the whole parish territory until the mid-seventeenth century. On their own, such parish centers generated an average hamlet or village size of around seventy people. However, the status of such parish centers was most enhanced when they were combined with the legally defined manors (with their additional court and administrative functions) and/or with what may be termed "manorial" style villages. Excluding the larger manorial towns, such "manorial" type settlements—which contained both church and castle—generated an average village size of around twenty houses or a total population of around 110.

Finally, the independent nucleating role of castles or towerhouses is particularly noticeable at the middle level of the rural settlement hierarchy—more powerful than that of the parish centers on their own but obviously weaker than the manorial or manorial-style parish center. The average size of this castle-village was about seventeen hearths, or a total population of around one hundred (more than forty adults). Many such castle-villages or castle-hamlets also contained their own "private" (non-parish) church or chapel-of-ease.

The preceding points to the intimate relationship between landlord patronage and settlement size. This, in turn, reflected the accumulation of rent surpluses at the center of such estates and the need for professional and military support in the management of medium-sized to large property units. It also reflected the need for a wide range of services at the center of such estates. Finally, in the turbulent decades of the late sixteenth and mid-seventeenth centuries, it also indicated the desire on the part of the weaker segments of the population for greater protection and security. Overall, then, the Tipperary evidence points to the towerhouse-castle as an autonomous force for concentrating settlement at specific nodes from the late medieval period onward. The Tipperary evidence also suggests that most castle-villages housed a more stratified and, in particular, a more significant artisan component than the clustered farm settlements.

Yet the Tipperary source materials still only allow for tentative generalizations about the nature and form of the mid-seventeenth-century settlement hierarchy. The evidence for County Kilkenny, in contrast, is far richer on the cartographic side but weaker in terms of social details. Unlike County Tipperary, where only one barony (Slievardah) is adequately covered by Down Survey parish maps, there are an outstanding series of barony maps for the whole county of Kilkenny as well as parish maps for six baronies, including the Liberties of Callan and Kilkenny. The barony maps for Crannagh and Ida, two of the most representative baronies in the county, are particularly instructive. Surviving traces of Down Survey parish maps from the Quit Rent Office also provide additional information for other baronies.

Whatever ambiguities remain as to the Tipperary settlement structure in the mid-seventeenth century, the evidence for County Kilkenny points overwhelmingly toward the dominance of a nucleated and clustered settlement pattern. For example, out of a total of seventy settlement units on the barony map of Ida, sixty-one, or 85 percent, were of village or hamlet type. Some of these were centered on a castle and/or church, others were simply clustered settlements without any visible nucleus. This is still farm-village country today, and allowing for the growth of new clustered settlements in its hilly regions in the late eighteenth and early nineteenth centuries, perhaps 50 percent of the seventeenth-century villages still survive. In contrast, the northern barony of Crannagh is now mostly bereft of farming villages, yet it was emphatically a world of villages and hamlets in the 1650s. Correlation of settlement details from the excellent Down Survey maps for Crannagh barony with its 1660 poll tax returns confirms the relevance of the tax returns to settlement analysis. In the barony, all the mapped townlands with adult populations of more than forty had complex nucleated settlements usually comprising both a church and a castle. Moreover, the great majority of townlands with an adult population of twenty to thirty-nine had at least one nucleating force at the center of the settlement, and this was usually a towerhouse-castle. In contrast, only one of the six settlements with both clustered settlements and an adult population of ten or less exhibited any such institutional locus. Indeed, recent aerial photographic work has confirmed the deserted status of many of these seventeenth-century settlement centers in County Kilkenny.

In the case of the barony of Iverk, the surviving map is uneven and incomplete, yet an examination of its Quit Rent parish maps in conjunction with the barony map confirms the ubiquity of its village structures, a not surprising finding given that the region still contains thirty-six farm villages in the late twentieth century. As another example, the scattered settlement structure of Fassadinin today contrasts with Nolan's detailed interpretations of its settlement structure in the mid-seventeenth century.[36] He noted that the cabin was the most numerous settlement item in around 1654. However, the collections of cabins were almost always recorded in conjunction with "more substantial edifices as castles, churches, thatched or stone houses or bawns—they were not found in isolation." Clearly, as Nolan noted, the clusters of cabins were the dwelling places of the dependent "tenantry" and their laborers.

Unlike Tipperary, the folk evidence in County Kilkenny is almost overwhelmingly couched in terms of a village culture—not just in the south but also in the north. Using the evidence of local informants, Owen O'Kelly, in his book *Placenames of County Kilkenny*, identified the sites of at least forty now deserted villages. In the villages of south Kilkenny, such as in Ballytarsney near Mooncoin, the locals regularly referred to the village as "the street." In the north of the county, the old village between Cloneen Bridge and Courtstown in Tullaroan parish was known as "Carroll's Street." O'Kelly noted numerous instances, as at Killeen (parish of Kilmanagh), where "there is an old graveyard called 'Seanchill' (the old church) and also a field called 'sean-sráid,' 'the old street.' " According to O'Kelly, the "latter name denotes an old [deserted] village everywhere throughout the county." Likewise, in Kildrinagh, there was a "place called 'sean-achadh,' 'the old field' also called 'the old street' where stood the old town of Kildrinagh." Similarly, there were a number of references to " 'páirc na sráide,' 'the street field,' evidence again of an old hamlet." Another indication of the deserted village is the field name *sean-bhaile*—as in Corstown in the parish of Ballycallan.[37] The terms *faiche* ("green") and *garraí/garraithe* ("gardens"), as well as references to forge fields (especially if adjacent to castle and/or church sites) may provide additional clues to other deserted villages and hamlets.

Although this folk evidence confirms the desertion of certain hamlet or village sites, it is by no means a comprehensive source or memory bank. For example, the Down Survey parish map of Tullaroan suggests at least ten hamlets or villages in the mid-seventeenth century, whereas only two were revealed by the assiduous research into the local folk traditions carried out by Carrigan and O'Kelly. Indirectly, therefore, the uneven oral traditions point to a much higher level of desertion in the county, especially in its northern and central parts. Ongoing aerial photographic work is confirming this pattern. Likewise, even a cursory inspection of the Ormond deeds confirms the service functions—as evidenced by the presence of butchers, tailors, weavers, clerks—in a number of places (such as Listrolin) that are now deserted in Kilkenny.[38] Like the Elizabethan fiants for Tipperary, these documents confirm a diversity of occupations at the local parish level.

The 1660 poll tax is the first reliable, if indirect, indication of the settlement hierarchy in Kilkenny after the Down Survey maps of 1654. Despite the facts that the tax came at the end of one of the bloodiest episodes in Irish history; that Kilkenny city and county, as the anchor point of the Catholic Confederation, constituted one of the cockpit regions in the Cromwellian conquest; and that the Cromwellian settlement itself created great turmoil, it is striking how many of the most populated denominations coincided with the residence of a "titulado" (i.e., a member of the local landlord/gentry class), regardless of whether the latter belonged to the new or the old elite. In examining the relationship between gentry residence and population size in all of Kilkenny's townlands, I found two key features. First, in the barony of Iverk the relatively weak settlement hierarchy was associated with an area dominated by the extensive estates of the duke of Ormond and the Cromwellian Ponsonby: only 36 percent of the relatively few, higher-order settlements were patronized by a gentry family. Fassadinin's settlement hierarchy, even more emphatically dominated by two great landlords (the duke of Ormond but more particularly the Wandesfordes), was likewise less well patronized by local resident gentry. In no other barony does the ratio of gentry to higher-order townlands (more than forty adults) go beneath 50 percent; and in Galmoy, Ida, Knocktopher, and the Liberties of Kilkenny and Shillelogher, two-thirds of all the larger settlements were associated with gentry residence. A second noticeable feature is the gentry

patronage of middle-order townlands (twenty to thirty-nine adults)—
especially in the wealthiest core baronies of Kells, Shillelogher, Crannagh, and the Liberties of Kilkenny. Ida and Iverk occupy a middle
position on this spectrum with Fassadinin (understandably) and Gowran less well patronized by gentry at the middle levels. Ida, Kells,
Shillelogher, and Crannagh also had a relatively strong gentry presence and patronage even at the lower levels of the settlement hierarchy (nineteen adults or under). Thus, although there are no comprehensive Civil Survey details on the location of castle owners in
Kilkenny in 1654, the preceding evidence reinforces the Tipperary
Civil Survey details as to the strong relationship between landlord
patronage, towerhouses, and higher population concentrations in particular townlands.

It also should be noted that the landowning patterns were often
closely tied into the parochial network. Indeed, this parish framework
was the oldest territorial framework in the counties and a powerful
force in shaping local identities. In this vein, it should be stressed that
the parish not only organized life at the religious level and not only
functioned as the territorial unit for collecting tithes, but also served
as a more "secular" administrative unit. The peoples of the different
townlands in the parish had numerous obligations. They had to
maintain the parish pound, they were obliged to keep watch on the
common grasslands of the parish (if these existed at the parish as
opposed to the joint townland level), they were expected to assist in
the maintenance of the king's highways if they passed through the
parish, and they were required to respect the offices of the parish
constable and his petty constables.[39] Until 1640, therefore, the parish
was a relatively powerful ecclesiastical, economic, and administrative
unit, even though its ecclesiastical function had been somewhat weakened by the Reformation and its aftermath.

It therefore is not surprising that the parish unit supported a strong
settlement at its center. In this context, we can relate parish and
village geographies by examining the distribution of the parishes in
which the centers had either greater or equal population as compared
to all the other townlands in the parish. What is striking about the
distribution in both counties, especially in Tipperary, is the recurring
polarities between better and poor land and, more particularly, between tillage and pastoral land. With some notable exceptions, it is
striking how the highly valued, grain-producing, mixed-farming,
single-property zones extending in Tipperary from the lower Suir to
the rich parishes of lowland Ormond around Nenagh sustained a
much more vigorous parish life and stronger parish centers. Equally

striking is the relative weakness of the parish centers in the pastoral zones of the county stretching from the Glen of Aherlow to the upland territories of Kilnamanagh, Keeper Hill, Barnane, and Owny and Arra. Instructive also are the exceptions, as on the better lands of Iffa and Offa in such parishes as Derrygrath and Ballybacon. These exceptions point to the central nucleating role played by the local landed families, such as the Keatings at Nicholastown and the Butlers of Gormanstown. Similarly, in Kilkenny, the dominance of the landlord residence as a focal point could reduce the status of the parish center. This was the case with the Fitzgeralds at Gorteen (parish of Rathpatrick), the Bryans of Bawnmore (parish of Erke), and the Blanchfields of Blanchfields Park (parish of Kilmacahill). Likewise, it is clear for County Kilkenny that in the hill plateau country of Crannagh and Fassadinin in the north and the area of the Walsh Mountains to the south, the greater scattering of settlement in these more pastoral regions often left the parish center in a relatively weaker position. In addition, the weaknesses of parish centers along the borders of Iffa and Offa and Middlethird and along the edges of the Liberties of Kilkenny highlight the already lost centers and villages of the late medieval period in places like Donaghmore. Such parishes may have suffered not only from absentee church administrators but also from absentee landlords. In both counties, the still relatively rare instances of absentee landlords were especially pronounced among the merchant families. This often depressed the settlement structure of such parishes while also leading to some confusion as to the number and status of smaller parishes in this age of growing economic change and rationalization.

While recognizing the twin pillars to settlement structure that parish administration and landlord patronage provided, it is noticeable by the early to mid-seventeenth century that the balance often had swung in favor of the secular arm of the settlement, a not too surprising development, given the turbulence of post-Reformation Ireland. One pivot of the nucleated settlement structure—that of the parish church—was under stress both before and particularly after the Reformation. Yet the extraordinary power of the twin anchors of castle and church—with the military and political arm becoming increasingly important—still provided the main raison d'être for the community structures in these counties as late as the mid-1660s. The longer-term consequences flowing from the belated, if effective, implementation of the Reformation, particularly the effects of the Cromwellian conquest and settlement and the subsequent greater commercialization and pastoralization of the economy, were to rupture this twin alliance with a ruthlessness and a thoroughness that allows one to speak of the "lost worlds" and "lost villages" of Tipperary and Kilkenny. But, as in life, things were not as simple as that—there were also communities and regions of greater continuities and adaptabilities (as in south Kilkenny) as well as regions of great transformations. To try to unravel this complex mosaic, I now turn to the impact of the Cromwellian conquest and settlement.

## The Cromwellian Conquest and Its Settlement Implications

Prior to 1641, Kilkenny and much of south and east Tipperary formed one of the richest, most developed parts of Ireland. These areas were inhabited by a large number of landed proprietors who were resident on their own lands and who managed their own territories and peoples. With some notable exceptions, particularly in Tipperary, these proprietors were Catholics of Anglo-Norman descent. By the end of the seventeenth century, this class had been largely supplanted by New English Protestant landlords, many of whom were Cromwellian officers and soldiers whose arrears of pay had been satisfied by grants of land. This final section provides an introduction to the diverse processes and patterns that underlay this great transformation in landownership, settlement, and society.

Exploring the hidden worlds of pre-Cromwellian Tipperary and Kilkenny with the help of relatively comprehensive source materials has been the central theme of this paper until now. These same documents, which help to reveal the general structure of, and local variations in, the economy, naming procedures, settlement, and so on, must also be seen for what they were primarily designed to achieve—the conquest and administration of "new" territories and peoples. The Civil and Down Surveys were in the first instance concerned with identifying and demarcating existing property units before redesigning these "chessboard" pieces to pay off the soldiers and adventurers who had ensured the Cromwellian conquest. The first mark of conquest everywhere is boundary definition, and the Civil and Down Surveys were above all about boundary making— not just at the topographic but also at the cultural and political levels. Thus, the Civil Survey described and defined many other things in addition to property lines. It ignored the subtle cultural distinctions and perceptions of the older populations—they were all characterized and henceforth would be categorized as "Irish Papists." Cromwellian planters regarded themselves, as Barnard observed, "as the chosen instruments of providence and looked upon their conquest as theirs by Divine Right. . . . The Irish offended their political (Republican) and religious (Puritanical) prejudices—the Irish were Papists and Jacobites and so inferior and alien."[40] A system of ethnic categorization and stratification was therefore embedded in these documents of conquest, and such categorizations provided the context that shaped and bounded future social relationships between these two groups.

The Civil and Down Surveys also sought to reduce the complexity of localized land measures to a single formula—the "plantation acre." Surveyors also sought to bring some order to the wide variety of denominations and territories that they met as they traveled across arable and pastoral land, bogland, and mountain. Hence, the future importance of that oldest and most critical of property chess pieces—the townland: it now became the key standardizing territorial unit at the base of the property system.

Conquest, therefore, not only involved a classification and appropriation of property units and their associated rent surpluses but also meant a reclassification and a renaming of places and peoples. The lyrical quality of the parish topographies in the Civil Survey derive mainly from the many ancient place-names embedded and perpetuated in these accounts. Yet here, as on the Down Survey maps, such place-names were rendered in English: Sir William Petty was anxious to standardize "those strange Irish names." Similar processes were at work (albeit over a longer period) on family names, as the centralizing state bureaucracy reshaped the words and worlds it encountered to better fit its image of how a "proper" language, economy, and society should sound, work, and behave.

The poll tax and hearth money records must be seen, therefore, in terms of what they set out to achieve: first, to act as paymaster to the Irish garrison and, second, to reach into almost every home in the country to support the superstructure of the Restoration state that now came to impinge so deeply on these counties that heretofore had been shielded by the earls of Ormond in their almost autonomous control of the "lordship." The state's instruments were the New English, acting out of self-interest no doubt—but also seeing themselves as representatives of this new, radical, and centralizing state and deeply imbued with notions of "superiority, improvement, and civility."

We still need much research on the social background of the varied groups and individuals that we collectively label the "New English." Some were early government officials, many were soldiers and officers of the Cromwellian army, others were essentially adventurers and speculators in land and money, and some were simply ordinary people seeking a better home and better opportunities. Suffice to note at this stage that they must have seen the landscape and resources of Tipperary and Kilkenny afresh—for they came with notions of exploitation and accumulation: most were relatively insecure, and getting rich quickly was an important priority. They belonged to a growing commercial nation, and they were to make a deep impression on the landscape and societies they encountered. They settled in areas about which they had little contemporary or historical knowledge. They were concerned instead with creating a new future. The landscapes, peoples, and place-names that they encountered were simply the instruments toward that end.

The new political-legal order was nowhere better epitomized than in the county towns of Clonmel and Kilkenny, which now, more than ever, became the fulcrums of the state's rule in the two counties. By 1667, Clonmel had the highest proportion of enumerated New English (49 percent) of any Tipperary town, and this figure had been significantly augmented since 1660, when Burke estimated the immigrant population at about one-fifth of the total.[41] The transformation of the city of Kilkenny was even more dramatic. The most significant inland city in the country, Kilkenny had long been dominated by such powerful merchant families as the Archers, Rothes, and Shees. It had its own complex and deeply rooted economic structures that supported a wide range of shops, services, and industrial activities, including as many as eighteen mills. New English control radically restructured the social geography of the city. As early as 1660, in the core of the city, in the High Street and elsewhere, over 72 percent of the population were of planter stock. In the surrounding ring of urban settlement, 40 percent of the population were settlers while in the outlying Liberties of the city, 24 percent were newcomers to a county where the New English comprised only 7.8 percent of the total adult population. The Cromwellians, therefore, had quickly established control over the core areas of the two counties.

Initial infiltration into these two county towns was in the administrative, legal, military, political, and ecclesiastical spheres. However, by the 1660s it was the merchants who dominated—men like Hamerton, Moore, and Perry in Clonmel and like Wareing, Warren, Wheeler, and Haydocke in Kilkenny. These were new leaders of an economic order in which merchant wealth was to help many of them acquire extensive estates in the surrounding regions. These two core towns thus were radically restructured, and although New English migrants literally occupied the homes of the old merchant families, they brought into these homes radically different assumptions, allegiances, and worldviews. They then attempted to remake Clonmel, Kilkenny, and their hinterlands in their own images. Such old county towns became anchorpoints of the new ruling elites and the centerpoints of their support populations.

This is not to suggest that the forces of transformation were all compressed into the Cromwellian period. Quite clearly, the expansion of Old English power and influence under the direction of the earls of Ormond over the previous century had paved the way for later intrusions. It was the post-Reformation takeover of the parochial glebelands that first initiated a small scattering of new immigrants into the region. Likewise, overspill from the earlier plantations of Laois and Offaly affected the northern edges of both counties—a process that underpinned the greatest rural concentration of Protestant populations in these border parishes in the eighteenth century. Similarly, the 1641 depositions indicate the deliberate introduction of New English tenants, miners, and leaseholders by both old "modernizing" and new landowners. The establishment of state-supported garrisons, as at Cullen, Golden, and Farney Bridge in Tipperary and places like Lodge Park and Knocktopher in Kilkenny, also brought in new people, as did rapid growth in the urban functions of the frontier towns of Nenagh, Roscrea, Clogheen, and Castlecomer. Finally, the central positions of Cashel and Kilkenny city in the new episcopal order provided additional impetus for immigration to, and expansion from, these old metropolitan foci—processes that also were reflected in new leasing patterns on the episcopal lands of the two bishops.

Figure 7.14 outlines the broad distribution of lands around 1670 for County Kilkenny. The now restored *duke* of Ormond had actually increased his Kilkenny holdings from fifty-five thousand to fifty-eight thousand plantation acres. This fact, in conjunction with the restoration of Lord Mountgarrett, the survival of the extensive Grace estate in Crannagh, and the continuation of the extensive Wandesforde estate in Fassadinin, meant that a sizable proportion of Kilkenny's real estate did not figure in the Cromwellian settlement. This was a crucial factor in the future, distinctive evolution of County Kilkenny society. On the other hand, figure 7.13 shows that Cromwellian grantees benefitted especially from the dismantling of the lands of many of the lesser Butlers, of the great Walsh estate in the south, and of practically all the other medium-sized and small estates held by that great phalanx of middle-order Old English gentry. There was therefore a close correlation between the areas of Cromwellian settlement and the lands shown in figure 7.8, which outlines the lesser

Butler and non-Butler lands of County Kilkenny in 1641. Thus, a solid group of Cromwellian estates at the level of five hundred to three thousand acres emerged among the Baker, Blunden, Bradshaw, Bushe, Loftus, and Warren families. Moreover, the creation of a Protestant ascendancy in Kilkenny, given the absence of an earlier New English presence, was overwhelmingly a function of such key Cromwellian families. However, it should be noted that only two of the new owners of the seven to eight estates of over five thousand acres, the Cuffe and Ponsonby families, were to become permanently associated with the county—the former at Inch and the latter at Kildalton and the landlord village of Piltown. In Tipperary, the most striking transformations were in the north and west of the county, where the "clan" lands and even the common lands were simplified and reduced to individually owned property units dominated by a small number of Cromwellian officers who bought out the debentures of many of their soldiers. In south and east Tipperary, in contrast, although there was actually a greater continuity in the shape and size of the estates, there was probably a greater transformation of the settlement and field patterns as old farming villages gave way to the newly enclosed geometric landscapes of individual farms and fields.[42]

A more detailed examination of the distribution of the Kilkenny gentry in 1660 provides further clues to the central priorities of the ruling group in the mid-seventeenth century. As we have seen already, control of the county and episcopal capital was a central feature of this design. Indeed, as illustrated elsewhere, the Cromwellian conquest was above all a conquest of Dublin, of all port cities, and of county towns (such as Kilkenny) by immigrant elites and peoples. The Cromwellian settlement, therefore, not only made for massive property transfers in the countryside; more significantly, Cromwellian policy and its associated economic processes saw the radical acceleration of planter command of urban properties, of agricultural surpluses, of external trade, and of a whole range of administrative and other positions in the cities and county towns. Underpinning this urban ascendancy were officers and soldiers, and the elaborate garrison fortifications that had been grafted onto the walls of the old cities.

Another feature of the Cromwellian elite distribution in Kilkenny was the control of key communication lines. Unlike the old lordships that had to administer and defend their own boundaries, the new elite could depend on the central state for this now broader function. In any case, much of Kilkenny's borderlands remained safely in Ormond Butler hands. The New English elite therefore moved to concentrate

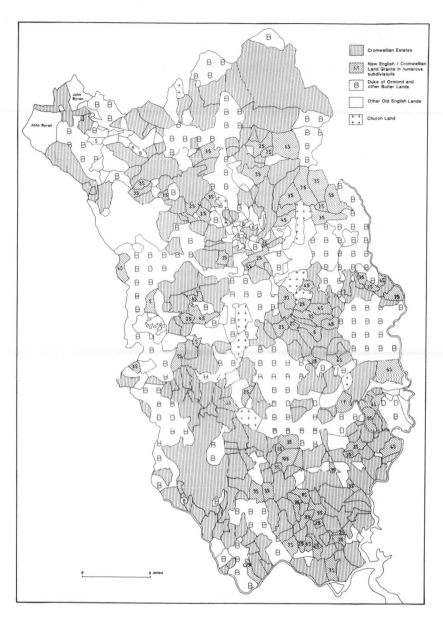

*Figure 7.14.* Distribution of Cromwellian Properties in County Kilkenny, c. 1670

282 WILLIAM J. SMYTH

its control not only in Kilkenny city but also outward into its hinterland in all directions: moving north through Ballyragget to the midlands, northwest by Freshford into mid-Tipperary, northeast to Dublin via Castlecomer, eastward along the rich core area to Gowran and the River Barrow, and finally, southwest along the corridor from Callan and Clonmel. Simultaneously, the New English moved to control the navigable stretches of the Nore River within the county and the lower stretches of both the Suir and Barrow rivers. Clear access from Kilkenny city south to Waterford port was also maintained, as was a central east-west axis along the northern foothills of the Walsh Mountains. Thus, the Cromwellians not only achieved landed control but they also established hegemony over the centers of trade and, above all, over the essential road and river networks that opened out from Kilkenny to Dublin, to Waterford, and to the Atlantic markets beyond. As indicated elsewhere, similar patterns and processes were found in County Tipperary.[43]

By the mid-1660s, a trinity comprised of a new ruling military and political order, a particular landed-commercial system, and an Established Church had together consolidated a geographical base. Burtchaell's unpublished work on the distribution of the New English in the two counties in 1660 highlighted the central role of the towns for the newcomers, the fanning out of the settlers along the major routeways, and the residual impact of the outlying garrison centers that were to wipe out the pockets of resistance that survived in the woodlands, boglands, and hills.[44] Yet there remained extensive areas in both counties where Cromwellian settlers were sparse.

The geography of this revolutionary transformation in the distribution and composition of elites was complemented by a geography of dislocation and trauma for the majority of people in both the old landowning and urban middle classes. These were required to make themselves, their families, and their retinues of stock and other material wealth known to the Revenue Commissioners before trekking to their new allocations in Connaught. In County Tipperary, 221 members of the former elite complied with these instructions, and in County Kilkenny 191 supplied the Cromwellian Commissioners with the relevant details.[45] Included in the Tipperary groups were the Butlers (Lord Dunboyne, Viscount Ikerrin, and Lady Mary Hamilton [Roscrea] as well as people like the Baron Purcell of Loughmoe and O'Meagher of Clonakenny. The Kilkenny contingent was led by such people as Walter Archer of Gowran, Nicholas Aylward of Aylwardstown, Thomas Butler of Kildellig, John Cantwell of Cantwellscourt,

Philip Purcell of Ballyfoyle, and Pierce Walsh of Ballyhubbock. In effect, all major and minor landowners were included except the earl of Ormond, his closest kin, and his immediate political allies. The Kilkenny Transplantation Certificates both highlight the zones of greatest dislocation and mirror the zones of greatest Cromwellian landed dominance (see figure 7.13).

However, the transportation summaries do not provide the whole story, for it appears that less than one-third of this group actually moved to Connaught. Instead, many of the rest hung on locally, hoping for reinstatement with the help of the now restored duke of Ormond. Thus, in 1660, the old Kilkenny gentry controlled the parishes of Clone, the Rower and Dungarvan in Gowran barony, and much of the middle lands of Ida—including the parishes of Ballygurrim, Kilbride, Kilmacknoge, and Kilcolme. Elsewhere on lands dominated by the Butlers, old elites retained control of such parishes as Killaloe, Conlaghmore, Dunamaggan, and Kells while competing with the new Cromwellian settlers along the Kilkenny city/Waterford port axis. Likewise, a great belt of old gentry survived in much of Crannagh barony, and some old elites also survived in north Kilkenny on the borders of Galmoy, Fassadinin, and Crannagh.

Further clues to the nature of local society are provided by the retainers named by landowners in the Transplantation Certificates as traveling to Connaught with their lords. The average number of retainers per transplanting owner countrywide was 20.5, almost precisely the norm for County Kilkenny. County Tipperary, in contrast, exhibited a larger number of retainers (39.1)—second only to County Kerry. For example, Corr of Tubberahany in Tipperary was recorded as being accompanied by 144 persons. It is therefore instructive that the Corr stronghold was one of the least populated centers in the lower Suir valley in 1667.

More generally, the 1664 Ormond list of dispossessed landowners in the two counties identified well over three hundred members of former elite families who still were hoping to be restored to at least some of their lands through the good offices of the duke of Ormond. Some few of these families, particularly those at the top of the social hierarchy, were able to renegotiate a place in the sun through their substantial wealth, social position, and political influence at the highest levels. The great majority of landlords were *not* restored, however, and with them went the patronage not only of the poets and the harpers but also of many of the old settlement foci and their populations. The Reformation and its aftermath had weakened some of the old villages, but it was the uprooting of the old landowner patrons in conjunction with the new economic forces of mercantilism—unleashed by a new elite—that finally shattered many of them.

The actual detailed breakdown of the complex combination of forces that led to the demise, shrinking, or survival of the village settlement structure will require careful research in the future. Yet a point that is clear is that such research will reveal that buried under many demesnes (the private, enclosed worlds that the landlords created for themselves in the late seventeenth and especially eighteenth centuries) are the remnants of the old settlement and social structures of both Counties Tipperary and Kilkenny. In this context, it is noteworthy that the surviving village world in south Kilkenny is one with very few, if any, demesnes. Clearly, it was north and middle Kilkenny where Cromwellian landlordism struck its deepest roots, as evidenced by the reconstituted towns and villages of this region and by the dense distribution of landlord demesnes. Practically every demesne in Lower Ormond (in Tipperary) and Galmoy (in Kilkenny) was built on a former focal point, and it is likely that a similar pattern prevailed elsewhere. Thus, in place of the old village communities were built parklands and high walls, enclosing forever the lost worlds of the seventeenth century.

The reverberations of such changes echoed well into the nineteenth century. On the one hand, in Tipperary, the old centers of Kilsheelan, Kilfeakle, and Ardmayle became only shadows of their former selves, and in subsequent decades, Castletownarra, Buolick, Kilcooly, Knockgraffan, Ballyclerahan, Solloghodmore, Lattin, Derryluskan, Clonakenny, and a host of smaller nuclei shrank or disappeared. Similarly, in Kilkenny, Kells was to become a small village, Newtownjerpoint disappeared completely, as did a whole host of parish centers throughout the lowland regions of the county. On the other hand, places such as Ballyhale, Ballyragget, and Inistioge were relocated or reconstructed, while new landlord villages or towns emerged at Johnstown and Goresbridge in Kilkenny and at Borrisokane, Templemore, and Cloghjordan in Tipperary. I have elsewhere detailed the depopulation of the Tipperary lowlands and the massive expansion of settlement in the bogland and upland regions between the 1650s and the 1850s,[46] but it is clear that these processes already were in motion in the two counties between the 1650s and the 1690s—probably at a swifter pace in the more pastoral county of Tipperary and more slowly—but with the same long-term results—in parts of County Kilkenny.

Although the local and regional displacement of populations and its associated settlement infrastructure was often related to the disappearance of the old landlord patrons, this was not the case everywhere. Using data for the national level, we can identify the contrasting regions in Ireland where old elites, as distinct from new elites, were preeminent. The sharpest contrast was between plantation Ulster and the regions "reserved" for the Irish in Connaught. Yet much of east and south Leinster and east Munster emerged as a battleground of conflicting interests. These were areas where the planters' more narrow ascendancy was matched by both the residual class power and greater population size of the older society. Members of the latter societies still held on to powerful hinge positions in the urban and rural social hierarchies and ensured that the relative success of the new landlord-inspired economy would both depend on and be in part mediated by them.[47]

This situation probably applied particularly to those parts of Tipperary and Kilkenny where the duke of Ormond and other Butler families, and those of their allies, survived as landlords for lengthy periods after the mid-seventeenth century. Ormond retained a massive 130,000 acres in Tipperary up to the early eighteenth century and likewise held close to sixty thousand acres in Kilkenny. This, as well as the survival or restoration of the Grace, Mountgarrett, Galmoy, Blanchfield, and other smaller estate units in Kilkenny, often sustained local communities in their respective areas.[48] Similarly, in County Tipperary, the survival of some of the key Butler families, such as those at Kilcash and Cahir, and other old families, such as the Mandevilles, Morrises, and O'Mearas, was probably associated with the continuity of local communities. In both counties, however, detailed research is still necessary to tease out the precise social impact of these surviving families.

A comparison of the 1660 poll tax with the hearth money records four to six years later also reveals variations in the dialectic between the Cromwellian and older forces at work in local communities and regions. In the barony of Fassadinin, Cromwellian settlement solidified between 1660 and 1664—a process marked both by the survival of the existing Cromwellians and by the emergence of new Cromwellian families at the elite (more than two hearths) level. Nolan confirmed this pattern for the end of the seventeenth century, when the barony was solidly in Cromwellian hands: even the duke of Ormond was selling off his interests here by the 1690s.[49] Similarly, in Galmoy, along the edges of the solidly planted midland belt of Laois-Offaly, a further solidification of the Cromwellian settlement was in motion between 1660 and 1664. This too was the case in the Liberties of Kilkenny and in the rich barony of Shillelogher, where an already established Cromwellian presence was entrenched.

In contrast, the Grace-dominated barony of Crannagh remained remarkably stable and resilient, with the old gentry families keeping a firm hold on their territories. Again in contrast, Knocktopher was a transitional case, where both "traditions" consolidated in different parts of the barony. In Gowran barony, apart from the Kilkenny city hinterland, the restoration of some of the major Butler families (including Lord Galmoy) and their allies saw a shift in favor of the old gentry families and the consequent relocation of some of the new Cromwellian grantees. Once again, in contrast, Ida and Iverk remained for the most part unchanged between 1660 and 1664. Ida showed a striking balance between the power of the two elite groups, whereas Iverk, given the dominance of the earl of Ormond and the Ponsonby family, experienced little change as its crescent of small Cromwellian grantees along the Suir simply persisted. Similar patterns of regional stability and change—as a result of the dialectic between old and new forces—have been documented for County Tipperary.[50]

However, there were further complications in landowning and landholding patterns that had significant implications for social and settlement structures. As Brennan noted, perhaps only fifteen to twenty of the approximately two hundred Cromwellian grantees in Kilkenny became so permanently associated with the county through residence and political representation as to form its so-called Protestant Ascendancy.[51] Although work needs to be done to tease out these early and continuing levels of absenteeism among the new landowners, it is clear that it was of a very significant order in both counties. Moreover, not only did absenteeism become a powerful feature, but, as figure 7.14 illustrates, the subdivision of formerly united properties among numerous grantees further complicated what was already a highly complex property framework. These two factors, absenteeism and complex property relations, had significant if still underresearched implications for the continuity or discontinuity of settlement patterns; for the development or nondevelopment of demesnes or landlord villages; for the encouragement or discouragement of an influx of "improving Protestant head tenants"; and for the survival or demise of old ways of managing territories and societies. In south Kilkenny, continuities clearly were related to higher levels of absenteeism. Yet it is unclear to what extent the survival of both old landlord patronage and parish structures in the richer lands of parts of Kilkenny and Tipperary actually inhibited the spread of enclosures, the greater commercialization of the agricultural economy, and the decline of the old village structures. The detailed unraveling of these processes is another day's work.

In any event, the most crucial continuities were not at the elite levels. Here the evidence suggests that Tipperary and Kilkenny were only half conquered. The hearth money records for both counties point to the continuing strength of both the middle and lower levels of the old society. They also show how sharp were the contrasting patterns of settlement in the middle and late 1660s. In Tipperary, the descendants of the Old Irish represented around 70 percent of the population, and they still retained 40 percent of the more substantial two-hearth houses. The descendants of the Old English, comprising 25 percent of the population, actually commanded an impressive 48 percent of the better houses. The New English, while only representing around 5 percent of the population, occupied 12 percent of the total number of houses with more than one hearth; but they occupied 70 percent of those houses with five or more hearths (i.e., the landlord mansions and largest town houses). The more limited Kilkenny hearth money evidence for 1664 suggests a similar pattern that surfaced even more emphatically at the time of the Williamite war between 1688 and 1691. Previously, during the short-lived reign of James II, the Irish in Kilkenny managed to define only sixty Cromwellians as "rebels"—a number of these being the widows of landlords "who were absent from the kingdom." In contrast, after the defeat of the Jacobites, nearly three hundred members of Kilkenny's old elite, some farmers, clerks, blacksmiths, and others were outlawed.[52] This list of "outlaws" shows the strength of, for example, the Brennans of Fassadinin—gone as landowners, but clearly a dominant force as middle gentry and local power holders in Castlecomer and adjacent parishes. Similarly, the Shortalls remained deeply enmeshed in the life and power structures of north Crannagh, even if none survived officially as landowners. The list of those outlawed also highlights the power that the old families retained in baronies like Gowran. Indeed, the list is in part a pointer to the last drive by the old "feudal" elite to regain the high ground. Moreover, judging by the distribution of surnames on the list, the southern half of County Kilkenny appears to have been less turbulent at this time— another factor in protecting this area from further upheaval. Finally, the list also makes clear how the core leadership of the Jacobite movement lay with the merchants, surgeons, and other gentry families of the city of Kilkenny: close to 20 percent of all Jacobite "rebels" resided there. Their failure enabled the Williamite conquest and confiscations to complete the Cromwellian "settlement" with a thoroughness, a ruthlessness, and a finality that would not be challenged at the political level for at least one hundred years. Yet beneath the landownership level, stubborn tenant farmers, and "agrarian combinations" were already constructing their own patterns of adaptation and resistance.

## Conclusion

Aidan Clarke, in his brilliant essay on the Irish economy between 1600 and 1660, observed:

> It was not, in short, Ireland that prospered in those years but those who controlled Ireland's resources and this distinction was to become increasingly plain in the years that followed. . . . There is, of course, a crude sense in which conquest was progressive; because it loosened traditional restraints on the use of land and allowed freer responses to market conditions; but the economic gains accrued to individuals, while the social cost was borne by the conquered community.[53]

Too true, but as this essay points out, perhaps historians (even the best of them) are inclined to overemphasize changes and discontinuities and to underemphasize the dialectic between continuity and change among a variety of communities in different regional settings. In Tipperary and Kilkenny, there are complex mosaics of communities that have remade themselves in history in a number of different ways. Of course, a whole host of questions still remain as this essay winds to a halt. I am not at all clear how local communities and local economies worked up to 1640. I still have not worked out the detailed consequences for the nature of settlement and society, of the survival or demise of old landowning structures, parishes, and economies.

However, I have worked long enough on these materials and counties to make the following conclusions. To do a proper study of how societies grow, change, decline, or reconstruct themselves, a full mastery of the relevant documents is essential: in the case of Counties Tipperary and Kilkenny the need, among other things, to explore further the meanings hidden in the Ormond deeds and related papers seems obvious. Second, a much deeper understanding of how the old society functioned and how the new settlers inserted themselves into, and attempted to reconstruct, the society is also essential. Here the anthropologist and ethnographer may have much to tell us. Third (and the geographer as fieldworker and explorer should be good at this), we need to have a much greater appreciation of the *terrain* (not just physical but infrastructural and cultural) in which people in these societies worked and made a living. We need to know more about where the populations actually lived, about the lie of the roads and about communications generally, about the role of the towns, about the nature of agricultural production, about trading patterns and linkages, and about a host of other cultural issues before we can provide a fuller picture of seventeenth-century Irish society and its transformation. However, at this stage, I think it may be clear why the Shortall-owned castle-village of Clomantagh is now deserted and why the villages of South Kilkenny survive into the late twentieth century both as living entities and as gateways into the lost worlds of the seventeenth century.

### NOTES

1. Burtchaell (1988:110–23).
2. Smyth (1976:29–49).
3. Smyth (1985:104–38); Smyth (1990:125–58).
4. Smyth (1988:55–83).
5. Smyth (1978:1–22).
6. Petty (1691:17–20).
7. This included County Leitrim but excluded the other counties of the province of Connaught and County Clare.
8. Simington (1934:iii–xvii).
9. National Library of Ireland (N.L.I.) Ms. 720.
10. Hardinge (1866:379–420).
11. Public Record Office of Ireland (P.R.O.I.).
12. Pender (1939:v).
13. Pender (1939:ii).
14. Pender (1939:ii–iii).
15. Pender (1939:iii).
16. Pender (1939:iii–iv).
17. Pilsworth (1943:22–24).
18. Belmore (1881:304–9, Appendix L).
19. Dickson, Ó Gráda, and Daultrey (1982:125–82).
20. Laffan (1911:201–5).
21. Walton (1985:33–47, 169–80).
22. Ormond Deeds (1932–43).
23. Smyth (1988:57).
24. N.L.I. Ms. D.4052.
25. Hardinge (1866:379–420).
26. Simington (1934:203–418).

27. Smyth (1988:60–62). I wish to thank Cork University Press for permission to include figures 7.5 and 7.11, previously published in Smyth and Whelan (1988). I also wish to thank Geography Publications, Dublin, for permission to include figures 7.7, 7.9, and 7.13, previously published in Nolan and Whelan (1990), and for permission to include figure 7.8, previously published in Nolan (1985).

28. Nicholls (1972:3–20).
29. Empey (1971:174–87).
30. Nolan (1979:65–148).
31. Walton (1985:33–47, 169–80).
32. Simington (1934:345); N.L.I. Ms. 720.
33. Smyth (1988:65–68).
34. Smyth (1985:118–30).
35. Burke (1907:420).
36. Nolan (1979:62–70).
37. O'Kelly (1985:1–192).
38. Ormond Deeds, vol. 8: 190–94.
39. N.L.I. Ms. 4052.
40. Barnard (1975:66).
41. Burke (1907:90).
42. Leister (1963:117–258).
43. Smyth (1985:130–38).
44. Burtchaell, personal communication.
45. Ryan (1977:58–60).
46. Smyth (1980:159–84).
47. Smyth (1988:70–72).
48. Burtchaell (1988:110–23).
49. Nolan (1979:83).
50. Smyth (1985:130–38).
51. Brennan (1985:134–71).
52. Carrigan (1905:396–404).
53. Clarke (1976:186).

# III

## APPROACHES TO THE PAST
## IN ANTHROPOLOGY,
## SOCIAL HISTORY, AND
## HISTORICAL SOCIOLOGY

# 8

# Colonialism and the Interpretation of Irish Historical Development[1]

■

## JOSEPH RUANE

Colonialism has been a recurring theme in Irish historical studies, and the issues it raises are important. But there has been no consensus on the subject; on the contrary, views have been diverse and contradictory. In this essay, I outline those views and consider whether a firm conclusion can be reached on the role of colonialism in Irish historical development. I argue that although the literature points to the questions that have to be addressed, it does not let us answer them. I also argue that Irish historical anthropology has much to contribute to resolving the issues in dispute.

Some writers have held that colonialism has been central to the Irish historical experience from the late medieval period onward, that it has shaped Irish society and culture in a crucial way, and that the Irish experience has been closer to that of colonized non-European countries than to that of mainstream Western Europe. Other writers have contested this, accepting perhaps the importance of colonialism at an earlier period of Irish history but questioning its later significance and stressing the parallels between Ireland and other European countries. Still others have adopted an intermediate position, pointing to the mixture of colonial and noncolonial elements in the Irish experience and the parallels with both colonial and noncolonial societies.[2]

Social scientists have now abandoned the notion that all societies follow a similar evolutionary path, differing only in the extent to which they have progressed along it. They stress instead that world society has developed in a highly differentiated way and will continue to do so.[3] The experience of colonialism is one of the crucial differentiating factors. If the Irish experience was colonial, in whole or in part, this has important implications for historical research. If it was not, a very different mode of interpretation is called for.

The question is of particular importance for Irish historical anthropology. More than the other social sciences, anthropology studies the entire range of societies and cultures. Much of its research has taken place in societies that were, or were until recently, colonized. If anthropologists are to draw on that literature to understand Ireland, they must first establish to what extent Ireland resembles those societies and where it should be placed in the array of societies they study. Even if their concern is noncomparative, they must establish what kind of society Ireland is and has been.

The task is far from simple. Determining if a particular historical experience has been colonial raises complex theoretical, ideological, and methodological issues; if these are not adequately addressed, the question cannot be answered. In the first part of this essay, I look at the treatment of the colonial theme in the different historical disciplines and then assess the adequacy of this treatment. Before I begin, however, a brief discussion of the concept of colonialism is necessary.

## Colonialism: A Definition

There has been no agreement on how colonialism should be defined. Virtually all definitions have stressed the theme of domination by an external power, but beyond that there has been much variation.

One theorist saw it as referring to a "state of inferiority or of servitude experienced by a community, a country, or a nation which is dominated politically and/or economically and/or culturally by another and more developed community or nation; applied especially when the dominant nation is European or North American, and the less-developed, a non-European people."[4] Another writer described it as the

> establishment and maintenance, for an extended time, of rule over an alien people that is separate from and subordinate to the ruling power.

. . . Colonialism has now come to be identified with rule over peoples of different race inhabiting lands separated by salt water from the imperial centre; more particularly it signifies direct political control by European states or states settled by Europeans, as the United States or Australia, over peoples of other races, notably over Asians and Africans.[5]

A third theorist defined it as the "settlement of foreign territories, the separation of foreign and indigenous peoples by legal means, and the growth of racialism" and as a special or direct form of imperialism defined as the "imposition of the power of one state over the territories of another, normally by military means, in order to exploit subjugated populations and to extract economic and political advantage."[6]

The scope for variation is indeed enormous. Colonialism can be defined with reference to relations between territories, peoples, communities, nations, states, societies, or cultures. The definition may limit colonialism to groups between whom there is a significant difference in level of technological or cultural development, or it may leave this question open. It may include reference to some or all of the following dimensions: economic, political, military, legal, cultural, psychological, racial. It may or may not refer to exploitation. It may place central emphasis on the role of metropolitan settlers in the process or ignore them. It may refer only to the activities of public bodies (states or governments) or cover also the activities of private operators. It may refer to a set of processes, or to a social system. It may concentrate on the internal characteristics of the colonized society or on the relationship between colonizer and colonized. It may be designed to fit the details of a particular case or to have global reference. It may be limited to particular moments in the historical process or particular geographical areas, or it may leave these open.[7]

The definition of colonialism that I employ here draws both on existing ones and on the ways—usually implicit—in which the term has been used in the Irish literature. I distinguish between colonial processes and colonial social systems. Colonialism as process refers to the intrusion into and conquest of an inhabited territory by the representatives (formal or informal) of an external power; the displacement of the native inhabitants (elites and/or commoners) from resources and positions of power; the subsequent exercise of economic, political, and cultural control over the territory and native population by the intruders and their descendants, in their own interests and in the name and interests of the external power.

A colonial social system is one in which the conflicts and contradictions associated with an initial colonizing process remain salient for its present structure and functioning. The degree of salience may vary from one time period to another and from one institutional sphere of the system to another (economy, politics, culture).

## Colonialism and Irish Historical Studies

### History

There has been no agreement among historians on the question of colonialism, though a general pattern is discernible. Historians have widely used the language and themes of colonialism—intrusion, conquest, displacement, control—for the late medieval period, the sixteenth and seventeenth centuries, and the eighteenth century. Thereafter, reference to colonialism has been unusual.[8]

Colonial themes have been paramount in the writings of historians for the late medieval period, covering such topics as the coming of the Anglo-Normans as intruders and conquerors; the displacement of the native lords and, to a lesser extent, the common people; the establishment of a structure of government and lordship of the English crown in Ireland; the struggles for power and control over land; the introduction of English law and the denial of legal rights to the native population; the perceptions of the Gaelic population as backward by the incoming Norman/English; the conflict between the two communities in the church. Together these themes amount to an essentially colonial view of Ireland during that period; in fact, many historians have explicitly used the language of colonialism. The emphasis on colonialism has also grown in recent years. The older view, that the conflicts and divisions of the initial period gave way from the fourteenth century onward to an integration of the two communities and cultures, has now been disputed. Current research has emphasized contact and mutual influence but within a context of separateness and division.[9]

Colonial themes have also dominated the literature for the sixteenth and seventeenth centuries (e.g., the reestablishment of English control over Ireland; the establishment of new, more effective forms of government; the arrival of new settlers of all classes; the confiscation of land and displacement of native elites of both English and Irish descent; the opening up of the economy to greater commercialism; the improvement of communications and founding of new towns;

the imposition of the Reformation; the destruction of the Gaelic legal and cultural system; the perception of the Irish, particularly the Gaelic Irish, as wild and uncivilized). Some historians have dealt with these simply as conflicts of religion, politics, and culture, but many have explicitly used the language of colonialism to characterize both the context within which the changes took place (English and, more generally, European expansion overseas) and the way in which they were implemented (ruthlessly and frequently bloodily). They also have drawn parallels between events in Ireland at this time and European intrusions, settlements, and imperialism in the New World.[10] There has been some difference of opinion as to how far the colonial view can be pressed; for example, one writer emphasized the complexities introduced by the nature of Scottish migration to Ulster, the role played by religion, the extent to which Ireland was a kingdom as well as a colony.[11] The degree to which English policies toward Ireland in the sixteenth century were of a piece with its policies in the New World has also been queried.[12] Others have argued that although colonialism was the outcome, this was less the original plan than the result of a complex and quite unpredictable set of events.[13] But these arguments qualify rather than counter the colonial view.

The eighteenth century saw the emergence of a more stable society in Ireland after the intrusions and disruptions of the previous two centuries, though conflict persisted. The literature has stressed the depth of the cultural and religious divide in the country; the dilemmas faced by a small minority ruling over a culturally and religiously different and disaffected majority; the legal and political restrictions it introduced to secure its position; the flowering of its culture in art and architecture; the expansion of economic activity and trade and the restrictions the British parliament placed on Irish trade; Ireland's subordinate position within the British colonial system; the emergence of conflict between the Anglo-Irish elite and the British parliament, and the beginnings of a form of nationalism; the ambivalence of the new ruling class toward Ireland and its two-way glance, partly toward Ireland, partly toward Britain; the progressive decline of the language and distinctive culture of the native population. Historians have differed in the extent to which they have characterized these divisions and developments in colonial terms. Some have ignored it; others have made it central.[14] Most have made some reference to it.

The themes in historical writing for the nineteenth and early twentieth centuries have been much more varied. Earlier themes—conflicts over land, religion, and political participation—have been continued, some in new aspects. However, new ones have emerged: population expansion and then decline; changes in the agricultural, industrial, and regional economies; the spread of markets and communications; commercialization; class struggles and restructurings; agrarian violence; urbanization; emigration; the growth of the state; the spread of literacy and formal education; the formation of mass parties; the emergence of nationalism. More important, the colonial frame of reference has been abandoned and a more complex and differentiated view taken. An eclectic combination of modernization (in its economic, class, political, and cultural dimensions) and an unspecified, and largely implicit, decolonization has provided the principal frame of reference for historical writing about this period.[15] The colonial view has not been totally rejected; for example, one historian argued that the society as a whole was still colonial and that modernization was taking place within a colonial framework.[16] However, most historians have distanced themselves from references to colonialism; this tendency becomes more marked as the century progresses.

Historical writing on the south since independence has focused mainly on political themes: the establishment of the structures of the new state, achievement of full sovereignty, political events and personalities, policies on Northern Ireland, foreign policy making. Economic, class, educational, cultural, intellectual, and ideological themes have also been dealt with, though to a more limited degree. These themes have been located within a frame of reference that, as for the previous period, eclectically combined modernization and decolonization, though the emphasis has shifted to achievements (or the lack of them) in state and nation building.[17] The more limited historical writing on the north also has dealt predominantly with political issues: the attempt at "state" and "community" building in a regional context marked by social division and constitutional uncertainty, its apparent success in the early period, and its later failure. These themes have typically been considered from a modernization perspective, although some writers have adopted a partly colonial view.[18]

Economics

Among economists who have written on Irish historical themes, Lynch and Vaizey and Kennedy, Giblin, and McHugh placed little emphasis on conflict or colonialism.[19] Mokyr referred frequently to the depth of the religious and cultural divide in Ireland but left its relationship to colonialism unclear. His analysis of the Famine did not refer to colonialism, and the question of whether the "perfidious policies of Albion" could account for Irish poverty was set aside on the grounds that it was a question to which "conventional empirical tests are . . . quite inapplicable."[20] Ó Gráda was similarly cautious.[21]

Some writers have gone farther toward a colonial interpretation. It was implicit at times in Black's analysis of British policy-making toward Ireland during the nineteenth century.[22] It was also suggested in Solow's conclusion that the land problem arose less out of actual economic conditions than out of a nationalism that had its roots in the earlier British decision "to maintain Ireland as a fully segregated society."[23] O'Malley referred explicitly to Ireland in colonial terms ("England's first colony"), though his analysis of the development (or lack of it) of the nineteenth-century Irish economy emphasized market relationships much more than colonialism.[24]

Crotty, uniquely, developed a fully fledged theory of colonialism and of Ireland as a colonial society.[25] He depicted the England-Ireland relationship as deeply colonial from the late medieval period. For Crotty it was just one of the many colonizations that stemmed from the expansion of capitalism beyond its northwest European heartland and that produced the four basic types of society found in the world today: capitalist societies, settler colonies, capitalist colonies and non-capitalist, and non-Western societies. Irish society fell into the third category, having been "capitalist colonised" in the sixteenth and seventeenth centuries. The legacy of that colonization has remained strong in both parts of Ireland. As a capitalist colony, Ireland was unique in Western terms, as a Western society, it was unique among the world's capitalist colonies. For Crotty, Ireland was geographically and racially part of Europe; historically, it was part of the Third World.

## Sociology

Sociologists also have differed in the extent to which they have emphasized colonialism. Some have made minimal reference to it. Keenan located the resource—organizational and political difficulties of the early-nineteenth-century Catholic church in the defeat and displacement of an earlier period—but he analyzed its recovery without reference to colonialism.[26] Clark identified the roots of the struggle for land in nineteenth-century Ireland in the conquests and confiscations of the sixteenth and seventeenth centuries, but he analyzed those struggles in terms of a theory of social movements that stressed economic, class, community, and political factors rather than decolonization.[27]

Inglis gave colonialism an important place in his explanation of the power of the Catholic church in Ireland from the late nineteenth century. Ireland was an external colony of England, though "like no other colony; being right next door and yet separated by a stretch of sea."[28] The lack of legitimacy of the colonial metropolitan power prevented the state, and enabled the Catholic church, to introduce and implement the "civilizing" process and to accumulate the power that could be derived from this role.

Gibbon stressed the role of colonialism in laying Ireland's economic and social foundations, including the basis for its subsequent division. Colonization in the northeast differed from the rest of the island. In the former, a "society of colons of British origin farmed holdings of a more or less uniformly small size," and development followed a broadly British metropolitan pattern. In the latter, a "few scattered colons grazed or sub-let large estates" and a "colonial mode of production" developed.[29] The emergence of unionism in Ulster and nationalism in the rest of Ireland reflected that structural division.

Hechter placed most emphasis on colonialism, testing and confirming the applicability to the British Isles of an "internal colonial" model of national development. He attributed the persistence of a sense of ethnic separateness and solidarity in Ireland, Scotland, and Wales to the "internal colonialism" to which the "Celtic fringe" was subject in the course of "British national development." Thus, for Hechter, English colonialism in Ireland was of an "internal" rather than an "external" kind—part of a process of national development in the British Isles rather than of empire building by Britain overseas.[30]


Political Science

Virtually all political scientists who have written on Irish historical themes have characterized the relationship between Ireland and Britain at some stage in its history in colonial, or nearly colonial, terms. The concept of the Republic of Ireland as a "postcolonial nation" or a "new nation" has been very strong in Irish political science, as has been the view that Irish political institutions and practices have diverged from those of the mainstream Western liberal democracies as a result of this experience.[31]

Chubb, for example, attributed the depth of British influence on

Ireland to the fact that Ireland was subject to British "political domin-
ion, social and economic domination and cultural blanketing. Ireland,
like Scotland and Wales, became an English province, her politics and
her economic and cultural life dominated by, and oriented to, England."[32] Similar themes, with explicit references to colonialism, are
found in Sacks, Garvin, Prager, and Rumpf and Hepburn.[33]

Garvin developed the theme of colonialism in greater depth. He
raised the complex question of Ireland's changing relationship to
Britain during the nineteenth century and concluded that Ireland was
a colony of Britain

> with its own acknowledged corporate status up to 1800, which London
> attempted to convert into a periphery in the nineteenth century by
> means of bureaucratic modernisation policies. London almost suc-
> ceeded, but in succeeding in the linguistic and economic assimilation of
> Ireland to Britain, political equality had also to be accorded, thus
> reviving or unleashing unsolved religious, regional and class animosi-
> ties deriving from the *English* national revolution of Tudor and Jaco-
> bean times.[34]

Irish nationalism was in part a response to colonialism, in part a
peripheral revolt: "Within the *United Kingdom* context, Irish nationalism was a classic example of a movement of peripheral protest,
reinforced by religious differences, economic contrasts and, of course,
both agrarian and urban labour/employer tensions, often entangled in
the traditional religion-based caste distinctions."[35]

Political scientists, concerned with the historical development and
current status of Northern Ireland, have differed significantly in their
emphasis on colonialism. For Wright the origins of the conflict today
lay in seventeenth-century colonialism, but over time the relative
equalization of conditions between "citizens" and "natives" meant
that the northeast of Ireland became an "ethnic frontier" rather than a
colony. Thereafter, the conflict became simply one of religion and
nationality.[36] In contrast, for MacDonald, the conflict was about the
continued dominance of the "settlers" over the "natives" and their
dependence on the external power.[37]

We may include here also the interdisciplinary, Marxist analysis of
Bew, Gibbon, and Patterson, who argued against the interpretation
of twentieth-century Ireland in "imperial" or "colonial" terms. Their
definition of these terms was the "classical Marxist-Leninist" one,
whereby "imperialism is a *special stage* in the development of the
capitalist mode of production, to which a *special form* of colonialism
corresponds." Imperialism in this sense began around 1900, too late

to shape modern Ireland, whose "basic lines of economic and political development (including its modern elements) were laid down in the last century." Thus, though an "imperial power, Britain, has maintained a colonial relationship to Northern Ireland," this did not prove that "struggles over the status of Northern Ireland involve the question of imperialism, or that contradictions involving imperialism have primacy in Ulster."[38]


Geography

Colonialism has been a frequent theme in Irish historical geography, although views have differed as to its nature, its centrality to the Irish experience, and how long it lasted. The introduction to a recent book relegated colonization to just one of a number of changes grouped under the general heading of "modernisation" that was taken as the "impact of forces, of exogenous or endogenous origin, on Ireland between 1600 and 1900, ranging from changes in farming technology to colonialism."[39]

Others have made colonialism more central, depicting Irish society and culture as built up out of the contributions of successive colonizations by new cultural groups—with elements of the new in part displacing, in part overlaying, in part sustaining themselves through the existing culture and social structure. Some have traced this process from prehistoric times, stressing its integrative, cumulative nature—with later cultures imposing themselves for a time on existing ones but then integrating with them. In this view, colonialism as a process laid the foundations for a society that later ceased to be colonial.[40] Others have focused on colonialism from the late medieval period onward and have emphasized the limited extent of integration, the continuing colonial nature of the society, and the degree to which earlier indigenous structures remained separate and intact underneath later colonial accretions.[41] Decolonization in the nineteenth century removed these accretions, exposing the still intact indigenous culture underneath: "the older partially submerged families and social structures reappeared as the backbone of a re-emergence which was to sweep away the superficial trappings of the colony and its urban appendages."[42]

An alternative approach to the colonial question—from political economy—is also found in the geography literature. In one version, Ireland was depicted as a colony from the early modern period up to independence and as a neocolony today.[43] In another, Ireland was colonial up until the legislative union between Britain and Ireland in 1800, when it became an integral part of the United Kingdom and ceased to be a colony.[44]

## Anthropology

Anthropologists have varied in their reference, implicit or explicit, to colonialism. There has also been variation between studies carried out in the Republic of Ireland and in Northern Ireland.

Most studies carried out in the south have referred to colonialism, though Silverman and Gulliver, in their detailed history of a local area from the mid-nineteenth century, did not.[45] Taylor attributed more importance to it, stressing its contribution to the social, political and cultural order that emerged in Ireland in the seventeenth and eighteenth centuries, some of whose legacy still remained. But for Taylor, in other respects, the Irish experience was similar to the broader European one, and colonial themes were not used to interpret the recent period (the late nineteenth century and later).[46] Bax stressed Ireland's status as an English colony from the seventeenth to the early twentieth centuries and colonialism as the context within which political modernization (center-periphery integration, democratization, bureaucratization) took place.[47] For Eipper there was "repeated advance, ossification and rupture, as the capitalist mode of production implanted itself in ever more developed (albeit 'impure') form in Britain's oldest colony."[48] A similar emphasis on colonialism and capitalism is found in Brody.[49]

Some writers have seen the colonial legacy as still very strong. For Messenger, the contemporary Irish displayed to a high degree many of the same psychological traits characteristic of colonized peoples everywhere.[50] Scheper-Hughes identified common traits in the Irish and Pueblo Indians, which she attributed to a common experience of colonialism—"a similar collective response to a similar collective tragedy: the violent and humiliating confrontation with a dominant, ambivalently despised and admired other culture."[51]

Anthropological studies in Northern Ireland have referred much less to colonialism. Only Bufwack depicted the Irish-British relationship in the past in explicitly colonial terms.[52] Colonial themes have appeared in references to the plantations of the seventeenth century, but no writer (even Bufwack) has interpreted the present conflict in, or condition of, Northern Ireland as a colonial one. Religious and cultural conflict and division in the present have been important themes, but they have not been related to colonialism.[53]

## Summary

There has been widespread agreement that the Irish historical experience has been colonial to some degree. But there has been much less agreement about the forces—economic, political, or cultural—that produced it, when it began, what form it took, how deeply it affected the society, how long it lasted, and what replaced it. In addition, there has been no agreement on the extent to which, on all these issues, the Irish experience has corresponded to colonial experiences elsewhere. For some writers, colonialism began in Ireland in the late medieval period; for others it only began in the sixteenth and seventeenth centuries. For some it took primarily an economic form; for others it took a political or a cultural one. For some it was an external intrusion into Ireland; for others it was an aspect of the internal development of the British Isles. For some it sank deep roots into the social structure and culture of the society; for others it was a surface phenomenon that decolonization swept away. For some it ended with the Act of Union in 1800; for others it ended later in the century; and for still others it ended only in 1922, and then only in the south. For some the societies, north and south, that emerged in the twentieth century were essentially modernizing ones based on the European model; for others the south was a postcolonial society that had yet to overcome its colonial origins, whereas the north was still colonial. For some the Irish experience of colonialism corresponded in its essential form to a general, worldwide pattern; for others there were limited similarities at specific times; for still others the Irish experience was unique.

## Assessing Colonialism in Ireland: Theoretical, Ideological, and Methodological Issues

There is a remarkable diversity of views on Ireland's relationship to colonialism. Which views do justice to the Irish historical experience? Is it possible to say at present?

Different interpretations of Ireland's past might be assessed using comparative studies designed specifically for that purpose.[54] But ultimately, the answers to questions of such complexity will emerge not in a final and precise form from a series of tests, but in a more tentative way, from the steady accumulation of historical research on all aspects of the case. Yet it does not follow from this that the accumulation of research alone will resolve the issue. It will do so only if the research takes adequate account of the theoretical, ideological, and methodological problems that colonial interpretations raise.

Among the theoretical problems is that of structural unevenness. Colonialism has often been discussed as if it were a single and uniform process affecting all areas of society equally. In fact, its impact is always uneven. The colonial dimension may be stronger in some sectors than in others (e.g., in the economy more than in politics or culture), in some parts of a sector more than in others (in land more than industry), or in the relationships involved (indirect rather than direct control). The process of decolonization may also be uneven, going farther and faster in some areas than in others.

A second theoretical problem concerns change. Colonialism has often been analyzed as if it were a static condition. Yet it is inherently dynamic. Not only are initial colonizing processes necessarily dynamic, but colonial social systems appear also to be dynamic, rooted as they are in conflict and contradiction, even if for long periods, the pace of change may be slow. Certainly the history of colonialism during the past four hundred years suggests this.

A third problem arises from the fact that colonialism rarely exists, or exists for long, in a "pure" form. Few social relationships are ever purely colonial in the sense of being wholly dominatory and exploitative and taking place between people who see themselves as totally alien to each other. They may begin that way, but very soon, other, less colonial dimensions will emerge. This may indeed be a functional necessity—to contain the tensions arising from the conflicts and contradictions associated with colonialism.

A fourth problem concerns the interests that colonialism serves. Colonizing powers frequently stress the benefits that the colonized derive from colonialism—the establishment of peace and political order, the building of roads and infrastructure, the introduction of a more advanced culture. These claims can easily be dismissed as the ideology of the colonizer. However, colonialism in operation may take a variety of forms, and it may, or may come to, serve at least some native interests, making it a more complex phenomenon than the purely exploitative model suggests.

A fifth problem concerns the distinction between intent and effect. Most definitions and theories of colonialism have assumed that the colonial power deliberately intended to colonize. But a colonial relationship may emerge without this initial intent. As in the British colonization of India, it may result from a complex and long-drawn-out process involving different agents pursuing their own private, and quite separate, ends.

A sixth problem concerns units of analysis, boundaries, and outcomes. The definition of colonialism offered earlier refers to the "intrusion into, and conquest of, an inhabited territory by the representatives of an external power," "native inhabitants," "intruders and their descendants," "the interests of the external power." These themes—which are common to virtually all definitions of colonialism—assume the existence of bounded social and territorial units. This assumption may be unproblematic if the two societies differ in race and culture and/or are separated by large stretches of ocean, if the intrusion is recent, and if the ideology of colonialism is overt. The situation is different if the initial distinctions in race and culture are minimal, the territories are adjacent, and the territory intruded upon is integrated into the intruding one. It is also different if, over time, there is a blending of race and culture and the legitimating ideology becomes vaguer. In such circumstances, the external power may not regard itself as external but claim the inhabited territory as its own. Some of the native inhabitants may agree with this but others may not; some may welcome the intrusion, whereas others may not; or some may welcome it at the outset but later come to reject it. The descendants of intruders may soon themselves claim to be natives, though still representing the external power. There may also be a time when, as a result of the intermingling of peoples and cultures, the society and culture cease to bear any resemblance to what existed at the time of the initial intrusion.

A final theoretical problem concerns explanation. Although the term *colonialism* may be used purely descriptively, it usually has been accompanied with some explanatory content—that is, with some view of what produces colonialism, what determines the responses of those subject to it, what leads to changes over time, and what roles are played by economic, political, and cultural factors; by structures or events; and by deeply rooted social forces or historical accidents. This explanatory aspect adds further complexity to colonial interpretations.

Though expressed in general terms, each of the preceding problems arises in any attempt to interpret the Irish case. For example, was colonialism more pronounced in English-Irish cultural relations than in economic relations? What were the stages of colonialism in Ireland? Were relations between settler and native in the seventeenth

century wholly conflictual, or was there also friendship and cooperation? Who were the beneficiaries of colonialism in Ireland? Did it
result from deliberate intent or from a succession of unforeseen events?
What significance should be attributed to the short geographical distance that separates Ulster and Scotland in assessing colonialism in
the north of Ireland? In raising such questions, I am not suggesting
that all applications of the concept of colonialism must be guided by
a comprehensive theory. Nevertheless, some account must be taken
of the theoretical problems it raises.

Ideological issues arise in one form or another in almost every area
of scholarly activity, but they pose particular problems in the case of
colonialism, with its emphasis on processes of intrusion, displacement, and control. Moreover, scholarly discussions on the matter
may occur in a political context of violent struggle. Scholars, even
those most committed to "value-neutral" science, are not immune to
the pressures generated by such conflicts, particularly when their
deliberations are available as ideological supports to those engaged in
the struggle.

The ideological problem posed by colonialism is further complicated by its relationship to nationalism and the impact of nationalism
on historical inquiry. There is no necessary relationship between
colonialism and nationalism; even at the ideological level the two
perspectives are analytically quite distinct. However, in practice, nationalism has been a core element in the ideology of many anticolonial
movements and has been a decisive ideological force in the formation
of the culture and identity of most postcolonial societies.[55] In such
circumstances, the ideological pressures to offer—or alternatively, to
counter—nationalist interpretations easily extend to colonial interpretations. The considerable overlap between colonial and nationalist
interpretations intensifies these pressures.

Both problems arise in the Irish case. Questions as to whether
Irish-British relations were ever colonial, when and how they may
have ceased to be, and whether there is a colonial dimension to
contemporary Northern Ireland are currently the subject of violent
conflict. The impact of scholarly work on this conflict, and of the
conflict on scholarly work, is debatable; but the wider Irish-British
political context at present is not conducive to a dispassionate consideration of the arguments for and against colonial interpretations.

The interrelationship between colonialism and nationalism has had
an impact on scholarship in Ireland. The fact that nationalist assumptions have pervaded much of the writing on, and popular understandings of, the Irish past has led many Irish historians, quite indepen-

dently of political considerations, to counter nationalist assumptions and mythology in their reinterpretations of Irish history.[56] A counter-nationalist interpretation could be constructed that remains open to a colonial view of Irish history, but this has been difficult in a situation of political conflict in which nationalist and anticolonial arguments overlap. No scholarly work can be freed entirely from ideological and political pressures, and all historical research reflects in varying degrees the period in which it is written. However, the distorting effects of ideology can be reduced if those pressures are understood and taken into account.

Finally, there are methodological issues. Colonial interpretations make specific statements about the relative importance of particular kinds of events and relationships: intrusions, displacements, strategies and mechanisms of control, interests. To assess whether a colonial interpretation is appropriate in a particular instance, one must first establish whether and to what extent such events and relationships occurred and how important they were. This requires in-depth understanding and a mode of analysis that attempt to build up a total picture of the society—in short, holistic analysis.

Colonial interpretations also make statements about social units and boundaries: about "natives," "intruders," and "external powers." But the boundaries between social groups and territories are rarely fixed and closed. Where societies are geographically and culturally contiguous they may be exceptionally open. To make a judgment that a colonial relationship obtains in a particular instance, therefore, one must determine the nature and meaning of all the relevant boundaries. This requires exploring the case in its wider social and cultural context—in other words, a methodology with a contextual approach.

Colonial interpretations also make statements of comparison, implicitly if not explicitly. Our understanding of colonialism is inextricably bound up with the common experience of a whole range of societies. Ultimately, to state that the experience of a particular society has been colonial is to state that its experience corresponds to those in that range. Colonial interpretations must therefore be grounded in comparative study.

The need for holistic, contextual, and comparative analysis is particularly important in the Irish case. Intervention and intrusion began many centuries ago, came from a neighboring island, and occurred during a period of very limited political centralization in Ireland. Over time, the mix of peoples and cultures has been extensive and the interrelationships complex. Throughout, the Ireland-England relationship was located in a wider European context.

## *Assessing Irish Colonialism: The Current Historical Literature*

To what extent has current research in Irish historical studies considered the theoretical, ideological, and methodological problems that the study of colonialism raises? Is a judgment now possible on the colonial question?

### History

Irish historians have not systematically addressed the kinds of theoretical issues that colonialism raises. Indeed, most studies that have used the concept have not defined it rigorously. This reflects a low level of concern with conceptual and theoretical issues generally among Irish historians. For example, the question of the appropriate units and boundaries in the Irish case has been raised only recently, for the relationship between Britain and Ireland has been viewed unquestioningly as one between two distinct and bounded units, with some recognition that the north of the island posed problems in this regard.[57]

There also has been very little discussion of the ideological questions that attend colonial interpretations of Irish history, though one historian recently argued that colonialism was being ignored for political reasons.[58] Most discussion has related to nationalism and to the controversy surrounding the revision of nationalist interpretations of Irish history.[59] The possible overlap between colonial and nationalist interpretations of Irish history has not been discussed.

From a methodological point of view, Irish historians have approached their research in a quite holistic way, providing considerable descriptive and incidental detail. Many of the topics covered have borne centrally on colonialism—changes in landownership; economic appropriation; and political, religious, and cultural struggles. This literature has much to offer to the assessment of the colonial question. Its main limitation lies in its concentration on struggle and conflict such that a view of the society "in the round"—necessary to assess the relative importance of colonial to noncolonial relationships—hardly emerges, particularly for the pre-1800 period.

Contextual and comparative analysis by historians has been uneven. The context of the British Isles has been dealt with at length, but selectively. The focus has been on the small number of individuals, groups, or institutions whose views, interests or actions impinged most immediately on Ireland. There has been little concern with analyzing the structure of British society as a whole and its implications for Ireland. The analysis has also concentrated on conflictual aspects of the British-Irish relationship. Systematic comparative analysis of different parts of the British Isles is still in its early stages.[60]

There has been much less concern with the wider European context. Typically, the European dimension has entered only when it could not be avoided or when it led to, or was bound up with, a disturbance in Anglo-Irish relations. It has usually been dealt with in a summary way and as a supplement to an otherwise Ireland-centered narrative. There has been little concern with grasping Ireland in a fully European context and relating it to the rhythms of European history as a whole. Although such studies have not been wholly lacking, no clear picture of Ireland's relationship to Europe down through the centuries has emerged from the historical literature.[61] Comparative work within continental Europe—particularly with central and Eastern Europe—has been very limited.[62]

Some wider international contexts have been explored (e.g., the emerging Atlantic world of the sixteenth and seventeenth centuries and the parallels between the colonization of Ireland and of the Americas).[63] Ireland's place in the British imperial system of the eighteenth and nineteenth centuries has also been examined, as have the pattern and experience of Irish emigration to the United States, Canada, Australia, and New Zealand as well as the reverse political and cultural impact of such emigration on Ireland itself.[64] However, most studies have concentrated narrowly on the "Irish dimension" of international processes and have not attempted to grasp global processes systematically in their own terms. Comparative analysis at this level has been very limited, and no study has attempted systematically to compare the development of Irish society as a whole with that of a non-European country.[65]

Economics

Though economists have shown a greater concern with theory in general, only Crotty dealt with the theoretical issues raised by colonialism. Most who have used the term took its meaning as given. Crotty went much further and elaborated a theory of "capitalist colonisation" and its legacy, which he applied systematically to the Irish situation.[66] However, even Crotty dealt with just some of the issues, ignoring, for example, the problem of the mix of colonial and noncolonial elements or that of units of analysis and boundaries.

Some economists have dealt with the ideological issues raised by nationalism. Again, only Crotty dealt with those raised by colonialism, and then indirectly. In contrast to most other economists, Crotty made no claims to value neutrality in his work. On the contrary, he advanced a radical economic and political project conceived in relation to colonialism: to identify the ways in which the "legacy of capitalist colonisation" in Ireland might be removed. Crotty argued that other social scientists also adopted ideological positions in their work as expressed in, among other things, their neglect of colonialism.[67]

Methodologically, the studies of economists have been less holistic than those of historians, concentrating more narrowly on economic relationships. They too have given much attention to topics that bear directly on colonialism (e.g., landownership and economic appropriation, struggles for status and power, British government policies and attitudes). However, although they have made an important contribution to the literature on those subjects, their focused approach has meant that they have added little to other aspects of the social whole.

As with historians, the primary focus of contextual and comparative analysis has been the British Isles, whereas the British context has been dealt with primarily in relation to Ireland. No study, with the partial exception of Crotty's, has attempted to deal with English development in its own terms or to analyze the structure of the British Isles economy as a whole or Ireland's relationship to it—though a general picture has emerged from some studies.[68] Comparative material from within the British Isles has also been limited.

Some writers have ignored the European context almost completely; others have dealt with it in terms of relative performances on selected variables without reference to the structure of European society or economy as a whole.[69] Again Crotty has been the exception: he identified basic patterns in European history and society and related Ireland systematically to them. Moreover, although some comparative material has been offered in some studies, Crotty has again been unique in his attempt to introduce wider international systems into his analyses and to relate the changes in the structure of the Irish economy to the pattern of development of the world economy as a whole.[70]

## Sociology

Among sociologists, only Hechter dealt at length with theoretical aspects of colonialism. He made an important contribution to resolving the problems associated with units and boundaries: his model of "internal colonialism" offered one way of conceptualizing colonial relationships between contiguous societies that later came under a single political authority.[71] Moreover, despite the general sociological concern with the ideological influences on social inquiry and despite the political resonance of the subjects that Irish sociologists have chosen to study—the land war, nationalism, unionism, the Catholic church—there has been almost no discussion of the ideological issues attaching to those subjects.

Methodologically, sociology as a discipline aspires toward holism, and it has made a significant theoretical contribution to the construction of a holistic understanding of Ireland's past. The studies by Gibbon, Inglis, and Clark in particular stand out.[72] However, at a more empirical level, their contribution has been limited by their neglect of descriptive and incidental detail. In addition, sociological attention to context and comparison has varied. Clark kept contextual material of any kind to a minimum.[73] The other writers placed some emphasis on the British dimension, although only Hechter analyzed the structure of British society in its own terms and attempted a comprehensive overview of the British Isles. He took the British Isles as his unit of analysis and traced its development over time, looking at its constituent units (England, Scotland, Wales, Ireland) in that context and comparing them systematically with one another.[74]

Only some studies have introduced the wider European context. Gibbon made little reference to it.[75] Hechter's argument that Ireland's experience of colonialism should be seen from the standpoint of state and nation building had an implicitly European dimension, but it was not developed.[76] Inglis made this dimension more central in his emphasis on the Europe-wide civilizing process, which in Ireland came to be guided and directed by the Catholic church.[77] Keenan also dealt systematically with the Roman dimension of changes in the Irish Catholic church during the nineteenth century. However, no study has attempted to grasp Europe as a totality, to deal with its diversity, or to delineate the specificities of Ireland's place within it. Other, wider international contexts have been even more neglected. Only Keenan, in his examination of the global extensions of the Irish Catholic church, developed this dimension to any degree—and then from an Irish standpoint only.[78]

Political Science

Although many political scientists have applied the concept of colonialism to Ireland, few have attempted to define it or to deal with the theoretical issues it raises. However, some contributions stand out. Garvin identified key issues with his question as to whether nineteenth-century Ireland was a "colony" of England or a "periphery" of the United Kingdom, and with his questioning of the context within which the contemporary politics of the Republic should be viewed.[79] Wright made an important contribution through his concept of the "ethnic frontier" and his concern for changing metropolitan-citizen-native relations and the possible impact of events in ethnic frontiers on the metropolis.[80] Bew and colleagues assessed the applicability of the classical Marxist-Leninist concept of imperialism and colonialism to modern Ireland.[81]

There has been little discussion of ideological issues in the political science literature on the Republic; instead, most has been written to conform with "value-neutral" norms.[82] A more political tone has entered analyses of Northern Ireland and there has been greater concern with the impact of ideology on interpretation, including the writers' own views.[83] However, as yet there has been no systematic treatment of the matter.

Methodologically, much of the research, while concentrating on political themes, has been holistic in its approach. It has contributed to the building of the larger social picture while deepening understanding of its political dimensions (e.g., Patterson's analysis of the interrelationship of class and sectarianism in nineteenth-century Ulster, Garvin's analysis of the forces that shaped the evolution of Irish nationalist politics, and Wright's analysis of the roots of the current conflict in Northern Ireland in the British-Irish "ethnic frontier").[84]

In their contextual analyses, all the writers have stressed the centrality of the British dimension in the formation of Irish political institutions and culture. Chubb stressed it repeatedly; Sacks presented Irish political culture as the product of two traditions—the British and the peasant; Garvin identified the British Isles as one of the three levels that had to be considered in any analysis of the contemporary political system of the Republic (the other two being the Republic itself and the whole of Ireland).[85] However, no writer has attempted an elaborate account either of British society or of the British Isles as a whole.

The European context has been dealt with to a lesser extent and in

a different manner. Many writers have stressed the limited importance of European influences on Irish politics and Ireland's distinctiveness in the European context. Prager's view that the Republic was
"more comparable in character and condition, in many respects, to
the new nations of the Third World than to Denmark, Switzerland,
or other small Western democracies to which it is more frequently
compared" has been shared by many political scientists.[86] Garvin,
however, while describing the Republic of Ireland as "untypical of
western liberal democracies in many ways" and a "fringe member of
the European group," emphasized the extent to which political development in nineteenth-century Ireland followed an essentially European path.[87] Elsewhere, he stressed the European context of Irish
nationalism.[88] Others have pointed to similarities in the Irish and
Eastern European experiences, particularly in the areas of ethnicity
and religion.[89]

The wider international context of Irish politics—parallels with
non-European countries or global influences on Irish politics—has
been much less developed. Some writers have made purely formal
comparisons by using political models of "new nations" and postcolonial societies derived from developing countries. But this is to
classify Irish politics rather than to analyze or systematically compare
them. Particularly rare have been studies of the impact of global
forces on Irish politics.[90]


Geography

Irish geographers (with the partial exception of those in the political
economy tradition) have not made explicit their theoretical models,
and they have not discussed theoretical approaches to colonialism.
However, geographers have thrown light on the problem of delineating boundaries and defining units of analysis. Heslinga provided the
most sustained critique available of the assumption that the island of
Ireland as a whole should be the primary focus of analysis.[91] However, its implications for the question of colonialism have not been
discussed.

There has been very little treatment of ideology in the geography
literature. Some writers have given explicit expression to ideological
judgments in their writings, though this has been unusual.[92] It has
been suggested that ideological factors may have influenced the choice
of subject matter in at least one area of Irish geography.[93] But the
possible impact of ideology on interpretation—on, for example, the

different approaches to colonialism found in the literature—has not been discussed.

Methodologically, Irish geography has been holistic in approach, particularly in its regional analyses. It has covered the entire range of social institutions, often with a strong emphasis on culture. However, the reliance on colonial models has been such that it is difficult to assess the relative importance of colonial and noncolonial elements.

There has been much emphasis on context in the geography literature—on the openness of Irish society and culture to influences from outside and on integration into wider systems of relationships. Most attention has centered on the British Isles. Many writers have stressed the extent and historic depth of contact between the two islands: the movements of population to and fro, the economic relations and cultural influences.[94] However, geographers have yet to study in detail this wider British Isles dimension and to clarify its mix of conflictual and nonconflictual elements. Comparative work on the British Isles in Irish geography has been unusual.

The European context has been dealt with to a much lesser degree. Some writers have been careful to locate the issues they have studied in a wider European context, but none has attempted to grasp "Europe" as a totality or to locate Ireland within it in a systematic way. The emphasis has been typically on Ireland's peripherality—its place at the end of a long chain of linkages as a selective recipient of European developments or as a conserver of archaic practices long abandoned elsewhere.[95] Regional interconnections have also been noted (e.g., the commonalities of the west of Ireland and other parts of the "Atlantic fringe" stretching from the Iberian peninsula to Scandinavia).[96] Systematic comparative work in a European context has been unusual, though the works of Flatrès and Simms are important examples.[97]

Contextual and comparative analyses at the wider international level have not been well developed. Studies have been made of the interconnections between Ireland and Irish communities abroad (e.g., in Newfoundland and in other parts of Canada).[98] Smyth examined Ireland's place within the Atlantic system of the sixteenth and seventeenth centuries and the parallels between the Irish experience and that on the other side of the Atlantic.[99] However, such studies have been rare and have had no counterparts for later centuries.

## Anthropology

Most studies in anthropology have given some discussion to theory but have not dealt with the theoretical issues raised by colonialism. Thus, the theoretical assumptions underlying the wide use of the concept in the southern-based studies and its neglect in the northern ones have not been articulated, nor have those underlying the different views as to when colonialism ended. Some writers have drawn on established theory for their approach to colonialism, whereas others have used more eclectic models but without clarifying their nature or dimensions.[100]

There has been some discussion of ideological themes in the anthropology literature, though usually in reference to the ideologies of others. For example, Messenger sought to establish the true nature of Inis Beag to counter its misrepresentation by "primitivists" and "nativists"; Shanklin opposed her view of Donegal to the "COBO" ("centuries of British oppression") view of Ireland's past held by locals.[101] Yet there has been little discussion of ideological influences on anthropological interpretations and none on the issues raised by colonialism.[102]

Methodologically, anthropological studies have been markedly holistic in approach and the ethnographies have offered a rich store of empirical materials for interpretative purposes. But there has been little attention in this literature to historical themes; in most cases, the historical analyses have been too schematic to be of value in the assessment of colonialism.

Beyond the national level, the dominant context for anthropologists has been the British Isles. The southern-based studies have emphasized the past importance of the British dimension. Perhaps surprisingly, the British dimension has received little attention in the northern-based studies. It has been mentioned infrequently and few comparisons have been made with other parts of the United Kingdom. No study has attempted to deal seriously with the British Isles as a totality, though Shanks's study, reflecting in part her subject matter, at times came close.[103]

There has been very little emphasis on the European context in Irish ethnographies and few comparisons of a systematic kind. At best, some initial general statement has been made to locate the study in relation to Europe (e.g., Fox's reference to Tory island as a region of survival, of "semifossilised history," of peasant Europe).[104] Some writers have offered comparative statistical material on Ireland and other European societies, but this has been unusual.[105] Other international contexts have also been poorly elaborated. Some studies, such as those by Brody and Eipper, located Ireland in relation to the international capitalist system. But the nature of that system was not elaborated; instead, the emphasis was on the way it impinged on Ireland.[106] Comparisons have been made from time to time with non-European societies on specific issues but in an incidental or ad hoc way and without implying any deeper similarities or dissimilarities. The exception was Scheper-Hughes's recent attempt to trace the implications of a single worldwide process of development for Ireland, with particular reference to colonialism.[107]

## Summary

Irish historical research has been at best uneven in its treatment of the theoretical, ideological and methodological issues that colonialism raises. There have been some important theoretical contributions on the subject (those of Pocock, Crotty, Hechter, Garvin, Wright, Bew and colleagues, Heslinga), but in general the literature has been distinguished by its indifference to theoretical issues. There has also been very little discussion of the ideological issues that colonialism raises or the ways in which such concerns may have influenced the willingness or unwillingness to interpret Irish development in colonial terms. The only issue that has aroused serious debate so far has been nationalism. Finally, from a methodological point of view, Irish historical research has been quite holistic; but contextual and comparative analyses within the British Isles have been limited, and even more so beyond that.

## The Colonial Question

If concern with theoretical, ideological, and methodological issues has been uneven in the literature, is it nevertheless sufficient to allow a judgment of Ireland's colonial question? A close look at two of the more complex issues will answer that question.

One of the most complex problems in the interpretation of colonialism in Irish historical development concerns the transition from the eighteenth to the nineteenth centuries. We saw that many historians viewed Ireland in the eighteenth century as colonial and as non-colonial in the nineteenth century. However, they have not clarified

why they saw the nineteenth century so differently from the eighteenth—the characteristics of the latter that made it colonial and those
of the former that made it noncolonial. The language of colonialism
simply stopped with the advent of the nineteenth century, without
explicit discussion or justification. But a host of questions arise. If a
transition occurred, did it take place suddenly or was it long and
drawn out? Did it occur at a different pace in different sectors of
society—economic, political, and cultural? Was it pursued as a conscious and intended process by all the actors involved or by just some,
or was it the result of wider social forces? Whose interests were served
by decolonization? If the transition from colonial to noncolonial status
took place in the early nineteenth century, how is the transition from
British to native rule in 1921 to be viewed? What is to be made of
those writings that have stressed the continued importance of the
colonial legacy today? Any precise statement on the colonial question
requires answers to those questions and a theoretical perspective adequate to the task. Such a perspective does not now exist.

The second problem concerns whether the Irish historical experience has been closer to that of colonized, non-European countries
than to that of mainstream Western Europe. We saw that, for Crotty,
English colonialism in Ireland was just one of the many colonizations
that stemmed from the expansion of capitalism beyond its northwest
European heartland. He placed Ireland into his category of capitalist
colonies, and argued that Ireland was unique because it was the only
Western society to have been colonized and the only colonized society
that was Western.[108] This view of Ireland as colonial and "non-
European" in its social structure has not been unique to Crotty; other
writers have also advanced it, if less strongly and explicitly.[109] However expressed, such views have offered a particular interpretation of
the nature of Irish-English/British relationships over time, the context in which they occurred, and the similarity between what happened in Ireland and elsewhere. Although such views may be accurate, the contextual and comparative studies on which a judgment
must rest do not at present exist. Despite the Anglocentric nature of
much historical research, Ireland's relationship to Great Britain and to
the development of the British Isles as a whole is still poorly understood.[110] Research into Ireland's place within the European system
and possible similarities with other peripheral areas of Europe, including much of Eastern Europe, has barely begun. No study has
systematically compared Ireland and a non-Western society over an
extended period of time. In such circumstances, no firm conclusion
on the matter can be reached. It should be noted too, in respect of

both issues, that although the current political climate is not conducive to detached discussion, there has been almost no consideration of the ideological issues they raise.

The general issue of Ireland's relationship to colonialism can now be addressed: the existing literature points to the questions that are outstanding and have to be answered, but it does not let us answer them. At the current stage of research in Irish historical studies, the questions of whether, for what period, or in what sense Ireland should be viewed in colonial terms are unanswerable.

## Irish Historical Anthropology and the Colonial Question

A conclusive statement on Ireland's relationship to colonialism is not possible now. This does not mean that the concept should be avoided. The questions it raises are important and the usefulness and limits of the concept must be discovered. Rather than being avoided, the concept should be used more critically and in a way that takes account of its theoretical, ideological, and methodological implications. Can Irish anthropology contribute to assessing the usefulness and limits of the concept of colonialism in Irish historical research?

As we have seen, colonialism is a multifaceted phenomenon that demands complex theory. A theory of colonialism able to deal with the complexities of the Irish case does not now exist. Its construction will be difficult because it will have to satisfy at once the conceptual and logical requirements of theory while doing justice to the empirical world. This will require a strong commitment to theory, to empirical inquiry, and to a dialectical view of their interrelationship. Anthropology as a discipline is distinctive in its commitment to such a view of theory and empirical research.

Anthropology has important insights to offer to the study of the ideological forces that impinge upon the question of colonialism. These insights have derived in part from the discipline's failure to address this issue in the past. Much early anthropological research was carried out in societies that were under colonial rule, but the study of colonial aspects was neglected.[111] Anthropologists today are especially sensitive to the pressures, evasions, and denials that colonialism imposes.[112]

We also have seen that the complexity of colonialism demands holistic analysis. Although many disciplines subscribe to this (anthropology, history, sociology, and geography), anthropology is most conscious in its commitment to it, particularly in empirical research.

The colonial question also raises contextual issues. Here too anthropology can make an important contribution. The primary focus in anthropology has been on local-area studies from which anthropologists have developed an appreciation of the importance of context and a theoretical and methodological expertise in dealing with it. This awareness and expertise can readily be transferred to higher levels of analysis: the region, the society, or larger units again.

The colonial question calls for comparative study. Here again, anthropology is important. It is not the only discipline committed to comparison but it has much to say on aspects of comparative study that have been largely ignored by other disciplines, particularly in respect of culture and meaning.[113] Moreover, its literature covers a wide range of societies, including many whose experience is now regarded as unambiguously colonial.[114]

In short, historical anthropology can make an important contribution to the study of the colonial question in Ireland. But it will depend on anthropologists' willingness to use the concept critically; to take account of the theoretical, ideological, and methodological issues it raises; and to address some of the outstanding matters in dispute.

## NOTES

1. This essay has benefited greatly from the comments of Jennifer Todd, Liam Kennedy, and the editors of this volume.

2. For a brief statement of opposing views, see Lee (1986) and Tucker (1986).

3. Wallerstein (1974, 1980); Wolf (1982).

4. Gould and Kolb (1964:101).

5. Sills (1968:1).

6. Abercrombie et al. (1984:106).

7. For discussions of problems of definition and typology, see Fieldhouse (1981:1–11) and Finley (1976).

8. This section deals with the writings of historians in a summary way. The much smaller literature by social scientists will permit a more detailed treatment.

9. For this period, see the contributions to Cosgrove (1987); also Frame 1981.

10. For examples, see Canny (1976), Ford (1985). and Pawlisch (1985).

11. Bottigheimer (1979).

12. Gillespie (1985).

13. Brady and Gillespie (1986).

14. Dickson (1987) is an example of the former category; Foster (1988—Part II), of the latter.

15. The change in frame of reference from eighteenth to nineteenth centuries is particularly evident in Foster (1988, parts II and III). For other applications of the new frame of reference, see Hoppen (1989) and the contributions to Vaughan (1989).

16. Miller (1985:362).

17. See Murphy (1975), Fanning (1983), and Lee (1990).

18. Harkness (1983) and Buckland (1981) offer examples of the first; Farrell (1976), of the second.

19. Lynch and Vaizey (1960); Kennedy, Giblin, and McHugh (1988).

20. Mokyr (1983).

21. Ó Gráda (1988, 1989).

22. Black (1960).

23. Solow (1971:201, 202).

24. O'Malley (1989:2).

25. Crotty (1986).

26. Keenan (1983).

27. Clark (1979).

28. Inglis (1987:103).

29. Gibbon (1975a:14, 1975b).

30. Hechter (1975).

31. See the discussion in chapter 1 of Carty (1981).

32. Chubb (1982:5).

33. Sacks (1976); Rumpf and Hepburn (1977); Garvin (1981); Prager (1986).

34. Garvin (1981:213).

35. Garvin (1981:213).

36. Wright (1987).

37. MacDonald (1986).

38. Bew, Gibbon, and Patterson (1979:19–29).

39. O'Flanagan (1987:x).

40. Evans (1981).

41. Hughes (1987); Smyth (1988); Whelan (1988a).

42. Whelan (1988a:41).

43. Regan (1980); Walsh (1980).

44. Pringle (1985:139).

45. Silverman and Gulliver (1986).

46. Taylor (1980a, 1980b, 1981, 1985).

47. Bax (1976).

48. Eipper (1986:18).

49. Brody (1973).

50. Messenger (1983).

51. Scheper-Hughes (1987:57).

52. Bufwack (1982).

53. For example, Harris (1972) and Shanks (1988).

54. This is a method employed in Hechter (1975).

55. On nationalism and colonialism, see Anthony Smith (1983).

56. For contrasting views on this issue, see Foster (1986), Fanning (1988), Ó Gráda (1988), and Comerford (1988); and from outside the discipline, see Fennell (1988, 1989).

57. See Boyce's comments and his endorsement of Pocock's call for a radical reconceptualization of British history. Boyce (1987); Pocock (1975, 1979). See also Ellis (1986) and the critical response by Bradshaw (1989).

58. Miller (1987).

59. The most recent contribution is Bradshaw (1989).

60. Comparison with Scotland is the most developed, the fruit largely of a series of conferences of Scottish and Irish economic and social historians. The latest is Mitchison and Roebuck (1988). For the first holistic/comparative survey of the history of the British Isles, see Kearney (1989).

61. Examples of contextual studies are Quinn (1958), Mansergh (1975), and Elliott (1982). The limited research so far is reflected in MacNiocaill and Ó Tuathaigh (1984).

62. Some progress has been made in comparative research with France but it takes the form largely of parallel, rather than truly comparative, studies. See the various proceedings of the Franco-Irish Seminars of Social and Economic Historians, for example Butel and Cullen (1986).

63. Andrews, Canny, and Hair (1979); Canny and Pagden (1987); Canny (1988).

64. James (1973); Simms (1988); McDowell (1979); Doyle (1981); O'Farrell (1986); Cook (1987); Elliott (1988).

65. The closest is the comparison of eighteenth-century Ireland and pre-revolutionary America by Doyle (1981).

66. Crotty (1986).

67. Crotty (1986).

68. Lynch and Vaizey (1960); Black (1960); Mokyr (1983).

69. Ó Gráda (1988) and (1989); Kennedy, Giblin, and McHugh (1988).

70. Crotty (1986).

71. Hechter (1975).

72. Gibbon (1975a); Inglis (1987); Clark (1979).

73. Clark (1979).

74. Hechter (1975).

75. Gibbon (1975a).

76. Hechter (1975).

77. Inglis (1987).

78. Keenan (1983).

79. Garvin (1981).

80. Wright (1987).

81. Bew, Gibbon, and Patterson (1979).

82. An exception is Bew, Hazelkorn, and Patterson (1989).

83. See the prefaces/introductions to Patterson (1980), Wright (1987), and MacDonald (1986).

84. Patterson (1980); Garvin (1981); Wright (1987).

85. Chubb (1982); Sacks (1976); Garvin (1981).

86. Prager (1986:12).

87. Garvin (1981:1–2).

88. Garvin (1987).

89. Coakley (1980, 1982, 1986); Wright (1987).

90. A partial example is in the application of a dependency perspective to the Blueshirts by Orridge (1983).

91. Heslinga (1979).

92. See the critical comments on Irish nationalism in Evans (1981).

93. Pringle suggested that the relative strength of urban social geography in Northern Ireland as compared to the Republic has been due in part to an "almost instinctive unionist rejection of anything even hinting of gombeen nationalism" (Pringle 1984:187).

94. For example, Evans (1981) and Heslinga (1979).

95. Evans (1981); also articles in Smyth and Whelan (1988).

96. Evans (1964).

97. Flatrès (1957); Simms (1988).

98. Mannion (1974); Houston and Smyth (1980).

99. Smyth (1978).

100. Examples of eclectic models may be found in Bax (1976) and Shanklin (1985).

101. Messenger (1969); Shanklin (1985).

102. The most serious criticism of ideological influences on Irish anthropology has come from outside the discipline. See Bell (1981).

103. Shanks (1988).

104. Fox (1978).

105. Cresswell (1969).

106. Brody (1973); Eipper (1986).

107. Scheper-Hughes (1987).

108. Crotty (1986).

109. For example, Tucker (1986).

110. The description of Irish history as "Anglo-centric" is in Foster (1988).

111. Asad (1973).

112. For a discussion of these issues in relation to contemporary Northern Ireland, see O'Dowd (1990).

113. Holy (1987).

114. The questions raised here about Ireland could of course be raised about any other case, however unambiguously "colonial" it may appear at present.

# 9

# Historical Anthropology, Historical Sociology, and the Making of Modern Europe

■

### SAMUEL CLARK

The purpose of this essay is to place the papers brought together in this volume into the wider context of Western European historical sociology and historical anthropology. The focus will be on historical studies of Western European society—by and large, on studies dealing with France and the British Isles, although a few other works will also be considered (mostly more global studies that include France and the British Isles). I am not assuming that these studies are typical of either historical sociology or historical anthropology in general. On the contrary, I think it is quite possible that the work on France and the British Isles is distinctive. This is, however, all the more reason to give it separate treatment.

Several conclusions will emerge from this review. First, we shall see that discipline does make a difference. Whether one is a sociologist, an anthropologist, or a historian affects the way one approaches the study of history; at least, it has for works on France and the British Isles. Second, if one compares what one is doing with the research carried out in another discipline, one learns much about the limitations, often self-imposed, of one's own discipline. Third, I shall argue that historians, historical sociologists, and historical anthropologists can all work together in the study of the making of modern Europe.

Since this paper is concerned with the orientations of academic disciplines, ideally we want our analysis to observe the boundaries of disciplines strictly. As a rule, I classify scholars according to their institutional affiliation and/or higher education. There are, of course, scholars in one discipline who behave more like those in another. Indeed, it could be said that the purpose of this paper is to determine (for research on France and the British Isles) the extent to which such intermixture occurs. To do this, however, we have to categorize scholars institutionally rather than intellectually. This means that some scholars the reader might expect to be cited will not be mentioned, such as William Sewell, Jr. (a historian who has written what could be considered sociology) or Peter Sahlins (a historian whose work might well be regarded as anthropology). Classifying scholars who live in the British Isles or in North America presents only a small number of difficulties, but classifying those who live in France, where the institutional distinctions are less clear, is extremely problematic. As a result, some arbitrary decisions have had to be made. For example, I classify Roland Mousnier, Emmanuel Le Roy Ladurie, and André Burguière as historians, and I classify Emmanuel Todd as an anthropologist. No doubt I even place a few British and North American writers in the wrong discipline, and for this I apologize.

## The Historical Sociology of Western Europe

In the early years of its development, sociology had a pronounced historical orientation. The social theorists whom sociologists regard as founding fathers—Auguste Comte, Herbert Spencer, Karl Marx, Emile Durkheim, L. T. Hobhouse, Vilfredo Pareto, and Max Weber—all made bold historical assertions. Yet little of their work resembled what historians did; as a matter of fact Comte, Spencer, and Durkheim held very disdainful views of historians.

During the first half of the twentieth century, this interest in history waned. Several reasons stand out. First, sociology developed empirical methods that encouraged researchers to engage in face-to-face interaction with their subjects, to mingle with them, or to interview them, to touch them directly in a way that is impossible for most historical research. Second, most sociologists were doing research on a society that seemed to have little history. Sociology became largely an American discipline, and American society had only a short history and one that seemed irrelevant. It could hardly have been expected that the Chicago School would have looked deeply into the past in its effort to understand the slums, gangs, racial riots, and public immorality of their city.[1] Third, the gap between what sociologists considered their territory and what interested most historians was particularly wide. History was still oriented toward political and constitutional history in the early twentieth century, whereas sociologists believed that their mission was to study "society," as opposed to the government or the economy. Fourth, a large number of sociologists sought to make sociology relevant to social problems and social planning.[2] Fifth, despite this applied orientation, many sociologists wanted to make sociology scientific. This meant drawing a sharp distinction between sociology and history. As Park and Burgess wrote:

> Both history and sociology are concerned with the life of man as man. History, however, seeks to reproduce and interpret concrete events as they actually occurred in time and space. Sociology, on the other hand, seeks to arrive at natural laws and generalizations in regard to human nature and society, irrespective of time and of place. In other words, history seeks to find out what actually happened and how it came about. Sociology, on the other hand, seeks to explain, on the basis of the study of other instances, the nature of the process involved. By nature we mean just that aspect and character of things in regard to which it is possible to make general statements and formulate laws.[3]

They placed history outside the bounds of science because it dealt with historical facts that were not repeated and thus not subject to verification. Finally, structural-functionalist models of order eventually came to dominate theoretically; the emphasis was on explaining stability and the persistence of social structure rather than on explaining change. For some or all of these reasons, most sociologists believed that historical research was of little use in answering the questions they were asking.

This is not to say that the study of history by sociologists ceased altogether. Even before 1950, a not insignificant number of sociologists engaged in historical research: Sorokin, Glass, Znaniecki, Elias, Teggart, Homans, Merton, and S. D. Clark.[4] Most of the historical sociologists in this period resided in North America, but not because Europeans less appreciated the importance of history. On the contrary, I think they had more appreciation of its importance, so much so that far fewer became sociologists. The people who read Marx, Weber, and Hobhouse were in other disciplines.

In any case, on both sides of the Atlantic, a greater number of sociologists became involved in history during the 1950s. Yet it was not really until the 1960s and 1970s that a new attitude began to emerge. I can suggest five aspects of historical research that have attracted sociologists.

First, some sociologists have been drawn to history because they wanted to study social change. The renewed interest in history was part of a larger transformation in sociology as a whole that saw a reaction against structural functionalism, particularly as represented in the work of Parsons. Since Parsons and his followers were charged with neglecting change, it is not surprising that at least some of their critics would turn to history to study change. Perhaps somewhat more surprising, though still understandable, is that a number of Parsons's own students were sensitive to the criticism and undertook historical research to offset it. An early example is Smelser's *Social Change in the Industrial Revolution;* a more recent example is Gould's *Revolution in the Development of Capitalism.* In fact, Parsons himself tried to demonstrate that his theory could be used to help understand historical change.[5]

Second, many sociologists have explicitly rejected the claim by some, such as Park and Burgess, that we should not concern our-selves with time and place.[6] Instead they have accepted the assumption of historians that causal relations have a certain chronology. All human behavior (collective or individual) consists of a series of events, and in this sense it is all history. Even mental attitude is a series of events. The historian's predilection for chronology is not some fetish to which she or he has become habituated. It is a recognition of the fundamental nature of all behavior. The events that occur in one period of time affect the events that take place in a subsequent period. Indeed, the structures that sociologists like to use to help understand human behavior are historically created, the result of human action in the past. Only through the study of history can sociologists explore how humans are both creators and creatures of the world in which they live.[7] All this has become accepted among an increasing number of sociologists.

Third, during the first half of the twentieth century, social history became stronger within the discipline of history, one of the most influential examples being the *Annales* school in France. By the mid-twentieth century, sociologists found that many of their colleagues in history departments were engaged in research that was much more like their own than was the case thirty or forty years earlier.

Fourth, the growth in popularity of Marxist thinking during the

1960s promoted historical research. An understanding of history is critical to Marxism, but Marx himself was not a good historian. Marxists were thus led to try to improve the Marxist historical literature. They also felt that history had been misinterpreted by "bourgeois" historians and that the working class had been neglected. They hoped to use history to elucidate the historical transition from feudalism to capitalism. It is true that the earliest converts to Marxism were slow to engage in historical research, assuming that Marx provided all the historical answers, which could then be debated at a theoretical level.[8] Eventually, however, a considerable number of Marxists became very good historical sociologists.

Fifth, sociologists were attracted to historical research because it extended the number and variety of cases they could examine. Restricting research to present-day phenomena meant that our sample was limited. Studying history could turn up a world greatly different from our own, which could be used to test theories or understand social processes on which sociologists have written. Nisbet became fascinated by the decline in kinship authority in ancient Rome because he saw it as an example of several sociological processes—shifts in authority, the rise of legal individualism, and the dislocation of important social groups.[9] In *Internal Colonialism,* Hechter was not especially concerned with the relationship between England and its Celtic fringe but with sociological theory. He chose to study England and its Celtic fringe because it was an example of an intermediate level of national integration:[10] "I am not specifically interested in the relationship between England and the Celtic fringe *sui generis.* However, these regions do provide an ideal research site from which to explore some fundamental issues in sociological theory. Perhaps not entirely by coincidence, these issues also relate to problems of social change in contemporary American society."[11] By studying migration to London and Paris during the nineteenth century, McQuillan sought to make a contribution to the general literature on migration.[12] Markoff took up the French Revolution primarily because he wanted to answer questions posed in the sociological literature on social conflict and rural revolt.[13] And Gould, as I have said, sought to use the English Civil War to illustrate Parsonian theory.[14]

In a similar spirit, many sociologists turned to the past to undertake comparative analysis. Historical sociology, by enlarging the variety of cases available for study, increased the dimensions that could be achieved by comparative research. The opportunities for comparative research that were opened up to sociology when it became more historical have been nothing short of revolutionary. I would venture to say that over half of the sociologists who have been engaged in historical work on Western Europe during the past two decades have done at least some comparative analysis.

The methods adopted by sociologists engaged in comparative history are diverse. The traditional method of the classical sociological theorists was to trace human evolution through stages or types of societies. Some historical works in sociology that appeared in the 1960s utilized this method.[15] The neo-evolutionary character of this approach made it less popular in the 1970s and 1980s, but the orientation of the classical sociological theorists has still had considerable influence, as I shall argue in a moment. First, however, let us consider the method that has the most similarity with conventional sociological method, what most sociologists in North America learn as undergraduates. This is correlation analysis: one tries to identify causal relationships by taking variation among regions on a dependent variable and correlating it with variation on one or more independent variables. As units of analysis, we can use administrative divisions within a country. Hechter, for example, did correlation analysis on counties.[16] McQuillan used French departments, both for his study of the relationship between modes of production and demographic behavior and for his study of migration to Paris, which he compared with migration to London, using English counties.[17] Markoff correlated data for French *bailliages*[18] to explain the Great Fear.[19] Brustein used cantons for his study of the relationship between modes of production and voting behavior in France from 1849 to 1981.[20]

Alternatively, countries may be used as units of analysis; if this is done, the number of cases is usually much smaller. Basing his inference on northwestern Europe, Holton tried to explain the rise of capitalism by asserting (wrongly, I believe) that those countries where capitalism developed earliest had relatively strong states and landed classes in a position to reorganize agricultural production.[21] Skocpol sought to explain the occurrence of "social revolutions" by comparing three countries where such revolutions occurred (France, Russia in 1917, and China) with countries where they did not occur (Japan, Prussia, England, and Russia in 1905).[22] Some sociologists have done correlation analysis with only two countries, often England and France.[23]

Correlation analysis is, however, fraught with problems. We first need to worry about the comparability of the data. The phenomena that our concepts seek to describe may change with time and place. "Labor unrest," for instance, can be quite different in one time and/ or place from what it is (or was) in another. Second, correlation analysis usually ignores important differences within cultures or nations. Depending on what is being studied, national states may make poor units of analysis because they can be extremely heterogeneous. Even French departments were too heterogeneous for McQuillan, who has moved to smaller units of analysis in an effort to understand demographic behavior in ninteenth-century France.[24] Finally, our cases may not be independent. Nations and cultures have mutual effects on one another. Similarities and differences may result from such effects rather than from endogenous causes. In fact, some writers argue that the whole logic of correlation analysis is open to question. The history of the world is not one of distinct nations following different paths of development. Instead, they insist, there is only one world history, in which almost every part of the world is involved.[25]

Not all sociologists engaged in comparative historical research have undertaken correlation analysis; and even many who have, such as Tilly, Holton, and Lachmann, have had additional objectives in mind. There is a sixth reason sociologists have been attracted to history, and it has led to a different kind of comparative approach. Many sociologists who study history do so because they want to understand how the society in which we live came to be. This is true even in Canada and the United States. That most Canadians and Americans are descended from immigrants who arrived within the past two hundred years is no longer accepted as sufficient reason for North American sociologists to ignore history.

This is all the more so true for sociologists working on Western Europe. Indeed, there are special reasons for sociologists to study Western European history. The vast social transformation that occurred in that part of the world during the eighteenth and nineteenth centuries was the underlying concern of the "classical" sociological theorists, most notably Spencer, Marx, Weber, and Durkheim. Although they were certainly trying to build general theory, they were also interested in coming to grips with the changes that had been taking place in the societies in which they lived. For better or for worse, sociology has been shaped by the intellectual epoch in which it was born and by the questions that excited students of social change at that time. This alone led some sociologists to study the making of modern Europe in order to advance the classical models, particularly those of Marx and Weber. In addition, however, doubts about the validity of these models stimulated interest among sociologists. The dominant "modernization" perspective was based on a misunderstanding of how the West developed.[26] It was abundantly clear what sociologists needed to do.

Sociologists interested in the making of present-day, Western Europe have used several research strategies. Many have undertaken correlation analysis. An example is the book by Holton already mentioned.[27] In addition, however, they have often focused on the evolution of major transformations or large processes over a number of countries.[28] Countries ceased to be units of analysis whose characteristics could be correlated to identify causes or conditions; instead they became part of a greater transformation. Such transformations included the rise of capitalism, the disappearance of the peasantry, proletarianization, the demographic transition, the development of national states, urbanization, and industrialization.

The logic behind this sort of analysis is different from that behind correlation analysis. For example, a correlation analysis of fertility decline in Europe would try to determine what social conditions characterized societies with sharply falling birth rates as compared with those where the rates fell more slowly. In contrast, demographic change in any one country could be studied as part of a larger historical process. Following this strategy, we do not seek to generalize from divergent "cases"; instead we endeavor to understand the diverse ways in which different parts of Europe or an even larger area shared a common experience. Often the sociologist identifies alternative "routes" or "paths" that various countries took.

I can briefly give four illustrations. The first is Moore's *Social Origins of Dictatorship and Democracy*. Although Moore sometimes used his countries for correlation analysis, his major objective was to chart different routes to modernity. The three principal routes were the "bourgeois revolution," taken by England, France, and the United States; the fascist route, taken by Japan; and the communist route, taken by China. That Moore never defined clearly what he meant by *modern* does not deny that the making of the modern world was the large-scale transformation that provided the foundation for his whole analysis.

Perry Anderson set himself the ambitious task of writing a three- or four-volume history of Europe from ancient times that would trace the various paths that have been followed by different countries, bringing into contrast, in particular, the Eastern European route and the Western European route. He also sought to compare the European way with Japanese feudalism and the Asiatic mode of production. The first two volumes have been written. *Passages from Antiquity to Feudalism* explained the unique characteristics of Western feudalism as a consequence of the much greater influence of Roman civilization and its slave mode of production on the West as compared with the

East. Anderson contrasted the sharply different circumstances in which eastern serfdom emerged in a later period. *Lineages of the Absolutist State* distinguished the quite dissimilar origins, development, and character of absolutism in Eastern as compared with Western Europe. Anderson employed correlation analysis. Yet he also violated certain basic methodological rules of correlation analysis. He did so, as Abrams argued, in order to identify particular sequences, or what Anderson called passages and lineages.[29]

The global transformation is even clearer—indeed, much more explicitly stated—in the work of Wallerstein.[30] It is the evolution of a "world system" from the sixteenth century. For Wallerstein the social structure and economic development of any country was reciprocally related to its position in this world system. In the early modern period, certain countries (England, Holland, and northern France) constituted the "core"; other countries provided the "periphery"; and still others constituted the "semi-periphery." There was a capitalist division of labor whereby the core exploited the periphery. The world system was a dynamic structure that changed over time, and the evolution of a particular country was determined by its location in, and by the development of, this world system. The ways in which different countries came to belong to the core, the semiperiphery, and the periphery were the focus of volume 1. In volume 2, Wallerstein examined the different paths by which countries fell out of the core. And in volume 3, he discussed how external countries became peripheralized.

Finally, in *Coercion, Capital, and European States,* Tilly plotted the evolution of states in Europe from the early Middle Ages to the late twentieth century. He observed that ultimately all of Europe became organized in "national states," that is, "states governing multiple contiguous regions and their cities by means of centralized, differentiated, and autonomous structures."[31] He showed, however, that the processes by which countries grew into national states varied greatly. He constructed a typology of three routes, among which there were infinite degrees of variation. The first was the "coercion-intensive" path. These states developed initially by means of the concentration of coercive resources, only later making use of concentrations of capital. Brandenburg and Russia provided illustrations. The second was the "capital-intensive" path, which was the exact opposite. Italian city-states and the Dutch Republic, for example, became strong states by drawing on concentrations of capital and only later made use of concentrations of coercive means or became parts of states relying more on such concentrations. The third route was the middle course taken most notably by England and France, in which both kinds of resources were developed simultaneously; this route produced national states earlier than the other routes.

All four of the these authors, but especially Wallerstein and Tilly, placed considerable emphasis on intersocietal forces. In this they were joined by Bendix, whose *Kings or People* called attention to the "demonstration effects" that the development of one country had on the development of another; by Skocpol, whose *States and Social Revolutions* gave explicit recognition to transnational economic effects and competition among states; and by Mann, whose *History of Power* traced the evolution of power networks in world history. It is here that we see the difference between this approach and the neoevolutionism of Parsons, Eisenstadt, and Lenski. The thrust of more recent work in comparative history by sociologists has been to replace the old idea that all countries experience or should experience the same pattern of development independently of one another (much as an organism goes through a developmental cycle independently of other organisms) with the idea that different countries mutually affect one another and their histories can only be understood if they are seen as part of larger transformations.

This perspective can lead us to question one of the most fundamental assumptions made by sociologists and economic historians: that the economic development of Western Europe is to be explained by determining the distinguishing charactersitics of Western Europe. If one believes that the world has experienced one common historical development, then the discovery of the uniqueness of the West only helps us, at best, to understand why the West came to dominate the world and why the industrial revolution occurred first in the West— and it may not even explain that. A major contribution to this reorientation in thinking has come from Abu-Lughod. She argued that the rise of the West resulted from a restructuring of world trade; European hegemony stemmed more from a decline of the East than from endogenous European characteristics.[32] It is also commonly assumed that an explanation of economic development within Western Europe lies in discovering the distinguishing charactersitics of England. Again, however, this approach may only explain why the industrial revolution occurred first in England, not why it occurred.

The study of global transformations does not mean a rejection of the usefulness of single-country studies as too particularistic. On the contrary, one of the nice features of this strategy is that it gives all the more purpose to single-country studies by setting them in a broader framework. An early example of this was Mendras's writings on the transformation of rural society, which focused on this phenomenon in France but as an example of a process that had taken place in other countries as well.[33] More recently, Lachmann (in *From Manor to Market*) and Martin (in *Feudalism to Capitalism*) illustrated the way in which a historical sociologist is inclined to relate a single-country study to general issues and to place it in a comparative framework. Lachmann's book was on the rise of capitalism in England. Nonetheless, he devoted considerable space to more general studies of the evolution of the state in Western Europe and the transition from feudalism to capitalism. Moreover, his book really needs to be understood in the context of the comparative work he has done on the role of elites in the evolution of states and capitalism in various parts of Europe.[34] Although Martin's book was, strictly speaking, on the English Midlands Revolt of 1607, his discussion of it was preceded by over 150 pages of discourse on theories of feudalism, English feudalism, theories of the transition from feudalism to capitalism, class struggle in medieval England, theories of absolutism, English absolutism, and finally, opposition between the landed class and the peasantry in England during the sixteenth and seventeenth centuries.

There is much still to be done. We are a long way from understanding the major transformations or large processes. I sometimes despair at how little we have progressed since the "classical" sociologists put their heads to the matter. Not just Marxists, such as Perry Anderson and Martin, but even non-Marxists, such as Holton and most recently Lachmann, are still trapped in the simplistic model of a transition from feudalism to capitalism. Demographic change and the development of the state are no longer neglected, yet other processes, such as urbanization and the evolution of status, are in need of much greater attention. Finally, although I despair less at the coverage we are now getting of Europe, in that northern, eastern, and southern Europe are now receiving the consideration that once was reserved for Western Europe, the small countries are still neglected. We shall never get a balanced picture so long as this is the case.

Not surprisingly, there are some dangers in the approach I have been describing. Most obviously, we have to be careful not to impose a major transformation or large process on a country. The involvement of any particular part of Europe in a major transformation is precisely what needs to be researched; it cannot be assumed. We also have to avoid the Whig fallacy of interpreting history in the light of what we know eventually emerged. Poggi explicitly acknowledged in his preface to *Development of the Modern State* that he was working backward:

The organization of my argument as a sequence of typological constructs puts it at variance with a properly historical account. From the continuity and diversity of the historical process are extracted a few highly abstract models, each treated as a closer approximation of the nineteenth-century constitutional state, which I consider the most mature embodiment of "*the* modern state."[35]

Similarly, the search for the origins of capitalism has led to an emphasis on those aspects of precapitalist Europe that relate to this question. Other questions are neglected, and periods of history are evaluated in terms of their contribution to the rise of capitalism.

Finally, this approach has difficulty providing explanations for the large transformations on which it focuses. It has to rely primarily on the sequence of events to determine cause. Without correlation analysis it is difficult to assess the causal importance of some historical forces and conditions. Brenner argued that the development of a class of large tenant farmers was responsible for the rise of agrarian capitalism in England.[36] The only way to test such an argument is to compare countries with and without large tenant farmers. As I have indicated, Holton, Moore, and Perry Anderson employed correlation analysis along with global transformation analysis. Even Mann, who has been highly critical of correlation analysis, has engaged in it; with Kane he examined turn-of-the-century agrarian politics in the United States, France, Denmark, Norway, Sweden, Austria-Hungary, and Russia to develop generalizations about the effect of political structure on peasant movements.[37] A careful correlation analysis, such as that of Fulbrook, can guard against the dangers of this methodology.[38] Although the assumptions of the two approaches are contradictory (global transformation analysis assumes intersocietal effects, whereas correlation analyis assumes independent cases), so long as we understand this and are cautious about our conclusions, the two strategies can be effectively used in conjunction. Indeed, the potential problems that intersocietal effects pose for correlation analysis can be minimized by studying these intersocietal effects; and this can best be done by illuminating global transformations.

## A Comparison of the Historical Sociology and Historical Anthropology of Western Europe

The ups and downs of historical research in sociology have had some parallels in anthropology. In the nineteenth and early twentieth centuries, we see schools of thought that paid attention to history but in

ways that were decidedly different from the historical anthropology
of today. Anthropology went through three early phases during which
something of a historical orientation could be found: evolutionism,
diffusionism, and American empiricism.[39] As in sociology, the historical interest waned in the first half of the twentieth century, and
several of the reasons were the same. Structural-functional models
gained ascendancy. Research methods led to face-to-face interaction
with subjects. The nonliterate societies studied by anthropologists
had no written records. (British anthropologists, in particular, were
critical of the errors that resulted from trying to study the history of
nonliterate peoples.) Finally, some anthropologists, though perhaps a
minority, admired the construction of abstract models, such as those
of Lévi-Strauss, that would apply everywhere, regardless of time or
place.

Yet if historical research never died out in sociology, this was even
more true in anthropology. Anthropologists were forced to be historical if they wanted to understand the conquest and acculturation of
so-called primitives. Some interest in the publication of documents
and descriptions of so-called primitives, particularly American Indians, persisted; and anthropologists developed better methods for investigating the history of nonliterate societies.

In the 1960s and 1970s, a new school of historical anthropology
emerged parallel to the movement that was emerging simultaneously
in sociology. We can observe a number of similarities between these
two movements. First, like the sociologist who wanted to understand
how capitalist societies or urban industrial societies came to be, the
anthropologist often wanted to know how the society she or he was
studying came to be.[40] An anthropologist likes to be thorough, to
study her or his community in all its aspects. This led naturally to
questions about the past. Second, both sociologists and anthropologists were interested in turning to history to increase the number and
variety of cases that could be explored. I shall say more later about
the anthropologists' search for traditional societies; let us simply note
at this time that, insofar as they were engaged in such a search, it is
not surprising that they turned to the past to find them. Third, both
historical sociology and historical anthropology were affected by a
recognition of the importance of social change, time, and chronology.
As Netting wrote in explaining why he became unhappy with conventional cultural ecology:

> It seemed to me that the strategy of ecosystem analysis had to be
> extended, beginning as it always had in a sound appraisal of how

people survived in their natural surroundings and how they responded to life-threatening conditions, but going on to those factors that were fundamentally different from one generation to the next, the ways in which people met novel challenges and unprecedented problems that often originated outside their local subsistence system.[41]

Only by studying change could anthropologists get away from studying society as a fixed order.[42] As in sociology, some anthropologists were unhappy with structural functionalism, and this led them to undertake historical research.

These are some of the similarities. There are, on the other hand, remarkable differences between historical sociology and historical anthropology, and it is these differences that I want to consider. With a few exceptions, I shall focus on research on France and the British Isles. The objective is to discover what is characteristic of this literature, not to generalize about historical anthropology or historical sociology as a whole.

There is a striking contrast in the attention accorded to social unrest, social movements, and revolution. The scholarship of Tilly obviously testifies to the sociological fascination with these social phenomena, but other historical sociologists have also taken an interest in social unrest and revolution in France or the British Isles. These have included Kimmel, Calhoun, Skocpol, Fulbrook, Goldstone, Markoff, and Gould, whose works have already been cited, as well as Aminzade, whose *Class, Politics, and Early Industrial Capitalism* examined collective action by workers in Toulouse. There is no comparable body of literature in the historical anthropology of France and the British Isles.

Closely related is the much greater concern of the historical sociologists with state and politics. I estimate that state or politics is central to well over half of the historical sociology on France and the British Isles. In historical anthropology on France and the British Isles, it is certainly much less than one quarter. In this regard, the articles in this volume are a little unusual: political behavior is central in the papers by Silverman and, to a lesser extent, Vincent. Vincent also had an article on political violence in *Ireland from Below*. Some space was given to state and politics in Silverman and Gulliver's *In the Valley of the Nore*. A number of anthropologists have dealt with the impingement of the state on a community. We find this subject treated in several of the preceding works as well as in Assier-Andrieu's *Communautés paysannes du Capcir*, Rosenberg's *A Negotiated World*, and Jenkins's *The Agricultural Community in South-west Wales*.

These three anthropologists also devoted space to local government, as did Segalen in *Quinze générations de Bas-Bretons*. Still, the state was in the background, not up front, as it was for Perry Anderson, Tilly, Wallerstein, Hechter, Hall, and Gould, to mention only a few historical sociologists who have focused on the state. Two exceptions among the anthropologists have been Gellner and Todd, who put the state or politics right up front in their comparative studies.[43] In any case, the historical anthropologists have been typically more interested in relatively less politicized conflict. The best example is *L'impossible mariage* by Claverie and Lamaison, which treated interpersonal conflicts among and within rural families in Gévaudan in southern France. Similar conflicts were examined by Silverman in her sensitive analysis of the life of "A Labouring Man's Daughter" and by Macfarlane in his analysis of witchcraft in Tudor and Stuart England.

Given their greater emphasis on the state, it is not surprising that the historical sociologists studying France or the British Isles have given more attention to elites than have the historical anthropologists.[44] The historical anthropologists have been more concerned with what historians would call the "common people." A good illustration is again Silverman's "A Labouring Man's Daughter." Generally, the historical anthropologists have studied the common people living in small towns or in the countryside. Claverie and Lamaison, Verdier, Jenkins, Segalen, Parman—the list could go on of historical anthropologists who have concentrated on rural peoples.[45] Although a good number of sociologists have followed Homans's lead and studied the Western European peasantry,[46] they have done fewer rural studies than anthropologists. Both the historical sociologists and the historical anthropologists have given less attention to the urban working class, but here the contributions are reversed: the sociologists have done more than the anthropologists. Examples include Hewitt's study of mothers and children in nineteenth-century factories, Calhoun's book on popular radicalism during the industrial revolution, Aminzade's book on Toulouse, Michael Anderson's analysis of family structure in nineteenth-century Lancashire, and Smelser's research on education in nineteenth-century Britain. Sociologists have been more interested in urban history than anthropologists, though less so than historians.[47]

The historical anthropologists have been especially interested in work, methods of agriculture, and the relationship of people to the environment. These concerns were exhibited in Segalen's *Quinze générations de Bas-Bretons,* Jenkins's *Agricultural Community,* Parman's *Scottish Crofters,* and many others. Some historical anthropologists have been fascinated by material artifacts, particularly tools.[48] They like to talk about the architecture of houses, the layout of living and working space, and the spatial distribution of houses and buildings.[49] The historical anthropologists have taken an interest in the daily lives of people that is found only rarely among the historical sociologists. The historical anthropologists have shown much more interest in individuals and their experiences.[50] The historical anthropologists have been more than usually concerned with the collective activities of communities, such as the "clipping bands" (cooperative sheep shearing) discussed by Littlejohn in his study of a Scottish parish.[51] There has been more interest in property ownership and land tenure among the anthropologists I am reviewing than among the sociologists. These subjects were treated by Macfarlane in *Origins of English Individualism,* Segalen in *Quinze générations de Bas-Bretons,* and Parman in *Scottish Crofters.* Regulation of the distribution of land and its use was important in a number of works, including Augustins's "Reproduction sociale," Assier-Andrieu's *Communautés paysannes du Capcir,* and Pingaud's *Paysans en Bourgogne.* The use of commons was given considerable attention in Segalen's *Quinze générations de Bas-Bretons.* It is central to Silverman's article in this volume.

As one would predict, the historical anthropologists have emphasized culture, customs, beliefs, folkways, symbolism, folk tales, ceremonies, and ritual. This has been especially true of such French historical anthropologists as Verdier and Segalen.[52] Although there may be others, the only historical sociologist studying France or the British Isles who has taken an interest in ritual, so far as I know, is Aminzade.[53] The anthropological fascination with customs and folkways has led some of them in a curious direction, toward an interest in law, particularly customary law.[54] One would have thought that their interest in culture would also have led them to study ideas and ideology, but it does not seem to have done so. Some exceptions are works by Gellner and Todd.[55] In contrast, a good number of historical sociologists have focused on ideas and ideology. Although Bendix is the best known, there have been others.[56]

The reader might also predict more literature on religion among the historical anthropologists, but this is not true for studies on France or the British Isles. Some anthropologists have paid attention to the church as an institution and to the clergy and their role in the community; this is found in Littlejohn's *Westrigg,* in Jenkins's *Agricultural Community,* and in Taylor's work.[57] Anthropologists, however, have not given enough attention to religious beliefs in French and British history. Macfarlane treated witchcraft in his *Witchcraft in Tudor and*

*Stuart England*; he analyzed the religious beliefs and preoccupations of a diarist in his *Family Life of Ralph Josselin*; Parman discussed superstition and religious beliefs in *Scottish Crofters*; and Taylor analyzes religious discourse in his essay in this volume. As with ideas, Gellner provided another exception, but religion was certainly not central for him. Sociologists have done more work on religion.[58] Still, it is not enough. Even sociological works on the English Civil War have played down the role of religion, though they have not ignored it completely.[59]

Sociology is a more quantitative discipline than anthropology, in the sense of using sophisticated quantitative techniques. Thus, one would expect that historical sociologists would be more quantitative than historical anthropologists, and this indeed has been the case. It should be noted, however, that, with the exception of Tilly, the dominant figures in historical sociology—Elias, Homans, Clark, Bendix, Eisenstadt, Moore, Wallerstein, and Perry Anderson—have been conspicuously nonquantitative. Some, in fact, are regarded by other sociologists as representatives of an antiquantitative movement in sociology. The sociological studies cited in this essay are less quantitative, proportionately, than the sociological literature as a whole. Nevertheless, we do find more quantitative analysis among historical sociologists engaged in research on France or the British Isles than among the historical anthropologists. In addition to Tilly, these sociologists have included McQuillan, Markoff, Goldstone, Maxim, Gillis, and others.[60] Quantitative historical anthropologists have included Almquist and Netting, but Netting's book was about a Swiss community and is thus not actually in the geographical area I am covering.[61] None of the papers in this volume uses sophisticated quantitative techniques.

A major difference between Western European historical sociology and historical anthropology has been the greater emphasis by anthropologists on love, sexual relations, marriage, family, and kinship. In such works as Macfarlane's *Marriage and Love in England,* Segalen's *Love and Power in the Peasant Family,* and Claverie and Lamaison's *L'impossible mariage,* marriage, family, and so on, were central. In other publications, family and kinship constituted a major element.[62] The historical anthropologists, especially the French, also have paid attention to the role of women and the sexual division of labor.[63] Even anthropological macroanalysis could devote space to kinship, in marked contrast with sociological macrohistory.[64] The historical anthropologists have also given more care to inheritance than the sociologists.[65] Exceptions in historical sociology on France or the British

Isles have included Hewitt's *Wives and Mothers,* Michael Anderson's *Family Structure in Nineteenth Century Lancashire,* Bourdieu's "Les stratégies matrimoniales dans le système de reproduction," and Watkins's "Spinsters."

There have not been as many demographic studies from the historical anthropologists as one might expect. A special case was Almquist's "Pre-famine Ireland and the Theory of European Proto-industrialization," though again Netting could be cited if we were to extend our geographical area to include Switzerland. In addition, some demographic analysis or discussion can be found in Macfarlane's *Origins of English Individualism* and his *Marriage and Love in England,* Segalen's *Quinze générations de Bas-Bretons,* Le Bras and Todd's *L'invention de la France,* and Todd's *The Causes of Progress.* At an individual level, fertility and mortality were treated in Macfarlane's *Family Life of Ralph Josselin.* Nevertheless, given the interest that anthropologists have taken in kinship and marriage, historical studies by anthropologists of fertility and mortality have been remarkably rare. In contrast, a good number of sociologists—McQuillan, Watkins, Sharlin, Treadway, Lesthaeghe, Goldstone, and Michael Anderson—have done demographic studies. Hewitt discussed age of marriage, fertility, and child labor in her analysis of women and children in Victorian industry; and Tilly has contributed considerably to our understanding of the consequences of demographic change.[66] At the same time, it must be recognized that the impressive work done in the past two or three decades on European demographic history has been carried out largely by demographers and historians.[67]

The neglect of family, kinship, and sex roles by the historical sociologists did not result from a neglect in the discipline of sociology as a whole. Few departments of sociology lack courses on these subjects. Rather, it is the particular orientation of the historical sociology of Western Europe in the direction of major transformations, large processes, political struggles, and elites that has led to a slighting of society's most fundamental institutions.

This orientation helps us understand why the historical sociology of Western Europe has had a stronger Marxist contingent than the historical anthropology of Western Europe. Perry Anderson, Martin, Corrigan, Sayer, and Comninel are self-confessed Marxists, whereas Tilly, Skocpol, Gould, Lachmann, and others have revealed considerable Marxist influence. It is not hard to understand why a Marxist doing Western European history should be drawn to sociology rather than to anthropology. The historical sociology of Western Europe has addressed the questions that interest Marxists—class struggle and the rise of capitalism—more than has historical anthropology. Another thing to note is that none of the preceding Marxist sociologists has studied the urban working class. The fine research that has been done on the history of the Western European urban working class has come mainly from historians, not sociologists. Marxist historical sociologists, like other historical sociologists in Western European studies, have been more concerned with the major transformations, the state, and elites. Marxism has had considerable impact on anthropology, but this influence has not been felt by the historical anthropologists, at least not those studying France or the British Isles. Assier-Andrieu, Wolf, and Goody have revealed a Marxist influence, but they are unusual.

It is not just that the historical anthropologists studying Western Europe have been less Marxist; they also have been less theoretical. Fitting their work into theoretical models or at least relating it to more general issues has been one of the distinguishing features of historical sociology. Many sociologists have explicitly sought to test the validity of two or more opposing sociological theories.[68] Most sociologists have carried with them theoretical baggage that consciously guided the inquiry. One of the best-known examples in European studies is the work of Bendix, almost all of which was built on the sociology of Weber. Some historical sociology has been almost as much theoretical as historical; Parsonian works stand out,[69] but among others are Holton's *Transition from Feudalism to Capitalism,* Michael Anderson's *Family Structure in Nineteenth Century Lancashire,* and Comninel's *Rethinking the French Revolution.* In a great number of sociological studies a theoretical framework played an important role.[70] It is true that some historical sociologists have questioned the need for "grand sociological theory"; and we have seen that many sociologists have become interested in specific large transformations for their own sake. Yet these historical sociologists have not rejected theory any more than did Marx and Weber. It is a measure of the strong theoretical orientation of historical sociology that sociologists such as Skocpol and Mann could become the focus of attack for being insufficiently theoretical.[71]

The historical anthropology here under review is much less theoretical. Some exceptions have included works by Assier-Andrieu, Macfarlane, Gellner, and Todd.[72] Otherwise, explicit theoretical references are few and far between.

It also has been less comparative than the historical sociology. Some grand comparative studies have been similar to the macrohistorical works in sociology (e.g., those by Goody, Wolf, Gellner, and

Todd).[73] Some of the historical anthropologists have referred to other societies and compared them with the society they were studying. Jenkins, Rosenberg, and especially Macfarlane did this.[74] So does Birdwell-Pheasant in this volume. She is, however, the only one in our book to do so. Furthermore, most of the historical anthropology that I cite in this essay focused on particular places and made few comparisons.

Similarly, the historical anthropologists have often ignored major transformations. Again the exceptions are Gellner, Goody, Macfarlane, Wolf, and Todd.[75] These are macrostudies. Many authors of community studies, in contrast, have paid insufficient attention to the external forces that impinged on their communities and the major transformations in which their communities were involved. This criticism cannot be leveled against some local studies by anthropologists,[76] but it is true of Verdier's *Façons de dire, façons de faire,* Claverie and Lamaison's *L'impossible mariage,* Segalen's *Quinze générations de Bas-Bretons,* Pingaud's *Paysans en Bourgogne,* Parman's *Scottish Crofters,* and many others. Augustins examined the effect of social change on land distribution and inheritance in the Baronnies, a region in the Pyrenees, but he focused almost exclusively on pressures caused by natural population increase; the only other force considered was the Civil Code, which only received a brief mention.[77]

Several examples can also be found in our volume. Silverman, perhaps more than any other author in this collection, needs to discuss the larger process with which she is dealing. Precisely because she is seeking to show how much of the transition to private property rights occurred at the local level, she needs to tell us how much of it did not occur at that level. The triumph of private property on the Nore River was also determined by the gradual ascendancy of private property throughout the British Isles in the eighteenth and nineteenth centuries. She also needs to compare it with what was happening elsewhere. The gradual decline in communal land was a Europe-wide process that began in the late Middle Ages and continued until the twentieth century. It went through a number of phases, moved at different paces in different regions and was responsible for variations in rural social structure in Europe that persist to this day. Gulliver's study of townsmen in Thomastown refers to my own work in Connacht. Still, he does not relate his findings to the more general literature on urban-rural relations in Western Europe. The larger question is the relationship between the petty bourgeoisie and the peasantry, how it varied, and how it changed over time. It is the question to which Gulliver's paper is really addressed and yet he never explicitly discusses it. Although Vincent is dealing with major changes that took place in provincial Ireland and the consequences of the encroachment of the English state and society on this country, she does not discuss these larger changes: the development of the British state, the rise of capitalism, the making of the capitalist bourgeoisie, and more locally, the evolution of an urban petty bourgeoisie. In her article in *Ireland from Below,* Vincent emphasized the importance of "global processes" but does little more than list them.

For the most part, these authors are doing what historians would do—more precisely, what local historians would do. Beyond an uncommonly large number of references to Arensberg and Kimball, there is little here that is distinctively anthropological. Why are these anthropologists behaving like historians?

It cannot be because they have no anthropological theory or comparative literature on which to draw. Anthropology has as much theory as sociology. As a discipline, it is actually more comparative than sociology, though it may be that there does not, to our authors at least, seem to be enough comparative literature relevant to nineteenth- and twentieth-century Ireland. It is no doubt also true that the local research in which these anthropologists have engaged has exhausted their time and energy, leaving them with little of either to tie their work to theory, to compare it with other societies, or to evaluate the impact of external forces. Finally, space is a very real limitation. The larger perspective often must be omitted in an article, whereas in a book it could be considered.

I believe, however, that the main reason for the neglect of theory, comparisons, and external forces in the case studies in this volume is the particular tradition of empirical work that has characterized anthropology. The conventional methods of anthropology are easier to adapt to historical research than are sociological methods. I was impressed during the conference at which these papers were given with the enjoyment that the anthropologists were getting from immersing themselves in the documents, much as they would immerse themselves in a community when doing fieldwork. In fact, all engaged in fieldwork as part of the research presented in this volume. For example, Gulliver and Silverman have spent extended periods living in Thomastown talking to the local people as they engaged in archival research.[78] Birdwell-Pheasant lived for a period in Ballyduff. The authors of other anthropological studies that I have cited in this essay also did fieldwork.[79] To be sure, ethnographic research has customarily been set in a larger framework in which comparison with other societies was natural. Nonetheless, it is also true that the ethnographic method of research, transferred to history, has produced a certain kind of research more empirically oriented than most historical sociology, more encouraging of work with primary rather than secondary sources, and more likely to focus on single communities than on the larger society.

European historical anthropologists have often looked for relatively out-of-the way societies, which they have studied in their entirety. Anthropologists have been particularly attracted to mountain communities. In French historical anthropology we have, as examples, *A Negotiated World,* by Rosenberg; "Reproduction sociale," by Augustins; and *Communautés paysannes du Capcir,* by Assier-Andrieu. Many anthropologists have looked for places that have not experienced great change. Verdier was part of a team of anthropologists investigating an out-of-the-way village in the Châtillonnais.[80] Claverie and Lamaison looked for a community that had experienced little change and into and out of which there was little mobility or marriage.[81] Gulliver and Silverman did not select an isolated community, but they explicitly wanted "to get away from national history, national trends and developments, nationally influential individuals and broad, national generalisations."[82] Local studies are exceptional among the historical sociologists studying France or the British Isles; and they are generally much different from the anthropological local studies.[83]

Anthropologists studying European history still like to find "traditional" societies less affected by forces of "modernization." The result has been a geographical bias, the reverse of what we find in historical sociology. The historical sociologists have been most interested in northwestern Europe, where major transformations, particularly the rise of capitalism, are perceived to be the most advanced. Historical anthropologists have been more interested in the Mediterranean region, which has modernized more slowly. Anthropological work on Italy has favored southern Italy over northern Italy because it is less industrialized.[84] Anthropological research on Ireland has favored the west of Ireland. Although some anthropologists—most notably Gulliver and Silverman—have tried to create a better balance, in this volume the west of Ireland receives more than its fair share of attention.

As I have just suggested, historical anthropologists also like to bring their research up to the present and combine it with fieldwork. Such a strategy can create problems. If a community is selected for study because of its suitability for nonhistorical research, it may not have the archival sources that permit good historical work. As a consequence, archival research can be weak, as it was in the works of Littlejohn, Jenkins, Pingaud, Verdier, Rosenberg, and Parman.[85] On the other hand, some historical anthropologists have been attentive to the availability of historical records in selecting their communities and thus have produced well-documented studies, often in combination with fine ethnographic research. A good use of historical material is found in Assier-Andrieu, Silverman and Gulliver, Claverie and Lamaison, and Segalen.[86] Moreover, the use of primary sources, however weak it may sometimes have been in historical anthropology, has been vastly superior to what we find in historical sociology, where the overwhelming majority of studies have been based on secondary sources. Only a small number of the historical sociologists studying France or the British Isles have engaged in primary research.

In addition, some anthropologists have become skilled in the use of present-day interviews to supplement archival research. The extreme was reached by Pingaud and Verdier, who based their historical analysis largely on discussions with living witnesses, but Parman, Littlejohn, Jenkins, Assier-Andrieu, Silverman, and Segalen provided a better mix of the two methods.[87] As Gulliver explained, there is an interaction effect when both methods are used. Describing his research with Silverman on Thomastown, he wrote:

> It is not a matter of contemporary anthropological research picking up where archival research stops; nor is it merely that one kind of research supports the other. Rather, there is an intertwining of both and of the data and understanding generated by both, such that each method becomes more productive in its results. As it were, each method builds upon and stimulates the other. For instance . . . archival data were expanded in various ways through discussion of them with a variety of informants, thus fleshing out the facts of a governmental report, a deed or a newspaper article. This, in turn, often induced us to return to the archives to re-check and to look for more; and it assisted in the evaluation of records. Conversely, we were able to use archival data as devices to start or stimulate informants' memories or to provide a focus for interviews.[88]

Anthropologists have been more sensitive than sociologists or historians to the significance of the meaning of history. Just as important as what actually happened is what people think happened and the importance they attach to it. Thus, historical research and fieldwork can enable the anthropologist to study the present-day meaning of past events, and how history is reinterpreted. A fine example of this kind of study is Parman's *Scottish Crofters*.

## Conclusion

One of the contributions that anthropologists are making has come from combining historical research with fieldwork. The approach has its advantages and disadvantages and has to be used with great care, but it is a powerful method when executed competently. Another contribution of historical anthropology comes from its attention to the daily lives of real people. This is what makes books such as Segalen's *Love and Power in the Peasant Family* and Claverie and Lamaison's *L'impossible mariage* a pleasure to read.

A third major contribution of historical anthropology is the study of the local community and the analysis of relationships between such communities and the larger society. Although some historical anthropologists can be criticized for ignoring major transformations and forces external to the community they studied—and I have so criticized several of the essays in our collection—a new awareness has emerged of the need to study the interaction of community and larger society. Led by Wolf, there has been a movement to recognize the importance of external forces and to analyse the interconnectedness of all parts of the world.[89] Blok argued that "the commmunity, though appropriate as a locus of study, proved hardly adequate as a unit of analysis."[90] Cole and Wolf were explicitly reproachful of traditional anthropological tendencies to study societies as closed systems.

> Such an approach . . . begs the question of how small social and cultural systems are related to the larger systems of which they form a part; and it precludes further questions as to how these different phenomena determine each other. It is soon obvious in fieldwork that the community is neither a closed system nor a homeostatic machine: the functional relationships that obtain within it are relations of adaptiveness and congruence, and not the causal components of a homeostatic motor. Underlying any process toward adaptation or congruence are causal impulses that flow from the requirements of the physical environment, on the one hand, and from the forces at work in the larger world, on the other. In complex societies, these larger "external" forces often dominate and reshape the forces at work in creating the local ecology.[91]

Even some earlier community studies, such as Littlejohn's *Westrigg* and Jenkins's *Agricultural Community,* paid attention to the effect of the larger society on the people they were researching. More recently, Assier-Andrieu and Rosenberg examined the impact of external forces on a community.[92] It can be done, and done well.

Historical sociologists have much to learn from historical anthropologists. Precisely because one of its strengths is theory, one of the dangers of historical sociology is that it can become too theoretical, too abstract. As a sociologist, I can only admire the resistance among anthropologists to forcing people into theoretical boxes. Sociologists also have a weakness for keys that they think will unlock the doors of history. For Wallerstein and Abu-Lughod it is the "world system"; for Mann it is "networks of power"; for Lachmann it is "elite conflict." As Taylor remarked, sociologists "seem to posit a novel theoretical position on every occasion."

The most encouraging development in recent work by sociologists on Western European history has been the renewed interest in the history of Europe for its own sake. Hechter and Gould are exceptions. Even Gould, who clearly has turned to history in order to apply a theory, accepted the importance of understanding the rise of capitalism in Western Europe as an objective in itself. Both Goldstone and Kimmel were as much interested in explaining early modern revolutions as in revolutions in general.[93] There has emerged in sociology a school of Western European historical specialists who read more history than sociology and who find themselves drawn into the debates and historical problems that concern historians.

One must give sociologists credit for courage, for asking the big questions, and for constructing frameworks for research. Sociologists have helped set the agenda for the megaproject on the making of modern Europe. Historical sociologists, historical anthropologists, and historians can all make a contribution to this project. Most historical sociologists have focused too much on the larger picture and have engaged in insufficient primary research; they need to pay more attention to the work that the historical anthropologists are doing, and even to take it as a model. Historical anthropologists, for their part, not only need to link their communities with the larger society but need to identify the major transformations that have affected their communities and in which their communities have been involved. Local studies are not just case studies of communities from which we can generalize about other communities. They are also communities that form part of the history of Europe.

NOTES

1. S. D. Clark (1962:225).
2. Banks (1989:527).

3. Park and Burgess (1969:11).
4. Glass (1938); Sorokin (1927, 1942); Znaniecki (1934); Teggart (1939); Elias (1978, 1982); Homans (1941); Merton (1970); S. D. Clark (1942, 1948).
5. Parsons (1966).
6. Tilly (1981, 1988); Abrams (1982).
7. Abrams (1982:xiv–xviii, 1–8).
8. Banks (1989:530–31).
9. Nisbet (1964).
10. Hechter (1975:21–22).
11. Hechter (1975:xiv).
12. McQuillan (1983).
13. Markoff and Shapiro (1985); Markoff (1985).
14. Gould (1987).
15. Eisenstadt (1963); Parsons (1966); Lenski (1966).
16. Hechter (1975).
17. McQuillan (1983, 1984).
18. *Bailliages* were judicial units of the Old Regime. There were over 400 of them.
19. Markoff (1985).
20. Brustein (1988).
21. Holton (1985).
22. Skocpol (1979).
23. Lachmann (1989); Kimmel (1988); Comninel (forthcoming).
24. McQuillan (1990).
25. Wallerstein (1974, 1980, 1988); Mann (1986); Hall (1986); Abu-Lughod (1989).
26. Burke (1980:83–89).
27. Holton (1985).
28. Tilly (1984a); McMichael (1990).
29. Abrams (1982:157–62).
30. Wallerstein (1974, 1980, 1988).
31. Tilly (1990:2).
32. Abu-Lughod (1989).
33. Mendras (1958, 1967).
34. Lachmann (1989, 1990).
35. Poggi (1978:xii).
36. Brenner (1976, 1985).
37. Kane and Mann (forthcoming).
38. Fulbrook (1983).
39. Hudson (1973:113).
40. Gulliver (1989:321).
41. Netting (1981:xiv–xv).
42. Blok (1974:xxix).
43. Gellner (1983); Le Bras and Todd (1981); Todd (1985); Todd (1987).
44. Most of the sociological works on the state have referred to elites. In

addition, there have been some publications that gave elites particular attention, such as Guttsman (1963), Bishop (1967), Elias (1983), Clark (1984), and Lachmann (1990).

45. Verdier (1979); Jenkins (1971); Segalen (1983); Claverie and Lamaison (1982).

46. Mendras (1958, 1967); Rambaud and Vincenne (1964); Tilly (1964); Moore (1966); Clark (1979, 1988); Martin (1983); Markoff (1985); Brustein (1988).

47. Mellor (1981, 1990); Sharlin (1978); McQuillan (1983); Tilly and Lodhi (1973).

48. Pingaud (1978). For an example of the anthropological concern with tools, see Segalen (1985).

49. One or more of these was treated in Segalen (1985) and Jenkins (1971).

50. For example, see Claverie and Lamaison (1982), Segalen (1985), Taylor (1985), Silverman (1989), Verdier (1979), and Parman (1990).

51. Littlejohn (1963).

52. Verdier (1979); Segalen (1983).

53. Aminzade (1981).

54. Assier-Andrieu (1981).

55. Gellner (1983, 1988); Todd (1985, 1987). See also Le Bras and Todd (1981).

56. Poggi (1978); Corrigan and Sayer (1985); Gould (1985); Hall (1986); Markoff and Shapiro (1985); Comninel (1987); Wuthnow (1985, 1989).

57. Taylor (1985, 1990a).

58. In addition to Bendix's work, see Swanson (1967); Markoff and Regan (1981); Fulbrook (1984); Hall (1986); Wuthnow (1985, 1989).

59. The significance of religion was underestimated in Kimmel (1988), Gould (1987), Goldstone (1986), but not in Fulbrook (1983).

60. Tilly (1972); McQuillan (1983, 1984, 1990); Markoff (1985); Markoff and Shapiro (1985); Goldstone (1986a); Maxim (1989); Gillis (1989).

61. Almquist (1979); Netting (1981).

62. Rosenberg (1988); Verdier (1979); Parman (1990); Assier-Andrieu (1981); Augustins (1977).

63. Segalen (1980); Assier-Andrieu (1981); Todd and Le Bras (1981); Todd (1987). Again Hewitt was an exception among the sociologists.

64. Compare Goody (1983), Wolf (1982), Todd (1985, 1987) with Moore (1966), Anderson (1974a, 1974b), Wallerstein (1974, 1980, 1988), Mann (1986), and Tilly (1990).

65. Augustins (1977); Goody (1983); Macfarlane (1978); Assier-Andrieu (1981); Segalen (1985); Jenkins (1971). Inheritance is also the subject of an essay in this volume by Birdwell-Pheasant.

66. McQuillan (1984, 1990); Tilly (1984b); Hewitt (1958). Among Watkins's writings see, in particular, 1986.

67. Works by historians include Levine (1977, 1983, 1987), Mendels (1972), Braun (1978), Wrigley and Schofield (1981), Wrigley (1961, 1969), Gullick-

son (1982), Lehning (1983), and Gutmann (1987, 1988). French historical demographers, such as Louis Henry and Jacques Houdaille, are probably best classified simply as demographers.

68. I have already given the example of Hechter (1975). Other examples include Snyder and Tilly (1972), Markoff (1985), Markoff and Shapiro (1985), Maxim (1989), and Gillis (1989), to mention only a few of the many that could be cited.

69. Smelser (1959); Eisenstadt (1963); Gould (1987).

70. Gillis (1989); Martin (1983); Corrigan and Sayer (1985); Poggi (1978); Mann (1986); Lachmann (1987, 1989); Skocpol (1979); Clark (1979); Calhoun (1982); Fulbrook (1983). (I would not want to try to provide a complete list.)

71. Kiser and Hechter (1991).

72. Assier-Andrieu (1981); Macfarlane (1978, 1986); Gellner (1983, 1988); Todd (1985, 1987).

73. Goody (1983); Wolf (1982); Gellner (1988); Todd (1985, 1987).

74. Jenkins (1971); Rosenberg (1988); Macfarlane (1970b, 1978).

75. Wolf (1982); Gellner (1983, 1988); Goody (1983); Macfarlane (1978, 1986); Todd (1987).

76. Taylor (1980b, 1985).

77. Augustins (1977).

78. Gulliver (1989:320, n. 1).

79. Pingaud (1978); Assier-Andrieu (1981); Segalen (1985), Rosenberg (1988); Parman (1990).

80. Verdier (1979); Pingaud (1978).

81. Lamaison (1979); Claverie and Lamaison (1982).

82. Gulliver (1989:335).

83. Tilly (1964); Aminzade (1981); McQuillan (1990).

84. Carroll (1992).

85. Littlejohn (1963); Jenkins (1971); Pingaud (1978); Verdier (1979); Rosenberg (1988); Parman (1990).

86. Assier-Andrieu (1981); Silverman and Gulliver (1986); Claverie and Lamaison (1982); Segalen (1985).

87. Pingaud (1978); Verdier (1979); Littlejohn (1963); Jenkins (1971); Blok (1974); Assier-Andrieu (1981); Silverman (1989); Segalan (1985).

88. Gulliver (1989:332–33).

89. Cole and Wolf (1974); Wolf (1982).

90. Blok (1974:xxvii).

91. Cole and Wolf (1974:20–21).

92. Assier-Andrieu (1981); Rosenberg (1988).

93. Goldstone (1986b); Kimmel (1988).

# 10

# The Anthropological Turn in Social History

■

## NICHOLAS ROGERS

History is fashioned on the basis of written documents, of course. When there are any. But it can and must be fashioned even without written documents if none are available. Then it can be made up of anything that the historian's ingenuity may lead him to employ, in order to make his honey, supposing he finds none of the usual flowers.                                    Febvre 1973[1]

Three or four months ago I had a brief conversation with Margaret Mead in Paris. I said to her that today in France historians want to have a field; they make interviews; they are studying oral traditions. She responded that the new anthropologists in America want to have records with precise chronology and so on.                                            Burguière 1978[2]

In my own work I have found that I can handle neither the congruities nor the contradictions of the deeper historical process without attending to the problems which anthropologists disclose.                                            E. P. Thompson 1979[3]

Thirty-five years ago, history and anthropology were not usually regarded as cognate disciplines. Although Lévi-Strauss saw them springing from the same impulse, the majority of practitioners in the two fields were engaged in very different enterprises. History was largely a matter of Great Events, Texts, and People, set within a conventional narrative mould and a Rankeian methodology. Anthropology, by contrast, was engaged in a natural science of society or the reconstruction of unique cultures. Often structural-functionalist in orientation, it drew its data from the present rather than from historical documents and took its disciplinary touchstones from archeology and biology as much as from history. Malinowski, whose book *The Argonauts of the Western Pacific* became paradigmatic, urged ethnographers to chart the rules, regularities, and autonomy of tribal cultures using sources "in the behaviour and in the memory of living men."[4] History became almost coterminous with myth; it was utilized insofar as it was remembered.

In the last decade or so this situation has been dramatically transformed. Anthropologists have begun to develop historical perspectives in their work and have invited historians to talk in interdisciplinary forums. Historians, for their part, have increasingly referenced and even reverenced leading anthropologists and deployed their perspectives to inform their own approaches to the past.[5] Burguière's remark, with which this paper began, is indicative of the renewed engagement between the two disciplines. How did this happen? What is its significance? It is the purpose of this essay to chart this convergence and offer some observations about it, particularly in the context of the current debates about the writing of social history.

Although the affiliations between anthropology and history have become a more visible preoccupation of current scholarship, there were always those who hoped for a closer relationship between the two disciplines, or at least noted some basic complementarities. The evolutionists, for example, had attempted to formulate laws of historical development in their anthropological studies, drawing their inspiration from the Enlightenment and positivism. Although their work frequently debased the complexities of the past in its search for unilinear lines of historical development and reinforced the ahistorical tendencies of structural-functionalist anthropology, it did prompt scholars to consider the ways in which diachronic and synchronic modes of analysis could be profitably combined. In 1961, when structural-functionalism was still a dominant mode of anthropological analysis, Evans-Pritchard attempted to stake out new ground for a more fruitful exchange between the two disciplines, urging anthropologists to heed the work of sociologically nuanced history in their construction of traditional societies instead of deriving their models from natural science. At the same time, he pointed to the ways in which anthropological perspectives on family, kinship, and non-Western cultures could enrich historical writing.[6] In his view, sociological history and anthropology had much in common—in their search for the dynamics of social change and the subtle transformations of seemingly unchanging habits or traditions, in their recognition of the importance of both written and oral testimony, and in their emphasis upon the general in the particular. "Anthropology," he declared, echoing

Maitland, "must choose between being history and being nothing."
Vice versa, the same was true of history.[7]

A new rapprochement between anthropology and history became
possible only when history began to reconstruct the popular experience in a systematic way. When Evans-Pritchard made his intervention in 1961, that shift was already under way. Social history was
already well established in France under the auspices of *Annales:
économies, sociétés et civilisations*. Founded in 1929 by Marc Bloch and
Lucien Febvre, and closely linked with the Sixth Section of the Ecole
Pratique des Hautes Etudes after 1945, the *Annales* school became the
powerhouse of French historical scholarship, with its own distinctive
style and methods. Dissatisfied with political histories that focused
simply upon the surface events of public life, it sought to probe the
deeper structures and rhythms of the past in ways that would inte-
grate history with the social sciences. This led its practitioners to
explore the influence of the environment upon human history, the
weight of numbers upon human resources and opportunities, and the
mental equipment of civilizations—the stock of ideas, assumptions,
and attitudes that defined the limits of the thinkable at any given
time. Underscoring and integrating this expansive project was a perception of the different temporalities of the past: of rhythms more
profound than the transient clatter of wars and diplomacy, rhythms
associated with the trade cycle or, more ponderably, with what Braudel described as a "history which almost stands still, a history of man
in his intimate relationship to the earth which bears and feeds him."[8]
In formulating this concept, what became known as the *longue durée,*
Braudel highlighted the theoretical breakthroughs of Lévi-Strauss,
whose emphasis upon the unconscious structures of social life corresponded with his own efforts to emancipate history from the "trap of
events."[9]

Braudel's contribution to the *Annales* paradigm was to formalize a
three-tiered model of historical analysis based on the differing temporalities of structure, conjuncture, and event: the long, medium, and
short term. In this history of continuities, so at variance with the
mobilities of orthodox political history, *Annales* scholars shared with
anthropologists an interest in material culture and in the dialectic
between man and nature. More directly, anthropological insights
helped shaped the *Annales* concept of *mentalité,* a notion associated
with the taken-for-granted habits of mind and attitudes underpinning
everyday beliefs, relations, and practices. The concept was adapted
from Levy-Bruhl's *La mentalité primitive,* first published in 1922, a
book that differentiated the rational disposition of modern man and

the "prelogical," superstitious disposition of his "primitive" counter-part.[10] However bogus such a distinction may now seem, however ridden with evolutionist assumptions, the concept did encourage scholars to investigate aspects of popular belief hitherto considered marginal to historical knowledge. It led Marc Bloch to analyze the healing rituals of early modern kings and to chart, with some precision, the rise and fall of sacred monarchy. It induced Febvre to explore the problem of unbelief in the sixteenth century and to set an agenda for a history of the emotional life of the past, a quest that subsequently took historians to the domain of private life, sexuality, childhood, and death.[11] In the hands of Vovelle, who investigated the funeral rituals and testamentary language of thousands of Frenchmen, the history of *mentalité* offered new insights into the changing forms of piety in eighteenth-century Provence and a socially nuanced chrongy of de-Christianization.[12] By this time, the concept no longer denoted the mental inertia of the past, but a more diverse, dynamic, if resolutely habitual set of attitudes, characteristic of past civilizations, whose distribution through place and time could be charted by quantitative analysis.

In a variety of ways, then, the historiography of the *Annales* school encouraged scholars to broach subjects common to both history and anthropology. It forced historians in particular to confront the issues of time, terrain, and habit, to develop a more sophisticated ecology and archaeology of the past, to probe its ethnology with a new sensitivity. Although anthropology was by no means the only source of inspiration to the *Annales,* its orientation remained central to the school's quest for a total history, if only to underscore the constraints (cultural, demographic, and environmental) upon preindustrial endeavor. Indeed, as the prospects of a total history receded somewhat in the 1970s, when the unity of the social sciences was blown apart by the controversy over structuralism, anthropologically nuanced history continued to be popular in France. Anthropological studies were consistently reviewed in *Annales E.S.C.* from the very beginning, but between 1969 and 1976, roughly 30 percent of all the essays published in the journal were explicitly oriented toward anthropology, most of them devoted either to mentalities, folklore, or food and eating habits.[13] In 1974, a special issue was devoted to history and anthropology, taking as its meeting ground the question of reciprocity in traditional societies, a theme central to the work of Mauss. Two years later, another issue focused upon the anthropology of France. In the late 1950s, when Braudel was still the leading spokesman for the *Annales,* the interdisciplinary exchanges were with sociologists as much as with anthropologists. Braudel's own invocations for a "global science" took him back to Durkheim and Simiand. His critique of sociology centered upon its ahistorical formulation of synchronic structures and its unwillingness to address the different, layered temporalities of historical change.[14] Twenty years later, when the social history of the *Annales* school appeared a more fragmented and epistemologically threatened discipline, its practitioners were increasingly turning to anthropology for interdisciplinary exchange and inspiration.

Despite the significant advances in historical knowledge pioneered by the *Annales* school, it was not until the 1960s that social history really began to penetrate the English-speaking world. In that decade the conventional boundaries of history were dramatically widened through the auspices of such journals as *Past and Present*. It was founded in 1952 by a group of British Marxists and liberals who sought to break with the academic specialisms of political and economic history and to pioneer a journal that would recapture the complexities of social transformations in the past, emphasizing the role that ordinary people played in the making of their own history. "Men are the active and conscious makers of history, not merely its passive victims and indices," its original manifesto declared. Consequently, "fashionable attempts to express history in terms of much simpler changes in the natural sciences (for instance, in terms of biological evolution, statistical growth-curves or invariant psychological mechanisms) oversimplify and falsify it."[15]

What distinguished this history, what later became known as "history from below," was its effort to recapture the experience of ordinary people in their own terms and to explicate the ways in which they negotiated, resisted, and sometimes challenged the prevailing structures of power and subordination. Rather than seeing subject or subaltern groups as an administrative or social problem, as passive recipients of change or of governmental policies, they were seen as historical agents in their own right. This involved a closer examination of the values, expectations, and modes of collective action by which people made sense of their lives; a more intensive exploration of popular culture than hitherto, and one, in contrast to earlier "populist" or folklorist histories, that detailed the dialectical interplay between rulers and ruled and its mediations. It also led to a fuller elaboration of social structures and social relations and to a reexamination of large-scale social transformations such as the birth of capitalism or industrialization. These themes had been central concerns of the historical group of the British Communist party during the 1940s, whose leading members constituted an important voice on *Past and Present*'s first editorial board.[16] Such a cluster of topics was clearly as pertinent to anthropology, or sociology for that matter, as it was to history. Indeed, the expansive agenda of *Past and Present* was reflected in the early admission of an anthropologist and sociologist to the editorial board and in the lines of communication that were opened up with members of the *Annales* school.[17]

Not all social historians in the English-speaking world, of course, followed the mandate of *Past and Present*. Many historians shared the journal's disposition to deal with the masses rather than the elites and to tackle large-scale transformations by attending to the collective experience of the groups involved, whether they be crowds during the American Revolution, workers in the early industrial mills, or European immigrants to the New World. But they did not necessarily follow its radical agenda.[18] In fact, the politically engaged history that the journal propounded, with its clear leftist resonances, was viewed with misgivings in some quarters. Hexter sought to take the wind out of left-wing sails by proposing a non–Marxist framework of social history that in effect echoed Pareto's sociology of elites. Perkin sought solace from a structural-functionalist perspective in charting a new course for social history. Stearns blew hot and cold at the "overcommitment to politics in social history," believing that the most appropriate agenda for the new subdiscipline was the "description and explanation of styles of life," a Trevelyanesque definition that stressed consumption, family organization, leisure, and private life rather than more public manifestations of collective struggle.[19] In practice, social history remained a contested yet expanding terrain in which modernization and behavioral models of social change were counterposed to Marxist ones and in which aspiring scholars drew insights from classical and contemporary sociologists as much as from Marx himself. Where American scholars drew inspiration from British historians such as E. P. Thompson, whose redefinition of class consciousness transformed labor history,[20] there were dissonant voices in defense of American exceptionalism and the peculiarities of its industrial experience, with its waves of immigration, high rates of mobility, and factory "ghettoes."

To some extent these tensions were held in check by the situation in which many social historians found themselves within the academy—that is, the need to create space for themselves in curricula still dominated by national, political histories. Even so, during the 1970s, dissonant voices were heard concerning the incoherent state of the field and the degree to which social historians had succumbed to a quantitative, nonpolitical history or to a populist exaltation of popular culture. Judt believed social history had disarmed itself by its vacuous application of modernization models and elision of class-based relations of power.[21] The Genoveses, anxious to return social history to the question of "who rides whom and how," targeted the ambiguous legacy of the *Annales* school, whose broadening historical vista, so they claimed, had been blunted by its unfortunate emphasis upon the constraints of human endeavor, thereby discounting popular agency and unsettling the balance between the structural and dynamic determinants of social life.[22] Ethnographic approaches to the past also came under attack for privileging description over explanation, eliding issues of power and second-guessing the intentions and actions of historical participants. As an answer to social history, claimed the Genoveses, the current anthropological fad was nothing less than a "bourgeois swindle."[23]

The interventions of Judt and the Genoveses offered an impassioned, if idiosyncratic, testimony to the confused state of social history in the 1970s. It did seem that the emanicipatory promise of the new history had been overwhelmed by academic overproduction and faddism as scores of scholars jumped on the social history bandwagon. Particularly disconcerting, as these authors recognized, was the facile enthusiasm with quantification, what E. P. Thompson was to term "positivism armed with a computer,"[24] which was openly trumpeted as a revolutionary means of unlocking the past. In the late 1960s and early 1970s, leading social historians, such as Furet, saw the construction of documentary series as promoting a "revolution in the historical consciousness," displacing the familiar narratives of *histoire événementielle* from the pinnacle of historical scholarship and affording new links between history and the social sciences. Le Roy Ladurie even predicted that "tomorrow's historian will have to be able to programme a computer in order to survive."[25] But the promised land of computer-driven history proved as elusive as ever, especially in the hands of counters who naively believed that the facts, once uncovered, would automatically disclose their own meanings. Census data revealed social taxonomies not classes, households not family relationships, men's work but seldom that of women and children. Serial history was not some privileged conduit to the past but a subgenre whose sources had to be interrogated like any other. Harnessed to a modernizing paradigm, it frequently resulted in a homogeneous, packaged history that marginalized popular agency and simply exalted the capitalist present. Handled sensitively, with apt comparisons and a judicious humility as to its limitations, quantitative history could elucidate the life chances of anonymous men and women, the commonalities of social groupings, the parameters of demographic regimes. It disclosed new angles to the past, prised open problems, but rarely by itself resolved them.

Judt and the Genoveses rightly condemned the arrogance and epistemological simplicity of much of the new quantitative history, although many of the pitfalls they highlighted have now been heeded by social historians, with the result that the question of quantification is less of a politically charged issue. As Dawley, an American labor historian in the Thompsonian vein, has recently remarked: "To count, or not to count; that is *not* the question. . . . So long as quantifiers ride herd on their techniques and do not allow their 'neat analyses' to take over the interpretation of 'untidy processes,' they will have much to contribute to the dialogue about the meaning of the past."[26] Judt and the Genoveses's indictment of history's exchange with anthropology, however, requires further comment. It raises important questions, both about the nature of that exchange and about the current direction of social history.

In the first instance, it should be emphasized that the historians' appropriation of anthropology has been characteristically eclectic and pragmatic. Confronted with the problems of reconstructing the experiences of subordinate classes through official sources and fleeting, fragmentary traces, historians have looked to anthropology for guidance in mapping their diverse representations and linking them to other parts of the social system. They have also availed themselves of anthropological insights to recapture the strangeness of the past, to make sense of the seemingly irrational or superstitious practices that underscored popular belief and behavior, whether these pertained to noneconomic forms of exchange, to family rituals, to festive rites, or to oral culture. Ethnographic accounts of sorcery, for example, have proved invaluable to historical investigations of witchcraft, enabling historians to explore the range of social, political, sexual, and psychological issues that informed witchcraft trials[27] or to probe the syncretism of magical belief and religious practice found in societies with limited technology and literacy.[28] Likewise, anthropological perspectives have helped historians understand the religious passions that divided early modern societies and the cultural differences—over time, space, leisure, work, and domesticity—that separated and helped demarcate the plebeian from the polite classes. In these endeavors, historians have been less interested in the theoretical differences among anthropologists than in their angle of vision and approach to alien cultures. And they have favored anthropologists whose approach is concrete and interpretive rather than logical and abstract. Despite Braudel's declared affinity with Lévi-Strauss, historians have largely remained unreceptive to structuralist anthropology because of its ahistorical or history-added perspective and because it collapsed the peculiarities and diversity of past cultures into a small number of underlying principles. Although Braudel applauded Lévi-Strauss's "geological" approach to the past, his own empirically driven, structural history was defined spatially and temporally, not in terms of a structured unity that was indiscernible to empirical investigation. Structuralism tended to elide historical process and, in a stridently antihumanistic fashion, to decenter the subject. In its more absolutist constructions, it has predictably encountered a hostile reception from social historians anxious to recapture the importance of popular agency in the past.[29]

Historians and anthropologists have found the world systems analysis developed by Frank and Wallerstein a more congenial meeting ground, particularly those engaged in Third World studies and in European expansion. This engagement, as Ortner stressed, has helped to historicize anthropology, which too frequently treated societies, and even villages, as if they were islands unto themselves, with homogeneous, bounded cultures.[30] As Ruane's essay in this volume suggests, a world system perspective has proved attractive to those who wish to question the peripheral nature of societies outside the mainstream of Euro-American cultures and to situate them more specifically within the contradictory trajectories of European capitalism. It has prompted some important debates about the historical definition of capitalist modes of production, and their purported reproduction on the periphery, and has helped to open up new ecological perspectives to the past. It has, however, proved difficult to reconcile the global and local determinants of change, what Wolf has recently termed the structural and organizational dimensions of power,[31] within the frame of one monograph. Although world systems analysis has continued to be an important point of genuine interdisciplinary exchange among historians, anthropologists, economists, and political scientists, and one that will undoubtedly thrive in the future as a historical referent for contemporary problems of economic development, it has thus far remained relatively marginal to the mainstream of social history.

Historians' interest in anthropology has, in fact, been principally in the field of cultural, especially symbolic, anthropology. Generally speaking, Anglophone historians have taken their cues from cultural anthropologists such as Geertz and Turner.[32] These prominent stylists of their discipline offered fresh insights into the semiology of culture, into those repetitive and public forms of social action through which one might decode the "webs of significance" that shape everyday life and sometimes transform it. Their actor-oriented definition of culture, particularistic, contextual, stressing process rather than structural laws or tendencies, has proved attractive to social historians who, like anthropologists, have had to wrestle with the problem of how to reconstruct popular mentalities. It offered an alternative to the *Annales* concept of *mentalité* that emphasized the dragnet of belief, the tenacious hold of the past, upon popular activities.

The historical appropriation of cultural anthropology has nevertheless produced ambiguous results. Techniques such as "thick description" have helped historians to recapture the complexities of small-scale dramas and have alerted them to the possibilities of reconstructing enthnographic or action-oriented histories, getting inside public actions, reconstructing the "relations, roles, rules, values, rituals and symbols" that "shape [their] logic and project [their] meanings."[33] More than this, cultural anthropology has forced historians to recognize that the "whole of social life, from such symbolically elaborate practices as religious festivals to such seemingly matter of fact activities as building houses or raising crops, is culturally shaped."[34] This recognition has reinforced the historical turn away from base/superstructure models of change, even within the Marxist tradition itself. "Marxists," reflected E. P. Thompson,

> if they wish to have an honest dialogue with anthropologists, *must* call in question the notion that it is possible to describe a mode of production in "economic" terms, leaving aside as secondary (less "real") the norms, the culture, the critical concepts around which this mode of production is organized. Such an arbitrary theoretical division into an economic basis and a cultural superstructure may be made in the head, and it may look all right on paper for a while. But it is only an argument in the head.[35]

At the same time, these preoccupations have sometimes led historians to reify culture or to defend versions of cultural determinism. Geertz's own work has veered dangerously in that direction in its insistence that "culture is a fabric of meaning in terms of which human beings interpret their experience and guide their action; social structure is the form that action takes, the actual existing network of social relations."[36] What is left unsaid in this statement is that social relations are constituted and reproduced in an asymmetrical fashion, privileging certain cultural meanings while displacing or marginalizing others.[37] As long as one recognizes the patterns of power and domination that reproduce cultural meanings, without completely barring the door to rival or alternative constructions, then thick description becomes a useful mode of analysis, playing out on a small scale the broader social processes, with their manifold tensions and contradictions, that lie beneath the surface of events.

Historians did not always heed these dangers, and sometimes even relapsed into a pre-Geertzian ethnography that sentimentalized and reified popular culture as a timeless, bounded system of shared meanings and practices—an evocation of the world, for better, for worse, that we have lost. Such misgivings were at the root of Judt and the Geneveses's criticism of the anthropological turn in history. At the same time, ethnographic strategies promised a better understanding of what Medick termed the "dual constitution of historical processes, the simultaneity of given and produced relationships" or what E. P. Thompson described as the codetermination of social being and social consciousness.[38] More contextually, ethnographic history grew out of a dissatisfaction with the way in which the dominant paradigm of the 1960s and 1970s—social science history—addressed this issue; that is, in terms of the dichotomous categories of objective and subjective processes. Within this framework, the overarching determinants of the past, frequently quantified in terms of economic or demographic indices, defined the terrain in which subjects then responded (and more often than not adapted) to change. What was lost in this mechanical explanation was a sense of how structural forces were handled in cultural terms, experienced in their "structuring." Ethnographic readings of the past offered one route out of this problem.

Two examples from different fields of historical inquiry may suffice to illustrate this point. Let us consider historical demography. In the 1950s, the emergence of historical demography as a discipline had important repercussions for understanding demographic regimes, allowing historians to reappraise the significance of Malthusian perspectives on the past and to grapple with such questions as the age of marriage, prenuptial pregnancies, illegitimacy, and the prevalence of the nuclear family before the advent of the industrial revolution. Yet the findings of historical demography by themselves posed as many problems as they solved. Prenuptial pregnancies could not be usefully interpreted without knowledge of courtship practices, or illegitimacy rates without some knowledge of common law marriages and the sexual politics of households. In England, population growth appeared to be marriage driven rather than to depend upon changes in fertility and nuptiality, but the social meaning of marriage, within and between classes, remained undisclosed. So did that of the family, whose social boundaries and sense of itself were culturally defined. Despite the new angles generated by demographic statistics, their interpretative significance could only be enriched by ethnographic inquiry. More than that, it was only through a combination of ethnographic and demographic data—the qualitative evidence of popular customs and the quantitative reconstruction of life cycles—that historians could begin to broach the question of how productive and reproductive relations were linked and gender relations reconstituted.[39]

As a second example, let us consider the case of collective action or protest, one of the staple features of "history from below." In the pioneering years, historians attempted to open up this subject by exploring the social composition of the crowd and the chronology of disturbance over time. This quantitative endeavor revealed some important negative truths. Crowds were not riffraff, as contemporaries frequently charged. Nor were their inventions neatly synchronized to periods of rapid industrial and urban growth, a fact that undermined sociological theories, drawn from Le Bon, Durkheim, and others, which presupposed that mass unrest was the product of social disequilibrium.[40] Yet important as these findings were, prosopographical and behavioral approaches to the crowd did not by themselves provide compelling explanations of collective action. What was required was a more sensitive appraisal of the language of popular protest and of the cultural conventions within which such interventions were situated. Hence, historians became increasingly interested in the songs, slogans, symbols, and rituals of crowd action and in the sociable settings in which it took place and germinated—such as the festival, the anniversary, the marketplace, the tavern. The decoding of the language and repertoires of collective action required an ethnographic eye and a capacity to read "against the grain"; that is, to make sense of documents recounting popular actions and attitudes that were written by men (and sometimes women) socially distanced from the popular classes themselves and frequently unsympathetic to them. Anthropologists offered some clues as to how this could be done because they were accustomed to observing the informal processes of social interaction, particularly in cultures alien to their own, and to decoding its symbolic universe and its plausible linkages to larger social systems. Such linkages became increasingly important to crowd studies because, as its scholars increasingly came to realize, the ways in which the dominant class sought to solicit consent were as important as the ways in which its rule was challenged. Crowd historians could not afford to wallow in radical subjectivity. They had to address what Wilentz called "those dramas of political expression—sometimes contrived, sometimes spontaneous—that reflect and help determine the boundaries of power."[41] In other words, crowd history could never be the history of the crowd per se. It also had to address both the strategies of containment and the politics of contention, the dialogue between rulers and ruled, the state of play among classes. Considerable headway was made in addressing these problems by bringing anthropological insights into conjunction with the Gramscian concept of hegemony. E. P. Thompson's exploration of plebeian culture in eighteenth-century England is a good case in point.[42]

Ethnography has proved a useful tool, then, in helping social historians interpret the past in ways that recaptured popular experiences and the complexities of historical process. Methodologically, it expanded the range of questions that historians could ask of their sources in their quest for popular experiences. In effect, it refined and expanded the oblique approach to the problems of popular culture, questioning in the process the narrow canons of historical criticism and enquiry propounded by orthodox, neo-Rankeian history, whose emphasis upon the narrative idiom, the particularity of the past, and the visibility of its principal actors, defined the limits of the knowable.[43] What is more, ethnography offered a potential solution to the dichotomous juxtaposition of the objective and subjective dimensions of the past that had informed social science history—one that privileged, through a technological fetishism, those features that alone could be measured.

How far the exchange between history and anthropology has been a two-way process remains a moot point. Commentators in the 1970s and early 1980s were usually of the opinion that historians had drawn more extensively upon anthropology than vice versa, although there were signs that a genuine dialogue was beginning. Development studies were one meeting ground; the reappraisal of culture in terms of the "historically developed forms through which the members of a given society relate to one another" has been another.[44] In this context, both anthropologists and historians have found the concept of hegemony a useful way of tackling the dynamic, processual flow of cultural forms within societies and the ways in which such forms have been inscribed within class-bound fields of force.[45] Indeed, as the illusion of bounded, autonomous, native cultures has become flagrantly untenable in an increasingly integrated world economy, so anthropologists have had to address the historical dimensions of their field of study. And in places such as Ireland, with its deep historical lineage and archival richness, such ventures have genuinely blurred the genres, as the essays in this volume reveal. To be sure, certain differences remain. Anthropologists tend to reference place over time, whereas historians reference time over place. In their exploration of the present, anthropologists also tend to make retrospective forays into the past, thereby stressing continuities rather than change. Field-work, moreover, is self-evidently dialogical in ways that archival research is not, so that the historian's task of listening to his or her subjects is of a somewhat different order—less synesthetic, more logocentric.[46] Unless they are blessed with a particularly loquacious and observant informer, historians have more difficulty determining *how* something was said. Lacking the direct experience of participant observation, they often have to attend to the tropes in the text and the techniques of intertextuality to decipher its meaning. Hence, they might be taken aback by the anthropologist's penchant for the reveal-ing anecdote as a source of structure bearing evidence (what we might call "Mrs. Murphy's aside"[47]), especially when such evidence is sim-ply hearsay.

These ethnographic differences are not, however, insurmountable. In fact, within the last decade, they have become central to the engagement with new developments in linguistic theory that have stressed the materiality of language, its codes, conventions, and dis-cursive strategies. The thrust of this theoretical intervention has been to decenter the importance of human agency in history and to ques-tion whether experience can be adequately recaptured without attend-ing to the ways in which such experiences are embedded in language itself. This antihumanist formulation has also furthered a discernible retreat from the goals of total history. It has fostered a disillusionment with master narratives and a belief that many social histories—in the strategies of their emplotment, in the coherent way in which they *order* the past, in their teleologies—have been mistakenly totalizing. As the right has consolidated itself in power in Western society and as feminism has wrestled with its marginality within existing labor movements (and too often within canonical social history texts), the notion that history—and social history a fortiori—was the handmai-den of social progress has been treated with a new skepticism. There has been a corresponding call for a new aesthetics in social history, a greater sensitivity and reflexivity to language, symbolism, and meta-phor, both in the materials of the past and in the way in which historians construct their own narratives.[48]

It is too early to pronounce upon how permanent this postmodern trend will be or, indeed, whether it will induce a significant abandon-ment of larger explanatory schemas in history.[49] Social history has encouraged a greater awareness of theoretical and methodological differences within the discipline, but it has not produced the paradigmatic warfare that has sometimes made anthropology seem like a "project in intellectual deforestation."[50] In feminist historiography, for example, the field that has thus far been most open to linguistic approaches to the past, particularly to the ways in which gender is constructed in discourse, there has already been a discernible negotiation of postmodern insights without necessarily buying into their absolutisms. Thus Walkowitz, in her recent exploration of sexual danger and upper-class seduction in Britain during the 1880s, adopted a Foucaultian approach to delineate the new discourse on sexuality, but in ways that remained sensitive to the social purchase of new ideas and to the networks in which they were situated. "Material reality," she insisted, always exists as a certain pressure, a destabilizing force on cultural production, forcing representations to be reworked, shored up, reconstructed; and the power of representations derives in good part from the material context in which they appear, from the social spaces where they are enunciated, and from the social and political networks that are organized around them.[51]

This is an important insight, for it forces us to consider cultural production as a dialectical process and a power relation, privileging certain meanings, displacing others, encountering resistance and challenge. Cultural meaning cannot be simply reduced to a linguistic deconstruction of this or that text, or to some narrow form of intertextuality. It is determined by social practices that shape the flow of cultural meanings as much as they are shaped by them. Both anthropologists and historians have much to offer on this score because they have remained attentive to the broader settings in which cultural meaning is reproduced. And they have done so in ways significantly different from those of Foucault: he sought to locate the power of discourse, what he termed *power/knowledge,* in a diffused and decentered field of institutional practices found in such places as the clinic, the prison, and the asylum, and subsequently transposed beyond their boundaries. Anthropological definitions of culture, by contrast, tended to be focused on "belonging" as much as on power and to be more centrally grounded in everyday life—in myth, ritual, work, kinship, and gender relations. Historians, for their part, have developed class-nuanced definitions of culture that were more restrictive in scope but more perspicacious on matters of power. Such definitions have not only been explored in the crucible of popular insurgency and revolutionary upheaval, when the articulations of power are more visible, but in periods of relative stability as well. Through the Gramscian concept of hegemony in particular—those taken-for-granted rules, strategies, and representations that distribute power and influence throughout society and solicit the consent of the subordinate—historians have remained attentive to the structuring of social life in ways that put process and change in the foreground.

Historians and anthropologists can thus add new dimensions to the Foucaultian insight that cultural and discursive formations are crucially related to social practices without endorsing his notion of a complex network of "micropowers" whose effects, in terms of discursive power, permeate every aspect of life. Such an endorsement would jettison structure and agency from history. Yet before this project can proceed, both disciplines will have to attend, perhaps more systematically than they have done to date, to the issues posed by the new literary theory concerning the materiality of language. As LaCapra noted, historians do sometimes "stripmine" texts without attending to the language codes and discourses within which they are situated.[52] Like anthropologists, they sometimes abuse ethnographic authority by ignoring the conditions and the dialogical interplay in which such data were recorded.[53] Culture is not simply out there, in the field or the archive, to be unproblematically reconstructed. Historical and ethnographic facts do not simply disclose themselves; they have to be interrogated, worked up, contextualized. At the same time they are not simply invented, as some postmodernists suggest. They do have determinate properties that exist outside the observer. Historians and anthropologists certainly invest their objects of knowledge with meaning, and their writing strategies, as postmodernists rightly claim, are part of that investment. But it does not follow from this that their enterprise is arbitrary and wholly relativistic, an evocative wordplay of representations upon representations whose limits are only bounded by language itself.

## Conclusion

In the last three decades there has been something of a convergence of interest between social history and anthropology—at the very least a growing fascination among social historians with anthropological perspectives. To be sure, this historical engagement with anthropology has been partial and eclectic, generated in large measure by the desire to recover aspects of the past that had hitherto remained outside or peripheral to the domain of political history. Because of the fragmentary and opaque nature of the sources so frequently used by social historians—particularly with respect to subaltern groups, their customs, beliefs, and rituals—historians looked to ethnography as a means of enriching their understanding of past cultures, discovering their "otherness," and mapping their interrelated configurations. At times, historians replicated the rather holistic, reified concepts of culture that some anthropologists advanced. Without doubt they remained largely innocent of the torrid theoretical debates within anthropology, usually taking their anthropological cues from brokers within their own discipline. Yet in the hands of such historians as E. P. Thompson, Davis, Young, and Isaac, such anthropological insights proved a boon.[54]

Yet the historical appropriation of anthropological perspectives has not been simply a matter of fleshing out the texture of popular history and addressing old problems in new ways. As Medick stressed, ethnographic ways of knowing have also offered a potential solution to the impasse that confronted second-wave social history in its juxtaposition of objective, material, structural factors in history against the subjective, cultural, symbolic ones.[55] This dichotomy was never resolved by orthodox social science history, particularly in its modernizing mode. As enthusiasm for cliometrics waned, historians increasingly turned to the possibilities of recapturing sense and meaning in the past through their public manifestations in the reciprocal but asymmetrical play of social relations. Two inherent dangers have been posed by this shift. One is culturalism, an overconcentration upon the cultural and symbolic aspects of history to the neglect of structural determinants. The other is an inattention to the materiality of language, to the ways in which language is socially constituted and socially constituting. Is, for example, the notion of culture-as-text epistemologically capable of recovering the "native point of view" rather than the competing discourses inscribed in the text itself? Would a more processual notion of culture that emphasized production as much as consumption allow one to recapture the battle for meaning inscribed within competing voices? These problems have not altogether been resolved, but both anthropologists and historians have begun to address them in what is likely to be a continuing rapprochement.

## NOTES

1. Febvre (1973:34).
2. Burguière (1978:206).

3. Thompson (1979:22).
4. Cited by Cohn (1981:232).
5. At a 1977 conference on American Intellectual History, the affinities between history and anthropology were explicitly proclaimed and Geertz was enshrined as the event's patron saint. See Walters (1980:537).
6. Evans-Pritchard (1964:172–91).
7. Evans-Pritchard (1964:190).
8. Braudel (1980:12).
9. Braudel (1980:25–54).
10. Burke (1978b:153).
11. Bloch (1973—first published in French in 1924); Febvre (1982—first published in French in 1942); Febvre (1973:12–26).
12. Vovelle (1973).
13. On this trend, see Burguière (1978).
14. See Braudel (1980:64–82).
15. Morris (1952:i).
16. Hobsbawm (1978:21–48).
17. See Hill (1983:3–14).
18. For a survey of trends in American social history, see Zunz (1985:53–101).
19. Hexter (1955); Perkin (1973:430–55); Stearns (1967:4–5).
20. Thompson (1963).
21. Judt (1979).
22. Fox-Genovese and Genovese (1976).
23. Fox-Genovese and Genovese (1976:215); see also Judt (1979:85).
24. Thompson (1978a:220).
25. Furet (1972:54); Le Roy Ladurie (1979:6).
26. Dawley (1985:22–23).
27. Davis (1981:267–75).
28. See, for example, Thomas (1971).
29. See Thompson (1978a:199–398).
30. Ortner (1984:142).
31. Wolf (1990:586–87).
32. For an interesting commentary on the historical fascination with Geertz, see Walters (1980:537–56). See also Brewer (1976, ch. 9) and Davis (1981:267–75).
33. Philipp (1983:350).
34. Sewell (1980:10).
35. Thompson (1979:18).
36. Geertz (1973:145).
37. For criticisms on this score, see Roseberry (1982:1011–28), Shankman (1984:216–70), and Scholte (1986:5–15).
38. Medick (1987:76); Thompson (1978a:200–1).
39. On these issues, see Gillis (1985), Levine (1987), and Segalen (1985).
40. On these themes, see Rudé (1964) and Tilly et al. (1975).

41. Wilentz (1985:3).

42. Thompson (1974, 1978b).

43. On this issue, see Burke (1976:69–84).

44. The quote is from Wolf, cited by Mintz (1982:505).

45. See Mintz (1982), Rebel (1989), Sider (1986), Thompson (1974, 1978b), and Wolf (1990).

46. On this question, see Fernandez (1988).

47. See the introductory essay by Silverman and Gulliver in this volume, p. 35.

48. See Hunt (1989:21) and Scott (1989:41–62).

49. See Hobsbawm (1980:3–8). Hobsbawm did not see the drift toward microhistory as a necessary abandonment of grand synthesis in historical research or a necessary preference for multicausality over monocausality. He offered these remarks as a response to Stone (1979). For a perceptive critique of the literary turn in social history, see Palmer (1990).

50. Wolf (1990:588).

51. Walkowitz (1989:31).

52. LaCapra (1983:339).

53. See Rosaldo (1986) for a deconstruction of the rhetorical strategies and epistemological assumptions behind two classic texts: Evans-Pritchard's *The Nuer* and Le Roy Ladurie's *Montaillou*.

54. See Davis (1975), Young (1984), and Isaac (1982).

55. Medick (1987).

# References

Abercrombie, N., S. Hill, and B. Turner, eds. 1984. *The Penguin Dictionary of Sociology*. Harmondsworth: Penguin.

Abrams, Philip. 1982. *Historical Sociology*. Ithaca: Cornell University Press.

Abu-Lughod, Janet L. 1989. *Before European Hegemony: The World System A.D. 1250–1350*. New York: Oxford University Press.

Akenson, Donald Harman. 1979. *Between Two Revolutions: Islandmagee, County Antrim 1798–1920*. Port Credit: P. D. Meany.

Almquist, E. L. 1979. "Pre-Famine Ireland and the Theory of European Proto-Industrialization: Evidence from the 1841 Census." *Journal of Economic History* 39:699–718.

Alter, George. 1991. "New Perspectives on European Marriage in the Nineteenth Century." *Journal of Family History* 16:1–5.

Aminzade, Ronald. 1981. *Class, Politics, and Early Industrial Capitalism: A Study of Mid-Nineteenth-Century Toulouse, France*. Albany: State University of New York.

Anderson, Michael. 1971. *Family Structure in Nineteenth Century Lancashire*. Cambridge: Cambridge University.

———. 1988. *Population Change in North-Western Europe, 1750–1850*. Houndmills, Basingstoke: Macmillan.

———. 1990. "The Social Implications of Demographic Change." In F. M. L. Thompson, ed., *The Cambridge Social History of Britain 1750–1950*. Vol. 2: *People and Their Environment*. Cambridge: Cambridge University Press.

Anderson, Perry. 1974a. *Passages from Antiquity to Feudalism*. London: New Left Books.

———. 1974b. *Lineages of the Absolutist State*. London: New Left Books.

Andrews, K. R., N. Canny, and P. E. Hair, eds. 1979. *The Westward Enterprise: English Activities in Ireland, the Atlantic, and America, 1480–1650*. Detroit: Wayne State University Press.

Arensberg, Conrad M. 1988 [1937]. *The Irish Countryman: An Anthropological Study*. Prospect Heights, Ill.: Waveland. Reprint.

Arensberg, Conrad M., and Solon T. Kimball. 1940. *Family and Community in Ireland*. Cambridge, Mass.: Harvard University Press.

Asad, Talal, ed. 1973. *Anthopology and the Colonial Encounter*. London: Ithaca Press.

Assier-Andrieu, Louis. 1981. *Coutume et rapports sociaux: étude anthropologique des communautés paysannes du Capcir*. Paris: Centre National de la Recherche Scientifique.

Augustins, Georges. 1977. "Reproduction sociale et changement social: l'exemple des Baronnies." *Revue Française de Sociologie* 18:465–84.

Badone, Ellen. 1990. *Religious Orthodoxy and Popular Faith in European Society*. Princeton: Princeton University Press.

Bailey, F. G. 1960. *Tribe, Caste, and Nation: A Study of Political Activity and Political Change in Highland Orissa*. Manchester: Manchester University Press.

———. 1963. *Politics and Social Change*. Berkeley: University of California Press.

Banks, J. A. 1989. "From Universal History to Historical Sociology." *British Journal of Sociology* 40:521–43.

Barnard, T. 1975. *Cromwellian Ireland: English Government and Reform in Ireland, 1649–60*. Oxford: Oxford University Press.

Barnes, John. 1951. *Marriage in a Changing Society*. Rhodes-Livingstone paper no. 20. Oxford: Oxford University Press.

———. 1954. *Politics in a Changing Society*. Manchester: Manchester University Press.

Bartrip, Peter. 1985. "Food for the Body and Food for the Mind: The Regulation of Freshwater Fisheries in the 1870s." *Victorian Studies* 28:2.

Bax, Mart. 1975. "On the Increasing Importance of the Small Community in the Irish Political Process." In Jeremy Boissevain and John Friedl, eds., *Beyond the Community: Social Process in Europe*, pp. 134–46. The Hague: Department of Educational Science of the Netherlands.

———. 1976. *Harpstrings and Confessions: Machine-Style Politics in the Irish Republic*. Assen, Netherlands: Van Gorcum.

———. 1987. "Religious Regimes and State Formation: Towards a Research Perspective." *Anthropological Quarterly* 60(1)1–11.

Behar, Ruth. 1986. *Santa María del Monte: The Presence of the Past in a Spanish Village*. Princeton: Princeton University Press.

Bell, D. 1981. "Community Studies: The Social Anthropological Heritage and Its Popularity in Ireland." *International Journal of Sociology and Social Policy* 1(2):22–36.

Belmore, Earl of. 1881. *The History of Two Ulster Manors.* London.

Bendix, Reinhard. 1978. *Kings or People: Power and the Mandate to Rule.* Berkeley: University of California Press.

Béteille, André. 1965. *Caste, Class, and Power: Changing Patterns of Stratification in a Tanjore Village.* Berkeley: University of California Press.

Bew, P., P. Gibbon, and H. Patterson. 1979. *The State in Northern Ireland, 1922–72: Political Forces and Social Classes.* Manchester: Manchester University Press.

Bew, P., E. Hazelkorn, and H. Patterson. 1989. *The Dynamics of Irish Politics.* London: Lawrence and Wishart.

Birdwell-Pheasant, Donna. 1986. "Domestic Process in the Transition from Labor-Flow to Cash-Flow Enterprise in Belize." *Urban Anthropology and Studies of Cultural Systems* 14(3):367–90.

Birnbaum, Norman. 1964. "The Zwinglian Reformation in Zürich." In W. J. Cahnman and Alvin Boskoff, eds., *Sociology and History.* New York: Free Press.

Bishop, T. J. H. 1967. *Winchester and the Public School Elite: A Statistical Analysis.* London: Faber and Faber.

Black, R. D. C. 1960. *Classical Economic Thought and the Irish Question, 1817–1870.* Cambridge: Cambridge University Press.

Bloch, Marc. 1954. *The Historian's Craft.* Manchester: Manchester University.

——. 1973. *The Royal Touch.* London and Montreal: Routledge and Kegan Paul.

Bloch, Maurice. 1986. *From Blessing to Violence: History and Ideology in the Circumcision Ritual of the Merina of Madagascar.* Cambridge: Cambridge University Press.

Blok, Anton. 1969. "Variations in Patronage." *Sociologische Gids* 16(6) 365–77.

——. 1974. *The Mafia of a Sicilian Village, 1860–1960: A Study of Violent Peasant Entrepreneurs.* Oxford: Basil Blackwell.

Bossy, John. 1970. "The Counter-reformation and the People of Catholic Europe." *Past and Present* 47:51–70.

Bottigheimer, Karl S. 1979. "Kingdom and Colony: Ireland in the Westward Enterprise." In K. R. Andrews, N. P. Cann, and P. E. Hair, eds., *The Westward Enterprise: English Activities in Ireland, the Atlantic, and America, 1480–1650,* pp. 45–65. Detroit: Wayne State University Press.

Bourdieu, Pierre. 1972. "Les stratégies matrimoniales dans le système de reproduction." *Annales, E.S.C.* 27:1105–25.

Bowen, John R. 1989. "Narrative Form and Political Incorporation: Changing Uses of History in Aceh, Indonesia." *Comparative Studies in Society and History* 31(4)671–93.

Boyce, D. G. 1987. "Brahmins and Carnivores: The Irish Historian in Great Britain." *Irish Historical Studies* 25(99):225–35.

Boyle, John W. 1988. *The Irish Labour Movement in the Nineteenth Century*. Washington, D.C.: Catholic University Press of America.

Bradshaw, B. 1989. "Nationalism and Historical Scholarship in Modern Ireland." *Irish Historical Studies* 26(104):329–51.

Brady, Ciaran, and Raymond Gillespie. 1986. "Introduction." In Ciaran Brady and Raymond Gillespie, eds., *Natives and Newcomers: The Making of Irish Colonial Society, 1534–1641*. n.p.: Irish Academic Press.

Braudel, Fernand. 1980. *On History*. Chicago: University of Chicago Press.

Braun, Rudolf. 1978. "Early Industrialization and Demographic Change in the Canton of Zurich." In Charles Tilly, ed., *Historical Studies of Changing Fertility*. Princeton: Princeton University.

Breen, Richard. 1982a. "Farm Size and Marital Status: County and Provincial Differences in Arensberg and Kimball's Ireland." *Economic and Social Review* 13(2):89–100.

———. 1982b. "Naming Practices in Western Ireland." *Man* (N.S.) 17: 701–13.

———. 1984a. "Population Trends in Late Nineteenth and Early Twentieth Century Ireland: A Local Study." *Economic and Social Review* 15(2): 95–108.

———. 1984b. "Dowry Payments and the Irish Case." *Comparative Studies in Society and History* 26(2):280–96.

Brennan, M. A. 1985. "The Making of the Protestant Ascendancy in County Kilkenny." Ph.D. dissertation, State University of New York at Stony Brook.

Brenner, Robert. 1976. "Agrarian Class Structure and Economic Development in Pre-Industrial Europe." *Past and Present* 70:30–75.

———. 1985. "The Agrarian Roots of European Capitalism." In T. H. Aston and C. H. E. Philpin, eds., *The Brenner Debate: Agrarian Class Structure and Economic Development in Pre-Industrial Europe*. Cambridge: Cambridge University Press.

Brewer, John. 1976. *Party Ideology and Popular Politics at the Accession of George III*. Cambridge: Cambridge University Press.

Brody, Hugh. 1973. *Inishkillane: Change and Decline in the West of Ireland*. Harmondsworth: Penguin.

Brown, Peter. 1981. *The Cult of the Saints*. Chicago: University of Chicago Press.

Brown, T. 1981. *Ireland: A Social and Cultural History, 1922–79*. Glasgow: Fontana.

Brustein, William. 1988. *The Social Origins of Political Regionalism: France, 1849–1981*. Berkeley: University of California Press.

Buchanan, Ronald. 1970. "Rural Settlement in Ireland." In N. Stephens and R. E. Glasscock, eds., *Irish Geographical Studies*. Belfast: The Queen's University Press.

Buckland, Patrick. 1981. *A History of Northern Ireland*. Dublin: Gill and Macmillan.

Buckley, Anthony. 1989. " 'We're Trying to Find our Identity': Uses of

History Among Ulster Protestants." In Elizabeth Tonkin, Maryon Mc-
Donald, and Malcolm Chapman, eds., *History and Ethnicity*. ASA Monographs 27:183–97. London: Routledge.

Bufwack, Mary. 1982. *Village Without Violence: An Examination of a Northern
Irish Community*. Cambridge, Mass.: Schenkman.

Burguière, André. 1978. "The New *Annales:* A Redefinition of the Late
1960s." *Review* 1:195–205.

Burke, Peter. 1976. "Oblique Approaches to the History of Popular Culture." In C. W. E. Bigsby, ed., *Approaches to Popular Culture*. London:
Edward Arnold.

———. 1978a. *Popular Culture in Early Modern Europe*. New York: New
York University Press.

———. 1978b. "Reflections on the Historical Revolution in France: The
*Annales* School and British Social History." *Review* 1:147–56.

———. 1980. *Sociology and History*. London: George Allen and Unwin.

Burke, W. P. 1907. *History of Clonmel*. Waterford.

Burtchaell, J. 1988. "The South Kilkenny Farm Villages." In W. J. Smyth
and K. Whelan, eds., *Common Ground: Essays on the Historical Geography of
Ireland*. Cork: Cork University Press.

Butel, P., and L. M. Cullen, eds. 1986. *Cities and Merchants: French and
Irish Perspectives on Urban Development, 1500–1900*. Dublin: Trinity College.

Calhoun, Craig. 1982. *The Question of Class Struggle: Social Foundations of
Popular Radicalism During the Industrial Revolution*. Chicago: University of
Chicago Press.

Canny, Nicholas. 1976. *The Elizabethan Conquest of Ireland: A Pattern Established, 1565–76*. Sussex: Harvester Press.

———. 1988. *Kingdom and Colony: Ireland in the Atlantic World, 1560–1800*.
Baltimore: Johns Hopkins University Press.

Canny, Nicholas, and Anthony Pagden, eds. 1987. *Colonial Identity in the
Atlantic World, 1500–1800*. Princeton: Princeton University Press.

Carney, Francis J. 1980. "Household Size and Structure in Two Areas of
Ireland, 1821 and 1911." In L. Cullen and F. Furet, eds., *Ireland and France,
17th–20th Centuries: Towards a Comparative Study of Rural History*. Ann
Arbor, Mich.: UMI Monograph Publishing.

Carrigan, W. 1905. *The History and Antiquities of the Diocese of Ossory*. 4 vols.
Dublin: Sealy, Bryers, and Walker.

Carroll, M. P. 1992. *Madonnas that Maim: Popular Catholicism in Italy Since the
Fifteenth Century*. Baltimore: Johns Hopkins University Press.

Carty, R. K. 1981. *Party and Parish Pump: Electoral Politics in Ireland*. Water-
loo, Ontario: Wilfred Laurier University Press.

Casey, James. 1989. *The History of the Family*. Oxford: Blackwell.

Census of Ireland. 1841. Dublin: Public Record Office.

Chapman, Malcolm, Maryon McDonald, and Elizabeth Tonkin. 1989. "Introduction." In Elizabeth Tonkin, Maryon McDonald, and Malcolm
Chapman, eds., *History and Ethnicity*, pp. 1–21. London: Routledge.

Christian, William A., Jr. 1972. *Person and God in a Spanish Valley*. New York: Seminar Press.

———. 1981. *Local Religion in 16th Century Spain*. Princeton: Princeton University Press.

Chubb, Basil. 1982. *The Government and Politics of Ireland*. 2d ed. London: Longman.

Clark, Samuel. 1979. *Social Origins of the Irish Land War*. Princeton: Princeton University Press.

———. 1984. "Nobility, Bourgeoisie, and the Industrial Revolution in Belgium." *Past and Present* 105:140–75.

———. 1988. "Landlord Domination in Nineteenth-Century Ireland." In *UNESCO Yearbook on Peace and Conflict Studies, 1986*. New York: Greenwood.

Clark, S. D. 1942. *The Social Development of Canada*. Toronto: University of Toronto Press.

——— 1948. *Church and Sect in Canada*. Toronto: University of Toronto Press.

———. 1962. *The Developing Canadian Community*. Toronto: University of Toronto Press.

Clarke, A. 1976. "The Irish Economy, 1600–60." In T. W. Moody, F. X. Martin, and J. Byrne, eds., *A New History of Ireland*. Vol. 3: *Early Modern Ireland, 1534–1691*. Oxford: Oxford University Press.

Claverie, Elisabeth and Pierre Lamaison. 1982. *L'impossible mariage: violence et parenté en Gévaudan, XVII^e, XVIII^e, et XIX^e siècles*. Paris: Hachette.

Clements, Lord, M.P. 1838. *The Present Poverty of Ireland*. London: Charles Knight.

Clifford, James and George E. Marcus. 1984. *Writing Culture: The Poetics and Politics of Ethnography*. Berkeley: University of California Press.

Coakley, John 1980. "Independence Movements and National Minorities: Some Parallels in the European Experience." *European Journal of Political Research* 8:215–47.

———. 1982. "National Territories and Cultural Frontiers: Conflicts of Principle in the Formation of States in Europe." *West European Politics* 5(4): 34–49.

———. 1986. "Political Succession and Regime Change in New States in Inter-war Europe: Ireland, Finland, Czechoslovakia, and the Baltic States." *European Journal of Political Research* 14:187–206.

Coale, A. J. and Roy Treadway 1986. "A Summary of the Changing Distribution of Overall Fertility, Marital Fertility, and the Proportion Married in the Provinces of Europe." In A. J. Coale and Susan Cotts Watkins, eds., *The Decline of Fertility in Europe*. Princeton: Princeton University Press.

Cohen, Abner. 1965. *Arab Border Villages in Israel*. Manchester: Manchester University Press.

Cohen, Anthony P. 1982. *Belonging: Identity and Social Organisation in British Rural Cultures*. Newfoundland: Memorial University Press.

————. 1987. *Whalsay: Symbol, Segment, and Boundary in a Shetland Island Community*. Manchester: Manchester University Press.

Cohn, Bernard S. 1981. "Anthropology and History in the 1980s." *Journal of Interdisciplinary History* 12:227–52.

————. 1987a [1962]. "An Anthropologist Among the Historians: A Field Study." In Bernard S. Cohn, *An Anthropologist Among the Historians and Other Essays*, pp. 1–17. Delhi: Oxford University Press.

————. 1987b [1980]. "History and Anthropology: The State of Play." In Bernard S. Cohn, *An Anthropologist Among the Historians and Other Essays*, pp. 18–49. Delhi: Oxford University Press.

————. 1987c [1981]. "Anthropology and History in the 1980s." In Bernard S. Cohn, *An Anthropologist Among the Historians and Other Essays*, pp. 50–77. Delhi: Oxford University Press.

Cole, John W., and Eric R. Wolf. 1974. *The Hidden Frontier, Ecology, and Ethnicity in an Alpine Valley*. New York: Academic Press.

Collard, Anna. 1989. "Investigating 'Social Memory' in a Greek Context." In Elizabeth Tonkin, Maryon McDonald, and Malcolm Chapman, eds., *History and Ethnicity*. ASA Monographs 27:89–103. London: Routledge.

Comaroff, Jean. 1985. *Body of Power, Spirit of Resistance: The Culture and History of a South African People*. Chicago: University of Chicago Press.

Comerford, R. V. 1988. "Political Myths in Modern Ireland." The Princess Grace Memorial Library, ed., *Irishness in a Changing Society*, pp. 1–17. Gerrards Cross: Colin Smythe.

Commissioners for Publishing the Ancient Laws and Institutes of Ireland. 1865. *Senchus Mor, the Ancient Laws of Ireland*, vols. 1–4. Dublin: Alexander Thom.

Comninel, G. C. 1987. *Rethinking the French Revolution: Marxism and the Revisionist Challenge*. London: Verso.

————. Forthcoming. "English Feudalism and the Origins of Capitalism."

Connell, Kenneth H. 1962. "Peasant Marriage in Ireland: Its Structure and Development Since the Famine." *Economic History Review* 14:502–23.

Connolly, Sean. 1982. *Priests and People in Pre-Famine Ireland*. Dublin: Gill and Macmillan.

Cook, Scott B. 1987. "The Irish Raj: Social Origins and Careers of Irishmen in the Indian Civil Service, 1855–1914." *Journal of Social History* 20(3): 507–29.

Corrigan, Philip, and Derek Sayer. 1985. *The Great Arch: English State Formation as Cultural Revolution*. Oxford: Basil Blackwell.

Cosgrove, Art, ed. 1987. *A New History of Ireland*. Vol. 2: *Medieval Ireland, 1169–1534*. Oxford: Clarendon Press.

Cresswell, Robert. 1969. *Une communauté rurale de l'Irlande*. Paris: Institut d'Ethnologie, Musée de l'Homme.

Crotty, Raymond D. 1966. *Irish Agricultural Production: Its Volume and Structure*. Cork: Cork University Press.

————. 1986. *Ireland in Crisis: A Study in Capitalist Colonial Development*. Dingle, Ireland: Brandon.

Cullen, L. M. 1972. *An Economic History of Ireland Since 1660.* London: Batsford.

Curtin, Chris, and Thomas M. Wilson, eds. 1989. *Ireland from Below: Social Change and Local Communities.* Galway: Galway University Press.

Curtis, E., ed. 1932–43. *Calendar of Ormond Deeds.* 6 vols. Dublin: Irish Manuscripts Commission.

d'Argemir, Dolors Comas. 1988. "Household, Family and Social Stratification: Inheritance and Labor Strategies in a Catalan Village (Nineteenth and Twentieth Centuries)." *Journal of Family History* 13:143–63.

Daly, Mary E. 1986. *The Famine in Ireland.* Dublin: Dundalgan Press.

Davis, John. 1989. "The Social Relations of the Production of History." In Elizabeth Tonkin, Maryon McDonald, and Malcolm Chapman, eds., *History and Ethnicity.* ASA Monographs 27:104–20. London: Routledge.

Davis, Natalie. 1975. *Society and Culture in Early Modern France.* Stanford: Stanford University Press.

———. 1981. "Anthropology and History in the 1980s." *Journal of Interdisciplinary History* 12:267–75.

———. 1987. *Fiction in the Archives. Pardon Tales and Their Tellers in Sixteenth Century France.* Stanford: Stanford University Press.

Dawley, Alan. 1985. "A Fable of the Bees: In Reply to Tilly." *International and Working-Class History* 27:20–25.

Dening, Greg. 1980. *Islands and Beaches: Discourse on a Silent Land—Marquesas, 1774–1880.* Chicago: Dorsey Press.

Dickson, David. 1987. *New Foundations: Ireland, 1660–1800.* Dublin: Helicon.

Dickson, D., C. Ó Gráda, and S. Daultrey. 1982. "Hearth Tax, Household Size and Irish Population Change, 1672–1821." *Royal Irish Academy Proceedings* 82C(6):125–82.

Donham, Donald L. 1990. *History, Power, Ideology: Central Issues in Marxism and Anthopology.* Cambridge: Cambridge University Press.

Donnelly, J. S. 1975. *The Land and People of Nineteenth Century Cork.* London: Routledge.

Douglass, William A. 1988a. "The Basque Stem Family Household: Myth or Reality?" *Journal of Family History* 13:75–89.

———. 1988b. "Iberian Family History." *Journal of Family History* 13:1–12.

Doyle, David. 1981. *Ireland, Irishmen, and Revolutionary America, 1760–1820.* Cork: Mercier Press.

Drudy, P. J. 1982. "Land, People, and the Regional Problem in Ireland." In P. J. Drudy, ed., *Ireland: Land, Politics, and People* (Irish Studies 2), pp. 191–216. Cambridge: Cambridge University Press.

Eipper, Chris. 1986. *The Ruling Trinity: A Community Study of Church, State, and Business in Ireland.* Aldershot: Gower.

Eisenstadt, S. N. 1963. *The Political Systems of Empires.* New York: Free Press.

———. 1968. *The Protestant Ethic and Modernization: A Comparative View.* New York: Basic Books.

Elias, Norbert. 1978 [1939]. *The Civilizing Process: Sociogenetic and Psychoge-*

*netic Investigations.* Vol. 1: *The Development of Manners: Changes in the Code of Conduct and Feeling in Early Modern Times.* New York: Urizen. Reprint.

———. 1982 [1939]. *The Civilizing Process: Sociogenetic and Psychogenetic Investigations.* Vol. 2: *State Formation and Civilization.* Oxford: Basil Blackwell. Reprint.

———. 1983. *The Court Society.* Oxford: Basil Blackwell.

Elliott, Bruce S. 1988. *Irish Migrants in the Canadas: A New Approach.* Belfast: Institute of Irish Studies.

Elliott, Marianne. 1982. *Partners in Revolution: The United Irishmen and France.* New Haven: Yale University Press.

Ellis, S. G. 1986. "Nationalist Historiography and the English and Gaelic Worlds in the Late Middle Ages." *Irish Historical Studies* 25(97):1–18.

Empey, C. 1971. "The Butler Lordship in Ireland." Doctoral dissertation, Trinity College, Dublin.

Ennew, Judith. 1980. *The Western Isles Today.* Cambridge: Cambridge University Press.

Evans, Estyn. 1964. "Ireland and Atlantic Europe." *Geographische Zeitschrift* 52:224–41.

———. 1981. *The Personality of Ireland: Habitat, Heritage, and History,* rev. ed. Cambridge: Cambridge University Press.

Evans-Pritchard, E. E. 1949. *The Sanusi of Cyrenaica.* Oxford: Clarendon Press.

———. 1951. *Kinship and Marriage Among the Nuer.* Oxford: Clarendon Press.

———. 1961. *Anthropology and History.* Manchester: Manchester University Press.

———. 1962. "Social Anthropology: Past and Present." In E. E. Evans-Pritchard, *Essays in Social Anthropology.* London: Faber and Faber.

———. 1964. *Social Anthropology and Other Essays.* New York: Free Press of Glencoe.

F. K. P. 1853. "The Peasant at the Shrine." *Duffy's Fireside Reader* 3:320.

Fallers, L. A. 1956. *Bantu Bureaucracy.* Cambridge: Heffer.

———. 1967 [1961]. "Are African Cultivators to Be Called 'Peasants'?" In Jack M. Potter, May N. Diaz, and George M. Foster, eds., *Peasant Society: A Reader,* pp. 35–41. Boston: Little, Brown.

Fanning, Ronan. 1983. *Independent Ireland.* Dublin: Helicon.

———. 1988. "The U.C.D. Debate: (a) The Meaning of Revisionism." *Irish Review* 4:15–19.

Farrell, Michael. 1976. *Northern Ireland: The Orange State.* London: Pluto Press.

Farriss, Nancy M. 1987. "Remembering the Future, Anticipating the Past: History, Time, and Cosmology Among the Maya of Yucatan." *Comparative Studies in Society and History* 29(3):566–93.

Febvre, Lucien. 1973. *A New Kind of History and Other Essays.* New York: Harper & Row.

————. 1982. *The Problem of Unbelief in the Sixteenth Century.* Cambridge, Mass.: Harvard University Press.

Feingold, W. L. 1984. *The Revolt of the Peasantry: The Transformation of Local Government in Ireland, 1872–1886.* Boston: Northeastern University Press.

Fennell, Desmond. 1988. "The U.C.D. Debate: (b) Against Revisionism." *Irish Review* 4:20–26.

Fernandez, James. 1988. "Historians Tell Tales: Of Cartesian Cats and Gallic Cockfights." *Journal of Modern History* 60:113–27.

————. 1990. "Enclosures: Boundary Maintenance and Its Representations Over Time in Asturian Mountain Villages (Spain)." In Emiko Ohnuki-Tierney, ed., *Culture Through Time: Anthropological Approaches.* Stanford: Stanford University Press.

Fieldhouse, D. K. 1981. *Colonialism, 1870–1945: An Introduction.* London: Weidenfeld and Nicolson.

Fienup-Riordan, Ann. 1988. "Robert Redford, Apanuugpak, and the Invention of Tradition." *American Ethnologist* 15(3)442–55.

Finley, M. I. 1976. "Colonies: An Attempt at a Typology." *Transactions of the Royal Historical Society* 26:167–88.

Firth, Raymond. 1951. *Elements of Social Organization.* London: Watts.

Fitzpatrick, David. 1977. *Politics and Irish Life.* Dublin.

————. 1982. "Class, Family and Rural Unrest in Nineteenth Century Ireland." In P. J. Drudy, ed., *Ireland: Land, Politics, and People* (Irish Studies 2). Cambridge: Cambridge University Press.

————. 1983. "Irish Farming Families Before the First World War." *Comparative Studies in Society and History* 25:339–74.

Flatrès, Pierre. 1957. *Géographie rurale de quatres contrées celtiques.* Rennes.

Ford, Alan. 1985. *The Protestant Reformation in Ireland, 1590–1641.* Frankfurt: Verlag Peter Lang.

Foster, George M.. 1967. "Introduction: What Is a Peasant?" In Jack M. Potter, May N. Diaz, and George M. Foster, eds., *Peasant Society: A Reader,* pp. 2–14. Boston: Little, Brown.

Foster, Roy. 1986. "We Are All Revisionists Now." *Irish Review* 1:1–5.

————. 1988. *Modern Ireland, 1600–1972.* Harmondsworth: Penguin.

Foucault, Michel. 1972. *The Archaeology of Knowledge.* New York: Pantheon.

Fox, Robin. 1967. *Kinship and Marriage: An Anthropological Perspective.* Cambridge: Cambridge University Press.

————. 1978. *The Tory Islanders: A People of the Celtic Fringe.* Cambridge: Cambridge University Press.

Fox-Genovese, Elizabeth, and Eugene D. Genovese. 1976. "The Political Crisis of Social History." *Journal of Social History* 10:205–20.

Frame, Robin. 1981. *Colonial Ireland.* Dublin: Helicon.

Friedrich, Paul. 1970. *Agrarian Revolt in a Mexican Village.* Englewood Cliffs, N.J.: Prentice-Hall.

Frykman, Jonas, and Orvar Löfgren. 1987. *Culture Builders: A Historical Anthropology of Middle-Class Life.* New Brunswick: Rutgers University Press.

Fulbrook, Mary. 1983. *Piety and Politics: Religion and the Rise of Absolutism in England, Württemberg, and Prussia.* Cambridge: Cambridge University Press.

Furet, François. 1972. "Quantitative History." In Felix Gilbert and Stephen R. Graubard, eds., *Historical Studies Today.* New York: W. W. Norton.

Garvin, Tom. 1981. *The Evolution of Irish Nationalist Politics.* Dublin: Gill and Macmillan.

———. 1987. *Nationalist Revolutionaries in Ireland, 1858–1928.* Oxford: Clarendon Press.

Gaunt, David. 1987. "Rural Household Organization and Inheritance in Northern Europe." *Journal of Family History* 12:121–41.

Geertz, Clifford. 1973. *The Interpretation of Cultures.* New York: Basic Books.

———. 1983. *Local Knowledge: Further Essays in Interpretative Anthropology.* New York: Basic Books.

Gellner, Ernest. 1983. *Nations and Nationalism.* Ithaca: Cornell University Press.

———. 1988. *Plough, Sword, and Book: The Structure of Human History.* London: Collins Harvill.

Gibbon, Peter. 1973. "Arensberg and Kimball Revisited" (a review of H. Brody, *Inishkillane: Change and Decline in the West of Ireland*). *Economy and Society* 2(4):479–98.

———. 1975a. *The Origins of Ulster Unionism: The Formation of Popular Protestant Politics and Ideology in Nineteenth-Century Ireland.* Manchester: Manchester University Press.

———. 1975b. "Colonialism and the Great Starvation in Ireland, 1845–49." *Race and Class* 17(2)131–39.

Gibbon, Peter, and Chris Curtin. 1978. "The Stem Family in Ireland." *Comparative Studies in Society and History* 20:429–53.

Gibbon, Peter, and M. D. Higgins. 1974. "Patronage, Tradition, and Modernization: The Case of the Irish 'Gombeenman.' " *Economic and Social Review* 6:27–44.

Gillespie, Raymond. 1985. *Colonial Ulster: The Settlement of East Ulster, 1600–1641.* Cork: Cork University Press.

Gillis, A. R. 1989. "Crime and State Surveillance in Nineteenth-Century France." *American Journal of Sociology* 95:307–41.

Gillis, John. 1985. *For Better, for Worse: British Marriages 1600 to the Present.* New York: Oxford University Press.

Gillmor, Desmond A. 1967. "The Agricultural Regions of the Republic of Ireland." *Irish Geography* 5:245–61.

Ginzburg, Carlo. 1980. *The Cheese and the Worms.* Translated by John Tedeschi and Anne Tedeschi. Baltimore: Johns Hopkins University Press.

Glass, D. V. 1938. *Changes in Fertility in England and Wales, 1851 to 1931.* New York: Hogben.

Glassie, Henry. 1983. *Passing the Time in Ballymenone.* Philadelphia: University of Pennsylvania Press.

Godelier, Maurice. 1966. *Rationalité et irrationalité en économie.* Paris: Maspero.

———. 1967. "La notion de mode de production asiatique et les schémas

Marxistes d'évolution des sociétés." In R. Garaudy, ed., *Sur le mode de production asiatique*. Paris.

Goldschmidt, Walter, and Evalyn Jakobson Kunkel. 1971. "The Structure of the Peasant Family." *American Anthropologist* 73:1058–70.

Goldstone, J. A. 1986a. "The Demographic Revolution in England: A Reexamination." *Population Studies* 49:5–33.

———. 1986b. "State Breakdown in the English Revolution: A New Synthesis." *American Journal of Sociology* 92:257–322.

Goody, Jack. 1983. *The Development of the Family and Marriage in Europe*. Cambridge: Cambridge University Press.

Goody, Jack, ed. 1958. *The Developmental Cycle in Domestic Groups*. Cambridge: Cambridge University Press.

Gough, Kathleen. 1968. "Anthropology: Child of Imperialism." *Monthly Review* (April).

———. 1981. *Rural Society in Southeast India*. Cambridge: Cambridge University Press.

Gould, Julius and William J. Kolb, eds. 1964. *A Dictionary of the Social Sciences*. New York: Free Press.

Gould, Mark. 1987. *Revolution in the Development of Capitalism: The Coming of the English Revolution*. Berkeley: University of California Press.

Gray, R., and P. H. Gulliver, eds. 1964. *The Family Estate in Africa*. London: Routledge and Kegan Paul.

Guinnane, Timothy. 1991. "Rethinking the Western European Marriage Pattern: The Decision to Marry in Ireland at the Turn of the Twentieth Century." *Journal of Family History* 16:47–64.

Gullickson, G. L. 1982. "Proto-industrialization, Demographic Behaviour, and the Sexual Division of Labour in Auffay, France, 1750–1850." *Peasant Studies* 9:106–118.

Gulliver, P. H. 1955a. *Labour Migration in a Rural Economy*. Kampala: East African Institute of Social Research.

———. 1955b. *The Family Herds: A Study of Two Pastoral Tribes in East Africa*. London: Routledge & Kegan Paul.

———. 1958. *Land Tenure and Social Change Among the Nyakusa*. Kampala: East African Insitute of Social Research.

———. 1963. *Social Control in an African Society*. London: Routledge and Kegan Paul.

———. 1969. *Tradition and Transition in East Africa: Studies in the Tribal Factor in the Modern Era*. London: Routledge and Kegan Paul.

———. 1971. *Neighbors and Networks: The Idiom of Kinship Among the Ndendeuli*. Berkeley: University of California Press.

———. 1989. "Doing Anthropological Research in Rural Ireland: Methods and Sources for Linking the Past and the Present." In Chris Curtin and T. M. Wilson, eds., *Ireland from Below: Social Change and Local Communities*. Galway: Galway University Press.

Gulliver, P. H., and Marilyn Silverman. 1990. "Social Life and Local Meaning: 'Thomastown,' County Kilkenny." In William Nolan and Kevin

Whelan, eds., *Kilkenny: History and Society*. Dublin: Geography Publications.

Gutmann, M. P. 1987. "Proto-industrialization and Marriage Ages in Eastern Belgium." *Annales de démographie historique*, pp. 143–73.

———. 1988. *Toward the Modern Economy: Early Industry in Europe, 1500–1800*. Philadelphia: Temple University Press.

Guttsman, W. L. 1963. *The British Political Elite*. New York: Basic Books.

Hajnal, J. 1965. "European Marriage Patterns in Perspective." In D. V. Glass and D. E. C. Eversley, eds., *Population in History: Essays in Historical Demography*. Chicago: Aldine.

———. 1982. "Two Kinds of Pre-industrial Household Formation System." In R. Wall, J. Robin, and P. Laslett, eds., *Family Forms in Historic Europe*, pp. 65–104. Cambridge: Cambridge University Press.

Hall, J. A. 1986. *Powers and Liberties: The Causes and Consequences of the Rise of the West*. Harmondsworth: Penguin.

Hammel, E. A. 1978. "The Income of Hilander: A Statistical Exploration." In Kenneth Wachter with Eugene A. Hammel and Peter Laslett, *Statistical Studies of Historical Social Structure*, pp. 137–52. New York: Academic Press.

———. 1984. "On the ✱✱✱ of Studying Household Form and Function." In Robert McC. Netting, Richard R. Wilk, and Eric J. Arnoud, eds., *Households: Comparative and Historical Studies of the Domestic Group*, pp. 29–43. Berkeley: University of California Press.

Hannan, Damian. 1979. *Displacement and Development: Class, Kinship and Social Change in Irish Rural Communities*. Dublin: Economic and Social Research Institute.

———. 1982. "Peasant Models and the Understanding of Social and Cultural Change in Rural Ireland." In P. J. Drudy, ed., *Ireland: Land, Politics, and People* (Irish Studies 2), pp. 141–65. Cambridge: Cambridge University Press.

Hansen, Karen Tranberg. 1989. *Distant Companions: Servants and Employers in Zambia, 1900–1985*. Ithaca: Cornell University Press.

Hardinge, W. H. 1866. "The Civil War in Ireland, 1641–1652." *Royal Irish Academy Transactions* 24(7):379–420.

Harkness, D. 1983. *Northern Ireland Since 1920*. Dublin: Helicon.

Harris, Rosemary. 1972. *Prejudice and Tolerance in Ulster: A Study of Neighbours and "Strangers" in a Border Community*. Manchester: Manchester University Press.

———. 1988. "Theory and Evidence: The 'Irish Stem Family' and Field Data." *Man* (N.S.) 23(3)417–34.

Hastrup, Kirsten. 1990. *Nature and Policy in Iceland, 1400–1800: An Anthropological Analysis of History and Mentality*. Oxford: Clarendon Press.

Hay, Douglas. 1975. "Property, Authority, and the Criminal Law." In D. Hay et al., *Albion's Fatal Tree: Crime and Society in Eighteenth Century England*. New York: Pantheon Books.

Healy, John. 1968. *The Death of an Irish Town*. Cork: Mercier.

Hechter, Michael. 1975. *Internal Colonialism: The Celtic Fringe in British National Development, 1536–1966*. London: Routledge and Kegan Paul.

Hedley, Max. 1979. "Domestic Commodity Production: Small Farmers in Alberta." In David H. Tuner and Gavin A. Smith, eds., *Challenging Anthropology*. Toronto: McGraw-Hill Ryerson.

Heiberg, Marianne. 1989. *The Making of the Basque Nation*. Cambridge: Cambridge University Press.

Herzfeld, Michael. 1987. *Anthropology Through the Looking-Glass: Critical Ethnography in the Margins of Europe*. Cambridge: Cambridge University Press.

Heslinga, M. 1979. *The Irish Border as a Cultural Divide: A Contribution to the Study of Regionalism in the British Isles*. Assen, Netherlands: Van Gorcum.

Hewitt, Margaret. 1958. *Wives and Mothers in Victorian Industry*. London: Rockliff.

Hexter, J. H. 1955. "A New Framework for Social History." *Journal of Economic History* 15:415–26.

Hill, Christopher et al. 1983. "Origins and Early Years." *Past and Present* 100:3–14.

Hobsbawm, Eric. 1978. "The Historians Group of the Communist Party." In Maurice Cornforth, ed., *Rebels and Their Causes. Essays in Honour of A. L. Morton*. London: Lawrence and Wishart.

———. 1980. "The Revival of Narrative: Some Comments." *Past and Present* 86:3–8.

———. 1983. "Mass-Producing Traditions: Europe, 1870–1914." In E. Hobsbawn and Terence Ranger, eds., *The Invention of Tradition*, pp. 263–307. Cambridge: Cambridge University Press.

———. 1990. "Escaped Slaves of the Forest." *New York Review of Books* 37(19):46–47.

Holmes, Douglas R. 1983. "A Peasant-Worker Model in a Northern Italian Context." *American Ethnologist* 10(4):734–48.

Holton, R. J. 1985. *The Transition from Feudalism to Capitalism*. Houndmills, Hampshire: Macmillan.

Holy, Ladislav, ed. 1987. *Comparative Anthropology*. Oxford: Basil Blackwell.

Homans, G. C. 1941. *English Villagers of the Thirteenth Century*. New York: Russell and Russell.

Hoppen, K. Theodore. 1979. "National Politics and Local Realities in Mid-nineteenth Century Ireland." In A. Cosgrove and D. McCartney, *Studies in Irish History*. Dublin: University College.

———. 1984. *Elections, Politics, and Society in Ireland, 1832–1885*. Oxford: Clarendon Press.

———. 1989. *Ireland Since 1800: Conflict and Conformity*. London: Longman.

Hoskins, Janet. 1987. "The Headhunter as Hero: Local Traditions and Their Reinterpretation in National History." *American Ethnologist* 14(4)605–22.

Hosp, Edward. 1960. "First Redemptorist Missions in Ireland." *Spicileqium Historicum* 7(2):453–85.

Houston, Cecil J., and William J. Smyth. 1980. *The Sash Canada Wore: An*

*Historical Geography of the Orange Order in Canada*. Toronto: University of Toronto Press.

Hudson, Charles. 1973. "The Historical Approach in Anthropology." In J. J. Honigmann,, ed., *Handbook of Social and Cultural Anthropology*. Chicago: Rand McNally.

Hughes, T. Jones. 1963. "Regionalism in Ireland." In P. O'Flanagan, P. Ferguson, and K. Whelan, eds., *Rural Ireland*, pp. 65–71. Cork: Cork Univrsity Press.

———. 1987. "Landholding and Settlement in the Counties of Meath and Cavan in the Nineteenth Century." In P. O'Flanagan, P. Ferguson, and K. Whelan, eds., *Rural Ireland: Modernisation and Change*, pp. 104–46. Cork: Cork University Press.

Hunt, Lynn, ed. 1989. *The New Cultural History*. Berkeley: University of California Press.

Inden, Ronald B. 1976. *Marriage and Rank in Bengali Culture: A History of Caste and Clan in Middle Period Bengal*. Berkeley: University of California Press.

Inglis, Tom. 1987. *Moral Monopoly: The Catholic Church in Modern Irish Society*. Dublin: Gill and Macmillan.

Irish Reports (Common Law Series) 1867. *Murphy v. Ryan*, pp. 143–55.

Isaac, Rhys. 1982. *The Transformation of Virginia, 1740–1790*. Chapel Hill: University of North Carolina Press.

James, Frederick G. 1973. *Ireland in the Empire, 1688–1770*. Cambridge, Mass.: Harvard University Press.

Jenkins, David. 1971. *The Agricultural Community in South-West Wales at the Turn of the Twentieth Century*. Cardiff: University of Wales.

Judt, Tony. 1979. "A Clown in Regal Purple: Social History and the Historians." *History Workshop* 7:66–94.

Kahn, Joel S. 1980. *Minangkabau Social Formations: Indonesian Peasants and the World Economy*. Cambridge: Cambridge University Press.

Kane, Eileen. 1977. *The Last Place God Made: Traditional Economy and New Industry in Rural Ireland*. 4 vols. New Haven: Human Relations Area Files.

Kearney, Hugh. 1989. *The British Isles: A History of Four Nations*. Cambridge: Cambridge University Press.

Keenan, Desmond. 1983. *The Catholic Church in Nineteenth-Century Ireland: A Sociological Study*. Dublin: Gill and Macmillan.

Kenealy, Mary. 1978. "Finn's Leinster Journal." *Old Kilkenny Review* 7:5.

Kennedy, Kieran, Thomas Giblin, and Deirdre McHugh. 1988. *The Economic Development of Ireland in the Twentieth Century*. London: Routledge.

Kennedy, L. 1983. "Farmers, Traders and Agricultural Politics in Pre-independence Ireland." In S. Clark and J. S. Donnelly, eds., *Irish Peasants, Violence and Political Unrest, 1780–1914*. Madison: University of Wisconsin Press.

Kennedy, Robert E., Jr. 1973. *The Irish: Emigration, Marriage, and Fertility*. Berkeley: University of California Press.

Kerry County Committee of Agriculture. 1972. *County Kerry Agricultural Resource Survey*. Tralee.

Kertzer, David I. 1984. *Family Life in Central Italy, 1880–1910*. New Brunswick, N.J.: Rutgers University Press.

——. 1989. "The Joint Family Household Revisited: Demographic Constraints and Household Complexity in the European Past." *Journal of Family History* 14:1–15.

Kertzer, David I., and Caroline Brettell. 1987. "Advances in Italian and Iberian Family History." *Journal of Family History* 12:87–120.

*Kilkenny Journal and Leinster Commercial and Literary Advertiser*, 1834–80.

*Kilkenny Moderator*, 1829–84.

Kimmel, M. S. 1988. *Absolutism and Its Discontents: State and Society in Seventeenth Century France and England*. New Brunswick, N.J.: Transaction Books.

Kiser, Edgar, and Michael Hechter. 1991. "The Role of General Theory in Comparative-Historical Sociology." *American Journal of Sociology* 97:1–30.

Kolbert, C. F., and T. O'Brien. 1975. *Land Reform in Ireland: A Legal History of the Irish Land Problem and Its Settlement*. Cambridge: Department of Land Economy, Cambridge University.

Kottak, Conrad Philip. 1980. *The Past in the Present: History, Ecology, and Cultural Variation in Highland Madagascar*. Ann Arbor: University of Michigan Press.

LaCapra, Dominick. 1983. *Rethinking Intellectual History: Texts, Contexts, Language*. Ithaca: Cornell University Press.

Lachmann, Richard. 1987. *From Manor to Market: Structural Change in England, 1536–1640*. Madison: University of Wisconsin Press.

——. 1989. "Elite Conflict and State Formation in 16th- and 17th-Century England and France." *American Sociological Review* 54:141–62.

——. 1990. "An Elite Conflict Theory of the Transition to Capitalism." *American Sociological Review* 55:398–414.

Laffan, T. 1911. *Tipperary Families: Being the Hearth Money Records for 1665–6–7*. Dublin.

Lamaison, Pierre. 1979. "Les stratégies matrimoniales dans un système complexe de parenté: Ribennes en Gévaudan, 1650–1830." *Annales: E.S.C.* 34:721–43.

Lamphere, Louise. 1987. *From Working Daughters to Working Mothers: Immigrant Women in a New England Industrial Community*. Ithaca: Cornell University Press.

Lan, David. 1985. *Guns and Rain: Guerillas and Spirit Mediums in Zimbabwe*. Berkeley: University of California Press.

Land League. n.d. Documents in National Library of Ireland. Dublin.

Larkin, Emett. 1972. "The Devotional Revolution in Ireland: 1850–75." *American Historical Review* 77:625–52.

——. 1980. *The Making of the Roman Catholic Church in Ireland, 1850–1860*. Chapel Hill: University of North Carolina Press.

Laslett, Peter. 1965. *The World We Have Lost*. London: Methuen.

——. 1972. "Introduction." In P. Laslett and R. Wall, eds., *Household and Family in Past Time*, pp. 1–89. Cambridge: Cambridge University Press.

Laslett, Peter, and Richard Wall, eds. 1972. *Household and Family in Past Time*. Cambridge: Cambridge University Press.

Law Reports (Ireland). 1884. Q.B., C.P., & Ex. Divisions, vol. 14:349–52.

Leach, Edmund. 1954. *Political Systems of Highland Burma*. London: Bell.

———. 1968. *Pul Eliya: A Village in Ceylon*. Cambridge: Cambridge University Press.

Le Bras, Hervé, and Emmanuel Todd. 1981. *L'invention de la France: Atlas anthropologique et politique*. Paris: Librairie Générale Française.

Lee, Joseph. 1973. *The Modernisation of Irish Society*. Dublin: Gill and Macmillan.

———. 1981a. "Preface." In J. Lee, ed., *Irish Historiography: 1970–1979*, p. vii. Cork: Cork University Press.

———. 1981b. "Irish Economic History Since 1500." In J. Lee, ed., *Irish Historiography: 1970–1979*. Cork: Cork University Press.

———. 1986. "Aspects of Irish Identity." In *Half the Lies Are True: Ireland/Britain; a Microcosm of International Misunderstanding*, pp. 22–28. Dublin: Trocaire.

———. 1990. *Ireland, 1912–1985: Politics and Society*. Cambridge: Cambridge University Press.

Lehning, J. R. 1983. "Nuptiality and Rural Industry: Families and Labour in the French Countryside." *Journal of Family History* 8:333–45.

Leister, I. 1963. *Das Werden der Agrarlandschaft in der Grafschaft Tipperary (Irland)*. Marburg: Universität Marburg.

Lenski, G. E. 1966. *Power and Privilege: A Theory of Social Stratification*. New York: McGraw-Hill.

LePlay, Frederic 1871. *L'Organisation de la famille selon le vrai modèle signalé par l'histoire de toutes les races et de tous les temps*. Paris, Tours.

Le Roy Ladurie, Emmanuel. 1979. *The Territory of the Historian*. Brighton: Harvester Press.

———. 1980. *Montaillou: Cathars and Catholics in a French Village*. Harmondsworth: Penguin.

———. 1981. *Carnival in Romans: A People's Uprising at Romans, 1579–1580*. Harmondsworth: Penguin.

Lesthaeghe, R. J. 1977. *The Decline of Belgian Fertility, 1800–1970*. Princeton: Princeton University Press.

———. 1983. "A Century of Demographic and Cultural Change in Western Europe: An Exploration of Underlying Dimensions." *Population and Development Review* 9:411–36.

Lesthaeghe, R. J., and Chris Wilson. 1986. "Modes of Production, Secularization, and the Pace of the Fertility Decline in Western Europe, 1870–1930." In A. J. Coale and Susan Cotts Watkins, eds., *The Decline of Fertility in Europe*. Princeton: Princeton University Press.

Levine, David. 1977. *Family Formation in an Age of Nascent Capitalism*. New York: Academic.

———. 1983. *Essays on the Family and Historical Change*. Austin: University of Texas Press.

———. 1987. *Reproducing Families: The Political Economy of English Population History*. Cambridge: Cambridge University Press.

Lewis, I. M., ed. 1968. *History and Social Anthropology*. London: Tavistock.

Leyton, Elliott. 1975. *The One Blood: Kinship and Class in an Irish Village*. Newfoundland: Memorial University (ISER).

Liguori, A. M. d'. 1978. *The Mission Book of the Congregation of the Most Holy Redeemer*. New York: Arno Press.

Lison-Tolosana, Carmelo. 1983 [1966]. *Belmonte de los Caballeros: Anthropology and History in an Aragonese Community*. Princeton: Princeton University Press. Reprint.

Littlejohn, James. 1963. *Westrigg: the Sociology of a Cheviot Parish*. London: Routledge and Kegan Paul.

Logan, Patrick. 1980. *The Holy Wells of Ireland*. London: Colin Smythe.

Longfield, Robert 1863. *The Fishery Laws of Ireland*. Dublin: E. Ponsonby.

Lynch, P., and J. Vaizey. 1960. *Guinness's Brewery and the Irish Economy, 1759–1876*. Cambridge: Cambridge University Press.

Lyons, F. S. L. 1979. *Ireland Since the Famine*. Great Britain: Collins/Fontana.

McClaughlin, Trevor. 1987. "Barefoot and Pregnant? Female Orphans who Emigrated from Irish Workhouses to Australia, 1848–50." *Familia: Ulster Genealogical Review* 2:31–36.

MacDonald, Michael. 1986. *Children of Wrath: Political Violence in Northern Ireland*. Oxford: Polity Press.

McDowell, R. B. 1979. *Ireland in the Age of Imperialism and Revolution: 1760–1801*. Oxford: Clarendon Press.

Macfarlane, Alan. 1970a. *The Family Life of Ralph Josselin, a Seventeenth-Century Clergyman: An Essay in Historical Anthropology*. Cambridge: Cambridge University Press.

———. 1970b. *Witchcraft in Tudor and Stuart England*. London: Routledge and Kegan Paul.

———. 1978. *The Origins of English Individualism: The Family, Property, and Social Transition*. Oxford: Basil Blackwell.

———. 1986. *Marriage and Love in England: Modes of Reproduction, 1300–1840*. Oxford: Basil Blackwell.

———. 1987. *The Culture of Capitalism*. Oxford: Basil Blackwell.

McGlinchey, Charles. 1986. *The Last of the Name*. Belfast: Blackstaff Press.

McGuire, J. I. 1981. "Index to Bulletin of the Irish Committee of Historical Sciences, 1939–1974." In Joseph Lee, ed., *Irish Historiography: 1970–1979*, pp. 225–38. Cork: Cork University Press.

MacLeod, Roy M. 1968. "Government and Resource Conservation: The Salmon Acts Administration, 1860–1886." *Journal of British Studies* 7:2.

McMichael, Philip. 1990. "Incorporating Comparison Within a World-Historical Perspective: An Alternative Comparative Method." *American Sociological Review* 55:385–97.

MacNiocaill, Gearóid, and M. A. G. Ó Tuathaigh. 1984. "Ireland and Continental Europe: The Historical Dimension." In P. J. Drudy and Dermot

McAleese, eds., *Ireland and the European Community*, pp. 13–32. Cambridge: Cambridge University Press.

McQuillan, Kevin. 1983. "Moving to the City: Migration to London and Paris in the Nineteenth Century." *Sociological Focus* 16:49–64.

———. 1984. "Modes of Production and Demographic Patterns in Nineteenth Century France." *American Journal of Sociology* 84:1324–46.

———. 1990. "Economic Structure, Religion and Age at Marriage: Some Evidence from Alsace." *Journal of Family History* 14:331–46.

Mann, Michael. 1986. "The Sources of Social Power." In *A History of Power from the Beginning to A.D. 1760*. Cambridge: Cambridge University Press.

Mannion, John J. 1974. *Irish Settlements in Eastern Canada: A Study of Cultural Transfer and Adaptation*. Toronto: University of Toronto Press.

Mansergh, Nicholas. 1975. *The Irish Question, 1840–1921*, 3d ed. London: George Allen and Unwin.

Marcus, George, and Michael M. Fischer. 1986. *Anthropology as Cultural Critique: An Experimental Moment in the Human Sciences*. Chicago: University of Chicago Press.

Markoff, John. 1985. "The Social Geography of Rural Revolt at the Beginning of the French Revolution." *American Sociological Review* 50:761–81.

Markoff, John, and Daniel Regan. 1981. "The Rise and Fall of Civil Religion: Comparative Perspectives." *Sociological Analysis* 42:333–52.

Markoff, John, and Gilbert Shapiro. 1985. "Consensus and Conflict at the Onset of Revolution: A Quantitative Study of France in 1789." *American Journal of Sociology* 91:28–53.

Martin, J. E. 1983. *Feudalism to Capitalism: Peasant and Landlord in English Agrarian Development*. Atlantic Highlands, N.J.: Humanities.

Maxim, P. S.. 1989. "An Ecological Analysis of Crime in Early Victorian England." *Harvard Journal of Criminal Justice*, 28:37–50.

Medick, Hans. 1987. " 'Missionaries in the Row Boat'? Ethnological Ways of Knowing as a Challenge to Social Change." *Comparative Studies in Society and History* 29(1)76–97.

Meillassoux, C.. 1964. *Anthropologie économique des Gouro de Côte d'Ivoire*. Paris: Le Monde d'outre-mer, 1 ser, xxvii.

Mellor, Rosemary. 1981. "The Capitalist City 1780–1920." In *Urban Change and Conflict*. Milton Keynes: Open University.

———. 1990. "Urbanization as Moral Project: Transitions in Twentieth-Century Britain." In Stephen Kendrick, Pat Straw, and David McCrone, eds., *Interpreting the Past, Understanding the Present*. Houndmills, Basingstoke: Macmillan.

Melody, William A., Liora Salter, and Paul Heyer, eds. 1981. *Culture, Communication, and Dependency: The Tradition of H. A. Innis*. Norwood, N.J.: Ablex.

Mendels, Franklin. 1970. "Industry and Marriages in Flanders Before the Industrial Revolution." In Paul Deprez, ed., *Population and Economics: Proceedings of Section V of the French Congress of the International Economic History Association, 1986*. Winnipeg: University of Manitoba Press.

————. 1972. "Proto-industrialization: The First Phase of the Industrialization Process." *Journal of Economic History* 32:241–61.

Mendras, Henri. 1958. *Les paysans et la modernisation de l'agriculture*. Paris: C.N.R.S.

————. 1967. *La fin des paysans: innovations et changement dans l'agriculture française*. Paris: S.E.D.E.I.S.

Merton, R. K. 1970 [1938]. *Science, Technology, and Society in Seventeenth Century England*. New York: Howard Fertig. Reprint.

Messenger, John C. 1969. *Inis Beag: Isle of Ireland*. New York: Holt, Rinehart and Winston.

————. 1983. *An Anthropologist at Play: Balladmongering in Ireland and Its Consequences for Research*. Lanham: University Press of America.

Miller, Kirby. 1985. *Emigrants and Exiles: Ireland and the Irish Exodus to North America*. Oxford: Oxford University Press.

————. 1987. "Review of T. W. Moody and W. E. Vaughan, eds., *A New History of Ireland*. Vol. 4: *Eighteenth-Century Ireland, 1691–1800*." *Albion* 19(2):315–19.

Mintz, Sidney W. 1974. *Caribbean Transformations*. Chicago: Aldine.

————. 1982. "Culture: An Anthropological View." *Yale Review* 71: 499–512.

————. 1985. *Sweetness and Power: The Place of Sugar in Modern History*. New York: Viking Penguin.

Mintz, Sidney W., and Eric Wolf 1950. "An Analysis of Ritual Co-Parenthood (Compadrazgo)." *Southwestern Journal of Anthropology* 6.

Mission Sermons. n.d. Redemptorist Archive, Marianella House, Dublin.

Mitchison, Rosalind, and Peter Roebuck, eds. 1988. *Economy and Society in Scotland and Ireland, 1500–1939*. Edinburgh: John Donald.

Mokyr, Joel. 1983. *Why Ireland Starved: A Quantitative and Analytical History of the Irish Economy, 1800–1850*. London: George Allen and Unwin.

Moore, Barrington, Jr. 1966. *Social Origins of Dictatorship and Democracy: Lord and Peasant in the Making of the Modern World*. Boston: Beacon Press.

Morris, John, et al. 1952. "Introduction." *Past and Present* 1:i–iv.

Murphy, John A. 1975. *Ireland in the Twentieth Century*. Dublin: Gill and Macmillan.

Nakane, Chie. 1972. "An Interpretation of the Size and Structure of the Household in Japan Over Three Centuries." In Peter Laslett, ed., *Household and Family in Past Time*, pp. 517–43. Cambridge: Cambridge University Press.

Nash, June. 1979. *We Eat the Mines and the Mines Eat Us*. New York: Columbia University Press.

National Library of Ireland (N.L.I.).

————. n.d. Down Survey Parish maps for County Kilkenny. Ms. 720.

————. n.d. *Ormond Deeds*, vols. 8 and 9 (in typescript).

————. 1637. Presentments at the Sheriff's Court in the County of Kilkenny. D. 4052.

Netting, Robert McC. 1981. *Balancing on an Alp: Ecological Change and Continuity in a Swiss Mountain Community*. New York: Cambridge University Press.

Netting, Robert McC., Richard R. Wilk, and Eric J. Arnoud. 1984. "Introduction." In Robert McC. Netting, Richard R. Wilk, and Eric J. Arnoud, eds., *Households: Comparative and Historical Studies of the Domestic Group*, pp. xiii–xxxviii. Berkeley: University of California Press.

Newbury, Catharine. 1988. *The Cohesion of Oppression: Clientship and Ethnicity in Rwanda, 1860–1960*. New York: Columbia University Press.

Nicholls, K. 1972. *Gaelic and Gaelicised Ireland in the Later Middle Ages*. Dublin: Gill and Macmillan.

Nisbet, R. A. 1964. "Kinship and Political Power in First Century Rome." In W. J. Cahnman and Alvin Boskoff, eds., *Sociology and History: Theory and Research*. New York: Free Press.

Nolan, William. 1979. *Fassadinin—Land, Settlement, and Society in South-East Ireland, 1600–1850*. Dublin: Geography Publications.

———. 1982. *Tracing the Past: Sources for Local Studies in the Republic of Ireland*. Dublin: Geography Publications.

———, ed. 1985. *Tipperary: History and Society*. Dublin: Geography Publications.

Nolan, William, and Kevin Whelan, eds. 1990. *Kilkenny: History and Society—Interdisciplinary Essays on the History of an Irish County*. Dublin: Geography Publications.

O'Brien, John. 1952. *The Vanishing Irish: Nation of Bachelors and Spinsters*. Portland, Ore.: Benedictine Press.

O'Carroll, J. P., et al. 1978. "Regional Aspects of the Problem of Restructuring Use and Ownership of Agricultural Land in the Republic of Ireland." *Economic and Social Review* 9(2)79–106.

O'Dowd, Liam. 1990. "New Introduction." In Albert Memmi, *The Colonizer and the Colonized*, pp. 29–66. London: Earthscan Publications.

O'Farrell, Patrick. 1986. *The Irish in Australia*. Kensington, New South Wales: New South Wales University Press.

O'Flanagan, Patrick. 1987. "Introduction." In P. O'Flanagan, P. Ferguson, and K. Whelan, eds., *Rural Ireland: Modernisation and Change*, pp. ix–xiv. Cork: Cork University Press.

Ó Gráda, Cormac. 1988. *Ireland Before and After the Famine: Explorations in Economic History, 1800–1925*. Manchester: Manchester University Press.

———. 1989. *The Great Irish Famine*. Houndmills: Macmillan.

Ó Healái, Pádraig. 1974–76. "Moral Values in Irish Religious Tales." *Béaloideas* 5(42–44):176–212.

———. 1977. "Cumhacht an tSagairt sa Bhéaloideas." *Léachtái Cholm Cille* 8:109–31.

Ohnuki-Tierney, Emiko. 1990a "Introduction." In Emiko Ohnuki-Tierney, ed., *Culture Through Time: Anthropological Approaches*, pp. 1–25. Stanford: Stanford University Press.

————. 1990b. "The Monkey as Self in Japanese Culture." In Emiko Ohnuki-Tierney, ed., *Culture Through Time: Anthropological Approaches*, pp. 128–53. Stanford: Stanford University Press.

O'Kelly, Owen. 1985. *The Placenames of County Kilkenny*. Kilkenny: Boethius Press.

O'Laoghaire, Díarmuid. "Marian Devotion." In Michael Maher, ed., *Irish Spirituality*. Dublin: Veritas.

O'Malley, Eoin. 1989. *Industry and Economic Development: The Challenge for the Latecomer*. Dublin: Gill and Macmillan.

O'Neill, Brian Juan. 1987. *Social Inequality in a Portuguese Hamlet: Land, Late Marriage, and Bastardy, 1870–1978*. Cambridge: Cambridge University Press.

O'Neill, Kevin. 1984. *Family and Farm in Pre-Famine Ireland: The Parish of Killashandra*. Madison: University of Wisconsin Press.

Orridge, Andrew W. 1983. "The Blueshirts and the 'Economic War': A Study of Ireland in the Context of Dependency Theory." *Political Studies* 31:351–69.

Ortner, Sherry B. 1984. "Theory and Anthropology Since the Sixties." *Comparative Studies in Society and History* 26:126–66.

O'Shea, James. 1983. *Priests, Politics, and Society in Post-Famine Ireland: A Study of County Tipperary, 1850–1891*. Dublin: Wolfhound Press.

Ó Súilleabhain, Séan, ed. 1951. "Scealta Craibhteachta." *Béaloideas*, special issue.

Ó Tuathaigh, Gearóid. 1981. "Ireland, 1800–1921." In Joseph Lee, ed., *Irish Historiography: 1970–1979*, pp. 85–131. Cork: Cork University Press.

Palmer, Bryan D. 1990. *Descent into Discourse: The Reification of Language and the Writing of Social History*. Philadelphia: Temple University Press.

Park, R. E., and E. W. Burgess. 1969. *Introduction to the Science of Sociology*. Chicago: University of Chicago Press.

Parliamentary Papers 1824. *Report from the Select Committee appointed to take into consideration the state of the Salmon Fisheries of Scotland and the United Kingdom, and the Laws affecting the same*. IUP 1824 [427] vii:1.

————. 1825. *Report from the Select Committee to take into consideration the state of the Salmon Fisheries of Scotland and the United Kingdom, and the Laws affecting the same*. IUP 1825 [173] v:283.

————. 1825. *Second Report from the Select Committee . . . and the Laws affecting the same*. IUP 1825 [393] v:315.

————. 1836. *First Report of the Commissioners for Inquiring into the Condition of the Poorer Classes in Ireland*. H.C. 1836 xxxi. Supplement to Appendix D:71.

————. 1837. *Second Report of the Commissioners of Inquiry Respecting the Present State of the Irish Fisheries, the Laws Affecting, and the Means and Expediency of Extending and Improving Them*. IUP 1837 [82] xxii:489.

————. 1843. *First Annual Report of the Commissioners of Fisheries, Ireland*. IUP [224] xxviii:17.

———. 1844. *Second Annual Report of the Commissioners of Fisheries, Ireland.* IUP [502] xxx:31.

———. 1845. *Third Annual Report of the Commissioners of Fisheries, Ireland.* IUP [320] xxvi:211.

———. 1846. *Fourth Annual Report of the Commissioners of Fisheries, Ireland.* IUP [713] xxii:175.

———. 1847–48. *Report of the Board of Public Works in Ireland in Regard to Fisheries in That Country.* IUP [983] xxxvii:213.

———. 1849. *Returns and Statements Respecting Fisheries in Ireland.* IUP [1098] xxiii:433.

———. 1849. *Report from the Select Committee on Fisheries (Ireland); Together with the Proceedings of the Committee, Minutes of Evidence, Appendix and Index.* IUP [536] xiii:1.

———. 1851 *Reports and Statements Respecting the Fisheries in Ireland, 1850.* IUP [1414] xxv:1.

———. 1854. *Report of the Commissioners of Fisheries, Ireland, for 1853, to His Excellency the Lord Lieutenant.* IUP [1819] xx:163.

———. 1856. *Report of the Commissioners of Fisheries, Ireland, for 1854, to His Excellency the Lord Lieutenant.* IUP [2021] xix:31.

———. 1857. *Report of the Commissioners of Fisheries, Ireland, for 1856, to His Excellency the Lord Lieutenant.* IUP [2272. Sess. 2] xvii:21.

———. 1860. *Report of the Commissioners of Fisheries, Ireland, for 1859, to His Excellency the Lord Lieutenant.* IUP [2727] xxxiv:663.

———. 1861. *Report of the Commissioners of Fisheries, Ireland, for 1860, to His Excellency the Lord Lieutenant.* IUP [2862] xxiii:27.

——— 1864. *Report of the Special Commissioners for Irish Fisheries for 1863.* IUP [3256] xxxi: 27.

——— . 1865. *Report of the Special Commissioners for Irish Fisheries for 1864.* IUP [3420] xxviii:431.

———. 1866. *Report of the Special Commissioners for Irish Fisheries for 1865.* IUP [3608] xxviii:355.

———. 1867. *Report of the Special Commissioners for Irish Fisheries for 1866.* IUP [3826] xviii:33.

———. 1867–68. *Report of the Special Commissioners for Irish Fisheries for 1867.* IUP [4056] xix:653.

———. 1870. *Report of the Inspectors of Irish Fisheries, on the Coast, Deep Sea, and Inland Fisheries, for 1869.* IUP [c. 225] xiv:193.

———. 1873. *Report of the Inspectors of Irish Fisheries, on the Coast, Deep Sea, and Inland Fisheries, for 1872.* IUP [c. 758] xix:607.

———. 1874. *Report of the Inspectors of Irish Fisheries, on the Coast, Deep Sea, and Inland Fisheries, for 1873.* IUP [c. 980] xii:591.

———. 1876. *Report of the Inspectors of Irish Fisheries, on the Coast, Deep Sea, and Inland Fisheries, for 1875.* IUP [c. 1467] xvi:555.

———. 1877. *Report of the Inspectors of Irish Fisheries, on the Coast, Deep Sea, and Inland Fisheries, for 1876.* IUP [c. 1703] xxiv:351.

————. 1881. *Report of the Inspectors on the Sea and Inland Fisheries of Ireland for 1880.* IUP [c. 2871] xxiii:401.

————. 1901. *Royal Commission on Irish Inland Fisheries.* Report: H.C. [Cd. 448] xii:1.

Parman, Susan. 1990. *Scottish Crofters: A Historical Ethnography of a Celtic Village.* Ft. Worth: Holt, Rinehart and Winston.

Parmentier, Richard J. 1987. *The Sacred Remains: Myth, History, and Polity in Belau.* Chicago: University of Chicago Press.

Parsons, Talcott. 1966. *Societies: Evolutionary and Comparative Perspectives.* Englewood Cliffs, N.J.: Prentice-Hall.

Patterson, H. 1980. *Class Conflict and Sectarianism: The Protestant Working Class and the Belfast Labour Movement, 1868–1920.* Belfast: Blackstaff Press.

Pawlisch, Hans S. 1985. *Sir John Davies and the Conquest of Ireland.* Cambridge: Cambridge University Press.

Peace, Adrian. 1989. "From Arcadia to Anomie: Critical Notes on the Constitution of Irish Society as an Anthropological Object." *Critique of Anthropology* 9(1):89–111.

Peillon, M. 1982. *Contemporary Irish Society.* Dublin: Gill and Macmillan.

Peletz, Michael Gates. 1988. *A Share of the Harvest: Kinship, Property, and Social History Among the Malays of Rembau.* Berkeley: University of California Press.

Pender, S., ed. 1939. *A Census of Ireland c. 1659.* Dublin: Irish Manuscripts Commission.

Perkin, Harold. 1973. "Social History." In Fritz Stern, ed., *The Varieties of History,* 2d ed. New York: Vintage.

Petty, W. 1691. *The Political Anatomy of Ireland.* London: Brown and Rodgers.

Philipp, June. 1983. "Traditional Narrative and Enthnographic History." *Historical Studies* 20:339–52.

Pilsworth, W. J. 1943. "Census or Poll-tax." *Royal Society of Antiquaries of Ireland Journal* 78:22–24.

————. 1951. "Thomastown Corporation." *Old Kilkenny Review* 4.

Pingaud, Marie-Claude. 1978. *Paysans en Bourgogne: les gens de Minot.* Paris: Flammarion.

Plakans, Andrejs. 1984. *Kinship in the Past: An Anthropology of European Family Life, 1500–1900.* Oxford: Basil Blackwell.

Pocock, J. A. 1975. "British History: A Plea for a New Subject." *Journal of Modern History* 47:601–21.

————. 1979. *The Limits and Divisions of British History.* Glasgow: Paper no. 31, Centre for the Study of Public Policy, University of Strathclyde.

Poggi, Gianfranco. 1978. *The Development of the Modern State: A Sociological Introduction.* Stanford: Stanford University Press.

Prager, Jeffrey. 1986. *Building Democracy in Ireland: Political Order and Cultural Integration in a Newly Independent Nation.* Cambridge: Cambridge University Press.

Price, Richard. 1990. *Alabi's World*. Baltimore: Johns Hopkins University Press.

Pringle, Dennis J. 1984. "Urban Social Geography." In *Irish Geography, Golden Jubilee, 1934–1984*, pp. 186–203. Dublin: The Geographical Society of Ireland.

———. 1985. *One Island: Two Nations? A Political Geographical Analysis of the National Conflict in Ireland*. Letchworth: Research Studies Press.

Public Record Office Ireland (P.R.O.I.). n.d. Books of Survey and Distribution for Counties Kilkenny and Tipperary.

———. n.d. Poll-money, Urny parish. Public Record Office Northern Ireland.

———. n.d. Poll Tax Return, Aghlow parish.

Quinn, D. B. 1958. "Ireland and Sixteenth-Century European Expansion." *Historical Studies* 1:20–32.

Rambaud, Placide, and M. Vincienne. 1964. *Les transformations d'une société Rurale: la Maurienne (1561–1962)*. Paris: A. Colin.

Rappaport, Joanne. 1985. "History, Myth, and the Dynamics of Territorial Maintenance in Tierradentro, Colombia." *American Ethnologist* 12(1): 27–45.

Rebel, Hermann. 1989. "Cultural Hegemony and Class Experience: A Critical Reading of Recent Ethnological-Historical Approaches." *American Ethnologist* 16:117–36, 350–65.

Redfield, Robert. 1930. *Tepoztlan: A Mexican Village*. Chicago: University of Chicago Press.

———. 1950. *A Village that Chose Progress: Chan Kom Revisited*. Chicago: University of Chicago Press.

Redfield, Robert, and Alfonso Villa Rojas. 1962. *Chan Kom: A Maya Village*. Chicago: University of Chicago Press.

Regan, Colm. 1980. "Economic Development in Ireland: The Historical Dimension." *Antipode* 12(1):1–14.

*Roinn Béaloideas:* National Folklore Archive, UCD, Belfield, Dublin.

Rosaldo, Renato. 1980. *Ilongot Headhunting, 1883–1974: A Study in Society and History*. Stanford: Stanford University Press.

———. 1986. "From the Door of His Tent: The Fieldworker and the Inquisitor." In James Clifford and George E. Marcus, eds., *Writing Culture: The Poetics and Politics of Ethnography*. Berkeley: University of California Press.

———. 1990. "Celebrating Thompson's Heroes: Social Analysis in History and Anthropology." In Harvey J. Kaye and Keith McClelland, eds., *E. P. Thompson: Critical Perspectives*, pp. 103–24. Philadelphia: Temple University Press.

Roseberry, William. 1982. "Balinese Cockfights and the Seduction of Anthropology." *Social Research* 49:1011–28.

———. 1983. *Coffee and Capitalism in the Venezuelan Andes*. Austin: University of Texas Press.

———. 1988. "Political Economy." *Annual Review of Anthropology* 17: 161–85.

Rosenberg, Harriet G. 1988. *A Negotiated World: Three Centuries of Change in a French Alpine Community*. Toronto: University of Toronto Press.

Rosenhaft, Eve. 1987. "History, Anthropology, and the Study of Everyday Life: A Review Article." *Comparative Studies in Society and History* 29(1): 99–105.

Ross, Eric B. 1986. "Potatoes, Population, and the Irish Famine: The Political Economy of Demographic Change." In P. Handwerker, ed., *Culture and Reproduction: An Anthropological Critique of Demographic Transition Theory*, pp. 196–220. Boulder, Colo.: Westview.

Ross, Michael. 1969. "A Regional Study of the Relative Prosperity of Irish Farms of Different Sizes." *Economic and Social Review* 1:77–107.

Ruane, Joseph. 1978. "The Analysis of Dependency in Rural Ireland: A Critique of Current Approaches." Proceedings of the Fifth Annual Conference of the Sociological Association of Ireland.

Rudé, George. 1964. *The Crowd in History, 1730–1848*. New York: John Wiley & Sons.

Rumpf, E., and A. C. Hepburn. 1977. *Nationalism and Socialism in Twentieth Century Ireland*. Liverpool: Liverpool University Press.

Ryan, T. 1977. "Mooncoin II: Landlords and Tenants, 1650–1977." Unpublished.

Sabean, David Warren. 1990. *Property, Production, and Family in Neckarhausen, 1700–1870*. Cambridge: Cambridge University Press.

Sacks, Paul. 1976. *The Donegal Mafia: An Irish Political Machine*. New Haven: Yale University Press.

Sahlins, Marshall. 1981. *Historical Metaphors and Mythical Realities: Structure in the Early History of the Sandwich Islands Kingdom*. Ann Arbor: University of Michigan Press.

———. 1985. *Islands of History*. Chicago: University of Chicago Press.

Samuel, Rafael. 1981. *People's History and Socialist Theory*. London: Routledge and Kegan Paul.

Saul, John S., and Roger Woods. 1971. "African Peasantries." In Teodor Shanin, ed., *Peasant Societies*, pp. 103–14. Harmondsworth: Penguin.

Scheper-Hughes, Nancy. 1979a. *Saints, Scholars and Schizophrenics: Mental Illness in Rural Ireland*. Berkeley: University of California Press.

———. 1979b. "Inheritance of the Meek: Land, Labor, and Love in Rural Ireland." *Marxist Perspectives* 5 (Spring):46–76.

———. 1987. "The Best of Two Worlds, The Worst of Two Worlds: Reflections on Culture and Field Work Among the Rural Irish and Pueblo Indians." *Comparative Studies in Society and History*, 29(1):56–75.

Schneider, Jane, and Peter Schneider. 1976. *Culture and Political Economy in Western Sicily*. New York: Academic Press.

Scholte, Bob 1986. "The Charmed Circle of Geertz's Hermeneutics: A Neo-Marxist Critique." *Critique of Anthropology* 6:5–15.

Schryer, Frans J. 1980. *The Rancheros of Pisaflores: The History of a Peasant Bourgeoisie in Twentieth Century Mexico*. Toronto: University of Toronto Press.

Scott, Joan. 1989. "Interview with Joan Scott." *Radical History Review* 45: 41–62.

Segalen, Martine. 1983. *Love and Power in the Peasant Family: Rural France in the Nineteenth Century.* Oxford: Basil Blackwell.

———. 1985. *Quinze générations de Bas-bretons: parenté et société dans le Pays bigouden sud, 1720–1980.* Paris: Presses Universitaires de France.

———. 1986. *Historical Anthropology of the Family.* Cambridge: Cambridge University Press.

Sewell, W. H. 1980. *Work and Revolution in France. The Language of Labor from the Old Regime to 1848.* Cambridge: Cambridge University Press.

Shanin, Teodor, ed. 1971. *Peasants and Peasant Societies: Selected Readings.* Harmondsworth: Penguin.

Shanklin, Eugenia. 1985. *Donegal's Changing Traditions: An Ethnographic Study.* New York: Gordon and Breach.

Shankman, Paul. 1984. "The Thick and the Thin: On the Interpretive Theoretical Program of Clifford Geertz." *Current Anthropology* 23:216–70.

Shanks, Amanda. 1988. *Rural Aristocracy in Northern Ireland.* Aldershot: Avebury.

Sharlin Allan. 1978. "National Decrease in Early Modern Cities: A Reconsideration." *Past and Present* 79:126–38.

Sharp, Lauriston, and Lucien M. Hanks. 1978. *Bang Chan: Social History of a Rural Community in Thailand.* Ithaca: Cornell University Press.

Sider, Gerald M. 1986. *Culture and Class in Anthropology and History: A Newfoundland Illustration.* Cambridge: Cambridge University Press.

Sieder, Reinhard, and Michael Mitterauer. 1983. "The Reconstruction of the Family Life Course: Theoretical Problems and Empirical Results." In Richard Wall, ed., *Family Forms in Historic Europe.* Cambridge: Cambridge University Press.

Sills, David L., ed. 1968. *International Encyclopedia of the Social Sciences.* New York: Macmillan.

Silverblatt, Irene. 1987. *Moon, Sun, and Witches: Gender Ideologies and Class in Inca and Colonial Peru.* Princeton: Princeton University Press.

———. 1989. "Imperial Dilemmas, the Politics of Kinship, and Inca Reconstructions of History." *Comparative Studies in Society and History* 30(1): 82–102.

Silverman, Marilyn. 1979. "Dependency, Mediation, and Class Formation in Rural Guyana." *American Ethnologist* 6(3):466–90.

———. 1980. *Rich People and Rice: Factional Politics in Rural Guyana, 1902–1970.* Leiden: E. J. Brill.

———. 1987. "Agrarian Processes Within 'Plantation Economies': Cases from Guyana and Coastal Ecuador." *Canadian Review of Sociology and Anthropology* 24(4):550–70.

———. 1989. " 'A Labouring Man's Daughter': Constructing 'Respectability' in South Kilkenny." In Chris Curtin and T. M. Wilson, eds., *Ireland from Below: Social Change and Local Communities.* Galway: Galway University Press.

Silverman, Marilyn, and P. H. Gulliver. 1986. *In the Valley of the Nore: A Social History of Thomastown, County Kilkenny, 1840–1983.* Dublin: Geography Publications.

Silverman, Marilyn, and R. F. Salisbury, eds. 1978. *A House Divided?: Anthropological Studies of Factionalism.* Newfoundland: Memorial University (ISER).

Silverman, Sydel. 1967. "The Community-Nation Mediator in Traditional Central Italy." In Jack M. Potter, May N. Diaz, and George M. Foster, eds., *Peasant Society: A Reader,* pp. 279–93. Boston: Little, Brown.

Simington, R. C., ed. 1931–34. *The Civil Survey* A.D. *1654–56, County of Tipperary.* 2 vols. Dublin: Irish Manuscripts Commission.

Simmons, William S. 1985. "Anthropology, History, and the North American Indian: A Review Article." *Comparative Studies in Society and History* 27(1):174–82.

Simms, A. 1988. "Core and Periphery in Medieval Europe: The Irish Experience in a Wider Context." In William J. Smyth and Kevin Whelan, eds., *Common Ground: Essays on the Historical Geography of Ireland,* pp. 22–40. Cork: Cork University Press.

Simms, J. G. 1986. "The Irish on the Continent, 1691–1800." In T. W. Moody and W. E. Vaughan, eds., *A New History of Ireland: Eighteenth Century Ireland,* vol. 4, pp. 629–56. London: Oxford University Press.

Skocpol, Theda. 1979. *States and Social Revolutions: A Comparative Analysis of France, Russia, and China.* New York: Cambridge University Press.

Smelser, N. J. 1959. *Social Change in the Industrial Revolution: An Application of Theory to the British Cotton Industry.* Chicago: University of Chicago Press.

Smith, Anthony D. 1983. *Theories of Nationalism,* 2d ed. London: Duckworth.

Smith, Carol A. 1985. "Local History in Global Context: Social and Economic Transitions in Western Guatemala." *Comparative Studies in Society and History* 26(2)193–228.

Smith, Cecil Woodham. 1962. *The Great Hunger: Ireland, 1845–1849.* New York: Harper & Row.

Smith, Gavin. 1989. *Livelihood and Resistance: Peasants and the Politics of Land in Peru.* Berkeley: University of California Press.

Smith, Michael. 1960. *Government in Zazzau.* London: Oxford University Press.

Smith, Robert J. 1972. "Small Families, Small Households, and Residential Instability: Town and City in 'Pre-modern' Japan." In Peter Laslett, ed., *Household and Family in Past Time,* pp. 429–71. Cambridge: Cambridge University Press.

Smyth, William J. 1975. "Continuity and Change in the Territorial Organisation of Irish Rural Communities" (Part I). *Maynooth Review* (June).

———. 1976. "Estate Records and the Making of the Irish Landscape." *Irish Geography* 9:29–49.

――――. 1978. "The Western Isle of Ireland and the Eastern Seaboard of America: England's First Frontiers." *Irish Geography* 11:1–22.

――――. 1980. "Land Values, Landownership and Population Patterns in County Tipperary for 1641–60 and 1841–50: Some Comparisons." In L. M. Cullen and F. Furet, eds., *Ireland and France, 17th–20th Centuries: Towards a Comparative Study of Rural History.* Paris: Editions de l'Ecole des Hautes Etudes en Sciences Sociales.

――――. 1984. "Social Geography of Rural Ireland: Inventory and Prospect." In *Irish Geography, Golden Jubilee, 1934–1984,* pp. 204–36. Dublin: The Geographical Society of Ireland.

――――. 1985. "Property, Patronage and Population: Reconstructing the Human Geography of Mid-Seventeenth Century County Tipperary." In William Nolan, ed., *Tipperary: History and Society.* Dublin: Geography Publications.

――――. 1988. "Society and Settlement in Seventeenth Century Ireland: The Evidence of the '1659 Census.' " In William J. Smyth and Kevin Whelan, eds., *Common Ground: Essays on the Historical Geography of Ireland.* Cork: Cork University Press.

――――. 1990. "Territorial, Social and Settlement Hierarchies in Seventeenth Century Kilkenny." In William Nolan, ed., *Kilkenny: History and Society.* Dublin: Geography Publications.

Smyth, William J., and Kevin Whelan, eds. 1988, *Common Ground. Essays on the Historical Geography of Ireland.* Cork: Cork University Press.

Snyder, David, and Tilly, Charles. 1972. "Hardship and Collective Violence in France." *American Sociological Review* 37:520–32.

Solow, Barbara. 1971. *The Land Question and the Irish Economy, 1870–1903.* Cambridge, Mass.: Harvard University Press.

Sorokin, P. A. 1927. *Social Mobility.* New York: Harper & Row,

――――. 1942. *Man and Society in Calamity: The Effects of War, Revolution, Famine, Pestilence Upon Human Mind, Behavior, Social Organization, and Cultural Life.* New York: Dutton.

South Tipperary Museum. 1661. Poll Money Book for Clonmel.

Southall, Aidan. 1962. *Social Change in Modern Africa.* London: Oxford University Press.

Spencer, Jonathan. 1990. "Writing Within: Anthropology, Nationalism and Culture in Sri Lanka." *Current Anthropology* 31(3):283–98.

Stearns, Peter. 1967. "Some Comments on Social History." *Journal of Social History* 1:3–16.

Stebbing, George. 1924. *The Redemptorists.* London: Burns, Oates and Washburn.

Stenning, D. 1959. *Savannah Nomads: A Study of the Wodaabe Pastoral Fulani of Western Bornu Province, Northern Region, Nigeria.* London: Oxford University Press.

Stoler, Laura Ann. 1985. *Capitalism and Confrontation in Sumatra's Plantation Belt, 1870–1979.* New Haven: Yale University Press.

Stone, Lawrence. 1979. "The Revival of Narrative." *Past and Present* 85: 3–24.

Swanson, G. E. 1967. *Religion and Regime: A Sociological Account of the Reformation*. Ann Arbor: University of Michigan Press.

Swartz, M., Victor Turner, and A. Tuden, eds. 1966. *Political Anthropology*. Chicago: Aldine.

Symes, David G. 1972. "Farm Household and Farm Performance: A Study of Twentieth Century Ballyferriter, Southwest Ireland." *Ethnology* 40(1) 25–38.

Tambiah, S. J. 1976. *World Conqueror and World Renouncer: A Study of Buddhism and Polity in Thailand Against a Historical Background*. Cambridge: Cambridge University Press.

Taylor, Lawrence J. 1980a "Colonialism and Community Structure in the West of Ireland." *Ethnohistory* 27(2):169–81.

———. 1980b. "The Merchant in Peripheral Ireland: A Case from Donegal." *Anthropology* 4(2):63–76.

———. 1981. "Man the Fisher: Fishing and Community in a Rural Irish Settlement." *American Ethnologist* 8(4):774–88

———. 1985. "The Priest and the Agent: Social Drama and Class Consciousness in the West of Ireland." *Comparative Studies in Society and History* 27(4):696–712.

———. 1987. "The River Would Run Red with Blood: Commons and Community in Donegal." In B. McCay and J. Acheson, eds., *The Questions of the Commons*. Tucson: University of Arizona Press.

———. 1989a. "The Mission: An Anthropological View of an Irish Religious Occasion." In C. Curtin and T. Wilson, eds., *Ireland From Below*. Galway: Galway University Press.

———. 1989b. "Bás InÉirinn: Construction of Death in Ireland." *Anthropological Quarterly* 62(4):175–87.

———. 1990a. "Stories of Power, Powerful Stories: The Drunken Priest in Donegal." In E. Badone, ed., *Religious Orthodoxy and Popular Faith in European Society*. Princeton: Princeton University Press.

———. 1990b. "The Healing Mass: Regimes and Fields of Religous Experience in Ireland." *Archives Sciences Sociales des Religions* 71:93–111.

Teggart, F. J. 1918. *The Processes of History*. New Haven: Yale University Press.

———. 1939. *Rome and China: A Study of Correlations in Historical Events*. Berkeley: University of California Press.

Terray, E. 1969. *Le Marxisme devant les sociétés primitives*. Paris: Maspero.

Thomas, Keith. 1971. *Religion and the Decline of Magic*. Harmondsworth: Penguin.

Thompson, E. P. 1963. *The Making of the English Working Class*. London: V. Gollancz.

———. 1972. "Anthropology and the Discipline of Historical Context." *Midland History* 1(3):41–55.

———. 1974. "Patrician Society, Plebeian Culture." *Journal of Social History* 7:382–405.

————. 1978a. *The Poverty of Theory & Other Essays*. London: Merlin Press.

————. 1978b. "Eighteenth-Century English Society: Class Struggle Without Class?." *Social History* 3:133–66.

————. 1979. *Folklore, Anthropology, and Social History*. Brighton: John L. Noyce.

Tighe, William 1802. *Statistical Observations Relative to the County of Kilkenny, Made in the Years 1800 and 1801*. Dublin: J. Archer.

Tilly, Charles. 1964. *The Vendée*. Cambridge, Mass.: Harvard University Press.

————. 1978. "Anthropology, History, and the *Annales*." *Review* 1(3/4): 207–13.

————. 1981. *As Sociology Meets History*. New York: Academic Press.

————. 1984a. *Big Structures, Large Processes, Huge Comparisons*. New York: Russell Sage.

————. 1984b. "Demographic Origins of the European Proletariat." In David Levine, ed., *Proletarianization and Family History*. Orlando: Academic Press.

————. 1988. "Future History." *Theory and Society* 17:703–12.

————. 1990. *Coercion, Capital, and European States, A.D. 990–1990*. Cambridge, Mass.: Basil Blackwell.

Tilly, Charles, Louise Tilly, and Richard Tilly. 1975. *The Rebellious Century, 1830–1930*. Cambridge, Mass.: Harvard University Press.

Tilly, Charles and A. Q. Lodhi. 1973. "Urbanization, Criminality and Collective Violence in Nineteenth-Century France." *American Journal of Sociology* 79:296–318.

Todd, Emmanuel. 1985. *The Explanation of Ideology: Family Structures and Social Systems*. Oxford: Basil Blackwell.

————. 1987. *The Causes of Progress: Culture, Authority, and Change*. Oxford: Basil Blackwell.

Trevelyan, Charles. 1848. *The Irish Crisis*. London: Longman, Brown, Green, and Longman.

Trevor-Roper, Hugh. 1983. "The Invention of Tradition: The Highland Tradition of Scotland." In E. Hobsbawn and Terence Ranger, eds., *The Invention of Tradition*. Cambridge: Cambridge University Press.

Trouillot, Michel-Rolph. 1988. *Peasants and Capital: Dominica in the World Economy*. Baltimore: Johns Hopkins University Press.

Tucker, Vincent. 1986. "Ireland: A 'Third World Microcosm?' " In *Half the Lies Are True: Ireland/Britain; a Microcosm of International Misunderstanding*, pp. 29–31. Dublin: Trocaire.

Turner, Victor. 1957. *Schism and Continuity in an African Society*. Manchester: Manchester University Press.

————. 1982. *Celebration. Studies in Festivity and Ritual*. Washington, D.C.: Smithsonian Press.

Van Velsen, J.. 1967. "The Extended Case Method and Situational Analysis." In A. L. Epstein, ed., *The Craft of Social Anthropology*, pp. 129–49. London: Tavistock.

Varley, Anthony. 1983. "The Stem Family in Ireland Reconsidered." *Comparative Studies in Society and History* 25:381–95.

Vaughan, W. E., ed. 1989. *A New History of Ireland: Ireland Under the Union.* Vol. 5 Oxford: Clarendon Press.

Verdery, Katherine. 1983. *Transylvanian Villagers: Three Centuries of Political, Economic, and Ethic Change.* Berkeley: University of California Press.

Verdier, Yvonne. 1979. *Façons de dire, façons de faire: la laveuse, la couturière, la cuisinière.* Paris: Gallimard.

Verdon, Michel. 1979. "The Stem Family: Toward a General Theory." *Journal of Interdisciplinary History* 10(1)87–105.

Verrips, Kitty. 1987. "Nobleman, Farmers and Labourers: A Civilizing Offensive in a Dutch Village." *Netherlands Journal of Sociology* 23(1)3–16.

Vincent, Joan. 1977. "Agrarian Society as Organized Flow." *Peasant Studies* 6:56–65.

———. 1982. *Teso in Transformation: The Political Economy of Peasant and Class in Eastern Africa.* Berkeley: University of California Press.

———. 1984. "Marriage, Religion, and Class in South Fermanagh, Ireland, 1840–1920." In Owen M. Lynch, ed., *Culture and Community in Europe: Essays in Honour of Conrad M. Arensberg,* pp. 175–93. Delhi: Hindustan Publishing.

———. 1987. "Dragon's Teeth." Paper presented at the spring meeting of the American Ethnological Society, San Antonio, Texas, May 1987.

———. 1989. "Local Knowledge and Political Violence in County Fermanagh." In Chris Curtin and T. M. Wilson, eds., *Ireland from Below: Social Change and Local Communities.* Galway: Galway University Press.

———. 1990. "The Pleasures and Problems of Place." Paper presented at Culture, History, Place: Local Discourses and Historical Anthropologies, 89th Annual Meeting, American Anthropological Association, New Orleans, Louisiana, November 1990.

———. Forthcoming. *The Culture and Politics of the Irish Famine: County Fermanagh, 1836–1856.*

Vovelle, Michel. 1973. *Piété Baroque et déchristianisation: les attitudes devant la mort en Provence au XVIIIe siècle.* Paris: Plon.

Wachter, Kenneth W., with Eugene A. Hammel and Peter Laslett. 1978. *Statistical Studies of Historical Social Structure.* New York: Academic Press.

Walker, Brian M. 1983. "The Land Question and Elections in Ulster, 1868–86." In Samuel Clark and James S. Donnelly, eds., *Irish Peasants: Violence and Political Unrest, 1780–1914.* Madison: University of Wisconsin Press.

Walkowitz, Judy, et al. 1989. "Patrolling the Borders: Feminist Historiography and the New Historicism." *Radical History Review* 43:23–43.

Wallace, Anthony F. C. 1970. *The Death and Rebirth of the Seneca.* New York: Knopf.

Wallerstein, Immanuel. 1974. *The World-System I: Capitalist Agriculture and the Origins of the European World-Economy in the Sixteenth Century.* New York: Academic Press.

————. 1980. *The Modern World-System II: Mercantilism and the Consolidation of the World Economy, 1600–1750.* New York: Academic Press.

————. 1988. *The World System III: The Second Era of Great Expansion of the Capitalist World Economy.* New York: Academic Press.

Walsh, Francis. 1980. "The Structure of Neo-Colonialism: The Case of the Irish Republic." *Antipode* 12(1)66–72.

Walters, Ronald G. 1980. "Signs of the Times: Clifford Geertz and Historians." *Social Research* 47:537–56.

Walton, J. 1985. "The Hearth Money Rolls of County Kilkenny: Extracted from the Carrigan Mss." *Irish Genealogist* 5(1):33–47, 5(2):169–80.

Watkins, Susan Cotts. 1984. "Spinsters." *Journal of Family History* 9:310–25.

————. 1986. "Regional Patterns of Nuptiality in Western Europe, 1870–1960." In A. J. Coale and S. C. Watkins, eds., *The Decline of Fertility in Europe.* Princeton: Princeton University Press.

————. 1990. *From Provinces to Nations: Demographic Integration in Western Europe, 1878–1960.* Princeton: Princeton University Press.

Weber, Max. 1963. *The Sociology of Religion.* New York: Beacon Press.

Went, A. E. G. 1955. "A Short History of the Fisheries of the River Nore." *Journal of the Royal Society of Antiquaries of Ireland.*

Whelan, Kevin. 1988a. "Town and Village in Ireland: A Sociocultural Perspective." *Irish Review* 5:34–43.

————. 1988b. "The Regional Impact of Irish Catholicism." In W. J. Smyth and K. Whelan, eds., *Common Ground: Essays on the Historical Geography of Ireland.* Cork: Cork University Press.

Wilentz, Sean, ed. 1985. *Rites of Power: Symbolism, Ritual, and Politics Since the Middle Ages.* Philadelphia; University of Pennsylvania Press.

Wilson, Godfrey, and Monica Wilson. 1945. *The Analysis of Social Change.* Cambridge: Cambridge University Press.

Wolf, Eric R. 1957. "Closed Corporate Peasant Communities in Mesoamerica and Central Java." *Southwestern Journal of Anthropology* 13:1–18.

————. 1966. *Peasants.* Englewood Cliffs, N.J.: Prentice-Hall.

————. 1971. "Aspects of Group Relations in a Complex Society: Mexico." In Teodor Shanin, ed., *Peasant Societies,* pp. 50–68. Harmondsworth: Penguin.

————. 1982. *Europe and the People Without History.* Berkeley: University of California Press.

————. 1990. "Facing Power: Old Insights, New Questions." *American Anthropologist* 92:586–96.

Worden, Blair. 1991. "Revising the Revolution." *New York Review of Books* 28(1/2):38–40.

Wright, Frank. 1987. *Northern Ireland: A Comparative Analysis.* Dublin: Gill and Macmillan.

Wrigley, E. A. 1961. *Industrial Growth and Population Change: A Regional Study of the Coalfield Areas of North-West Europe in the Later Nineteenth Century.* Cambridge: Cambridge University Press.

————. 1969. *Population and History*. New York: McGraw-Hill.

Wrigley, E. A., and Schofield, R.S. 1981. *The Population History of England, 1541–1871: A Reconstruction*. London: Arnold.

Wuthnow, Robert. 1985. "State Structures and Ideological Outcomes." *American Sociological Review* 50:799–821.

————. 1989. *Communities of Discourse: Ideology and Social Structure in the Reformation, the Enlightenment, and European Socialism*. Cambridge, Mass.: Harvard University Press.

Young, Alfred. 1984. "English Plebeian Culture and Eighteenth-Century American Radicalism." In Margaret and James Jacob, eds., *The Origins of Anglo-American Radicalism*. London: George Allen & Unwin.

Znaniecki, Florian. 1934. *The Sociology of the Struggle for Pomerania*. Turan, Poland: Baltic Institute.

Zonabend, Françoise. 1984. *The Enduring Memory: Time and History in a French Village*. Manchester: Manchester University Press.

Zunz, Olivier. 1985. "The Synthesis of Social Change: Reflections on American Social History." In O. Zunz, ed., *Reliving the Past*. Chapel Hill: University of North Carolina Press.

# Index

Cantwell, John, 282
Cantwell family, 258; lands of, 256
Capital-intensive development of national states, 332
Capitalism, 64n83, 331, 335, 345; and agrarian economy, 83, 85–86; and colonialism, 318; correlation analysis, 329; Crotty's view of, 299, 310–11, 318; and Eniskillen politics, 88; in Ireland, 303; world systems analysis and, 360
Carlow: political leadership of, 194
Carrick, earl of, 116, 104, 126; and cot fishing, 121
Carrick (market town), 148
Carrick-on-Suir, 253, 267
Carrigan, W., 245, 273
Carroll's Street, 272
Case studies: historical, 29; of inheritance patterns, 216–17, *217;* and Irish history, 48–49; local, 25
Cashel (episcopal capital), 258, 263, 279
Cashen River: salmon fishing in, 232n37
Castle villages, 269, 270–71, 275
Castlecomer, 246, 258, 279; and Brennan family, 287; Cromwellian settlement of, 282
Castlegrace (manorial village), 269
Castletownarra (village), 284
Categorizations, 44; Cromwellian conquest and ethnic, 277
Catholic Church, 25; chapels, 148; and holy wells, 156; nineteenth-century influences of, 312
Catholicism: anthropological view of, 144; charismatic, 146; civil, 146, 164; and competing discourses, 143, 144; ethnography of European, 144–45; Irish, 144, 145, 147, 148, 149, 152–56; popular, 31; sociological views of, 299–300
Catholic population, 97n8, 98n16; of Donegal, 143; of seventeenth-century landed proprietors, 276; and workhouse admission, 93, 98n20
Causal relations: chronology of, 327; correlation analysis of, 329, 335
*Causes of Progress, The* (Todd), 341

Causeway parish, County Kerry, 211
Cavan (county), 97n9; missing poll tax returns in, 243
*Census of Ireland c. 1659, A* (Pender), 241–45, *242*
Census records, 41, 43, 63n70, n71, 231–32n32, 232n33, 233n45, 358; and designation of heir, 215; and Small Area Population Printouts, 211; and stem family study, 211; Thomastown, 5
Change: anthropology and, 53; areal distributions and process of, 41; and breakdown of social systems, 13; dynamic process and, 11–12; and economic innovations, 258; historical analyses of cumulative process of, 132–33; nineteenth-century, 147–48; social, 14, 36, 42, 327, 357; studies of, 337
Chapels, 148; private, 270
Charity: by landlords, 79, 84–85; shopkeepers and, 191
Charles II, King of England, 239
Chartist movement, 94
Chicago School: sociological research of, 326
Child labor: studies of, 341
Children: in Eniskillen workhouse, 91, 92, 98n20; and Thomastown history, 11; workhouse deaths of, 93; and workhouse regulations, 98n18
Cholera: deaths from, 93
Chronologies, 32; local people and, 9–10; overlapping, 33
Chubb, Basil, 195, 300–1, 313
Churches: and nucleated settlements, 269; and social control, 157, 175n23; *see also* Catholic church; Chapels
Church of Ireland, 97n8
Civil revolution: Fermanagh, 89
Civil Survey (1654), 240, 245, 260, 266; Cromwellian conquest and, 276–77; Tipperary, 253, 268
Civil War, 58n13; and destruction of archives, 69n129
Clachan, 148
Clans, 235n76
Clanwilliam, 253, 263, 266
Clare (county), 266; political leadership of, 195, 197